BENTON COUNTY ARKANSAS

BIOGRAPHICAL AND HISTORICAL MEMOIRS

Goodspeed

Heritage Books
2025

HERITAGE BOOKS

AN IMPRINT OF HERITAGE BOOKS, INC.

Books, CDs, and more—Worldwide

For our listing of thousands of titles see our website
at
www.HeritageBooks.com

A Facsimile Reprint
Published 2025 by
HERITAGE BOOKS, INC.
Publishing Division
5810 Ruatan Street
Berwyn Heights, MD 20740

Previouly published:
Mountain Press
Signal Mountain, Tennessee
2005

International Standard Book Number
Paperbound: 978-0-7884-9819-0

HISTORY OF BENTON COUNTY

LOCATION AND BOUNDARY.

THE county of Benton lies in the extreme northwestern corner of the State of Arkansas, and is bounded north by McDonald and Barry Counties in the State of Missouri, east by Carroll and Madison Counties in Arkansas, south by Washington County in the same State, and west by the Indian Territory. The meridian of longitude 94 west from Greenwich, England, or 17 west from Washington, passes through the eastern part of the county near the village of Garfield, and the parallel of latitude 36° and 20' north, passes east and west through the county near its center. The boundary lines of the county are described as follows, to-wit: "Commencing on the State line between Missouri and Arkansas at the northeast corner of fractional Section 8, Township 21 north, Range 27 west; thence south to the southeast corner of Section 8, Township 18 north, Range 27 west; thence west eight miles to the southwest corner of Section 7, Township 18 north, Range 28 west; thence south two miles to the southeast corner of Section 24, Township 18 north, Range 29 west; thence west eighteen miles to the northeast corner of Section 25, Township 18 north, Range 32 west; thence south five miles to the southeast corner of Section 13, Township 17 north, Range 32 west; thence west three miles to the northeast corner of Section 21, in the same township and range; thence south three miles to the southeast corner of Section 33; thence west nine miles (more or less) to the southwest corner of the county at the corner, to Townships 16 and 17, and Ranges 33 and 34; thence north on the eastern boundary line of the Indian Territory, on a bearing of about 10° west, twenty-nine miles, more or less, to the northwest corner of the State; thence east on the State line to the place of beginning."

TOPOGRAPHY AND NATURAL HISTORY.

The site of Benton County is the plateau of the Ozark Mountains, the greatest unbroken portion of which in this State lies west of White River, in the counties of Benton and Washington. The elevation of the county above sea level averages from 1,400 to 1,600 feet, and the summit of Poor Mountain, in the northeastern part, is probably the highest point. With the exception of a strip of land about two miles wide, extending from Rogers to the southern boundary, the whole surface of the county lying east of the St. Louis & San Francisco Railroad is so broken and uneven that it is mostly unfit for cultivation, except in the valleys of the streams. In the north central portion of the county, extending several miles on both sides of Sugar Creek, is also a large tract of broken and hilly land. There is an elevated, broken and uneven ridge, or water shed, extending north and south through the county, mostly in Range 32 west, along the line of which much of the land is too rough for cultivation. With these exceptions, together with the steep hills or bluffs bordering on the streams, the balance of the county, and by far the greater portion thereof, consists of elevated plateaus of gently undulating or rolling prairie and timbered lands, all of which are susceptible of a high state of cultivation. These latter lands are classed as the table lands of the State, and are in fact the beginning of the prairie region which covers the southern part of the Indian Territory.

"The ascent from the level of White River, on the east, to the table lands, is 375 feet; the ascent from the level of Elk River, a tributary of the Grand River fork of the Arkansas, is 406 feet; and the ascent from the Illinois fork of the Arkansas is 394 feet. The area of the county is 900 square miles, or 576,000 acres. The proportion of unmodified prairie is, approximately, 86,000 acres; oak barrens or modified prairie, 175,000 acres; wooded mountain or ridge territory, 200,000 acres; and river and creek valley lands, 86,000 acres."

Streams, Springs, etc.—The southeastern and extreme north-eastern portions of the county are drained by White River and its tributaries. This river enters the county on its southern boundary, near the line dividing Ranges 28 and 29, and flows thence in a northerly, northwesterly and northeasterly direction, and in fact toward all points of the compass, in its tortuous route, and finally leaves the county at its eastern boundary, from Section 5, in Township 20 north, Range 27 west. Its principal tributaries on the east are War Eagle and Little Clifty Creeks, and on the west are Spider, Indian, Prairie and Esculapia Creeks. White River, after crossing the northwest corner of Carroll County, enters the State of Missouri, in which it forms a bend, and then returns to Arkansas, and flows in a southerly direction, and empties into the Mississippi about twelve miles above the mouth of the Arkansas River. A portion of the extreme northeastern part of the county is drained by tributaries of Big Sugar Creek, flowing generally in a northwestern direction. The north central part of the county is drained by Little Sugar Creek and its numerous tributaries. This creek rises in the northeastern part of the county, and, after flowing in a general western direction about fifteen miles, it bears to the northwest, and enters the State of Missouri near the middle of Range 31 west, being also near the center of the north boundary line of the county. The south central and southwestern portions of the county are drained by the Osage fork of the Illinois River and its various tributaries, the main one of which has its source at the noted Osage Spring, at the home of Ezekiel Dickson, in Section 16, Township 19 north, Range 30 west. The Osage fork flows in a general west-southwest direction, and leaves the county near its southwest corner, where it enters the Indian Territory. The west central portion of the county is drained by Flint and Spavinaw Creeks and their tributaries. The former runs in a direction west of southwest, and crosses the western boundary line of the county in Section 23, Township 18 north, Range 34 west, and the latter runs in about the same direction, and leaves the county from Section 10, Township 19 north, Range 34 west. The extreme northwestern portion of the county is drained by creeks which flow mostly in a northwestern direction, and empty into the Neosho River. All the streams here mentioned, excepting White River and its tributaries, eventually flow into the Arkansas. On the larger streams, especially White River and War Eagle, excellent mill-sites abound, and a few have been improved, the most noted of which is at War Eagle Mills, on War Eagle Creek. This creek was named after an Indian chief called "War Eagle."

Benton County has the great advantage of having many springs from which flow pure, soft water, "as clear as crystal," and of a quality unsurpassed in any country. There are several groups or systems of springs distributed throughout the county, the most noted of which are White Sulphur Springs, in the northwestern part; Siloam Springs, in the southwestern part; Crystal Springs, near Bentonville, and the Electric and Esculapia groups, near Rogers. Some of the springs have medicinal qualities, mention of which will be made elsewhere in this work. There are also hundreds of individual springs, some of which produce a stream large enough to furnish good water-power, if properly utilized. Prominent among the individual springs is the one at Springtown, another one at the residence of Oliver I. Anderson, in Anderson Township, and the Osage Spring, before mentioned. According to tradition the latter derived its name from the following incident: An Indian belonging to the Osage tribe visited the spring to quench his thirst, and was shot and killed by one belonging to the Delaware tribe, who had concealed himself in a tree-top overlooking the spring, hence the name. These tribes are said to have then been at enmity. An abundance of good water on the uplands is obtained by digging or boring for it at various depths, ranging from fifteen to eighty feet, and much water is obtained from this source. Cistern water is also used to some extent by many who prefer it to any other water. Away from the streams stock water is frequently obtained from ponds of rain water kept in artificial excavations, the sub-soil or bottoms thereof being of such a nature as to hold the water and prevent its sinking. Upon the whole the supply of water is abundant, and its quality is first-class.

Timber.—The table lands and ridges of the county, where not improved, are mostly covered, and in some places densely covered, with the several varieties of the oak, the black, or "jack oak," predominating, and hickory. Some chestnut is also found on these lands. In the valleys and along the streams sycamore, hackberry, elm, black walnut, butternut, gum, ash, several kinds of oak, and other varieties of timber exist. Many trees of sycamore, hackberry and elm grow from two to five feet in diameter at the base, but all of them have a short, scrubby growth, so that but few trees will produce more than two saw-logs each. In the southeast corner of the county is a tract of land, six miles north and south by about eight miles east and west, covered with pine timber, much of which is large enough for lumber, and of it there is a seemingly inexhaustible supply. The best white oak timber is found in the gulches of the mountainous portion of the county, the ridges being covered with black oak of a short, scrubby growth. When the settlement of the county began (in the early part of the present century) all of the comparatively level upland was called prairie, while in truth there was but little real prairie. The timber was then very thin, the trees stood far apart, and the country which is now covered with a dense growth of young timber was then so open that the wild deer could be seen anywhere at a distance of several hundreds of yards. The entire surface of the earth was then covered with a rank growth of vegetation, consisting of the native grasses and wild flowers, which gave to the landscape, especially in the timbered lands, a more beautiful appearance than it now has. Annually, after this rank growth of vegetation became dead and dry, the Indians set fire to it, and burned it from the entire surface of the country. This they did to destroy the places of concealment for the wild game, the better to enable them to secure their prey. This burning of the decaying vegetation also destroyed the germs or sprouts, and thus prevented the growth of young timber. When this practice ceased the germs of underbrush and young timber began to grow, and the surface of the timbered lands, where they have not been cleared, are now covered with a dense growth of young timber and bushes. The supply of this young timber, all of which has grown in the present century, is so abundant that there is much more wood now in the county than when its settlement began. As yet not much of the young timber is large enough for lumber, but much of it can be made into rails.

Geological.—But little can be definitely said upon the subject of geology, as there never has been made a geological survey of the county. The surface, especially the broken portion thereof, is underlaid with limestone, sandstone, vermicular and cavernous rocks, and in many places in the bluffs along the streams the rock crops out and forms perpendicular walls of immense height. Where the rock is thus exposed many caves are found, and from many of them streams of pure, cold water are flowing. The surface of the ridges and broken lands is composed of earth intermixed with pieces of flint and chert rock about the size that rock is generally broken into for the making of macadamized roads. This rock is so abundant that it is only necessary to clear a highway and use it in order to have a road as good in quality as the best of macadamized roads. In the beds of the streams and along their margins a sufficient supply of this naturally prepared rock can be found to thoroughly macadmize all the roads in the county.

At a point on White River, about five and a half miles southeast of Rogers, there is a large deposit of rock composed of fine, white sand, which is believed to be of the best quality for the manufacture of glass. It has, however, not been tested. Minerals are believed to exist in considerable quantities at various places in the county. Lead has been taken out at Cherokee City and on Spavinaw Creek, and specimens have been found at other places in the county; but no measures have yet been taken to ascertain its quantity. Indications of the existence of copper and zinc have been discovered in the county. It is believed also that silver exists, but in such limited quantities that its mining cannot be made profitable. A controversy is at present going on between the State geologist and certain citizens of the State, in regard to the existence of silver in Arkansas. The former claims that with the possible exception of Silver City, there is not sufficient silver in the State to pay for its mining.

Soils.—" As due to geological origin and the local modification—the soils having been derived from the red and yellow upper strata of the sub-carboniferous group, and also from disintegration of magnesium and sub-carboniferous limestone—the following distinct bodies of land are found distributed throughout the county: A rich and strong barren soil, a gravelly and cherty ridge soil, a compact soil on a foundation of stiff clay; a fourth, a dark brown soil lying in the valleys adjacent to the streams; and a fifth, the best of all, a soil of brown color, upon a foundation of red clay, and with a timber growth of black and red oaks, sugar maple, locust, hickory and walnut. This is in the interior. In the marginal areas, as in the broken country forming the eastern and northern boundaries, the characteristic types of interior lands are lost to an extent in coarser soils of a pale brown, and of a darker color, more silicious or more compact, as the case may be, and imposed upon a subsoil of no greater depth above the bed rock, excepting, of course, from this classification, the alluvial valley lands of White River."*

The soils of Benton County are well adapted to diversified agriculture, a system that has been adopted and practiced by the farmers. With proper cultivation, corn, oats, wheat, rye, potatoes and all kinds of vegetables can be produced in great abundance, and a large proportion of the soil produces the finest quality of tobacco. While the county is well adapted to diversified agriculture, its greatest advantage, perhaps, is its complete adaptability to horticulture. Apples, peaches, pears, plums, grapes and all manner of small fruits are grown in great abundance. The climate being mild and the atmosphere pure, all manner of fruits adapted to this latitude grow in Benton County to perfection. It has acquired the cognomen of "The apple orchard of America," this fruit being so successfully and so extensively grown. Hereafter, in its proper place, more will be said about the agricultural and horticultural interests of the county. Comparative tables of the quantities produced, and the future prospects for obtaining wealth in Benton County will be mentioned.

Climate.—"Benton County is generally accepted to have a climate as that of the Piedmont region of Virginia, which is borne out in its annual mean temperature of approximately 60° F., and in the following approximate temperature: Spring, 60°; summer, 78°; autumn, 60°; winter, 40° F. The annual rainfall is from thirty-two to forty-four inches."

*Col. M. L. DeMalher.

SETTLEMENT.

The First.—While it is not positively known, it is believed that Adam Batie, who settled on the prairie that now bears his name, near the present site of Maysville, was the first settler in Benton County. The date of his settlement has not been ascertained, but it is presumed to have been prior to the year 1830. Batie Prairie and the creek that flows from it are both named in honor to this early and first settler. In 1830 John McPhail and his father settled on that prairie. Soon thereafter Martin Mays settled on the present town site of Maysville, and William Bird Keith settled near by. The above named five persons were the only residents on Batie Prairie in 1838. Soon thereafter Judge English, Robert Cooper, Lemuel Tynnon and several others followed, until the whole of the prairie was occupied.

One of the first settlers of the county was William Reddick, who settled early in the thirties or late in the twenties at the place since known as Elkhorn. He and his son-in-law, Samuel Burks, also an early settler, came from Illinois. Reddick was a politician and a prominent citizen. For many years he controlled the politics of the Sugar Creek settlement, and that settlement usually controlled the politics of the county. Jacob Roller, from Hawkins County, Tenn., settled where his son William now lives, on Roller's Ridge. This ridge lies northeast of Garfield, and is about four miles long, east and west. It is so called by reason of Roller's settlement thereon. Two improvements had been made on this ridge prior to Roller's settlement, one on the east and one on the west end. Mr. Roller erected and for a number of years kept a whisky distillery where he settled. He was thrice married and had twenty-four children. His third wife, who survived him, is still living. There were other settlers in that neighborhood by the name of Roller. James Jackson, from Overton County, Tenn., settled near the site of Garfield in 1829. Daniel Ash was a very early settler near the State line north of Garfield, and in 1849 Jacob R. Forgery, from Scott County, Va., settled in the same neighborhood. The Pascals were early settlers in the country southeast of the site of Garfield. Before the organization of the county Henning Pace, from Tennessee, the father of the first sheriff of the county, settled on Sugar Creek, a few miles north of Bentonville, and one or two of his sons settled lower down on the same creek. Chris. C. Pace, who is still living at a very advanced age, settled south of Bentonville. Henry Ford, and other Fords, were also among the early settlers on Sugar Creek.

Others.—Three miles east of Bentonville was the Woods' Settlement, where Samuel and William Woods, of Tennessee, located. They both raised large families, and lived there until their deaths. George P. Wallace, at whose house the county was organized, settled one mile and a half east of Bentonville. He was a large and powerful man, being nearly seven feet in height, and had several sons who were his equal in stature. He subsequently sold his first improvement and moved to another place in the county, a few miles further north. It is said that when he wanted to raise a house he did not invite his neighbors to assist, for he and his stalwart sons were always equal to the task. John B. Dickson, the first clerk of the county, settled on what is now Deming's Addition to the town of Bentonville. He subsequently settled at Osage Springs, where Ezekiel Dickson now lives, and afterward moved to Texas, where he died. He came to this county from Bedford County, Tenn. James Jackson and his sons, and Samuel Williams, his father-in-law, settled one mile west of Bentonville, and the locality was afterwards known as the "Jackson and Williams Settlement." Robert Dickson and his son Joseph settled one-half mile west of Bentonville, and Uncle Ezekiel Dickson, a brother to Robert, settled about eight miles west from Bentonville. The Dicksons all came from Bedford County, Tenn. James, Joseph and David McKissick settled from five to eight miles west of Bentonville, and Edward Cunningham settled at the Cunningham Springs, about six miles from Bentonville. About a mile south of these springs William Pelham settled. He subsequently became surveyor-general of the State. He was a brother-in-law of ex-Gov. Conway. Rev. James Harris, a Cumberland Presbyterian minister, and probably the first preacher in the county, settled about three-fourths of a mile west of Bentonville. In 1836 Col. Hugh A. Anderson brought his family from Kentucky, and settled

where his son Oliver I. Anderson now resides, nine miles southwest of Bentonville. A large spring, heretofore mentioned, is
at this place, and Col. Anderson used to keep a deer park so
enclosed that the deer had access to the spring branch.

Phineas Holmes settled about five miles southwest of Bentonville, and John Kinchelve settled near the same place on
Osage Creek. The latter took an active part in the organization of
the county, and was for many years a justice of the peace for his
township. A few miles southeast of Bentonville was the Graham settlement, where George and Joseph Graham located with
their families. An early settler, still surviving, says "there were
a host of the Grahams." Robert and James Cowan settled about
eight miles south of Bentonville. A brother-in-law of the Cowans, by the name of Colville, settled in the same locality. Colville Township derives its name from the latter. Colville went
to California in 1850, and on one occasion he left the camp of
himself and comrades and went out prospecting, and was never
afterward heard from. Robert Hubbard, the first representative
of Benton County in the State Legislature, settled near the
Cowans, and Benjamin and Jefferson Hubbard settled lower down
on the Osage. The Maxwells also settled in the Cowan neighborhood. Isaac Horton, from Tennessee, settled near the site of
Lowell, in 1830. All of the foregoing named individuals, whose
date of settlement is not mentioned, were living at the places
mentioned in 1838, when Judge Alfred B. Greenwood came from
Georgia and settled in Bentonville. Many of them had settled
several years prior to that time.

In 1833 Felix G. Lindsey came from Kentucky and settled
about three miles west of Sulphur Springs. In 1835 Christopher C. Pace and his son J. H. Pace, also from Tennessee, settled about six miles east of Maysville. In 1840 Solomon Phillips
and his son Pleasant, from Tennessee, settled about one and a
half miles north of Maysville. Among the first children born in
Benton County were John and Elijah Keith, who were born about
three miles southeast of Maysville, the former in 1834 and the
latter in 1836. Among the later settlers near Maysville was A.
T. Hedges, from Indiana, who located one and a half miles southeast of that place in 1844. Henry R. Austin and his mother,

Ellen Austin, came from Bedford County, Tenn., in 1845, and settled west of Nebo, where Elijah Austin, son of Henry R., now lives. Mrs. Ellen Austin has survived her son, and is now living with her grandson, at the advanced age of one hundred and one years, and is yet active and intelligent. She was well acquainted with Gen. Jackson and with President Polk, and is such a stanch Democrat that she declares that if she could control a thousand votes she would give them all to "Grover."

In 1839 Richard Burgess and his family, including W. W. Burgess, who now lives at Springtown, came from Bedford County, Tenn., and settled on Lick Branch, near the Osage, where Ed. Maxwell now lives. The same year Walter Thornberry and his son-in-law, David Brickey, came from Virginia, and John Edwards from Tennessee, and settled on the same branch. About the same time Joseph Neal and Charles Kincheloe settled on Brushy Creek. In the fall of 1840 Archey Wilson and his brother Samuel, also from Bedford County, Tenn., settled in the Burgess neighborhood. This made quite a colony of Tennesseans. David Brickey was a famous hunter, and on the first night after the arrival of the Burgesses he and W. W. Burgess went out and shot and killed six turkeys. Certainly the new comers were not "out of meat." The first settlers on Flint Creek, in the vicinity of Springtown, were as follows: Isaac and Hasting Dial, the latter settling about a mile east, where John Reynolds now resides. In 1850 Robert Duckworth, Matthew Vaughan, Perminter Morgan, Wiley Jones and Maj. Jack Russell all came from Georgia, and settled in that vicinity. The following year Robert Hall and his sons, Jesse and Young, Rolly Hood, Joseph Thomas and his son Joseph, also from Georgia, Hiram Thomason and his sons, John and Sanford, and several others, settled on Flint Creek, and William Addington settled in "Coon Hollow."

Simon Sager, a German, after whom Sager's Creek was named, is believed to have been the first settler in the Hico-Siloam vicinity. He settled on the creek where John De Armon now lives, near Siloam. About the year 1844 Dr. Henry Powell settled with his family on Flint Creek, four miles north of the site of Siloam. His widow, Mrs. Anna Powell, still resides on the place. About the same time James Riddle also settled on Flint Creek, in that vicinity. John Quinton was the first settler of the place now occupied by Col. D. Gunter, at Hico. The latter came from Tennessee in 1844, and settled where he now resides. Daniel Copeland was also a very early settler near Hico.

P. M. Phillips, of Bedford County, Tenn., came to Benton County in 1838, and in 1847 settled on Round Prairie. Col. Henry Hastings came from Tennessee in 1836, and settled seven miles west of Bentonville. He subsequently located at Corner Spring (Decatur), where he lived until his death. Thomas Quarles, from Georgia, settled on the northeast part of Round Prairie about the year 1840, and in 1844 Col. John Phagan, from North Carolina, settled at the Double Springs, on the Line Road. In 1846 David Chandler, also from North Carolina, settled on the farm which he still owns, one and a fourth miles southwest of Bloomfield. He now resides in Bloomfield. Rev. John Givens, a Baptist minister from Tennessee, was an early settler on Butler Creek. About the year 1845 Z. M. Winnery, from Tennessee, settled on the site of the village of Sulphur Springs. Near the same time Frank Lauderdale, James Thomason and Daniel Tittle, all from Tennessee, settled in that neighborhood.

The first settlement on War Eagle Creek, in Benton County, was made by two brothers known as bear hunters, their names being Isaac and Levi Borne. They came from Illinois early in the spring of 1832, and settled above the present War Eagle Mills, and each one raised three acres of corn that year. The following fall Absalom Thomas, Henry Taber, Lewis Russell, Robert Taber, William Brazeel and a Mr. Nelson all settled with their families in that neighborhood, and in December of that year Sylvanus Blackburn, Josiah Blackburn, Julius Kirk and Matthew Brewer with their families, all from Hickman County, Tenn., settled in the same neighborhood. The latter party came by way of Springfield, Mo., and, crossing what is now the line between Missouri and Arkansas, on the old State road passing north and south, they reached the cabin of John Fitzgerald, then living near the present village of Lowell, and stayed there over night. The next day, leaving their families at Fitzgerald's, they prospected for and selected their respective locations, and then moved thereon. Sylvanus Blackburn located on the place, at the present War Eagle Mills, where he and his estimable wife, who then accompanied him, are still residing, he being in his eightieth year at this time, and she being about the same age. Julius Kirk settled on the creek about half a mile below the mill site and Matthew Brewer about three-fourths of a mile above it. Mr. Blackburn and his wife are the only survivors of these settlers. The next year John, David and Abram Stanley, James Borne, James Matthews and Daniel Flannery settled in that neighborhood, and soon after George Crabaugh and his son-in-law, Oliver Miller. About the same time two famous hunters, Stephen Coose and John Scennett, settled on White River. The former, in order to illustrate the crookedness of this river, once related that he traveled one entire night on the river in his canoe from a point near his residence, and on landing in the morning found that he had gained so little distance that he walked home to get breakfast.

The first death that occurred in the War Eagle settlement was that of a little daughter of David Stanley, and hers was the first grave in the Austin graveyard, about four miles above War Eagle Mills. The second death was that of John B. Kirk, son of Julius Kirk, and he was buried in the first grave in the Blackburn graveyard, near War Eagle Mills. Among the first marriages that took place in that neighborhood were those of John Highland and Rachael Borne, James Blackburn and Sarah Crabaugh, Joseph Stanley and Millie Blalock, Oliver Miller and Miss Blalock, the latter being a sister to Millie.

Later Settlers.—About 1848 William Wells, from Washington County, Ark., settled one mile south of Sulphur Springs. In 1851 G. W. Mitchell, from Tennessee, settled on the site of the present village of Bloomfield, and H. T. Gillespie, from North Carolina, settled where he now lives on the Line Road, two miles south of Cherokee City. About the year 1855 James Ingle settled two and a half miles northeast of Bloomfield. In 1855 Jesse Benton settled where he now lives on Honey Creek, eight miles west of Sulphur Springs. He came from Georgia. Prior to 1853 the following persons settled in the upper Pea Ridge neighborhood, near the famous battle-field, to-wit: Enoch Trott, from Tennessee; James Wardlaw, from Illinois; Mat. Cavaness, George Miser, from Tennessee; Lewis Pratt, Rev. Jasper Dunagin, Wash. Ford, John and Samuel Reddick, Wiley Foster and his two brothers, and Granville Medlin. J. Wade Sikes and his father and family, from Tennessee, settled there in 1853. H. H. Patterson and his two brothers, William Marsh, John Lee and the Morgans were also early settlers in the Pea Ridge vicinity. In 1851 Young Abercombie and his sons, James, William, John, Samuel, Hiram, La Fayette and Floyd, settled on Round Prairie.

For other early settlers the reader is referred to the biographical department of this work. It must also be borne in mind that many other persons hereinafter mentioned in connection with the organization of Benton County were early settlers thereof.

Nativity and Character of the Settlers.—By far the greater portion of the first citizens of Benton County came from Tennessee. Many came from Georgia and North Carolina, and a goodly number came from Virginia and Kentucky, with here and there a man from the free States. Many were descendants of the first settlers of the States from whence they came, and were thoroughly acquainted with pioneer life, and thus well qualified to open the country and establish new homes on the wild western frontier. Nearly all were farmers and hunters, without much education or polish, and with moderate ambitions and wants easily satisfied. To establish a home on a farm of greater or less extent, to live plainly, frugally and honestly, to enjoy comfort and not to work too hard seems to have been their chief desires. The majority were poor and they never became wealthy. As is the case everywhere the few only became rich. Of cultured, scholarly, enterprising and ambitious men there were a few. Many brought some money, slaves and other property to the county, established themselves comfortably from the first, and soon or eventually reached conditions of affluence. Some of the merchants and other business men were shrewd and successful. The doctors and lawyers were fair representatives of their professions. There were no gentlemen of leisure, all had duties to perform, and though they were a little rough, uncouth and unpolished, they were free and hearty, generous and hospitable, and on the whole just the right kind of people to brave the storms, "subdue the wilderness" and press forward the line of civilization.

Some people sigh for a return of "the good old times," but there was no more morality in the first decade of the county's existence than in the one just past; and on looking over the first indictments in the courts one would conclude that there was not so much. There were not then so many churches, schools and school books in proportion to the population as at present. Indeed, some of the "noble old pioneers" were a little "tough." One of the first enterprises was the establishing of whisky distilleries, and in those "good old days," when the intoxicating fluid was cheap, and free from government gaugers and revenue collectors, nearly everybody drank it. And notwithstanding the declaration that some are disposed to make, that intemperance is on the increase, the truth is just the opposite, as there is not nearly as much whisky consumed now, in proportion to population, as there was then. It is customary to indulge in a great deal of extravagance in extolling the virtues of the first settlers of any country. Their good qualities are extolled immoderately, while it is seldom, or ever, hinted that they had any vices. Our first settlers were men and women, with all of the virtues and graces, and all of the vices and frailties possessed by their ancestors, and retained by their descendants. They were hospitable and generous, as a rule, and their successors practice the same virtues.

The Pioneer's Cabin.—Log cabins were the domiciles of the pioneer settlers, and the building of one was a notable event. The first two or three settlers had to erect their own, with the assistance of their families. Later, the pioneer, upon arrival into the country intended for his future operations, would stop and camp at the house of some former settler, and leaving his family there would, under the guidance of the former settler, set out and hunt and select a place to his liking, usually at a spring or some creek, and then return and move his family thereto. The next thing to be considered was a cabin in which to dwell. A day for its erection would be appointed, and the former settler would mount a steed and ride far and near to the habitations of the

few scattered settlers and notify them when and where the "raising" was to take place. They would come from within a radii of fifteen to thirty miles, and on the day appointed the cabin would
go up; meanwhile the newcomer would clear the spot for the new
house, and live with his family in the "covered wagon." Axes,
with which to cut and prepare the logs, froes, with which to rive
the clapboards, and augers, with which to bore holes for pins
and to prepare the wooden hinges for the doors, were all the
tools required. If there were enough helpers, the logs would
be hewed, otherwise put up round. Ridge poles would be placed
in order, and the clapboards placed thereon and weighted down
with poles, and thus the cabin would be covered. A huge fire-
place cribbed with logs at one end of the building, lined with
stone and mud, and topped out with a stick and mud chimney,
constituted the heating apparatus. The floor and door would be
made of puncheons, and the door hung with wooden hinges.
Thus the pioneer's cabin would be completed. With the use of
the ax and auger bedsteads were made of small poles in the corners of the building. In such humble houses the pioneers dwelt,
wore plain apparel and fed on humble fare—lived comfortably,
happily and well. They did not sport fine clothes, but had plenty of comfortable and durable linsey and jeans and homespun
cotton, much better suited to their rough-and-tumble life.

Population.—The increase in the population of Benton
County, since its settlement, was very gradual until since the
year 1880. In 1860 it was 9,285; in 1870, 13,782; in 1880,
20,255, and now it is 31,000; an increase of 10,745 since 1880.
This unusual increase is due mostly to the large influx of immigrants that have come into the county since the completion
of the St. Louis & San Francisco Railroad through it, and
since the fact has been advertised that this region is unexcelled
in the United States for the growing of all kinds of fruit. The
population of Benton County, by race, for the dates here given,
is as follows: For 1860, white, 8,905; negro, 385; Indians, 16.
For 1870, white, 13,640; negro, 182; Indians, 9. For 1880,
white, 20,167; negro, 128; Indians, 33. Of the present population the number belonging to each race cannot be accurately
given. By a comparison of these figures it will be noticed that

while the white population is rapidly increasing, that of the colored is decreasing, there being only one-third as many of the latter in 1880 as there were in 1860, and more than three times as many whites as there were then. It will also be noticed that the small Indian population doubled in the same period of time.

Wild Animals, Game, etc.—The wild animals that originally inhabited the territory of Benton County were buffaloes, bears, wolves, wild cats, catamounts, panthers, elk, deer, foxes, raccoons, opossums, rabbits, squirrels, etc. The buffaloes fled in advance of the approach of the white man, and but few lingered after his coming. Sylvanus Blackburn remembers having seen two soon after he settled, in 1832. Probably these were the last ones seen in the county, or, at least, among the last. Unlike other wild animals, they did not remain to annoy or be annoyed by the settlers, but sought new pastures farther toward the setting sun. The bears, not willing to abandon their native haunts, lingered and struggled with their exterminators. Many were killed by the "bear hunters," who loved the dangerous sport. In the open country they have become extinct, but occasionally one is yet found in the mountain fastnesses. They were very annoying to the early settlers, and destroyed many of their hogs. The wolves were very numerous and troublesome, and destructive to sheep, pigs and young cattle. Sylvanus Blackburn relates that they killed nine of his sheep for two successive nights.

The bears would kill the largest hogs, and the wolves would generally take the pigs. The bears were hunted and killed for their meat and skins, and for their extermination. Many were killed simply to gratify the love of the adventure. The wolves being unfit for food, and their skins being of no value, were hunted and killed with a view of their extermination. They are not wholly exterminated, but are no longer troublesome. A few yet remained in the broken country distant from the settlements. The wild cats, catamounts and panthers, once very numerous and annoying, have become so nearly extinct as to cease to be troublesome. The elk became extinct many years ago. The deer were numerous but not annoying. They were hunted and killed for food. Their skins were also valuable. Josiah Blackburn, son of Sylvanus Blackburn, was a great hunter. He killed forty deer one winter on one "hunting snow." The old gentleman, though not a professional hunter, sometimes killed as high as three deer per day. Many of the surviving old settlers say that they often went out and killed a deer before breakfast. Many a deer lost its life by approaching too near the "clearings" of the old settlers, who always had their trusty rifles near at hand. The other animals mentioned above, though not so numerous as they formerly were, still abound in considerable numbers.

Wild fowl, of various kinds, especially turkeys, were numerous. The turkeys, like the deer, were easy of acquisition, and were extensively used by the early settlers for food. The wild fowl still exist, but in very limited numbers. The varieties are those common to all parts of America in this latitude. In the hollow trees of the forests wild bees and their honey were found in great abundance by the early settlers. Had there been a market near at hand, the quantity of honey that could have been gathered from the forests would have been a considerable source of revenue, but, as it was, it was only gathered for home consumption. When a bee tree was found, the next thing to be done was to kill a deer and skin it. Then the deer skin, by true pioneer ingenuity, was formed, and tied up so as to form a sack that would hold about two bushels. Into this deer skin sack the honey would be placed and carried home, the sack hung up in a safe place, and left hanging until the honey was consumed. The reader may think this was a novel vessel in which to put the honey, and so it was. In those days the people were not close to market where they could purchase earthen and wooden vessels to suit their conveniences, and consequently were obliged to improvise many things that we would not think of using at the present day. Sylvanus Blackburn and other surviving pioneers can testify to the truth of the foregoing concerning the wild bees and their honey.

Hardships, Advantages, Disadvantages, etc.—The first settlers labored under great inconvenience from the want of grist and saw-mills, post-offices, blacksmith and other mechanical shops, there being none within convenient distance. The pioneer, before entering the extreme frontier, would provide himself with a supply of meal, which would last for a short time after making his settlement, then a new supply had to be obtained. Then came the test of pioneer life—some corn had to be obtained by making a long trip to some point back from the frontier, or to some distant settler, who had "made" a crop and had a few surplus bushels. Mr. Sylvanus Blackburn, of War Eagle, and those that settled with him, went to Richland, about twenty-five miles distant, to get their corn. Many others had to go a greater distance. The corn being obtained the next thing to be done was to reduce it to meal, and in the absence of mills how was it to be done. The following is the method as related by the old settlers, who of necessity had to use it: First a large tree was felled, so as to leave a stump with a level surface, then a fire was kindled and kept burning on the center of the top of the stump, while the outer portion or rim thereof was kept wet to prevent its burning. In this way a hole would be burned into the stump, and when it was of sufficient depth to form a good bowl, the fire would be taken out and the hole cleaned, the coals adhering to the wood would be scraped out with some edged instrument, and a bowl thus formed sufficient to hold a quantity of corn. Then a pole with one end hinged to a forked post set near the stump, and extended horizontally over the stump, and a pedestal or maul suspended to the pole over the bowl in the stump, completed the pioneers' grist-mill. The corn would then be placed in the bowl, and one or two persons (often the settler and his good wife) would take hold of the loose end of the pole or "sweep" and move it up and down, thus causing the pedestal to pound the corn into meal. Such were the pioneer grist-mills on which the corn was ground for the hardy settler, his wife and little children. The first few grindings would be considerably mixed with the black, burned wood of the stump, and the meal would be of a dark color. Bread or "hoe-cakes," made of such meal, together with wild meat, of which they had a great abundance, and a little coffee and sugar—the two latter articles being very inconveniently obtained—usually constituted the diet of the pioneers for the first year and until they could raise a crop.

Clothing.—Their clothing consisted of what they brought

with them, which they subsequently made out of cloth manufactured at home with the spinning wheel and loom; and while it was not the finest in quality or of the most fashionable style, it was withal very comfortable. Until stores were opened on the frontier, it was very inconvenient for the settlers to obtain such goods as they could not manufacture. Another great inconvenience was the absence of post-offices. It took as many months, or more, as it now takes days for the news of the East to reach the settlers on the frontier. Many were the inconveniences, too numerous to mention here, which they were compelled to endure. Children should remember with gratitude the parents who endured these hardships and deprivations for their benefit.

Later Mills.—The stump and pedestal mills were superseded by "horse mills," and these by small water mills. Among the first of the latter kind erected was one put up by John E. Turner, on War Eagle Creek, about six miles below the present War Eagle Mills. This was probably in what is now Washington County. There is no mill there now. The first mills at War Eagle were put up in 1848. The early settlers in the western part of the county went to the Elk Mills, in Missouri, to get their grinding done. Subsequently the Hilterbrandt Mills were erected on Flint Creek, in the Indian Territory, about twelve miles southwest of the present village of Bloomfield. For many years these mills were patronized by the people of the western part of the county. Finally the Hico, the Bloomfield and other mills were erected within the county, and now it is well supplied with both saw and grist-mills. Several of the flouring mills are supplied with the latest improved machinery and apparatus for making the roller process flour. The most noted ones are mentioned in the history of the towns in which they are located.

Although the early settlers had to endure many hardships and privations, they certainly had many of the sweets of life along with the bitter. After having raised and gathered a crop, and thus secured a supply of breadstuffs and vegetables for their families, they lived on the fat of the land, which was then "flowing with milk and honey." The milk was supplied by the cows that fed upon the luxuriant wild grasses, and the honey was procured from the hollow trees, where the busy little bees had stored it in

great quantities, the latter costing nothing but the labor of securing it, and, perhaps, an occasional sting. Yes, with plenty of
bread and vegetables, wild honey, venison, turkey and other wild
game to suit their tastes, they could certainly prepare meals such
as kings and potentates, in the midst of magnificent splendor,
never dreamed of enjoying.

Pioneer Weddings.—The courting of the young people, in
the frontier settlements, was attended with some inconveniences.
For the want of house room it was often difficult to visit and woo
a young lady except in the presence of her parents. No costly
parlors furnished with upholstered chairs, into which the young
couple might retire to tell of their loves and expectations, then
existed, and it was seldom that a young man had the pleasure of
escorting his lady love to church or to Sunday-school. But there
were " frolics " and dances on the puncheon floors, and in spite of
the many inconveniences the young people enjoyed themselves.
The climate being mild, there is no doubt but that the native
forests were often utilized by young lovers for pleasure walks, and
that on such occasions, underneath some beautiful shade tree, the
question was asked and the answer given that forever bound
their hearts together. A pioneer wedding could not compare, in
point of elegance and finish, with one of these days, for there
were lacking the paraphernalia of display, and the pomp and circumstances attendant, in this äge, upon affairs of that character.
In those days the wedding trousseau was not costly and elegant,
but plain and simple. The bridal toilet was neither expensive,
elaborate, fanciful or showy, but it was sensible, for it was sufficient and appropriate to the times, the manners and circumstances.
Yet she was as well dressed as the groom with his coon-skin cap,
his jeans coat, his linsey or cotton shirt, his jeans or coarse linen
trousers, his feet in home tanned shoes, and without a glove to his
hand or name. But for all the discomforts and disadvantages,
the marriages were as fortunate and felicitous, and the weddings
themselves as joyous, as any of those of modern times.

Early weddings were sometimes attended with some public
amusement. A shooting match was sometimes common, and foot
races and other athletic sports were frequently indulged in. At
night a dance, in which all participated, was common. The

wedding feast was well worthy the name. The champagne was good old whisky, manufactured at some local distillery, clear and pure as mountain dew. Then there were venison steaks and roasts, turkey and other wild meats, and other delicious edibles, sufficient to appease the appetites of the most fastidious guests. The particulars of the first marriage or marriages in Benton County cannot now be given, nor the names of the first parties married, unless they were some of those mentioned in connection with the War Eagle Settlement. If any public record of the early marriage was made, it has been lost or destroyed, as no such record can be found in the clerk's office prior to the year 1860.

The record was commenced in 1861, and records only three marriages for the year 1860, viz.: March 28, Thomas Wells and Miss Adaline Baker; August 30, James Riddle and Mrs. Emla* McWilliams; October 9, T. J. Holum, aged twenty-three years, and Mrs. Elizabeth Thomas, aged forty-one years, all being solemnized by Rev. H. Powell. Sixty marriages are recorded for the year 1861, and six in January, 1862, and then no more are recorded until July, 1865, after which forty-two are recorded for that year. The war suspended marriages, or else they were not recorded. For subsequent years the record shows the number of marriages in the county to have taken place as follows: For 1866, 108; for 1870, 133; for 1880, 142; for 1887, 243, and for the present year, up to August 7, 142.

INDIANS.

Tribes.—At the beginning of the settlement of the territory now embraced in this county, it was occupied by roving bands of the Osage and Delaware tribes of Indians, though it was not then and had not been the permanent location of these tribes. While the tribes were at enmity with each other, they were at peace with the whites, and friendly to the early settlers.

Removal.—The Indians were not numerous here, and did not remain long after the settlement by the whites began. In 1837 the removal of the Cherokee Indians from Georgia to the Indian Territory began. There were several thousand of them, and

---

* So spelled on the record.

before the removal took place they were divided into two parties, under the respective leadership of two chiefs, named John Ross and John Ridge. They were accordingly designated as the " Ross Party " and the "Ridge Party." In treating for their removal, the Government recognized the Ridge Party, whereupon Ross and his party claimed that Ridge and his party had no authority to enter the treaty, and at first refused to be removed. But upon further negotiations Ross entered into a contract with Gen. Scott to remove his party, by which it cost the Government about $54 per head for their removal. In making the removal the Cherokees were divided into several detachments of about 1,000 each, and each detachment was properly officered with white men. A military escort and provisions were furnished by the Government.

They started on their journey in the fall of 1837, but, like Moses in the wilderness, they lingered by the way, and did not reach their " promised land " until the spring of 1838. They congregated at and started from Calhoun, on the Hiwassee River, in McMinn Co., Tenn. The detachments started at different times, and one of them, belonging to the Ridge party, traveled westward, and crossed the Mississippi at Memphis. The others came by way of Nashville, Tenn., crossed the Ohio River at Golconda, and the Mississippi at Green's Ferry, thence westward, passing through Benton County to their destination, some of them passing directly through Bentonville.

Judge A. B. Greenwood, now of Bentonville, then a young man, was appointed commissary for one of the detachments, and came with it as far as Nashville, then resigned, and returned to Georgia for his family, and moved directly to Bentonville, where he has ever since resided. He was here to witness the passing of the Indians on their way to the Territory.

For a number of years following the Indians would come out of the Territory and establish camps in Benton County from which to hunt game. Being unmolested they became bold and a little treacherous, and did not at all times confine themselves to the capture of wild game, but began to appropriate the hogs which the settlers had turned out to feed upon the mast. Being discovered in their thefts they were finally ordered by the citizens to retire from the county, and not return again for the purpose of hunting. The order was obeyed, and no further trouble was had. On one occasion, in 1840, a band of Indians encamped on Flint Creek, about a mile above the present site of Springtown. After committing some thefts a body of armed citizens met to drive them out, peaceably or otherwise. W. W. Burgess, now of Springtown, was in this party, and on their way he killed a deer, near the site of Springtown, and threw it into the big spring there to keep it cool until their return. Arriving near the Indian camp the citizens notified them to leave instanter, which they did, and thus all further trouble on that occasion was avoided. Aside from killing a few hogs and committing some petty thefts the early settlers of Benton County were not molested by the Indians.

COUNTY ORGANIZATION.

First County Court.—Benton County was organized in accordance with an act of the General Assembly passed or approved September 30, 1836. In accordance with the act the first term of the county court, Judge George P. Wallace, presiding, was held in April, 1837, at the residence of said Wallace, one and a half miles east of the present site of Bentonville, when and where the organization of the county was completed. The first county officers were as follows: George P. Wallace, judge of the county court; John B. Dickson, county clerk; Gideon G. Pace, sheriff; Henry C. Hastings, treasurer; Henry Ford, coroner, and A. McKissick, surveyor.

The County Seat.—According to the act creating the county, an election was held for the selection of three commissioners to select and fix upon a site for the county seat. On counting the returns it was found that Robert Cowen, Robert Weaver and Thomas Swaggerty were elected as such commissioners. On the 7th of November, 1837, they filed with the county clerk a report of their proceedings in the words and figures following, to-wit:

We, the undersigned commissioners elected under an act of the General Assembly of the State of Arkansas, after having been duly qualified, and giving the notice required by law, and having duly examined the various situations, donations and conveniences, beg leave to report that we have selected a site, to-wit: The south half of the southeast quarter of Section 30, in Township 20 north, Range 30 west of the fifth principal meridian, as presenting to your commissioners, duly considering its situation, the donations offered, and its eligibility for a county seat, more advantages and conveniences than any other situation which was presented for the consideration of your commissioners. They have, after selecting the same, in accordance with the powers vested in them as commissioners, proceeded to lay off a town thereon, leaving a square and 136 lots, and have named and called said town Bentonville; all of which is respectfully submitted to the court.

[Signed.]   ROBERT COWEN.
                         ROBERT WEAVER.
                         THOMAS SWAGGERTY.

The report was addressed to the circuit court, to which tribunal the law required it to be made, and on the second day of the first term of that court, which was held in November, 1837, the report was presented to the judge thereof, and the following entry was ordered to be made of record, viz.:

And now on this day comes the commissioners elected to locate a county seat for the county of Benton, and present their report, which is approved by the court and ordered to be filed and recorded. And it appearing to the court here that a court-house will be prepared for the reception and use of the court by the next term thereof, it is therefore ordered by the court that the clerk of the Benton Circuit Court do move all the files, records and papers of his office to the town of Bentonville, the county seat so selected by said commissioners, or within one mile thereof, at least thirty days before the next term of this court. And that the town so selected be established as the seat of justice for said county, and be called and known by the name of Bentonville, in honor to the Hon. Thomas Hort Benton, and that all writs and process hereafter issued from this office, shall bear test and be made returnable at the court-house in the town of Bentonville, county of Benton.

In accordance with this order the books and papers of the court were moved to the court-house in Bentonville before May, 1838, in which month the second term of the court was held in the established county seat, which has ever since remained as such.

Lost Records.—The records of the proceedings of the county court from its organization to the year 1857, and again for a number of years including the war period, have been lost or destroyed. It is thought that many of them were destroyed by soldiers during the war. In consequence of the absence of the records some important items of the proceedings of the county court, that might otherwise appear, will necessarily have to be omitted.

The major part of the business of this court in the early history of the county consisted in the appointment of commissioners to lay out and establish public roads, and to accept and approve, or reject, their reports, to audit accounts, to make contracts for public improvements, to examine and approve the reports of guardians and administrators, to exercise jurisdiction over all county and probate business in general and to levy and superintend the collection of revenues for both county and State.

PUBLIC BUILDINGS.

Court-houses.—The first court-house was a small hewed log building, which stood on the north side of the public square, in Bentonville. It was built in 1837. Being only a temporary "makeshift," to be used only until a better building could be constructed, it stood only two or three years, or until the second court-house, a more permanent building, was completed. This was a two-story brick structure about fifty feet square, and stood upon the center of the public square, where the well is now located. The court room was in the first story, and the county offices and jury rooms in the second. John and William Walker were the contractors, who built it, as it is said, at a loss to themselves. This house stood until some time during the late Civil War, when it was destroyed by fire.

Immediately after the close of the war a temporary court-house was built on the lot near the old jail, it being on the north side of the street, a short distance east of the northeast corner of the public square. This was a two-story frame building, costing in the neighborhood of $1,000. It was used until the present court-house was erected, after which it was moved to and now stands on the county "poor farm."

On Monday, January 4, 1870, the county court made the following entry on the record of its proceedings: "Whereas, there being no suitable court-house in the county of Benton in which to hold the courts of said county, and no jail for said county, therefore it is hereby ordered by the court that a court-house and jail be erected in the town of Bentonville, in said county of Benton, in the State of Arkansas." William W. Reynolds was then appointed commissioner of public buildings within and for the county, "and there being no suitable ground belonging to the county on which to erect said buildings," the commissioner was ordered to select a proper piece of ground in the town of Bentonville for that purpose, and to purchase the same and take a good and sufficient deed of conveyance in fee simple therefor, and to make report of his proceedings to the court at his earliest convenience. Commissioner Reynolds accepted his appointment, and on the same day filed his report in the words and figures following:

Hon. County Court of the County of Benton, State of Arkansas:
The undersigned commissioner of public buildings, instructed by order of your honorable court to purchase a suitable lot of ground for the erection of a court-house and jail thereon, beg leave to submit the following report: That he has (subject to your approval) purchased, of Joseph R. Rutherford's estate, Lots Nos. 90, 91, 94 and 95 of the town of Bentonville, Benton Co., Ark. In arriving at the consideration for the property purchased, the kind of payment was considered, and from the fact that such payment would be made in county warrants, the sum of $1,250 was agreed upon as the consideration for said lots. These lots could have been purchased with greenbacks for the sum of $1,000. The deed for said lots to the county of Benton, in fee simple, is herewith submitted and asked to be taken as a part of this report. As a confirmation of the contract of your commissioner, he would ask your honorable court that county warrants to the amount of $1,250 be issued to the said Joseph R. Rutherford in consideration of said property. Most respectfully submitted.
[Signed.]   W. W. REYNOLDS,
                                                 Com. of Public Buildings.

The report was accepted and approved by the court, and county warrants to the amount of $1,250 were ordered to be drawn in favor of J. R. Rutherford in full payment for the lots named therein, the warrants to be issued in such sums as he might desire. The commissioner was then ordered to make out and submit to the court, at its next term, a plan or plans, with an estimate of the probable cost of a court-house and jail, to be erected on the grounds purchased for that purpose. At the next term of the court Commissioner Reynolds submitted plans and specifications for the proposed building, drawn by W. T. Ritter, architect, together with an estimate of its cost, at $35,000. The plans and specifications were adopted by the court, and spread in full length upon its records. ["A" pages 121 to 127 inclusive.]. The commissioner was then ordered to proceed to let the contract for the building of the court-house and jail combined to the lowest responsible bidder, after giving at least twenty days' notice of the time and place and terms of the letting, the commissioner to receive sealed bids from any and all parties until 12 o'clock of the first day of May, 1871, and to open all bids on that day in the presence of the Court. A sufficient amount of bonds, not exceeding $50,000, was then ordered to be issued for the purpose of raising funds for the construction of the proposed building, the first $10,000 to be made payable in one year after date, the second $10,000 in two years after date, and so on until the contract should be fully paid, or the $50,000 exhausted; all bonds to bear interest at the rate of 10 per cent.

On the first day of May following, the court being in session, the following entry was made upon its record of proceedings: " Now, on this day comes W. W. Reynolds, commissioner of public buildings of the county of Benton, and at 12 o'clock M. of this day, proceeded and did open, in the presence of this Court, the several bids for the erection of the court-house and jail, in accordance with the advertisement of the commissioner in this behalf. Whereupon the following bids were presented, to-wit: J. H. Neely and Samuel H. Kelton, of Bentonville, $33,000; A. H. Leady, of Springfield, Mo., $36,575; M. A. Rowles, of Illinois, $36,500; W. T. Ritter & Co., of Springfield, Mo., $34,735; J. Oliver, of Springfield, Mo., $31,910."

After an examination of the several bids, the contract was awarded to John H. Neely and Samuel H. Kelton, at $33,000, whereupon the contractors immediately filed their bond conditioned for the fulfillment of their part of the contract, in the sum of $66,000, with good and sufficient security to the satisfaction of the court. In June following Commissioner Reynolds reported to the court the progress of the work, and that the work done on the new court-house and jail, together with material purchased, amounted to $7,900. The next month he reported the sale of bonds made by him on the 24th day of June preceding, amounting to $7,669, with the following credits, to-wit: Receipt of Neely & Kelton, contractors, $6,115.51; receipt of R. & T. A. Ennis for printing bonds, $80; receipt of Cory & Cook and A. B. Cory, printing, $24; receipt of M. B. Maxwell for surveying, $6.25; total credits, $6,225.76.

On the 15th day of August, 1871, a petition signed by John A. Dickson, J. V. Lee, J. C. Woods and twenty-eight others was presented to the court, praying for the abandonment of the bond system.   The petition reads as follows:

We, the undersigned tax payers of Benton County, would most respectfully represent to the Honorable County Court, that, whereas, they did, at the April term of said court, according to Act 66 of the Acts of the Assembly of 1871, authorizing them so to do, order the commissioner of public buildings to have $50,000 in interest-bearing bonds struck, $10,000 of which have already been sold; and whereas, said bonds cannot be cashed except at such rates as proves ruinous sacrifice to the people, we would therefore pray your honorable body to dispense with the use of the remaining Benton County Court House and Jail Bonds amounting to $40,000, and make such modification with the contractors as will be equitable and satisfactory to them and the court, for the erection of the building, levying cash tax according to the law for raising revenue for county expenses; provided you find you are authorized so to do by the law. Believing that you will save the public money on the balance of the bonds, and meet the approval of almost the entire population, who feel deeply aggrieved by the bond system.   All of which is most respectfully submitted by your petitioners.

Then, in response to a citation issued to them, Messrs. Neely and Kelton came into court, as also did the petitioners by their attorney, and the Court took into consideration the matter of the petition.   The contractors refused to accept any change from the bond system, showing that they could not use county scrip at all, and that the bonds would furnish them cash in hand, and further that they could not accept the payments from a direct tax in lieu of their contract, for the reason that it would take eight or ten years to realize the amount due them.

Then follows of record the following entry: "Therefore the Court, after due and respectful consideration, is of the opinion (as the petitioners have wholly failed to show any plan that is satisfactory to the contractors, by which one cent would be saved to the county, but on the contrary the plans submitted would cost the county a large amount in excess of the present system), that it would be unwise to change the present bond system." Upon request of the contractors, the court then ordered the second year's bonds, being for $10,000, to be offered for sale by the commissioner of public buildings, to the highest bidders for cash, at the door of the court-house, on Monday, September 4, 1881.   In October following, Commissioner Reynolds reported a further sale of bonds, and that the whole amount then paid to the contractors was $14,569.25.

In January, 1872, the court (having undergone a change in its formation, being then composed of a board of supervisors) found that the contractors could not proceed with the building without additional aid, and that unless the bonds could be converted into money the enterprise would of necessity be retarded in its progress, and that the deplorable condition of the finances of the people of the county, as shown by the last effort of the commissioner to sell the bonds, satisfied the court that the policy of again offering the bonds for sale at public outcry would be attended with failure, as in the sale of the last installment. It further appeared to the court by written assurance of Denton D. Starke, a banker of Fayetteville, that he had negotiated with the contractors for the purchase of the bonds, at such price as to enable them to proceed with their work, and complete the building within the time specified, provided the court would issue the whole of the bonds remaining unsold, and turn them over to the contractors. To remove all obstacles and to secure the speedy completion of the building, the court ordered that the remaining $30,000 in bonds should be issued, and turned over to the contractors at 75 cents on the dollar, in full payment of their contract for the construction of the building, and that the commissioner should take their receipt in duplicate for the same, and file one with the clerk of the court and retain one in his possession. It was further ordered that before turning over said bonds the contractors should give bond to the court, in the sum of $30,000, conditioned for the delivery of the bonds to said Starke, as aforesaid, within fifteen days from date of the order. And it was further provided that the funds arising from the sale of the bonds should be drawn from said Starke, as follows: $500 on or before April 1, 1872, and $2,500 monthly thereafter, unless otherwise ordered by the court, until the whole amount of the proceeds of the sale should be exhausted, except the proceeds arising from the sale of the $7,500 of reserve fund, which was to remain in the bank subject to the special orders of the court. The contractors filed their bond as required, received the bonds for the $30,000, and turned them over to Starke, the banker, at

Fayetteville, and filed his duplicate receipt for the deposit of the same, with the court, as directed.

In May following Commissioner Reynolds filed with the court the following report, to-wit: "To the Honorable County Court of Benton County: The commissioner of public buildings respectfully submits the following report, to wit: The amount paid contractors as per last report, $14,569.25. Amount of contingent fund, $175.75. Work done to this date: Excavation, $150.00; stone wall, $1,500.00; cut stone, $800.00; guion corners, $1,000.-00; door sills, $50.00; brick in wall, $8,500.00; cut stone window sills, $300.00; well and pump, $100.00; rods and anchors, $350.00; carpenter work, $1,700.00. Total, $14,450.00. Material ready for use, $500.00; cut stone ready, $600.00; cut post ready, $150.-00; iron cornice, $1,400.00; vault doors, $375.00; iron columns, $500.00; ceiling joists, $160.00; oils and paints, $300.00; 35,000 feet lumber, $1,050.00; 5,000 feet walnut, $160.00. Total, $5,195.00. Whole amount of work done and material ready for use, $19,645.00."

At this time the court found that the constructors had failed to negotiate with D. D. Starke for the sale of the $30,000 in bonds, or to realize any money from the bonds. The contractors then returned the bonds for that amount to the court and took up their receipt, whereupon the court rescinded its former order by which the bonds were issued, and they were burned by order of and in the presence of the court. The commissioner was then ordered to prepare three hundred interest-bearing bonds of the denomination of one hundred each, and to offer for sale a sufficient number of them to raise the sum of $5,075.75, less 15 per cent on said amount in currency. "That said bonds should bring five cents on the dollar, and should be sold one at a time at the court-house door of said county, for cash to the highest bidder, commencing on Saturday June 1, 1872, and to continue from day to day until the full amount required was sold," and it was further provided that if no sales were made, the commissioner should pay to the contractors the amount in bonds at 75 cents on the dollar. On the 3d of July following the commissioner reported that the bonds had been offered for sale as per order, and that one of them, No. 54, was sold to C. H. Davis for $75.05

and all the others were sold to the contractors for 75 cents on the dollar.

In January, 1873, the court found that the contractors, Neely & Kelton, had failed to finish and complete the court-house and jail by the 1st of September, 1872, according to contract, and called upon them to show why their said contract should not be declared forfeited. In response the contractors replied that they had nothing to say; whereupon the court declared and ordered the contract forfeited by the default of the contractors, Neely & Kelton. On the 15th day of February following the offered resignation of Commissioner Reynolds was accepted, and S. G. Elliott was appointed his successor. In April, 1873, the court ordered that forty-six one hundred-dollar interest-bearing bonds should be issued, and that the commissioner should proceed at once to negotiate their sale by private contracts to the best advantage of the county, provided that he should not sell any of them for less than 75 cents on the dollar, and if he could not thus dispose of them he was authorized to offer them for sale at public auction to the highest bidder for cash. He was also authorized, as soon as practicable, to contract with one or more responsible persons "for the completion of the walls, roof, windows, doors and second-story rooms of the court-house of said county." And if he failed to get money by the sale of the bonds, he was to pay the workmen with the bonds at such discount as in his judgment justice would be done the county.

In May, 1873, the county court, then consisting of a board of supervisors, ordered Commissioner Elliott to let out to the lowest bidders the contract for finishing the work on the court-house, the bids to be received June 2, 1873, and the work to be completed on or before the second Monday of September following. Accordingly, on the 3d of June, contracts were entered into as follows: To F. A. Johnson, Robert Anderson and P. Q. O. Rabb, the wood work remaining undone, for the sum of $800; to J. C. Alexander, the tin roofing, spouting and capping and covering cornice for $230; to James Haney, the brick, stone and plastering work remaining undone, for $830. In July following the court found the court-house completed as per the last aforesaid contracts.

In July, 1874, W. C. Lefors, the county treasurer, submitted the following report:

To the Honorable Board of Supervisors of Benton County, Ark.:

I hereby certify that all the court-house and jail bonds that has ever come into my hands as collector of revenue for 1871, and as treasurer for the years 1872 and 1873, amount to the sum of $37,570, and that I have paid out on 254 bonds...................$29,599 71

On court-house warrants and coupons............   7,236 37

Total amount paid out less commission......$36,836 08
Leaving in treasury July 22, 1874............... $124 18
All of which is respectfully submitted.
(Signed)   W. C. LEFORS, *County Treasurer.*

It is not known just what the court-house and jail actually cost the county, but it is estimated that on account of the interest and discount on the bonds actually issued and sold, and the depreciated county scrip, that it cost nearly $60,000. It is, according to the plans and specifications, a three-story brick building, 56x76 feet in size, set on a stone foundation. The first story, twelve feet in height, contains the county offices, halls and stairs; the second story, eighteen feet in height, the court-rooms, and the third story, twelve feet in height, the jail with cells, etc., for prisoners.

The County Jails.—The first jail for Benton County, which was erected immediately after its organization, stood on the north side of the east and west street, about sixty yards east of the northeast corner of the public square, in Bentonville. It was a small building, consisting of a double wall of squared logs, with a cavity of several inches space between the walls. In this cavity poles were stood upon end, thus making what might be called a third or interior wall.

In April, 1860, the county court made the following entry upon the record of its proceedings, to-wit:

This being the day heretofore appointed by this Honorable Court to take the vote whether a direct tax should be levied for the purpose of building a county jail, and the court being satisfied that notices have been put up in every township, as required by law, and there being a number of the justices of the peace of the county present, and they having unanimously voted for the levying of a direct tax * * * on all property now assessed for the year 1860, for

34   BENTON COUNTY, ARKANSAS - BIOGRAPHICAL AND HISTORICAL MEMOIRS

****

county purposes, and also a poll tax of 25 cents per capput, which said tax can only be paid and received by the sheriff in gold or silver.

It is therefore ordered by the court that a county jail be built, and that a direct tax of twenty per cent* be levied on all property now assessed for the year 1860, for county purposes, and also that a poll tax of 25 cents per capput for the year 1860 be levied, and the sheriff is hereby ordered to receive and collect in discharge of both of said taxes only gold or silver.

At the July term following plans and specifications were adopted for the building of a jail, forty feet long by twenty-two feet wide, from outside to outside, the wall of the first story to be eighteen inches thick and nine feet high, with two partition walls thirteen inches thick across the building. The second story of the building was to be eleven feet high, and the whole was to be set upon a solid stone foundation. Full details for the construction of the building were given in the plans and specifications. At the following August term of the court the contract for the erection of the building was awarded to E. R. McKeen, the lowest bidder, for $3,475.

The political campaign of 1860 was now on, and probably the results which followed were foreseen or apprehended by the contractor, for nothing further was done with this jail, it never being built. The next county jail was the one constructed in the third story of the present court-house. Proceedings pertaining to the construction of the present jail were commenced in October, 1887, when Robert N. Corley was appointed commissioner, to let the contract or contracts for its construction, and to superintend the work. The contracts were let in January, 1888, to different parties, as follows: Stone mason work to H. G. McWhirter for $1,693; brick work to William D. Kelton for $475; carpenter work to Duffey & Fristoe for $475; iron work to Clapp, McGruder & McAdams for $682; steel cages, etc., to the Paulling Jail Co. for $3,000; tin work (roofing, etc.), to Hobbs & Co. for $82; excavation to different parties, estimated at $50.

At this writing the building is not wholly completed; the painting, construction of sewerage, etc., remains to be done. It will cost when completed, according to the plans and specifications, including sewerage, about $7,500. It is located on the

---

* This must have been intended for 20 cents on each $100, instead of twenty per cent, as written on the record.

court-house grounds on the north side thereof. It is a one-story building, forty-two feet two inches by thirty-two feet two inches in size, outside measure. It contains a hall, which extends all around the building inside of the brick wall, and on the interior the place proper for the prisoners is a space thirteen feet square, containing two cells six and a half feet square, and a corridor six by thirteen feet. It is so arranged that the prisoners cannot have access to the outer wall. It sets about three feet below the level of the ground, and has an excavation of that depth, and about six feet wide, all around it. The roof of the building extends over this surrounding excavation. Upon the whole, it is a very substantial building, and so arranged that the jailor need never come in contact with the prisoners.

Poor-House.—In April, 1857, the county court, finding it necessary and expedient to establish a poor-house in the county of Benton, ordered that Samuel Woods, James Jackson and Dysert Woods be appointed to act as commissioners to select a proper site for such building. At the following October term of the court two of these commissioners, James Jackson and Samuel Woods, reported that they had not been able, as yet, to select such a place as in their judgment would be suitable for such purpose, and asked for further time, which was granted until the next regular term. The court then ordered its clerk to make or draw a warrant upon the treasurer of the county, in favor of the commissioners, for the sum of $1,200, provided they or a majority of them call for the same, to enable them to purchase a farm or site for a poor-house. It seems, however, that this order was not called for. In January, 1858, the commissioners, all joining, reported to the court that they had selected a site for the poor-house on forty acres of land lying north of Bentonville, owned by William Clements, together with five acres off of a tract owned by William McDaniel, including a spring or interest in the spring, and had made a contract, therefor, at the sum of $300. They further reported that there was a log house on the same without floor, ten acres in cultivation, and about four acres in wheat, and recommended the place as the most eligible site they had been able to select, and asked the adoption of their report.

The report was adopted, and a warrant for the $300 was

ordered to be issued and paid to the said Clements upon his making, to the commissioners and their successors in office, a warrantee fee simple deed for the lands aforesaid. The court then authorized the commissioners to enter at the United States Land office at Fayetteville, forty acres of land lying due north of the forty-acre tract already purchased. Afterward, in April, 1858, Jacob Candill, county surveyor, in obedience to a former order issued to him, made to the court a survey of the poor-farm, showing that it embraced the east half of the southwest quarter, and four and a half acres out of the southeast corner of the southwest one-fourth of the southwest quarter of Section 20, in Township 20 north, Range 30 west, as surveyed by him February 26, 1858. As soon as the neccessary buildings on the poor-farm were put in order, the paupers of the county were removed thereto and placed under the care of a superintendent engaged for that purpose. In November, 1875, the court appointed Zach. Baker commissioner to let the contract to the lowest responsible bidder, after giving ten days' notice, for the removal of the old frame court-house to the poor-farm, and for repairing the same so as to make it suitable for a poor asylum. In January following Commissioner Baker reported in full to the court, whereupon it was ordered that a county warrant for the sum of $330 should be issued, payable out of the public building fund, to William Stewart and J. V. Lee, for removing the old court-house to the poor-farm, and for materials for fitting it up and putting it in order; and that another warrant for the sum of $120.50 should be issued to James Haney for materials furnished and work and labor performed by him in fitting up the same building.

The pauper inmates of the poor-house average from eight to ten in number. The method of keeping them is by letting or renting the poor-farm to a superintendent, who takes care of them for a stipulated price. Temporary relief is also administered in a limited degree, to a few persons not confined in the poor-house, by small appropriations from the county treasury.

MUNICIPAL TOWNSHIPS.

Roller Township.—The loss of records prevents the formation and organization of the original municipal townships of Benton

County from being satisfactorily ascertained and given. The first change appearing of record was made in January, 1857, when John Roller and sixty-one other citizens filed a petition with the county court asking for the formation of a new township in the northeast corner of the county, within the following boundary lines, to-wit: "Commencing at Henry Moor's on the line of Walnut Township, and running to Burks' tanyard; thence with the State road north to the Missouri line, including all the inhabitants on said road; thence east to the Madison County line; thence south with the Madison County line to the Walnut Township line; thence with said line to the beginning." The prayer of the petition was granted, and the territory included, with boundary lines described therein, was declared to be a new township by the name of Roller, and Jacob Roller, Samuel Burks and David Gunner were appointed judges of elections, with the election precinct at the house of William Herds. The name of the township has since become " Roller's Ridge."

Prairie Creek Township.—In April, 1859, John B. Putnam, with fifty other citizens of Sugar Creek, White River and Big Spring Townships, filed with the county court a petition for the formation of a new township taken from the above townships and bounded as follows, to wit: "Commencing at Henry Moor's; thence to the mouth of Prairie Creek; thence up White River to William Graham's farm; thence to George Callahan's on the State road; thence to and with Osage Township line to Sugar Creek; and thence up Sugar Creek, making the bed of said creek the line up to Blankenship's farm, and thence to Henry Moor's at the beginning." The prayer of the petitioners was granted, and the township was named Prairie Creek, and the voting place was established at Job R. Mona's mill.

Alterations.—No further proceedings pertaining to the municipal townships appear on record until March, 1873, when the following entry was made of the proceedings of the court:

Ordered, that the sixteen political townships or voting precincts as existed in 1860, in the county of Benton, be recognized and re-established as they stood in said year 1860, and that all elections hereafter held in said county be held at the original voting precincts in each original township, respectively, as they were in 1860; and that this order take effect from and after the tenth day of March, 1873.

Ten years later, at the October term, 1883, of the court, the following order was made:

Now, on this day it appearing to the court that the records of the county court have been destroyed, showing the true boundary lines between the townships of the county. It is therefore ordered by the court that the township lines as shown by the map of Benton County, Ark., issued by S. B. Robertson, in 1883, be, and the same are hereby declared to be the correct and true lines between said townships of Batie, Sulphur Springs, Dickson, Osage, Mount Vernon, Sugar Creek, Roller's Ridge, Walnut, War Eagle, Esculapia, Bright Water, Colville, Big Spring, Anderson, Wager, Ball, Flint, Hico, Round Prairie, Eldorado Springs and Wallace. That said townships be as they are hereby established and set forth, and designated in said map as published by said S. B. Robertson in 1883.

Decatur Township.—Following the above proceeding, a petition was filed for a new municipal township, to be called Decatur Township, whereupon the court, after due consideration of the matter, ordered that " the said new township, which is called Decatur, should be composed of and bounded as follows: Commencing at the northwest corner of Section 34, in Township 20 north, Range 32 west, and running due south along the west boundary of Section 34, and on west side of Sections 3, 10, 15 and 22, Township 19 north, Range 32 west, to the southwest corner of Section 22, thence on south boundary of Sections 22, 23 and 24, Township 19 north, Range 32 west, and on south boundary of Sections 19, 20 and 21 to the southeast corner of Section 21, Township 19 north, Range 31 west; thence due north along the east line of Sections 21, 16, 9 and 4, Township 19 north, Range 31 west; thence west to southwest corner of Section 33, Township 20 north, Range 31 west; thence north to the nortwest corner of Section 33, Township 20 north, Range 31 west; thence due west along the north line of Sections 31 and 32, Township 20 north, Range 31 west, and on the north side of Sections 36, 35 and 34, to the northwest corner of Section 34, Township 20 north, Range 32 west, to the place of beginning."

By clerical error the above description places Decatur Township just six miles east of where it is actually located. To correct the error, Township 31 west should read 32 west, and Township 32 west should read 33 west.

Garfield Township.—In July, 1884, A. J. Wilks, J. N. Ingram, J. B. Lamkins, J. C. Vandagriff and others filed with the court a petition for the formation of a new township within the following boundary lines, to-wit: "Beginning at the northeast corner of Section 26, in Township 21 north, Range 28 west; thence west to the northeast corner of Section 29; thence north to the northeast corner of Section 20; thence west to the northwest corner of Section 19; thence south in Range 29 to the northeast corner of Section 25; thence west to the northwest corner of same; thence south to the township line between 20 and 21; thence east to the range line of 28 and 29; thence south to the southwest corner of Section 18, in Township 20 north; thence east to the southeast corner of Section 14; thence north to the beginning." The prayer of the petition was granted—the township being established as prayed for, and it was named Garfield, and the voting place for the township was established at Garfield Station, on the railroad.

Yell Township.—On the 29th day of April, 1886, A. Twiggs and others presented to the court a petition for the formation of a new township, to be composed from parts of Ball, Flint and Hico, and bounded as follows, to-wit: "Commencing at section corner between 15 and 16 and 21; thence north one mile and a half to center of sections 9 and 10; thence west on said half mile line to the line of Hico Township; thence north to the line of Flint Township; thence northwest with said line to the center or half-mile corner between Sections 15 and 22, Range 33; thence east on said section line to the present line between Flint and Ball; thence with the original line to the starting point." The prayer of the petition was granted—the township as thus described being established and named Yell.

Washington Township.—On the 1st day of May, 1886, J. C. Hopkins, B. C. Martin, Martin R. Walker and others presented to the court a petition for the formation of a new township within the following boundary lines, to-wit: "Beginning at the southwest corner of Section 22, in Township 18 north, Range 30 west, and running north to the northwest corner of Section 27, in Township 19 north, Range 30 west; thence east to the northeast corner of Section 30, in Township 19 north, Range 29 west; thence south to the Washington County line; thence west to the place of beginning." The prayer of the petitioners was granted, and the township organized as prayed for, and named Washington. The voting place was established at the village of Lowell.

The descriptions of the boundary lines of the civil townships, formed since the county map was published, in 1883, have been given in full, so that the reader can trace and mark them on the map if he so chooses. The names of all the civil or municipal townships in the county, beginning in the northeast corner and going west on the north tier to northwest corner, thence east and west successively, after the manner that sections are numbered in Congressional townships, are as follows, viz.: Roller's Ridge, Garfield, Sugar Creek, Mount Vernon, Dickson, Sulphur Springs, Batie, Eldorado, Wallace, Osage, Bright Water, Walnut, War Eagle, Esculapia, Anderson, Decatur, Round Prairie, Flint, Wager, Colville, Washington, Big Spring, Yell, Hico and Ball— twenty-five in all. Some of them are very irregular in shape.

PUBLIC HIGHWAYS.

Line and State Roads.—There are two noted highways passing through Benton County, known as the "Line Road" and the "State Road." The former passes on or near the boundary line of Benton County and the Indian Territory, hence the name "Line Road." It is also known as the "Old Military Road," having been cut out and established by the general government from Fort Scott, in Kansas, to Fort Smith, in Arkansas, for the purpose of opening and establishing communications between those important points. In some places this road runs on the boundary line, especially at and for a few miles south of Maysville, but it lies mostly on the Benton County side. It passes through Maysville, Cherokee City and Silvan in Benton County. The State Road leading from Fort Smith, bearing a little to the east of north, passes through the eastern part of Benton County, along the general route of the "Frisco" Railroad, into the State of Missouri. Before transportation was provided by the railroads, this State Road was the great thoroughfare over which Texas cattle were driven in large droves to the north, and mules were driven southward. All along this road, at convenient points accessible to water, were formerly "taverns" or "stands," as they were called by the drovers. There were two such noted taverns in Benton County, one at Bright Water and one at Cross Hollows. Large yards for confining stock were always connected with these "stands." The remains of the old tavern at Cross Hollows are still standing.

Ferries.—The particulars concerning the laying out of the early highways cannot be given on account of the loss of the records. In January, 1857, a license was granted to Abner Jenning to establish and keep a ferry "across White River, at the crossing of the Blackburn mill road," and he was authorized to charge the following rates of ferriage: Each footman, 5 cents; man and horse, 10 cents; one-horse carriage, 20 cents; two-horse carriage, 25 cents: four-horse carriage or wagon, 35 cents; three yoke of oxen, or six-horse wagon, 50 cents; each head of loose stock of all kinds, 2 cents. It was ordered that the ferry should be known and called by the name of Jenning's Ferry, and that Mr. Jenning should pay for his license or privilege a county tax of $1 per annum.

The same year, in October, William Early was granted permission to establish and keep a ferry across White River, at or near the crossing of the Bentonville and Huntsville road, and the same was declared a public ferry. He was authorized to charge the following rates of ferriage: Footman, 5 cents; man and horse, 25 cents; wagon and two horses or oxen, 50 cents; wagon and four horses or oxen, $1; wagon and six horses or oxen, $1.50; each head of loose stock, $2\frac{1}{2}$ cents. He was charged $1 per annum for his license.

Other Roads.—In 1857 a road was established "to commence on the State line near Shell's mill, at the termination of a road leading from Neosho, thence running to the Elkhorn tavern, to meet a road leading from said tavern on the road to Huntsville, in Madison County." At the same time Joseph Blackburn was appointed overseer of the Blackburn Mill road from the first crossing of Cleptny to where it intersects the War Eagle road. David Baylston was appointed overseer of the same road from the Poor Mountain to the crossing of White River. C. C. Squires was appointed overseer of the Smith Mill road down Sugar Creek, to commence at the first crossing of the creek, and terminating at the State line. John F. Jenkins was appointed overseer of " class No. 1, of the Springfield road, commencing at Bentonville on the line near James Woolsey's, thence to A. C. Young's; thence along a neighborhood road to near the corner of Mrs. Jefferson's field; thence along said road to where the same intersects the old Springfield road near Warren Wright's, or Sugar Creek road; thence along said old road to the first crossing of the river channel of Sugar Creek." John L. Booth was appointed overseer of the State road from Robert Sikes' place to the Cross Hollows district. The Sikes place is now the site of Rogers.

There are no macadamized roads in Benton County, but many of the ridge roads in the broken and mountainous portions are equally as good, the surface of the lands being so completely filled with small chert and flint rocks of the proper size, that all that is necessary to have a road macadamized by nature is to clear it and travel it. Of course this does not apply to the roads through the prairie and more level lands of the county, which form by far the greater portion. There is an abundance of this small chert and flint rock of proper size along the ridges and in the beds of the streams to thoroughly macadamize every mile of the public roads of the county without breaking a stone. Of course in some places it would have to be hauled a long way.

RAILROADS.

An effort to secure the building of a railroad through Benton was made prior to the breaking out of the Civil War, as will be seen by reading the following order of the county court, made at its July term in 1860: "Ordered by the court that the sum of $500 of the industrial improvement funds, so soon as that amount shall be accumulated in the hands of the commissioners of Benton County, be paid over by said commissioners into the hands of C. W. Rice, Sr., to be retained by him and disposed of in the manner following: "It is contemplated to have a survey made in order to determine the nearest and most practicable route for building a railroad from Van Buren, Crawford Co., Ark., through the counties of Crawford, Washington and Benton, to intersect at the most practicable point the southwest branch of the Missouri Pacific Railroad. Now, if the counties of Crawford and Washington, or the citizens of each in their individual capacity, shall appropriate and expend upon said survey an equal amount, then the said Rice shall, and is hereby authorized, to pay to the person or persons bearing the expenses of said survey the said sum of $500, he taking his or their receipts therefor, and filing the same in the clerk's office of Benton County, provided that the same shall be expended exclusively within the limits of Benton County upon said survey. The said Rice is required to retain said funds until it is certain that the same will be expended as last above directed. It is further ordered that the order heretofore made by this court for a similar purpose is annulled."

This was the effort made on the part of the county to secure a railroad; but for some reason, perhaps the apprehended danger of the trouble following the result of the political campaign of 1860, the proposed survey was not made, and, consequently, the $500 appropriated for that purpose was not expended.

The St. Louis & San Francisco Railroad, which runs through the eastern part of Benton County, giving an outlet to the great States both north and south, was completed through the county in the summer of 1881. It has stations within the county at Garfield, Bright Water, Avoca, Rogers and Lowell. The railroad leading from Bentonville to Rogers was built by the Bentonville Railway Company, at a cost of about $42,000. It was completed in 1883.

PUBLIC LANDS AND THEIR SURVEYS.

The rectangular system of surveying the public lands now in use by the United States, and by which the lands in Benton County were surveyed, was inaugurated and adopted by Congress at or near the beginning of the present century. The first surveys made under the system, and before it was fully perfected, were made in what is now the State of Ohio. Under this system the lands are surveyed into strips six miles wide, running both east and west, and north and south, those running east and west are called "townships," while those running north and south are called "ranges." The squares—six miles each way— formed by the crossing of these strips, are called Congressional townships, each of which (if full) is subdivided into thirty-six sections, containing each 640 acres, more or less. The "townships" are numbered north and south from a given base line, and the "ranges" are numbered east and west from a named meridian, called a principal meridian. The "first principal meridian" is the State line between the States of Ohio and Indiana; the "second principal meridian" runs through the State of Indiana only, a few miles west of the city of Indianapolis; the "third principal meridian" runs through the central part of Illinois, a few miles west of Bloomington; the "fourth principal meridian" runs through the western part of Illinois, from a point near Bardstown, on the Illinois river, to the Mississippi on the north; the "fifth principal meridian," which in part governs the surveys of this county, passes through Arkansas near the ninety-first degree of west longitude from Greenwich, or the fourteenth degree from Washington. It extends northward through the States of Missouri and Iowa. The "base line," which, together with the last named principal meridian, governs the surveys of Arkansas and the States north of it, runs east and west through the central part of Arkansas, from a point on the Mississippi River near the mouth of St. Francois river, to the Indian Territory on the west, passing about five miles south of the city of Little Rock.

From this base line and the fifth principal meridian the lands of Benton County are found to embrace parts of Townships 17, 18, 19, 20 and 21 north of the base line, and Ranges 27 to 34, inclusive, west of the meridian. The public surveys in Benton County were made late in the thirties and early in the forties. Among the persons making them were Elias Conway, Robert W. Mecklin and Matthew McClellan. As soon as surveyed the public lands became subject to entry at the land office, then at Fayetteville. Scattering entries were made by the early settlers prior to 1858, and from that date to 1861 the entries for the greater bulk of the lands that have been taken up were made. Land entries still continue, and there still remains a large quantity of land subject to entry. The unentered lands are mostly broken and undesirable. They will probably become desirable on account of their timber, and their adaptability to growing fruits.

AGRICULTURE AND HORTICULTURE.

Farm Statistics.—Benton County has been mainly an agricultural county, other industries not having been, until recently, introduced. While the soil is not as rich as it is in some counties, it produces well, although but little scientific farming has ever been applied to it. The farm areas and farm values of the county, as ascertained by the census of 1880, were as follows: Number of farms, 2,725; acres of improved lands, 121,874; value of farms, including land, fences and buildings, $2,256,424; value of farming implements and machinery, $112,193; value of live stock, $580,425; cost of building and repairing fences, $30,621; cost of fertilizers purchased, $1,272; estimated value of all farm productions (sold, consumed or on hand) for 1879, $509,458. From the same census it is found that the principal vegetable productions of the county for the year 1879 were as follows: Barley, 200 bushels; buckwheat, 183 bushels; Indian corn, 1,119,834 bushels; oats, 245,382 bushels; rye, 1,300 bushels; wheat, 156,087 bushels; value of orchard products, $4,265; tons of hay, 2,376; cotton, 126 bales; Irish potatoes, 28,165 bushels; sweet potatoes, 14,058 bushels; tobacco, 395,982 pounds. Also from the census of 1880 the "live stock and its productions" of Benton County are found to have been as follows: Number of animals—Horses, 5,864; mules and asses, 2,233; working oxen, 69; milch cows, 5,397; other cattle, 6,307; sheep, 12,919; swine, 46,516; pounds of wool, 36,764; pounds of butter, 298,346; pounds of cheese, 700.

By comparing these statistics with like statistics of all other counties in the State, it is found that according to the census of 1880 Benton stood first in the production of oats, Irish potatoes, tobacco and butter, and second in the production of Indian corn and wheat (Washington being first), and in the number of horses, sheep and swine, and in the production of wool. Where Benton County stands second Washington generally stands first, and where Benton stands first Washington is second. Benton was pre-eminently first in the production of tobacco, as she produced more than ten times as much as any other county in the State. Boone was the next best tobacco producing county, and its product was 34,089 pounds. White with 28,184 pounds was next, and Washington with 26,357 pounds next. Benton County's large production of tobacco accounts for its being second in some other things.

The following quotations from the pen of Col. M. L. DeMalher, who has recently written up the resources of Benton County, show the increase and decrease of products since 1880: "Number of bushels of corn produced in 1887, 1,679,751; increase over the production of 1879, 559,917 bushels. Bushels of oats produced in 1887, 378,093; increase over 1879, 122,691. Bushels of wheat produced in 1887, 234,130; increase over 1879, 78,143. Bushels of rye produced in 1887, 2,040; increase over 1879, 680. Value of orchard products in 1887, $500,000; increase over value of orchard products in 1879, $496,735; number of tons of hay mown in 1887, 3,519; increase over 1879, 1,173 tons; pounds of tobacco raised in 1887, 400,000; pounds of wool clipped in 1887, 31,480; bushels of potatoes produced in 1887, 42,247; dozens of eggs marketed in 1887, 485,000, valued at $52,000."

The value of live stock in the county assessed for taxes is $639,065, divided as follows: Number of horses 7,774, value $298,854; number of mules 3,184, value $151,072; number of cattle 18,123, value $144,290; number of sheep 10,732, value $6,806; number of hogs 31,653, value $29,043. The abstract of the tax books also brings out the fact that the number of wagons in use in the county is 3,333.

Tobacco.—"Intimately related to the mixed farm pursuits and to the present and prospective total production, argued in the fact of the subdivision of its territory into small farms, is the production of tobacco. It is both the chief tobacco county of the State, and one of the few districts in which, together with other varieties, the famous White Burley attains perfection. But at the same time this is established, its agricultural conditions being flexible, and the farmer left free to avoid the pressure of the tobacco market, it transpires that from 1880 until the improvement last year in price, Benton County had almost lapsed in the production of tobacco. The industry was not killed, but so long as the farmer had to work against his interest, and recourse was had in other profitable crops, its production was lessened until the price of tobacco had improved, and indeed, that in its adaptable agriculture, which applies to tobacco, may be said to apply to every other production of the county. If, upon economic grounds, the production of one kind of crop does not pay, the pressure can be overcome by the production of another kind, for nothing is truer of Benton than its agricultural conditions, affording the farmer perfect freedom to adopt his methods, and his productions to varying states of the market.

"Of the area of the county it is accepted that 200,000 acres are adapted to the profitable growth of tobacco. The varieties grown are notably the White Burley, Virginia Golden Leaf, Yellow Pryor and Orinoco. The production of 1877 was the same as in 1880, approximately, 400,000 pounds. The relative proportion of types was as follows: Dark shipping leaf, 15 per cent; fillers, 25 per cent; bright wrappers, 10 per cent; nondescript, 35 per cent.

"In this connection it should be added that instead of going wholly abroad, much of the crop, the best at least, finds a market at home, the Arkansas Tobacco Company, of Bentonville, being large consumers of the superior product of the county. The company, dating from October, 1887, is a successor of Trotter & Wilkes, who had for the first time in the history of the county worked up the tobacco manufacture to the advantage offered in the superior production of the region. Flowing out of the experience of the old firm, and the acquisition of good manipulators and a superior equipment, they have already carried the business of the present year to twice the volume of 1887, with a prospect of a like result following during the remainder of the year. It is an incorporated stock company, backed with capital sufficient to the purchase of the production of the county, and hereafter in turn may be expected to control the tobacco crop of Benton County.

"The secretary and general manager of the company is J. W. Trotter, formerly of the firm of Trotter & Wilkes. Their superintendent has had a life-long experience in handling tobacco, acquired in Virginia. The president is W. B. Deming, a local capitalist, formerly of Abilene, Kan."

Fruit Growing.—Fruit growing has recently become one of the leading industries of Benton County, and the prospects are that with one or two more railroads to give sufficient transportation, it will become the leading industry, and will bring the greatest income.   The completion of the "Frisco" Railroad through the county, giving it an outlet north and south, gave a great impetus to the business of growing fruit.   A great surplus of fruit has long been grown in the county, but, until the completion of this railroad, there was substantially no way of getting it to market. Since an outlet has thus been obtained men have set out and are still setting out large orchards of various kinds of fruit, such as apples, peaches, pears, plums, etc.   Many have also gone into the cultivation of small fruits, strawberries, raspberries and blackberries.   Fruits grow here to great perfection, and the crop is always certain.   The young apple orchards that have been set out consist of trees that have been grafted into the best varieties suitable for growing in this climate, and the same may be said of the peach orchards that have recently been set out by professional or skillful fruit growers.   It seems, however, that before the fruit growing interest was opened up but little attention was paid to raising a good quality, especially of peaches.   One will observe in passing through the county, that the great bulk of bearing peach trees are only seedlings, and many of them occupy the fence corners along the highways.   At this writing (August), they are loaded with small and inferior fruit.   It will soon be discovered that budded peach trees produce a superior and more profitable fruit than seedlings, and will take the place of the latter.

The climate and natural conditions are so superior for the production of fruit that this is destined to be a great fruit center. It is estimated that if all the orchards in Benton County now in cultivation were consolidated into one, it would cover a tract of land equal in size to a congressional township—six miles square. At the rate that new orchards are now being planted and established, the area now devoted to the raising of fruit will soon be doubled and tripled.   Now is the time to purchase the lands and establish the orchards, so that they will come into bearing by the time the greater facilities for transportation are obtained.

Certainly there can be no place found in the States where fruit trees grow more thrifty, or with cleaner bark, or where a greater quantity can be grown, that in Northwestern Arkansas. In consequence of the large amount of fruit already produced, a number of evaporators, or drying factories, have been erected, and more are contemplated. A canning factory is also in full and successful operation, and more are projected. It is believed that enough of these factories will soon be established to dry or can all the surplus fruit that cannot be shipped to market in the natural state. The factories already running have established a home market for the fruits, and given employment to a large number of men and women. These factories will be mentioned individually in connection with the history of the towns where they are located.

Another important industry of Benton County is its fruit tree nurseries, the largest of which is located near Bentonville, and of which G. C. Davis is the proprietor. There is no need of sending abroad for trees, as all kinds best adapted to the place can be purchased at the home nurseries.

Benton County Horticultural, Agricultural and Mechanical Fair.—This fair association was organized in the summer of 1888 at Rogers, where its exhibitions will be held. The officers of the association are J. Huffman, president; W. R. Felker, treasurer; W. J. Todd, secretary. The directors, aside from the officers, are Charles Warbritton, W. A. Miller, J. A. C. Blackburn, J. S. Miser, J. W. Scroggs and G. F. Kennon. The association has secured several acres of land at Rogers for a fair ground, and have fitted it up with a race track and appropriate buildings, and have published their catalogues announcing premiums offered, and the dates of October 10, 11, 12 and 13, 1888, for the first annual fair. Very liberal premiums are offered.

BENTON COUNTY FINANCES.

The financial condition of Benton County is so good that but little pertaining to it has to be said. The following is the recapitulation of the taxable property of the county for the year 1887: Number of acres of land assessed, 349,940; assessed value of the lands, including town lots, $1,780,018; assessed value of personal property, $1,672,568; total value of real and personal property, $3,452,586.   This is the assessed value of the property for the purpose of taxation, but by no means the true value.   Property is not usually assessed for taxation at half of its real value; so in order to ascertain the true value of the taxable property of Benton County its assessed value must at least be multiplied by two.   This would make the approximate real value stand at about $7,000,000 in round numbers.

The amount of revenue collected in 1887 for both State and county purposes was $37,733.30.   To this should be added $10,279.93, special school tax collected, making the total amount collected $48,013.23.   These taxes were divided as follows: State tax, $6,905.17; State sinking fund, $3,452.58; State school tax, $6,905.17; county tax, $15,191.37; poll tax, $5,279; special school tax, $10,279.93.

Benton County has no bonded indebtedness whatever.   It has, however, a small indebtedness in the way of outstanding county scrip, which, according to the report for the last fiscal year ending June 30, 1888, amounted to $1,693.30.   It may, therefore, be said to be substantially out of debt.

SOCIETIES.

Benton County Medical Society.—The Benton County Medical Society was organized in 1875, with only five members.   It was organized auxiliary to the State Medical Society, and it now has seventeen members.   All graduated physicians of the county, possessing other proper qualities, are eligible to membership. The present officers are Dr. Theo. A. Coffett, president; Dr. Thomas W. Hurley, secretary; Dr. W. R. Davis, treasurer.   The society meets monthly, usually at the city of Bentonville.

Harmonial Vegetarian Society.—This society was organized in 1860, and on the 29th day of October, in that year, J. E. Spencer and Martha, his wife, for the consideration of $6,000, conveyed by warranty deed to A. D. Tenney, John Murphy and Milton Vale, trustees of the society, the following parcels or tracts of land, to-wit: The southwest quarter and the west half of the southeast quarter of Section 12, the northeast quarter and the east half of the northwest quarter of Section 13, Township 20 north, Range 34 west and the southeast quarter of the southeast quarter of Section 23, Township 21 north, Range 34 west, containing in all 520 acres more or less.   These lands were conveyed, as expressed in the deed, "for the following uses and purposes, or trusts, and for no other purposes:

"*First*, in trust, to hold the same for the sole use and benefit of the said Harmonial Vegetarian Society, composed of the following named persons, to-wit: A. D. Tenney, Rachel S. Tenney, William Tenney, J. D. Potter, Irena Potter, John Murphy, Milton Vale, Mercy G. Vale, John M. Adams, Henry E. Dewey, Sarah J. Dewey, Benjamin F. Stites, Charles G. Foster, Ada M. Foster, Deborah Brackett, Phebe A. Rodgers and Angeline A. Dunn.

"*Second*, in trust for the use and occupancy of the said society, for agricultural, mechanical, mercantile and manufacturing purposes.

"*Third*, in trust, to convey said lands and premises in fee simple absolute, to such person or persons, and upon such terms, as the members of said society, or a majority of them, shall direct."

According to the rules of this society, "they had all things in common," and all married persons joining it had to renounce their marriage contracts, and contribute to the society all their property, so that there was no individual ownership thereof—all property being owned in common.   While marriage was not recognized in the society, the members were allowed to choose or select their "mates," by lot, and it was intended that the children born of members were to be considered the offspring of the society rather than that of the parents.   No meats or greasy substances therefrom were allowed to be used for food—the diet was strictly vegetable, as it was believed that a purely vegetable diet would prolong life.

Immediately after purchasing the lands the society took possession, and as soon as possible erected a large three-story building, containing from eighty to ninety rooms, for a home and hospital, a large bath house, machine shop, a spring house over the spring, a saw and grist-mill, blacksmith shop, and a building for a general store, also a printing office, and opened up and cultivated the large farm, and made everything prosperous.   For about one year they published a paper called the *Theocrat*, in which they advocated the theory of living in societies, with all things in common, and upon a purely vegetable diet.

They lived exclusively to themselves in a social way, and had but little to do with the outside world except in a commercial capacity. They had their own physicians and teachers, and while marriage was not recognized, strict order and strict rules were enforced for their government. The society was in operation about four years, during which time they were not known to have a death. In case of sickness they would admit "outsiders" into the hospital, where they would treat them for a consideration. Water was pumped from the spring, by means of a hydraulic ram, to every room in the home and hospital. During the civil war the buildings of this society were used part of the time by the armies, and about the close of the war they were all burned. Soon thereafter the property was sold and the proceeds divided among the members, all of whom left the county except Henry E. Dewey, who remained and ran a grist-mill for a few years on Honey Creek. The male members of the society dressed in the Quaker style, and the females wore "bloomers." They were all active and industrious and had no drones.

ELECTIONS.

The first general election in Benton County was held in August, 1838, being for the election of governor, members of the Legislature and county officers. The whole number of votes cast in the county on that occasion was 272. Politically the county has always been strongly Democratic, and that party has always elected its officers with the exception of the period following the war, when Democrats who had participated in the Rebellion were disfranchised. During that period Republican officers were elected, and since that time up to the present year the Republicans of Benton County have not had a ticket in the field. The Democrats being so largely in the ascendancy, there is not now, and never has been, much political excitement in the county. On the 21st day of July, 1888, the Republicans met in convention in Bentonville and nominated a full county ticket. They had a fine procession, which marched entirely around the public square, led by a martial band. At the head of the procession Mr. C. G. Metheny, of Sulphur Springs, carried the "stars and stripes," and it was claimed that this was the first time for thirty years that the old flag had been carried around the public square of Bentonville by a political procession. Following this, on the Saturday prior to the late election, the Democrats met in convention in Bentonville and nominated a full county ticket, all of which was elected at the election following. On the day of their convention the Democrats raised a handsome pole and hoisted thereon the "stars and stripes," all now recognizing it as "the flag of our country."

At the late election the question of granting licenses for the sale of intoxicating liquors, and also for the call of a convention to amend the State constitution, was submitted to the voters. The following are the returns of the election held in Benton County in September, 1888:

Total vote cast, 4,561.

Governor—J. P. Eagle, 3,049; C. M. Norwood, 1,384.

Secretary of State—B. B. Chism, 3,094; G. R. Terry, 1,369.

Treasurer—W. E. Woodruff, 3,101.

Auditor—W. S. Dunlop, 3,094; A. W. Bird, 1,338.

Attorney General—W. E. Atkinson, 3,101; W. J. Duval, 1,338.

State Land Commissioner—Paul M. Cobb, 3,098; R. H. Morehead, 1,335.

Superintendent Public Instruction—Wood E. Thompson, 3,085; B. P. Baker, 1,334.

Chief Justice—S. R. Cockrill, 3,095; O. D. Scott, 1,339.

Prosecuting Attorney—J. W. Walker, 1,194; M. R. Baker, 1,670; S. M. Johnson, 1,227.

Representatives—D. M. Setser, 3,177; P. A. Rodgers, 3,050; A. Hollingsworth, 1,146; Eli Bacon, 1,242; W. N. Hemingway, 119.

For County Judge—S. A. Cordell, 3,037; I. B. Lawton, 1,291.

Circuit Clerk—C. C. Huffman, 3,114; E. L. Allen, 1,236; C. R. Craig, 83.

County Clerk—E. L. Taylor, 3,155; James C. Tune, 1,279.

Coroner—R. N. Corley, 3,083; J. C. Pennington, 1,246.

Sheriff—E. P. Galbreaith, 2,445; W. C. Lefors, 1,721.

Treasurer—H. C. Smith, 3,243; James Elam, 1,159.

Assessor—W. H. Haines, 3,229; P. W. Roberts, 1,247.

Surveyor—J. A. Murray, 3,145; M. B. Maxwell, 566.

For license, 2,311; against license, 1,760.

For convention, 600; against, 3,035.

COUNTY AND DISTRICT OFFICERS.

The following are lists of public officers serving in, or representing Benton County, from the date of its organization to the present time, together with dates of service:

Circuit Court Judges.—Joseph M. Hoge, 1837–39; Lewis B. Tully, 1839–40; Joseph M. Hoge, 1840–44; Sebron G. Sneed, 1844–48; William W. Floyd, 1848–50; Alfred B. Greenwood, 1850–53; Felix I. Batson, 1853–58; John M. Wilson, 1858–61; Joseph J. Green, 1861 (vacant during war period); Elias Harrell, 1865–67; William Story, 1867–68; E. D. Ham, 1868–73; J. H. Huckleberry, 1873–75; J. M. Pittman, 1875–79; James H. Berry, 1879–83; J. M. Pittman, present judge, elected in 1882 and re-elected in 1886.

Circuit Court Clerks.—John B. Dickson, 1836–42; John Smith, 1842–48; Joseph D. Dickson, 1848–52; A. G. Williams, 1852–56; John Galbreath, 1856–58; R. S. Williams, 1858–60; J. R. Woods, 1860–64; Charles W. Rice, 1864–66; J. W. Sikes, 1866–68; J. R. Rutherford, 1868–72; Hugh A. Dinsmore, 1872–74; John Black, 1874–80; B. F. Dunn, 1880–86; C. C. Huffman, present incumbent, elected in 1886.

Sheriffs.—Gideon G. Pace, 1836–42; John H. Hammock, 1842–46; John Galbreath, 1846–56; H. Hammock, 1856–58; J. R. Wood, 1858–60; Joseph Henry, 1860–62; R. E. Doak, 1862; Alfred Dean, coroner, acting sheriff, 1865–66; J. W. Norwood, 1866–67; John W. Simmons, 1867–68; W. C. Lefors, 1868–72; William Isbell, 1872–74; John W. Simmons, 1874–78; J. H. McClinton, 1878–82; R. A. Hickman, 1882–84; F. P. Galbreath, 1884–86; W. H. Cloe, present incumbent, 1886–88.

County Court Judges.—George P. Wallace, 1836–38; Matthew English, 1838–40; T. M. Duckworth, 1840–42; David Mitchell, 1842–44; J. A. P. Carr, 1844–46; T. M. Duckworth, 1846 to September; James Jackson, from September, 1846, to 1848; J. M. Rogers, 1848–50; W. J. Howard, 1850–52; J. W. Cowan, 1852–54; William McDaniel, 1854–56; Enoch Trott, 1856–58; John Kincheloe, 1858, resigned, and J. W. Cowan filled the vacancy to 1860; H. Marley, 1860–64; D. Woods, 1864–68; J. McPherson, 1868–72; D. Woods, 1872–74; Harvey Marley, 1874–76; S. N. Elliott, 1876–82; T. D. Bates, 1882–86; S. A. Cordell, 1886–88.

County Court Clerks.—Prior to the year 1872 there was but one clerk for both the offices of circuit and county courts. During the years 1872–74 the law required a clerk for each office. In 1872 John Black was elected clerk of the county court, and Hugh A. Dinsmore was appointed by the governor as clerk of the circuit court. From 1874 to 1880 the law only required one clerk for the two offices. In 1880 the offices were permanently separated, and since that time the office of the county court clerk has been continuously in the hands of John Black, the present incumbent.

Treasurers.—Henry C. Hastings, 1836–46; S. Langston, 1846–48; William McDaniel, 1848–54; H. C. Hastings, 1854–58; E. W. Smith, 1858–60; S. Langston, 1860–62; E. W. Smith, 1862–64; S. Langston, 1864–68; Joseph Thomas, 1868–72; John Galbreath, 1872–74; Haley Jackson, 1874–76; B. F. Dunn, 1876–80; Thomas Wood, 1880–82; T. H. Wood, 1882–86; H. C. Smith, 1886–88.

Coroners.—Henry Ford, 1836–38; James Beaman, 1838–40; James Jackson, 1840–48; W. B. Covey, 1848–50; H. O. Gilbert, 1850–54; John Wilcox, 1854–56; Hardy Wilson, 1856–58; William Morgan, 1858–60; Alfred Dean, 1860–62; John Galbreath, 1862–64; Alfred Dean, 1864–66; I. S. Reynolds, 1866–68; J. C. January, 1868–72; J. E. Plummer, 1872–74; J. H. Hogan, 1874–76; J. W. Bland, 1876–78; P. H. Throne, 1878–80; R. W. Hansard, 1880–82; R. N. Corley, 1882–88.

Surveyors.—A. McKissick, 1836–38; W. H. McLean, 1838–40; James White, 1840–42; W. H. Woods, 1842–44; Dr. Hayden, 1844–46; D. Chandler, 1846–50; J. McBrown, 1850–52; * * * M. B. Maxwell, 1854–56; J. Candill, 1856–58; M. B. Maxwell, 1858–64; * * * M. B. Maxwell, 1866–72; S. Peak,

1872–74; M. B. Maxwell, 1874–82; D. W. German, 1882–84; M. B. Maxwell, 1884–86; S. B. Robertson, present incumbent, 1886–88.

Assessors.—J. N. Curtiss, 1868–72; W. L. Cowan, 1872–78; H. Higfill, 1878–80; A. G. Gamble, 1880–84; W. H. Haynes, 1884–88.

Representatives in Congress.—Following is a list of Representatives in Congress from the district of which Benton County has composed a part: Archibald Yell, 1836–39; Edward Cross, 1839–45; Archibald Yell, 1845–47; Robert W. Johnson, 1847–53; A. B. Greenwood, 1853–59 (three terms); Thomas C. Hindman, 1859–63 (the civil war prevented him from taking his seat in 1861); W. W. Wilshire (ousted by T. M. Gunter, contestant), 1873–75; T. M. Gunter, 1875–83 (four terms); Samuel W. Peel, the present Representative, was elected in 1882, and re-elected in 1884 and again in 1886, and has served continuously since entering Congress in 1883. Prior to 1847 the whole State had but one member of Congress. The State having been divided into two districts, there were two Congressmen elected in 1847. Subsequently other districts were formed, until the State became divided, as at present, into five Congressional Districts, this being the fifth, composed of the counties of Benton, Washington, Madison, Carroll, Boone, Newton, Searcy, Marion, Baxter, Fulton and Izard.

United States Senators from Arkansas.—A. H. Sevier (resigned), 1836 to 1849; Solon Borland (resigned), 1848 to 1855; R. W. Johnson, 1855 to 1861; Chas. B. Mitchell,* 1861; B. F. Rice, 1868 to 1873; S. W. Dorsey, 1873 to 1879; J. D. Walker, 1879 to 1885; J. K. Jones, 1885 to 1891; W. S. Fulton (died), 1836 to 1841; Chester Ashley (died), 1844 to 1848; W. K. Sebastian,† 1848 to 1865; ‡1865 to 1868; Alex McDonald, 1868 to 1871; Powell Clayton, 1871 to 1877; A. H. Garland, 1877 to 1889;§ J. H. Berry, 1885 to 1889.‖

---

*Mitchell was elected for the term ending March 4, 1867, but did not occupy his seat after the secession of the State.

†Sebastian was expelled from the United States Senate on suspicion of sympathy with the rebellion of 1861. In 1878 the resolution of expulsion was reversed by the Senate. Sebastian was elected for the term ending March 4, 1865, but did not occupy his seat after the winter session of 1860–61.

‡Both seats were unoccupied or vacant for the remainder of the term of Sebastian and Mitchell after March 4, 1861.

§Appointed Attorney General of the United States.

‖ Elected to fill Garland's unexpired term. During the first session of the (Murphy) Legislature

Senators of the Arkansas Legislature.—Following is a list of State Senators of the senatorial districts of which Benton County formed a part, from its organization to the present time, to-wit: Benton, Madison and Washington Counties, O. Evans and A. Whinnery, 1836–40; Benton and Madison, A. Whinnery, 1840; Benton and Madison, J. G. Walker, 1842–45; Benton and Madison, J. B. Dickson, 1846–49; Benton and Madison, J. Berry, 1850–55; Benton and Madison, I. Murphy, 1856–57; Benton and Madison, M. Douglas, 1859–62; Benton County, J. Dungan, 1862; Benton and Madison, E. D. Ham, 1864–65; Benton County, J. Dungan, 1864; Benton and Madison, J. Dungan, 1866–67; Seventh District, Benton and Washington, T. J. Hunt, 1868–69; A. Caraloff, 1871–73; J. Dunagin, 1874; Twenty-fourth District, Benton and Madison, C. J. Reagan, 1874–77; E. P. Watson, 1879–81; J. T. Walker, 1883–85.

Representatives in the Arkansas Legislature.—The following is a list of representatives sent from Benton County to the State Legislature, beginning with 1840: Robert Hubbard, 1840; Alfred B. Greenwood, 1842–43; A. B. Greenwood and R. Hubbard, 1844–45; J. H. Hammock and William Thompson, 1846; J. H. Hammock and W. H. Howell, 1848–49; D. Chandler and J. Jackson, 1850–51; J. H. Hammock and W. J. Howard, 1852–53; M. Douglas and A. Whinnery, 1854–55; M. Douglass and T. Quarles, 1856–57; R. E. Doak and T. Quarles, 1858–59; J. Dunagin and J. P. Putnam, 1860–62; J. H. Hammock and W. B. Fain, 1862; R. H. Wimpey and J. Shortis, 1864–65; W. B. Fain, 1864; William E. Gould and W. W. Reynolds, 1866–67; Seventh District, Benton and Washington Counties, S. Bard, J. Yoes, E. D. Fenno, and J. F. Owen, 1868–69; J. F. Owen, Martin F. Tygart, Thomas Wilson and James M. Pittman, 1871; David Chandler, James H. Berry, D. Bridenthal and T. W. Thomason, 1873; * * * Benton County, James Putnam and J. H. Rice, 1874–75; J. Dunagin and E. P. Watson, 1877; D. H. Williams and W. M. Keith, 1879; E. S. McDaniel and J. Dunagin, 1881; H. H. Patterson,

of 1864 Elisha Baxter, on May 2, 1864, W. M. Fishback, on May 5, and W. D. Snow, on December 30, were respectively elected to the Senate for the terms ending March 4, 1865 and 1867. None of them were admitted. Charles B. Mitchell and Robert W. Johnson, in 1862, were elected Confederate State Senators, and served as such. Mitchell died September 18, 1864, and A. H. Garland was elected to his vacancy. Johnson and Garland served until the fall of the Confederacy. John T. Jones and Andrew Hunter were elected senators by the Legislature of 1866; Hunter resigned. Neither were admitted by the Senate.

Jr., and S. S. Graham, 1883; James A. Rice and Z. Baker, 1885.

Delegates to Constitutional Conventions.—The first constitutional convention of Arkansas was held January 4 to January 13, 1836. This was prior to the organization of Benton County. The next constitutional convention was held March 4 to 21, and May 6 to June 3, 1861, and the delegates in this convention from Benton County were A. W. Dinsmore and H. Jackson.

Another constitutional convention was held from January 4 to January 23, 1864, in which there were no delegates from Benton County. In the convention held January 7 to February 18, 1868, Benton County was represented by W. W. Reynolds. In the last constitutional convention, held July 14 to October 31, 1874, Benton County was represented by H. H. Patterson and A. M. Rodgers.

Notaries Public in Benton County—as per report of Secretary of State published in 1886, with dates of expiration of terms: Hugh Elliott, October 7, 1886; James S. Harris, January 18, 1887; G. P. Rogers, February 6, 1887; L. H. McGill, April 28, 1887; E. S. McDaniel, May 9, 1887; O. V. Wager, February 11, 1888; John F. Mitchell, April 28, 1888; W. D. Wasson, April 30, 1888; Charles R. Bruce, May 17, 1888; Sydney H. Denham, August 1, 1888; J. D. Walter, September 3, 1888; David Chandler, November 1, 1888; B. C. Martin, January 2, 1889; S. A. Cordell, February 28, 1889; W. J. Blackburn, March 7, 1889; Samuel Box, March 20, 1889; Thomas Keith, July 21, 1889; James M. Tucker, January 2, 1890; D. Shafer, January 23, 1890; S. D. Bullock, February 13, 1890; Charles R. Craig, February, 13, 1890; M. E. Smith, April 9, 1890; Dr. R. Hammer, April 16, 1890; B. S. Beach, June 18, 1890; A. J. Wilkes, July 7, 1890; W. T. Hudson, February 27, 1887; H. C. King, October 6, 1888; William Keever, November 22, 1888; J. K. Gibson, January 26, 1889; F. M. Garvin, January 31, 1889; R. E. Underwood, February 26, 1889; R. S. Armitage, November 20, 1889; James F. Gillick, February 22, 1890.

THE COURTS.

County Court.—The origin of the county court of Benton County, and the time and place of holding its first term, has been given under the head of "Organization." For many years

—up to 1873—the court was composed of a county judge and two associate justices. The judge was elected by the people, and the associate justices by the several justices of the peace, who met at the county seat in January each year for that purpose. In 1873, under a change in the law, the court was made to consist of a board of supervisors consisting of three persons, Dysert Woods, John W. Phagaen and B. F. Davis, who were appointed by the governor. The first term of the court thus organized was held in May, 1873, when the supervisors met and selected Dysert Woods as president of the board. The court continued thus organized until January, 1875, when, according to another law, it was composed of a single judge elected by the people, and so it has ever since remained.

The county court has always had, and still retains, jurisdiction over the levying and collection of revenues; the erection of public buildings; making of contracts for public improvements; laying out of highways; auditing all accounts against the county, and of all county business proper. It also had jurisdiction of all probate business from its original organization until 1873, at which time the probate business was, by law, transferred to the circuit court. The circuit court had jurisdiction of this branch of business one year, until 1874, and then the separate probate court was established, with full original jurisdiction over all probate business. The county court judge is also judge of the probate court. The county court meets in regular session four times a year, commencing the sessions on the first Mondays of January, April, July and October, and the probate court meets the same number of times, commencing the sessions on the third Mondays of the same months.

First Probate Business.—The first letters of administration granted in Benton County were granted April 17, 1837, to Mrs. Mary Blair, to administer on the estate of John C. Blair, deceased. Also to Elizabeth Johnston, to administer on the estate of Spencer B. Johnston, deceased. In September following letters of administration were issued to James McKissick, to administer on the estate of Madeline Catharine White, deceased.

The following is a copy of the first " will " on record in Benton County:

I, Samuel Tenan, of the County of Benton and State of Arkansas, being weak in body, but of strong mind and memory, thanks be to God for the same, do make and ordain this my last will and testament in the manner and form as follows:

First: I give my soul to God, who gave it to me, and my body to earth, to be decently buried by my executor hereafter named.

Second: I request that my negro boy, Jack, be sold, and that some of my connection buy him, and that the money be divided equally between my brother, L. Tenan, and my two sisters, Mary Allen and Zebe Yunt.

Third: I require my executors to take all my personal property, with notes and accounts, and pay all my just debts; and after all are paid, together with my funeral expenses, then the balance to be divided equally between my brother and sisters as before named. I do hereby appoint Abner Allen my executor, and also request that my executor take my negro boy, Jack, and attend to selling him.

Given under my hand and seal this twentieth day of August, 1837.

Test: W. B. Woody, }
    William Reed. ∫

His
SAMUEL **X** TENAN.
mark.

This will was probated January 15, 1838, and letters testamentary to Abraham Allen* as sole executor of the will were granted.

First Deed Recorded.—Though not belonging to probate business, the following, which is a copy of the first deed recorded in Benton County, will be read with interest, inasmuch as the property conveyed consisted of slaves, conveyed in manner and form the same as real estate, viz.:

Know all men by these presents, that for and in consideration of the sum of $400 to me in hand paid by James M. Dickson, the receipt of which is hereby acknowledged, I, Ezekiel Dickson, of the County of Benton, in the State of Arkansas, do hereby bargain and sell unto the said James M. Dickson, a negro woman named Till, about forty-five years of age, also a negro boy child named Jack, about five or six years of age, which said negroes I hereby sell and convey as slaves for life. And I do hereby warrant and defend the title of said negroes to the said James M. Dickson, his heirs and assigns forever.

In witness whereof I have hereunto set my hand and affixed my seal this 7th day of February, 1837.   EZEKIEL DICKSON.
    Witness, JAMES McKISSICK.

The next instrument found on record was dated January 26, 1837, and was for the conveyance by Phineas Holmes and Rachel, his wife, of Lucinda, Guilford, Andy and Clarisa, four slaves, to James H. Wallace, for the consideration of $3,000.

The first instrument on record for the transfer of real estate in Benton County is that of Samuel Whitehead and wife to

*This name appears Abner Allen in the will, as recorded, and Abraham Allen in record of the probate.

Singleton Lankston, for the east half of the northeast quarter of Section 31, Township 20 north, Range 30 west, being now a portion of the site of Bentonville. It was dated February 27, 1838.

Circuit Court.—When the State of Arkansas was organized it was divided into but few circuits, each containing many counties, or at least much more territory than at present. As the population and business increased, the State was redistricted, or certain circuits were changed from time to time. Additional circuits were formed and the size of the old ones reduced. Prior to the last change, the fourth judicial circuit, of which Benton County composes a part, embraced Marion, Boone, Searcy, Newton, Madison, Carroll, Benton and Washington. In 1887 the General Assembly reduced it in size, and made it to contain, as it is now organized, only the counties of Benton, Carroll, Madison and Washington. Only two sessions of this court are held during the year, and the sessions in Benton County commence on the first Mondays of January and July. For a list of the names of the judges who have presided over the Benton Circuit Court, see " County and District Officers."

Following is a copy of the caption of the record of the proceedings of the first session of the circuit court held in Benton County:

" At a circuit court begun and held at the house of George P. Wallace (the temporary seat of justice of Benton County), for the county of Benton, State of Arkansas, on the second Monday after the fourth Monday in October, A. D. 1837. Present, the Hon. Joseph M. Hoge, judge of said court."

First Grand Jury.—The court being convened, the sheriff returned the following " panel of good and lawful men " to serve as the first grand jury, to-wit: Joseph McKissick, foreman; Philip Dumas, William Reddock, William Ford, Christopher S. Pace, George Graham, Joseph Dickson, Robert Cooper, John B. Robinson, Jonathan Duff, Samuel P. Woods, Dioclesian Jackson, Ezekiel M. Dickson, Ambrose G. Williams and Henry Ford, who, being duly sworn and charged, retired to consult of their duties. Being selected as grand jurors, it follows that these were representative pioneers of Benton County. All are now dead excepting Christopher S. Pace and Ambrose G. Williams, who are still living in the county.

First Petit Jury.—The first petit jury was selected on the same day to try a civil case between Samuel Vaughan and John Rose. Their names were James Anderson, Robert Hubbard, John Maxwell, George W. Ford, Samuel B. McLean, Ezekiel J. A. Dickson, Henry Hastings, John Hammock, Nathan Coughman, Samuel Black, David Woods and Samuel Woods. The only survivor of these twelve old pioneers of Benton County is Ezekiel J. A. Dickson, who now lives at Osage Springs, a few miles southeast of Bentonville.

Important Trials.—The first case before the Circuit Court was that of the State against Samuel Vaughan, George W. Vaughan, Abram Hamilton, Price McMurty, John Meeks and Reese Butler for committing a "riot." The indictment not having been preserved, the full particulars of the matter cannot be given. Some of the defendants did not live in Benton County, neither was the riot committed in this county. On being arraigned for trial the defendants moved to quash the indictment, and after hearing the arguments of counsel on the motion, the court ruled that the indictment was not sufficient in law to maintain the action, and thereupon discharged the prisoners. They were immediately re-arrested and held under bonds for their appearance at the next term of court. Hon. L. D. Evans was then the prosecuting attorney. The next day a new indictment was returned by the grand jury against these defendants for the same offense. At the next term of the court, which was held at the new court-house in Bentonville, beginning May 7, 1838, the defendants were tried, and four of them, Samuel Vaughan, George W. Vaughan, William Vaughan and John Meeks, were found guilty as charged, and Samuel Vaughan was fined $85, George W. Vaughan $75, and the other two $50 each. The defendants' attorneys then made a motion for arrest of judgment and reduction of fines, whereupon the judge reduced the fine of Samuel Vaughan to $25, and that of the others to $20 each. At this trial John Rose was fined $1 for contempt of court, it being for using profanity when deposing as a witness.

The first civil suit in the Benton Circuit Court was that of

Parnell, Lamont & Co. *vs.* J. and J. M. Holmes on attachment. On being called the plaintiffs' attorney dismissed the case, and the costs were assessed to plaintiffs. The next civil case was that of Robert Weaver against Socrates Stone on an appeal from a justice of the peace. The parties appeared and submitted their case to the judge, who gave judgment in favor of the plaintiff for $15. This was the first actual trial in the Benton Circuit Court, though not the first on the docket. The first jury trial was that of Samuel Vaughan *vs.* John Rose, which was tried by the first petit jury heretofore named on the first day of the court at its first term. The jury disagreed and the case was continued. At the same term an indictment was found against Edward Cunningham for assault and battery, and another was found against John Rose for forgery. This ended the business of the first term of the court.

State of Arkansas *vs.* Mary Ridinghour and William Spencer: At the third term of the court, commencing November 3, 1838, these defendants were indicted for adultery, it being the first prosecution in the county for that misdemeanor. Mary was arrested, but Spencer escaped. On being arraigned she plead "not guilty." The trial was by jury, and the verdict was " guilty as charged in the indictment," and her fine was fixed at $40. Judgment was rendered accordingly, and she was to stand committed until the fine and costs were paid. Thereupon she appeared in court and made oath that she had no effects out of which to pay the fine and costs assessed against her, whereupon she was discharged from custody, and thus freed from further punishment. It seems that her accomplice, Spencer, remained away, and was never apprehended.

First Trial for Murder.—State of Arkansas *vs.* Edward Welch: The first trial in Benton County for murder took place at the May term of the court in 1841. The prisoner, Edward Welch, was arraigned on an indictment for murder, and plead not guilty. He was then tried by the following jury, to wit: Thomas Carle, William Hammock, Warren Wright, Daniel Mayes, John B. Walker, David McKissick, Joseph McKissick, James M. Pope, Alfred M. Wallace, Nicholas Skillern, Hampton Clark and Benjamin Hubbard. The verdict of the jury was, " We, the jury, do find the within named Edward Welch not guilty of murder, but guilty of manslaughter, in manner and form as charged in the within bill of indictment, and do say that he be punished by imprisonment for the term of seven years, and that he be fined the sum of $10,000," Thomas Carle, foreman.

The court then passed the following sentence, to wit: "It is therefore considered, adjudged and sentenced by the court here, that the said Edward Welch do pay unto the State of Arkansas the sum of $10,000 as assessed, and that he be imprisoned in the common jail of the county of Benton and State of Arkansas for the term of seven years next ensuing, and that this day be computed as one day thereof, and that he stand committed until the fine aforesaid and costs of this prosecution be fully satisfied and discharged." This trial was on a change of venue from some other county, consequently the crime was not committed in this county.

State of Arkansas *vs.* Harrison Oliver: The first prosecution in Benton County for retailing liquors without license was that of Harrison Oliver, who was tried for that offense in November, 1841. The trial was by jury, the verdict was "guilty as charged," and he was fined $1, and sentenced accordingly.

State *vs.* John B. Dickson: At the same term of court John B. Dickson was indicted for shooting at some one with whom he had some difficulty. He was tried before a jury, which found him guilty, and assessed his fine at $50 and his imprisonment at one minute. He was sentenced accordingly. Mr. Dickson was then clerk of the court.

State *vs.* Edward Brown *et al.:* Also at the same term of court Edward Brown, John Moore and Joseph Kear were indicted for murder. On being arraigned for trial the defendants plead "not guilty." They were tried and acquitted.

State *vs.* Wat Foreman: At the November term, 1842, Wat Foreman, a Cherokee Indian, was indicted for the murder of another Indian. On being arraigned he plead not guilty, and the case was continued to next term, when he was tried and found guilty of murder in the first degree. The following is a copy of the sentence of the Court. "It is therefore considered adjudged and sentenced by the Court here that the said Wat Foreman, the defendant, on Friday, the 16th day of June, 1843, between the hours of 11 o'clock in the forenoon and 2 o'clock in the afternoon, be hung by the neck on the public gallows, in the county of Benton, in the State of Arkansas, until he is dead. And it is further ordered by the Court that the clerk make out a warrant directed to the sheriff of Benton County requiring him to execute the foregoing sentence." For some reason the sentence was not executed at the time specified, and in May, 1844, the prisoner was taken before the judge of the circuit court on a writ of *habeas corpus*. The Court finding that the prisoner could give no sufficient reason why the foregoing sentence should not be executed, ordered that the sentence should be executed between the hours of 10 A. M. and 3 P. M. on the 14th day of June following. Defendant then appeared by his attorney and filed his reasons why the sentence of death should not be carried into execution. The Court did not consider the reasons sufficient in law, and overruled them. Defendant excepted and filed his bill of exceptions, which was signed, sealed and made part of the record. On appeal to the supreme court the judgment of the lower court was confirmed, and the defendant was executed according to the foregoing sentence.

State *vs.* Robert Armstrong. In May, 1845, the defendant, Robert Armstrong, was indicted and tried for the crime of murder, and acquitted. The offense was committed in another county.

State *vs.* Charles G. Duncan. In May, 1847, Charles G. Duncan was indicted for the crime of murder, and on being arraigned for trial plead not guilty. He was tried and acquitted.

State *vs.* Henry Miser. Some time prior to April, 1851, Henry Miser and Joseph Hardwick had a fight in a church near Miser's Springs. Hardwick was stabbed, the wound causing his death. In April, 1851, Miser, the defendant, was indicted for the murder of Hardwick, and in October following he was tried and acquitted. The State failed to prove to the satisfaction of the jury that the defendant did the stabbing.

State *vs.* Doghead Glory. In April, 1852, Doghead Glory, a Cherokee Indian, was indicted for the murder of another Indian named David Scoutie. In October following he was tried for the offense, and the following is the verdict of the jury: " We, the jury, find the within named defendant, Doghead Glory, guilty of the murder of the within named David Scoutie in the first degree, in manner and form as charged in the within indictment in this behalf.   (Signed)   WILLIAM WHITE, *Foreman.*"

A bill of exceptions was filed and made part of the record. A motion for a new trial was overruled, and a second bill of exceptions was filed and made part of the record. The prisoner was than sentenced as follows: "It is considered, sentenced and adjudged by the Court, that you, Doghead Glory, be remanded to the common jail of Benton County, from whence you came, there to remain until the nineteenth day of November, 1852; from thence you will be taken on said day by the sheriff of said county to the place of execution, and between the hours of ten o'clock in the forenoon and three o'clock in the afternoon of said day, there be hanged by the neck until you be dead! dead!! dead!!! And may the Lord have mercy on your soul." An order followed to the sheriff to execute the sentence. The defendant then prayed an appeal to the supreme court, which was granted, and the Court then ordered the appeal to operate as a stay to all proceedings in the cause, until the 4th day of February, 1853, when, between the hours of 10 o'clock in the forenoon and 3 o'clock in the afternoon of said day, aforesaid sentence should be executed. The supreme court confirmed the judgment of the lower court, and the unfortunate wretch was hanged accordingly.

State *vs.* Cow-sa-low-a. In April, 1852, Cow-sa-low-a, an Indian, was indicted for the murder of another Indian. In April, 1853, he was tried and found "not guilty as charged in the indictment."

On account of the loss of all the trial papers of the circuit court, before the Civil War, it has not been possible to give the names of the killed or murdered, for whom the aforesaid defendants were prosecuted.

State *vs.* Franklin Saunders and William King. At the March term, 1871, of the circuit court, Franklin Saunders and William King were indicted for the murder of James M. Lefors. The indictment charged that on the 25th day of January, 1871, at Mitchell's Mill, in Benton County, Franklin Saunders, with a club, struck and killed Lefors, and that William King was present, aiding and abetting. Both were charged as principals. King was arrested and arraigned for trial in September, following. The case was continued until March, 1872, when he was tried and acquitted. Saunders ran off and has never been apprehended.

State *vs.* Girsham P. Hoytt and Cornelius Hammon. In October, 1875, these defendants were indicted for the murder of Columbus Hancock, which took place in White's Hollow, near White River, in Benton County, on the 4th day of August, 1875. The murder was committed in Section 16, Township 19, Range 28. On being arraigned, the prisoners plead "not guilty." Hoytt asked for a separate trial, which was granted, and upon application he was granted a change of venue to Washington County, where he was afterward tried and found not guilty. Hammon was put upon trial, and from the evidence it appeared that on the occasion of the murder he and Hancock, in company with a lewd woman, went to White's Hollow, where the dead body of Hancock was found. The verdict of the jury was as follows: "We, the jury, find the defendant, Cornelius Hammon, guilty of murder in the first degree, as charged in the second count of the indictment. Signed—John W. Floyd, foreman." A motion for a new trial was made by the defendant, and overruled by court. On application an appeal to the supreme court was granted. The next day the prisoner appeared before the court and was addressed as follows:

Cornelius Hammon, you have been indicted by the grand jury of Benton County, State of Arkansas, at the present term of this court, for the murder in the first degree in killing Columbus Hancock. On this indictment you were arraigned, and interposed thereto your plea of not guilty. Upon that issue you were tried by a jury of said county, selected and chosen by yourself, and they have found you guilty of murder in the first degree. You have had at each step of the progress of the trial the advice and assistance of able counsel, appointed by the Court to defend you. They have been zealous and untiring in their efforts in your behalf; nothing within their power has been left undone by them that would in the slightest degree tend to show your innocence or extenuate your offence. Now have you any legal cause to show why the judgment of the court should not be pronounced upon you?" To this the defendant answered: "No other except what has already been interposed." The Court then proceeded:

The judgment which the law provides for murder in the first degree is death by hanging, and it now becomes the painful duty of the Court to pronounce that sentence upon you. For the short time which the law in its mercy extends you for a preparation of soul to meet the Almighty Judge of mankind,

I earnestly exhort you that you betake yourself to that earnest work. I can hold out for you no hope on earth, and your only hope is in the mercy of the Giver of all life. The judgment and sentence of this court is that you be taken hence to the jail of this county, thence on the 14th day of January, 1876, to be taken by the sheriff of Benton County, Ark., to some point to be selected by him, within two miles of the court-house of said county, and to a gallows to be by him erected, and there, between the hours of ten o'clock in the morning and two o'clock in the evening of said day, to be by him hanged by the neck until you are dead! And may God have mercy upon your soul!

He was executed accordingly. Hoytt was tried at Fayetteville and acquitted.

State *vs.* Jesse Thompson. In April, 1884, Jesse Thompson was indicted for the murder of his wife, Annie Thompson, which was alleged to have been committed on the first day of that month. The case was continued until the fall term, when, upon application, the defendant was granted a change of venue to Washington County, where he was afterward tried and acquitted.

State *vs.* S. J. Yantis and her children. In October, 1884, a party consisting of F. M. Yantis and his alleged wife, S. J. Yantis, and their children, William, Oliver and Ida, were moving through the county toward the Indian Territory, and camped over night near Siloam. On this occasion F. M. Yantis was killed. Afterward the woman, S. J. Yantis, and the children were indicted for the murder. In April, 1885, the children were tried separately from their mother and were acquitted. The mother was tried, and from the evidence it appeared that she killed her husband in self-defense, and thereupon was acquitted. The killing was alleged to have been done with an ax.

State *vs.* Jack Gates. In October, 1885, Jack Gates was indicted for the murder of Ferdinand Cherry, which took place on the tenth day of the preceding August. In March following he was tried and found guilty of manslaughter, and his punishment was assessed at two years' service in the penitentiary. A motion for a new trial was overruled, and his sentence was pronounced in accordance with the verdict of the jury.

State *vs.* R. O. Chambers. On the 1st day of October, 1886, R. O. Chambers was indicted for murder in the second degree. The indictment charged him with the killing of a man named Ellis, a few miles west of Bentonville. He was tried April 21, 1887, and found by the jury "not guilty."

Benton County Bar.—The first attorney of the Benton County bar was A. B. Greenwood, now familiarly called "Judge" Greenwood. He settled at Bentonville the year the county was organized, and except when absent on official business has resided here ever since. For the first four years of the existence of the county he constituted the whole bar, being the only resident attorney. Attorneys from abroad, however, came here to practice. At a ripe old age the Judge is vigorous and active. He has had much to do in making the history of this county, and has imparted much information to the compiler of this work. [See his biography.]

Judge Joseph M. Hoge, the first judge of the Benton Circuit Court, resided in this county from about 1840 to 1845, and then went to Texas. Until recently the bar of Benton County was small, but now it has grown to be large. The following is a list of the names of the members of the bar at this writing, to wit: Judge A. B. Greenwood, E. P. Watson, James A. Rice, E. S. McDaniel, L. H. McGill, W. D. Mauck, A. Nicodemus, J. M. Peel, S. W. Peel, D. H. Hammons, W. S. Floyd, S. E. Davis, S. N. Elliott, S. A. Cordel, E. R. Morgan, F. H. Foster, C. M. Rice, A. T. Rose, E. D. Fenno. All of these reside within the county.

WAR RECORD.

A company of soldiers was raised in Benton County, by Capt. Henry L. Smith, for the Mexican War. They went as far as Fort Smith, but the quota having been filled they were not accepted. A portion of them, however, then joined the company of Capt. Wells, a company that was accepted but not yet full. In this company they went forward, and served in that war. On the approach of the late Civil War, when the question of "secession" was being agitated, the people of Benton County, in general, were opposed to that measure, and did not wish to sever their connection with the Federal Union. They were, however, almost unanimously in favor of the Southern cause, and when it became evident that nothing but war would suffice to settle the difficulties between the opposing sections of the country, they cast their lot with their friends of the South, and went into the conflict with a determination to fight to the end of the struggle to secure what they believed to be their rights, and how well they did this the sequel will show.

In the spring of 1861, after the "dogs of war" had been let loose, Capt. T. T. Hays raised an infantry company on Pea Ridge, in Benton County, and Capt. Dan. McKissick raised a cavalry company, mostly from the southern part of the county, both of which companies joined the State service, and remained therein until a short time after the battle of Wilson's Creek was fought, and were then disbanded. These companies did not happen to be engaged in any fights. Nearly all the men composing these companies afterward joined other companies, and went into the Confederate service.

The Fifteenth Regiment Arkansas Infantry.—The first company that went into the Confederate army from Benton County was Company A, of the Fifteenth Arkansas Regiment. It was raised in midsummer of 1861, by Capt. J. H. Hobbs. Soon thereafter Companies F and G of the same regiment were raised in Benton County. The former went out under Capt. William Thompson, and the latter under Capt. J. M. Richards. The regiment was organized in a camp near Cross Hollows, in this county, in the fall of 1861, served to the close of the war, and surrendered at Marshall, Tex., in May, 1865. Its first colonel was D. McRea, and afterward Capt. Hobbs, of Company A, became the colonel, and he finally resigned on account of ill health. Among the important battles in which this regiment was engaged were Pea Ridge, in Benton County, Ark.; Iuka Springs and Corinth, in Mississippi; Fort Gibson, Baker's Creek, defense of Vicksburg during the siege thereof, Prairie De Ann, Mark's Mill and Jenkins' Ferry. After the surrender at Vicksburg the regiment went into a parole camp at Washington, Ark., where it remained until after it was exchanged. Its loss during the war was somewhat heavy.

The Thirty-fourth Regiment Arkansas Infantry.—Company F, of this regiment, was raised in Benton County, in July, 1862, and went out under Capt. C. L. Pickins. The regiment was organized at Mount Comfort, in Washington County. The more important battles in which it was engaged were Prairie Grove, Helena and Jenkins' Ferry. It also surrendered at Marshall,

Tex., in May, 1865. Company F, of Col. King's Arkansas Regiment, was raised in Benton County, and went out under Capt. John Miser, of Pea Ridge. This regiment was organized at Mulberry, in Franklin County, was brigaded with the Thirty-fourth Arkansas, and participated in the same battles and surrendered at the same time and place.

Capt. Tom Jefferson raised a company of cavalry in Benton County, for Col. Carl's regiment of Arkansas cavalry. This regiment served through the war, mostly in Missouri and Arkansas. Capt. Hugh Tinnin, of Maysville, and Capt. W. H. Hendren, each raised a company in the western part of Benton County, both of which served during the war in the Indian Territory. Capt. James Ingram raised a company of cavalry in the eastern part of Benton County, and it served in Northwestern Arkansas until October, 1863, when it went south, dismounted, joined and became a part of the Thirty-fourth Arkansas Infantry. Capt. "Bill Buck" Brown raised a company of cavalry in the southern part of Benton County, which served in Northwestern Arkansas during the continuance of the war. The captain was killed in a skirmish in the winter of 1864–65. Capt. James Cooper also raised an independent company of cavalry, which served in Northwestern Arkansas.

This gives eleven companies which were raised in Benton County for the Confederate army, all of which averaged 100 men each, thus making 1,100 men that served in the Confederate army from this county, besides several hundred who went into the service as recruits. No Federal troops were organized in this county for actual service in the war. A few months before the close of the war two or three companies of militia were organized, under the provision of the Federal Government, for the purpose of protecting the citizens from the depredations of the thieving and marauding parties not belonging to either army, that were prowling around through the country plundering, murdering and robbing the citizens.

Skirmish on Dunagin's Farm.—In February, 1862, when Gen. Price retreated from Missouri to join McCulloch in Arkansas, he was pursued through Benton County by the Federal forces under Gen. Curtis. His rear guard, under command of

Gen. James S. Rains, was annoyed considerably by the Federal advance, and to get rid of this Rains halted on the farm of Rev. J. Dunagin, at or near the present station of Avoca, on the St. L. & S. F. Railroad, and planted a battery in a seemingly unprotected position, at the same time having it well protected by troops concealed along the side of the approach to it. Not discovering the support to this battery, the Federal advance (cavalry) charged it, and received the cross fire of the concealed troops of the enemy. Twenty Federal soldiers and sixty horses, and two or three Confederate soldiers, were killed at once. This, of course, repulsed the Federal advance, and checked their pursuit. This was the first fight and the first reception of Federal troops in Benton County, and on this occasion the residence of Rev. J. Dunagin was set on fire and burned by the Federals, it being the first house burned in Benton in the war period. This house stood one-half mile east of the present village of Avoca. It was probably the 18th day of February, 1862, when this skirmish took place. The facts concerning it were furnished the compiler by Rev. Dunagin, who is well known to the people of Benton County.

Battle of Pea Ridge.—This great battle, having been fought in Benton County, deserves a prominent place in its history. On the 18th day of February, 1862, the Federal army, commanded by Maj.-Gen. Samuel B. Curtis, crossed the State line from Missouri and went into camp on Sugar Creek, near Brightwater, in Benton County, Ark. "The Third and Fourth Divisions advanced from this position twelve miles farther south to Cross Hollows, where also the headquarters of Gen. Curtis were established, and the First and Second to Bentonville, twelve miles to the southwest, while a strong cavalry force, under Gen. Asboth, went to Osage Springs. On the 23d Gen. Asboth made a dash into Fayetteville, twenty miles in advance, found the city evacuated, and planted the Union flag on the court-house." On March 1, Col. Jeff. C. Davis' division withdrew from Cross Hollows and he took his position immediately behind Little Sugar Creek, covering the Fayettville and Springfield road, and fortified his position in anticipation of an attack from the south. On the 2d of March the First and Second Divisions, under Gen. Sigel, moved to McKissick's farm, four and a half miles west of Bentonville. Col. Schaefer, with the Second Missouri Infantry and a detatchment of cavalry, was sent to Osage Mills, six miles south by a little east of McKissick's farm, as a post of observation toward Elm Springs, and for the purpose of running the mill to grind flour for the troops.

Another detachment of cavalry was sent to Osage Springs, five miles southeast of Bentonville, to hold connection with the division at Cross Hollows. On the 5th a detachment under Maj. Conrad was sent from McKissick's farm to Maysville, on the State line, twenty-one miles west of Bentonville; and another detachment under Maj. Mezaros went to Pineville, twenty-five miles northwest, while a detachment under Col. Vandever had been sent to Huntsville, in Madison County. Meanwhile the Confederate army, commanded by Maj.-Gen. Earl Van Dorn, concentrated in the Boston Mountains south of Fayetteville, and on the 3rd it was on the march to Fayetteville and Elm Springs, its advance arriving at the latter place on the evening of the 5th. On this march Price's troops in the lead were followed by McCulloch's division, while Gen. Pike with a brigade of Indian troops brought up the rear. The Federal officers did not learn of this movement until the 5th, when the Confederates were only a day's march from Sigel's position at McKissick's farm. It was the intention of the Confederate commander to move early on the 6th, and if possible cut off and capture Sigel's two divisions before they could prepare for defense or effect their retreat. Sigel, however, was advised of the advance of the enemy in time to prevent this disaster. Col. Schaefer's outposts were attacked on the evening of the 5th, and during that night he fell back, under instructions from Gen Sigel, to Bentonville. " At 2 o'clock A. M. of the 6th Gen. Asboth's division left McKissick's farm with the whole train, followed by the division of Osterhaus. They passed through Bentonville from 4 to 8 o'clock A. M., and arrived at the camp behind Sugar Creek at 2 P. M., where the Union army was to concentrate."

For the purpose of defending the main column on its retreat, and to make observations regarding the Confederates' advance, Gen. Sigel remained at Bentonville, with about 600 men and a battery of six pieces, after all the troops had left the place. At 10 A. M. he discovered that the Confederates were forming a battle line about a mile south of the village. With all possible haste and caution he then set out with his rear guard to follow his main army. The Confederate troops quickly followed, and skirmished with his command until they gained a point on Sugar Creek, about seven miles northeast of Bentonville. Here Sigel went up the creek toward Brightwater, where he joined the main army under Curtis. Van Dorn, the Confederate commander, left his wagon train at the crossing of Sugar Creek, and posted Green's division there to protect it, and to prevent the Federals from retreating down the valley in case of their defeat. He then advanced his army on the Bentonville and Keetsville road, passing the right of the Federal army as it was then in position facing southward, and passing north of Big Mountain, until, with Price's command, he reached the Fayetteville and Springfield road at a point north of the Elkhorn Tavern, and in the rear of the Federal army. He expected to reach this point before daylight on the morning of the 7th, but, on account of obstructions placed in the road by Col. Dodge's Iowa regiment, he did not reach it until nearly 10 A. M. of that day. During the night, while passing along the north side of Big Mountain, McCulloch's command countermarched, and returned to the west end of Big Mountain, taking position immediately west and south thereof, with his lines facing south and southwestwardly. During the night of the 6th the Federal army rested in line of battle, facing southward from behind Sugar Creek. Gen. Asboth's division held the extreme right, Col. Osterhaus was on his left, Col. Davis next, and Col. Carr, with his division, on the extreme left. The extreme right was so retired as to face southwest. Curtis expected to be attacked from the south, and had made preparations accordingly, but early on the morning of the 7th he learned that his enemy was in his rear instead of the front; and, after consultation with his division commanders at Pratt's store, he faced about and directed Col. Carr to take position at Elkhorn Tavern, while Col. Bussey was directed, with the cavalry of the different commands (except the Third Illinois) and with three pieces of Elbert's battery, to move by Leetown against the enemy supposed to be advancing in that direction. A brigade of infantry and another battery from Sigel's command were sent to support the cavalry, and Col. Osterhaus was also directed to accompany Col. Bussey for the purpose of taking control of the movement. Davis' division then moved to the support of Osterhaus on the left to contend with the Confederate forces under McCulloch, while Asboth moved to the support and assistance of Carr's division on the right to contend with Price's command. The lines of the latter faced south, southwest and west, forming a sort of semi-circle, the left of which overlapped the right of the Federal lines.

As the lines of the respective armies were formed on the morning of the 7th, before the engagement began, Price's command of the Confederate army, under the immediate control of the commanding general, Van Dorn, lay east of Big Mountain, while McCulloch's forces lay west and southwest thereof, and thus all immediate communication between the two portions of the Confederate army was cut off. The Federal army was also divided, as before stated, in order to contend with the divided forces of the Confederates, but Gen. Curtis established his headquarters near Pratt's store, and kept up communication between the two portions of his army. When the battle opened on the morning of the 7th the Federal cavalry sent out from Sigel's command to meet McCulloch's advance was repulsed, and in turn the Confederates were checked in their onslaught by the command of Osterhaus. "At this point," says Gen. Sigel, "the speedy arrival of Col. Jeff. C. Davis' division on the right of Osterhaus, and its energetic advance, turned a very critical moment into a decisive victory of our arms. McCulloch and McIntosh fell while leading their troops in a furious attack against Osterhaus and Davis. Hebert and a number of his officers and men were captured by the pickets of the Thirty-sixth Illinois (cavalry), under Capt. Smith, and of the Forty-fourth Illinois Infantry, under Capt. Russell. Thus the whole of McCulloch's column, deprived of its leaders and without unity of command, was thrown into confusion and beaten back. Though a great advantage was gained on our side by the death and capture of those leaders, the principal cause of our success was rather the quick rallying and excellent maneuvering of Osterhaus' and Davis' forces, as well as the coolness and bravery of their infantry, supported by Welfley's, Hoffman's and Davidson's batteries. Osterhaus changed his front twice, under the fire of the enemy, to meet the dangerous flank attack and pressure of Hebert's Louisiana and Arkansas infantry, while the brigades of Davis, by striking the left of McCulloch's advancing column, threw it into disorder and forced it to retreat."

During the day the left wing of the Confederate army, under Van Dorn and Price, was eminently successful, as conceded by Gen. Sigel, who says: "In spite of the heroic resistance of the two brigades of Dodge and Vandever, and the re-enforcements sent them during the afternoon, they were forced back from position to position until Elkhorn Tavern was taken by the enemy, and our crippled forces, almost without ammunition, their artillery reduced by losses of guns, men and horses, their infantry greatly reduced, had to seek a last shelter in the woods and behind the fences, separated from the enemy's position by open fields, but not farther than a mile from our trains. They formed a contracted and curved line, determined to resist, not disheartened, but awaiting with some apprehension another attack. Fortunately the enemy did not follow up his success, and night fell in, closing this terrible conflict."

Of the Indian forces in McCulloch's column Col. Drew with his Cherokee regiment retreated to the southwest toward Bentonville, while Col. Greer, who succeeded McCulloch in command of the wing, moved with the remainder of the force during the night and joined Van Dorn, taking position on his extreme left the next morning. Col. Stand Waitie, with his Cherokee regiment, retreated to Bentonville during the second day of the fight. It is said that the hardest fighting in this battle took place between the forces of the Confederate left and the Federal right. When the battle opened the position held by the Federal right was stoutly maintained, and it was with a fearful struggle and heavy loss to both sides that they were dislodged and compelled to fall back. With repeated attacks on the Federal line it was compelled to fall back, so that when the day's engagement closed the left of the right wing rested near the foot of Big Mountain and the right a short distance east of Pratt's store. This was confronted by the advanced line of the Confederates, who had captured Elkhorn Tavern, and formed their line west and south thereof, with their right resting at the foot of the mountain. The withdrawal of the Confederates' right wing from in front of the Federal left enabled Sigel to move eastward, with the division of Osterhaus along the south side of the mountain, to the relief and support of the right wing, which had been sorely pressed during the day. During the night of the 7th the division of Col. Davis was called in from Leetown, and this brought the Federal army all together.

On the first day of the fight, while Van Dorn and Price were so vigorously pushing their columns forward with marked success, they hoped that the right wing under McCulloch was equally successful. But learning of his death, and that of McIntosh, the repulse of the right wing, and the state of affairs in general, Van Dorn concluded to retreat, and during the night Green's division, that had been left back on Sugar Creek to guard the wagon train, was ordered to fall back and secure the train from exposure to capture. Early on the morning of the 8th the Federal line was re-formed, with the division of Asboth on the left (near the mountain), Osterhaus' division in the center, and that of Davis on the right, with Carr's division in a retired position to the rear of Davis' right, and immediately in front of Pratt's store, the whole facing generally to the east, and confronting the Confederate line. The latter, as formed on the morning of the 8th (Saturday), was as follows: Little on the right, next to the mountain and directly in front of the Federal forces under Asboth and Osterhaus; Frost next on the left; Greer and Hill next, with Gates' cavalry on the extreme left. Gen. Curtis opened the battle on the second morning with cannonading, and having selected a good position he moved on to the Confederate forces, who seemed to fight more on the defensive than on the offensive, as they had the day before. "However, opposite the left of the Federal line, near Elkhorn Tavern, Van Dorn made a determined effort to hold the spur of hills, the top of which was crowned and protected by rocks and bowlders. Some of Price's infantry had already taken possession of it, and a battery was being placed in position, when Hoffmann's and Elbert's batteries were ordered to direct their fire against them, chiefly with solid shot. Not more than fifteen minutes elapsed before the enemy evacuated this last stronghold." [Sigel.] About the same time two Federal regiments advanced from the center and right into the woods, engaged the Confederate infantry and drove it back, and another Federal regiment (the Twelfth Missouri) captured the Dallas battery. At this juncture the Federal right advanced on to the Confederate left, the latter yielding, and the general retreat of the Confederate army now began. It fell back over the same ground it had gained the day before, and the main army, which remained in order, retreated to the southeast on the Van Winkle road. Some detachments cut off from the main army retreated in other directions, being followed by Federal forces toward Keetsville, in Missouri, and to a point beyond Bentonville, in Arkansas.

It is claimed by those who served in the Confederate army that Van Dorn's only object in maintaining the fight on the second day was to enable his trains and forces to make a successful retreat. The retreat took place before noon. The Federal army remained on the field, having won the victory which the Confederates felt confident of winning during the first day of the fight. The plan of attack adopted by Gen. Van Dorn was a wise one, and could he have reached the vicinity of Elkhorn Tavern by daylight on the morning of the 7th, as he expected to, he would have found the Federal army unprepared to receive his attack, and would in all probability have won the victory. Again, as it was, if the column of McCulloch had been properly handled, the Confederates might have gained the day. But be that as it may, it was a great victory to the Union cause, inasmuch as to a great extent it kept the war out of Missouri for the next two years, and completely defeated Van Dorn's contemplated project of capturing St. Louis and extending the war into Illinois. It is the province of this work, however, only to give *the history*, and not to make extended comments on what "might have been."

On the second day of the Pea Ridge battle Brig.-Gen. William Y. Slack, commanding a force under Gen. Price, was mortally wounded in a charge made on a part of the Federal line. His home was in Chillicothe, Mo. He was a lawyer by profession; was a captain in the Mexican War under Sterling Price, who was then a colonel.

Composition, strength and losses of the contending armies at Pea Ridge:

Federal Army: Brig.-Gen. Samuel R. Curtis, commander.

First and Second Divisions, Brig.-Gen. Franz Sigel.

First Division, consisting of two brigades of infantry and two batteries of artillery, commanded by Col. Peter J. Osterhaus.

Second Division, consisting of the First Brigade, some unattached troops, and two batteries: Brig.-Gen. Alexander Asboth.

Third Division, consisting of two brigades, one battery and some cavalry: Col. Jeff. C. Davis.

Fourth Division, consisting of two brigades, one battery and some unattached cavalry and infantry: Col. Eugene A. Carr.

Effective force of Union army, 10,500 infantry and cavalry, with forty-nine pieces of artillery. [See "Official Records" VIII, page 196.]

Total loss of Union army: 203 killed, 980 wounded, and 201 captured or missing. Total 1,384.

Confederate Army: Maj.-Gen. Earl VanDorn, commander.

Missouri State Guards: Maj.-Gen. Sterling Price.

Confederate Volunteers: Various commands.

State Troops: Second, Third, Fifth, Sixth, Seventh, Eighth and Ninth Divisions.

McCulloch's Division (various commands): Brig.-Gen. Ben. McCulloch.

Pike's command, consisting of Indians and a squadron of Texas cavalry: Brig.-Gen. Albert Pike. Other troops not included in the foregoing.

Effective force of Confederate army: Price's command, 6,818, with eight batteries of artillery [Official Records, VIII, page 305]; McCulloch's command, 8,384, with four batteries of eighteen pieces [Official Records, VIII, page 763]; Pike's command, 1,000 [Official Records, VIII, page 288]; aggregate, 16,202 infantry and cavalry. This, of course, includes the number left back with Green to guard the trains. The Confederate loss has been reported at 800 to 1,000 killed and wounded, and between 200 and 300 prisoners, which, if correct, would make the loss about equal to that of the Federal army.

Elkhorn Tavern.—The site of this famous tavern was settled in 1832 by James Hannors, of Illinois, who, in 1834, sold it to William Redick, also from Illinois. The latter built the house known as the "Elkhorn Tavern." It was an ordinary two-story frame, with a front porch to each story, and a brick chimney on the outside at each end, and was adorned on top with a huge pair of elk-horns taken from an animal killed by Mr. Casedy, who settled the site of Pratt's store, which still remains on the Pea Ridge battle-field. During the battle of Pea Ridge Mr. Cox, who lived in the tavern, was obliged, with his mother and his young wife, to seek protection in the cellar. The Federals took the elk-horns from the building, and sent them finally to New York, and during the latter part of the war the house was burned. In 1886 Mr. J. C. Cox, who still owns the property, rebuilt the tavern upon the original plan and on the original site. Then, through the assistance of Col. Hunt P. Wilson, of St. Louis, who, with the Confederate army, participated in the battle, he procured the return of the elk-horns and placed them upon the new building, where they are now gazed upon by the many who visit that historic place.

Devastations of War.—From the date of the battle of Pea Ridge to the close of the war Benton County was alternately possessed, overrun and devastated by the opposing armies. Provisions, crops and other property was appropriated for the use of the troops; houses were pillaged and burned, and the fences on many farms, especially in the vicinity of the soldiers' camps, were entirely consumed for fuel. Good, dry rails burned so much easier than green wood, made better fires, and saved the labor of chopping. However, the soldiers only took the "top rails," but it was understood that after these were taken off the next ones in turn became "top rails," and so on down to the bottom. Many citizens were wantonly killed, some for their money, and others for no cause whatever. Some were even tortured with fire to compel them to give up their money, or tell where it was concealed. The taking of provisions, horses and other animals for the use of the armies, and the burning of rails for fuel,

was authorized by the officers of both; but the burning of buildings, with but few exceptions, if any, the killing of defenseless
citizens, and the torturing of others for the purposes of robbery,
were not authorized by the officers unless by some inferior subor-
dinates of either army.

War gives an excellent opportunity for thieves and robbers
to practice their fiendish profession, and on the occasion of the
late war this class of men armed themselves and organized as
bandits, and scoured the country, stealing, plundering, burning
and murdering as they went. To them and the bushwhackers
the greatest atrocities were chargeable. Of the depredations
generally authorized by the "usages of war," the Federal army
is undoubtedly chargeable with the greater portion in Benton
County, as the citizens were not generally in sympathy with it,
while they were in sympathy with the Confederate army, hence
the reason. There were bad men in both armies, who committed
many misdeeds, for which neither could be held responsible.
War is a terrible thing, and it is hoped and fully believed that
the people of the United States now living will never see any
more of it, especially among themselves. The many individual
incidents that occurred in Benton County during the late struggle,
if related, would fill a volume in themselves, and consequently
cannot be inserted in this work.

Confederate Reunion at Pea Ridge.—On the first day of
September, 1887, over twenty-five years after the battle of Pea
Ridge was fought, the people, with the surviving veteran soldiers,
met on that famous field to commemorate the event, and to witness the unveiling of the monument erected to the memory of
Gens. McCulloch, McIntosh and Slack, and other brave Confederates who fell on that occasion. The camp-ground for the
reunion was established one mile southwest of Elkhorn Tavern,
near a fine gushing spring in a densely shaded grove. Here
thousands of people, including many veterans, assembled to
enjoy the occasion. From this lovely spot in plain view lay
the high point where once stood Sigel's battery, and off to the
southwest of him was the Round Mountain, where stood the Confederate battery. The points where McCulloch and McIntosh
lost their lives were still a mile or so further west and southwest
of Sigel's battery.

About 100 yards southwest of the old tavern stands the monument built by the people of Benton County to the memory of their fallen heroes. The square pedestal that rises from the base has an inscription on each side, as follows: On the north, "Gen. W. Y. Slack, of Missouri;" on the west, "Gen. Ben McCulloch, of Texas;" on the south, "Gen. James McIntosh, of Arkansas," and on the east, "The brave Confederate dead, who fell on this field March 7 and 8, 1862." It is a plain, unpretentious shaft of marble that does credit to the donors. Below the pedestal and above the sandstone base is a marble block, upon which the following verses are inscribed:

> Oh give me a land where the rains are spread,
> And the living tread light on the hearts of the dead;
> Yes, give me a land that is blest by the dust
> And bright with the deeds of the downtrodden just.
>
> O give me the land with a grave in each spot,
> And names in the graves that shall not be forgot.
> Yes, give me the land of the wreck and the tomb;
> There's a grandeur in graves, there's a glory in gloom.
>
> The graves of our dead, with green overgrown,
> May yet form the footstool of liberty's throne,
> And each single wreck in the war-path of might,
> Shall yet be a rock in the temple of right.

A few yards from the spot where the monument is erected stood Capt. Bledsoe's battery, which included the famous cannon, "Old Sacramento," which had seen service through the Mexican War.

The address of welcome was delivered by Col. S. W. Peel, member of Congress from that district, and the response thereto was made by Judge C. A. DeFrance. The latter drew a contrast between the welcome extended to the large number of Federal soldiers who were present, and the terrible reception given them on the spot twenty-five years before. They were then welcomed with bloody hands to gory graves, and now they were welcomed as friends and neighbors, and were happy to accept and extend hospitalities.

Ex-Gov. Lubbock, of Texas, delivered the general address, concluding it by commending both the "Blue and the Grey" for their bravery, and by exhorting his hearers "to stand by the old constitution as it now is, and be a loyal and conservative people." He was followed by Senator Berry, Judge DeFrance, Col. T. J. Patton and others, who made appropriate short speeches.

In compiling the history of the battle of Pea Ridge the writer acknowledges assistance from Hon. D. H. Hammons and others, who participated in the battle on the Confederate side, as well as from a few Union soldiers who participated therein, and also from the Benton County *Journal*, which contains a brief sketch of the battle. Acknowledgments are also due to the *Journal* for the account of the Confederate Reunion on the occasion of unveiling the monument to Gen. McCulloch and others.

TOWNS AND VILLAGES.

AVOCA.

This little village is prettily located on the St. Louis & San Francisco Railroad, five miles north of Rogers. It was laid out in 1881 by Albert Peel, who built the first house and opened the first store in the place. It now contains the railroad depot, two stores, kept, respectively, by Albert Peel and J. R. Dunagin, a blacksmith shop and grain warehouse, also a district school-house. Grain, railroad ties, fence posts and fruits, especially small fruits, are extensively shipped from this station.

BRIGHTWATER.

Brightwater is a station on the St. Louis & San Francisco Railroad, two miles northeast of Avoca. As a village it was established about the year 1840, by an old pioneer settler, Enoch Trott, who kept a tavern or "stand" and a grocery, principally for the use of the drovers and other travelers on the old State road. A leading article sold at the grocery was in liquid form. It was called "Trott's Stand." At the breaking out of the war Judge Long kept the only store in the place. This store-house and the few other buildings there were burned on the occasion of the battle of Pea Ridge. The first improvement there, after the war, was made by Albert Peel (now of Avoca), who bought the land and put up a dwelling-house and a store-house. It now consists of the general store of Joe Dickson & Son, the drug store of Drs. T. M. & R. S. Rice, the grocery store of Hill & Lynch, a

blacksmith shop and a fruit evaporator, the latter by Kimmons &
Son. The capacity of the fruit evaporator is about 200 bushels
per day, and when operated the proprietors employ about twenty-
five hands. The place has a district school-house, but no church
edifice. The only organized church there is the Christian, and
the members thereof worship in the school-house. Pea Ridge
Lodge No. 119, A. F. & A. M., is located at Brightwater. In
amount of shipments the place compares well with other stations
on the road.

BENTONVILLE.

The origin and location of Bentonville, the county seat of
Benton County, has been given in connection with the organization of the county. Being established in 1837, the first
store opened in the place was managed by Dr. Nicholas Spring,
under the firm name of Blythe & Spring, and the next one was
opened by two brothers, John G. and William T. Walker. Blythe
& Spring had a pretty fair stock of goods, but the Walkers had
a broken stock, worth only about $800. In 1840 or 1841 another
store was opened by some parties from Fayetteville, and in 1850
the town had about five business houses and a few mechanics'
shops. Being so far inland, and in a new country, the settlement
of which was slow, the growth of the town was also slow and
gradual. In 1860, just before the outbreak of the Civil War, it
contained five general stores, kept respectively by A. W. Dinsmore, James Woolsey, Greenwood & Hobbs, J. M. Vestal and
James A. Dickson; the furniture store of Henry Baumeister, the
saddle and harness-shop of J. W. Clark, the Clark Hotel by J. W.
Clark, the Vestal Hotel by W. R. Vestal, and three or four mechanics' shops. It also contained the county public buildings,
and two churches, Cumberland Presbyterian and Methodist
Episcopal, South, and the building of the Masonic lodge and
school-house, and had a population of about 500. Of professional
men there were four physicians—Drs. C. D. Talliaferro, D. H.
Hobbs, William Wilson and John Gray. There were also a few
attorneys and local officers, together with the county officers. In
addition to the foregoing there were one or more "dram-shops"
or saloons in the town.

Bentonville, especially, suffered terribly from the ravages of war. In February, 1862, when a portion of Federal troops belonging to Gen. Curtis' army passed through the town, a soldier lingered behind, either with or without authority, and was killed by one in sympathy with the Southern cause. Some of the Federal soldiers returned to the town next day, and on learning of the fate of their comrade became exasperated, applied the torch in revenge, and on this occasion thirty-six buildings were consumed by fire. In justice to the commander of these troops, who were then encamped a few miles southwest of the town, it must be said that as soon as he learned the state of affairs he sent orders back to stop the burning of the town. Afterward, from time to time, buildings continued to be burned in the town, and in the country surrounding it, by both Federal and Confederate soldiers, and some were burned by thieves and plunderers belonging to neither army. Both contending parties now claim that the court-house was burned by the other. According to best authority, the two churches, the Masonic hall and school building, and the jail, were burned to prevent their being used by the Union armies. After the first burning, scouting parties of either army, passing through and finding houses standing, would imagine that they were left because their owners were in sympathy with the other army, and would therefore burn them. This work of burning property was carried on to such an extent that when the war closed only about a dozen houses were left standing in Bentonville.

At the close of the war the county was devastated and the towns likewise, but the people were inured to hardships, and were determined if possible to retrieve their lost fortunes. With but little capital they applied themselves to the work, and the following directory and sketch of the present business and institutions of Bentonville will show how well they have succeeded in their efforts. It is true, however, that much of the success of Bentonville is due to its immigration from other States.

Bentonville was incorporated by the county court at its January adjourned term in 1873. At the present writing (1888) its officers are Hon. W. D. Mauck, mayor; Henry Cowan, recorder; W. S. Black, treasurer; councilmen, Dr. John Smartt, Dr. J. M. Thompson, N. S. Henry, Robert Brashear, George P.

Jackson; W. T. Woolsey, marshal. The town contains several large brick business blocks, besides many frame business houses, and many beautiful residences. The latter are mostly surrounded with large lawns well filled with shade and fruit trees. Though the oldest town in the county, it is yet a young town, having been nearly all built since the close of the late war, and mostly within the last ten years. Its population is between 2,500 and 3,000.

Bentonville Directory.—Banks, Benton County Bank, The Peoples Bank; dry goods, W. A. Terry & Co., Craig & Sons, Woods & Claypool, George Jackson; auction store, W. E. Goodwin; groceries, J. C. Knott, Morris & Co., J. H. & J. P. Burns, Wagner & Jefferson, G. M. Bates & Co., P. S. Powell, drugs, Dr. C. D. Taliaferro, E. H. Looney, W. S. Black; confectioneries, Inson & Larick, W. R. Hoffman, M. M. Harkins, P. McBride; furniture, T. C. Barney, J. L. Pluck; hardware, Hobbs & Co., Maxwell & Hickman; harness and saddles, H. A. Rogers, Stahl & Crough; clothing, Lincoln & Arthur; boots and shoes, Laughlin & Brashear; watchmakers and jewelers, R. J. Laughlin, M. M. Hawkins; undertakers, J. Huffman & Son; marble works, McWhirter & Robbins; bakery, J. K. Putman; candy factory, H. C. Turner; agricultural implements, C. W. Clapp, F. C. Hawkins; millinery, Wakefield & Deming, J. A. Sanderson & Co., Miss Julia Loomis; boot and shoemakers, Roberts & Thomas, D. R. Thompson; produce dealers, McHenry & Bryan, R. Y. Nance; blacksmiths, W. H. Ferguson, W. A. Smith, A. Marcum; feed store, Corley & Son; meatmarkets, S. N. Price, J. H. Houston; livery, Smartt & Brown, Faircloe & Brim; brickyards, J. Haney, Z. Mitchell, M. T. Carroll; contractors, J. Haney, C. A. Blanck, A. W. Duffie, J. Cook, Carney & Dodson, Robert Carley; Eagle Mills, H. W. Schrader, proprietor; Bentonville Mills, John Curtis, proprietor; tobacco manufactory, Arkansas Tobacco Company; canneries and evaporators, Bentonville Canning and Evaporating Company; wagon factory, McGruder, McAdams & Co., proprietors; lumber yard, Hall, Guthrie & Co.; cooperage, Dungie & Hunter; hotels, Rogers House, Western Hotel, Eagle Hotel, Eclipse Hotel; physicians, T. W. Hurley, J. M. Thompson, John Smartt, C. D. Taliaferro, B. F. Smith, J. R. Lucas, W. R. Davis,

J. M. Hobbs, J. A. Gill, N. B. Cotton; dentists, D. A. Watson, S. H. Petit, M. B. Vaughter; collector and conveyancer, F. M. Bates; insurance, C. E. Bruce, Cotton & Craig; attorneys, see " Benton County Bar."

Churches.—Cumberland Presbyterian, Rev. F. T. Chaston, J. D. Ritchie, temporarily in charge; Methodist Episcopal Church, South, Rev. T. J. Reynolds; Presbyterian, Rev. D. C. Boggs; Baptist Missionary, Rev. J. M. McGuire; Christian Church, J. R. Lucas, M. D.; Methodist Episcopal Church, Rev. W. M. Brock.

Sales Transactions in 1887.—Four dry-goods, notions, etc., $122,000; five groceries, $90,000; one clothing and gents' furnishing, $21,000; one boots and shoes, $10,000; two furniture, $20,-500; one undertaker, $1,500; two saddlery and harness, $11,000; two hardware, $37,000; two agricultural implements, etc., $61,-000; two drugs, $17,000; one watch-maker, $4,000; two millinery and ladies' furnishing, $5,000; four hotels, $10,000; two butchers, $11,000; one bakery, $2,600; one tobacco, $15,000; one lumber, $25,000; two produce and fruit, $81,000; one evaporating plant, $25,000; grain and grain products, $116,000; live stock, $41,000; railroad ties, $16,500; railroad earnings, $12,953; miscellaneous, $100,000.   Total, exclusive of banking and loans, $896,000.

Bentonville Railroad Company.—Length of railroad in miles, $5\frac{1}{4}$; cost of construction, $42,000.   Passengers carried west, 5,077; passengers carried east, 4,182; total tickets sold in 1887, 9,259.   Tons of freight received. 2,833; tons of freight forwarded, 5,477; total tons of freight handled in 1887, 8,310.   Tons agricultural products handled, 661; tons animal or live stock, 260; vegetable foods and products, tons, 738; manufactured articles, tons, 168; merchandise, tons, 2,838; products of forest, tons, 3,450; eggs, 195.   Total tons handled, 8,310.

Officers Bentonville Railroad.—President, John Smartt; vice-president, J. H. McClinton; general manager, N. S. Henry; traffic manager, D. H. Woods; conductor, C. M. Robinson.

The Benton County Bank was organized in May, 1885, by John Black, president; J. A. Rice, vice-president; S. F. Stahl, cashier; Jesse Motter, assistant cashier, and J. G. McAndrews, with a paid-up capital of $20,000.   In May, 1887, the bank was reorganized, and the capital stock was increased to $50,000, all paid up.   The present officers are W. A. Terry, president; A. J. Bates, vice-president; S. F. Stahl, cashier; N. B. Cotton, assistant cashier; J. A. Rice, attorney.   Other stockholders aside from the officers named are J. W. Langford, John Black and J. G. McAndrews.   The bank is located in the Terry Block, opposite the People's Bank, at the southwest corner of the public square. This fine brick block is three stories high, and is the most attractive and imposing structure in the city.   The lower story contains the banking room on the corner and a large store-room, with one front on the north side of the bank facing eastward, and another front west of the bank facing southward.

The People's Bank was organized and began business in June, 1888, with a capital stock of $50,000.   Its first and present officers are John Smartt, president; I. B. Gilmore, vice-president; F. E. Gilmore, cashier; A. W. Dinsmore, assistant cashier. Board of directors: John Smartt, J. A. C. Blackburn, I. B. Gilmore, A. W. Dinsmore, W. R. Davis, I. R. Hall, W. H. Fry. Stockholders: John Smartt, J. A. C. Blackburn, A. W. Dinsmore D. H. Woods, I. B. Gilmore, George T. Lincoln, E. S. McDaniel, C. A. Blanck, W. R. Davis, James Haney, F. E. Gilmore, J. B. Mayo, W. H. Fry, Leonard West, G. Ambrose, T. A. Woods, I. R. Hall, F. M. Bates, B. F. Dunn, A. W. Taylor, G. H. Moore.

Bentonville Mercantile Company.—This is a joint stock company, with a paid-up capital of $30,000, the stockholders being W. A. Terry, R. E. Brashear, Alex. Hall, B. F. Burks and J. W. and Asa E. Langford.   This company keeps a wholesale and retail general store in the Terry Block, occupying all the stories and all the space in the entire building, aside from the banking room, with their goods.

The Eagle Mills were erected in 1881, and have since been equipped with the roller process apparatus.   The capacity is sixty barrels per day.   The business is so pressing that the mills are being run both day and night.

The Bentonville Canning and Evaporating Company is of recent origin, and its officers are I. B. Gilmore, president; W. B. Lyon, secretary, and F. E. Gilmore, treasurer.   The capital stock of the company is $20,000; cost of plant, $10,000, of which

$5,000 was for machinery. Their main building is 30x80 feet, and three stories high. It was built in February, 1888, by Plummer & Son, of Leavenworth, Kas., and is equipped with the Plummer process for evaporating fruit. Its capacity is 800 bushels of apples per day, and from fifty to sixty hands are employed. The contemplated canning factory is not yet erected. W. L. Plummer & Son have received for their process of evaporating fruit the medals from five world's fairs: Centennial, in 1876; Paris, in 1878; New Orleans; Melbourne, Australia, and Chili, South America.

The Arkansas Tobacco Company, dating from October, 1887, is a succession of Trotter & Wilkes. The secretary and general manager of the company is J. W. Trotter, of the former firm. The president is W. B. Deming, original proprietor of "Deming's Additions" to Bentonville, formerly of Kansas. They manufacture several brands of plug and smoking tobacco, and do an extensive business.

The Bentonville Mills, located on the spring branch below town, were erected in 1869 by T. K. Blake and J. Claypool. John Curtis has been proprietor since April, 1884. It is supplied with two run of buhr stones, with a capacity of 100 bushels of wheat and 200 bushels of corn per day. A carding machine is run in connection with the mills.

Societies.—Bentonville Lodge No. 56, A. F. & A. M., was chartered November 4, 1852, with J. D. Dickson, W. M.; J. H. Hobbs, S. W., and James M. Rogers, J. W. The present membership of this lodge is about sixty-five, and the present officers are R. J. Laughlin, W. M.; T. T. Blake, S. W.; C. W. Clapp, J. W.; C. R. Bruce, Secretary; S. F. Stahl, Treasurer; Josephus Huffman, Tyler. This lodge is in a good financial condition, and dispenses all its surplus for charitable purposes.

The Benton Chapter, R. A. M., was chartered October 23, 1874, on petition of R. S. Armstrong, John Black, W. B. Roper, S. H. Kelton, Josephus Huffman, Thomas J. Webster, H. W. Glover and others. It was reorganized under its first charter in June, 1887. The present officers are R. J. Laughlin, H. P.; J. M. Thompson, King; J. H. Burns, Scribe; R. N. Corley, C. H.; T. J. Reynolds, P. S.; P. Gotcher, R. A. C.; G. T. Lincoln, T.

T. Blake and Isaac Cook, G. M. S.; J. P. Burns, Treasurer; J. W. Taliaferro, Secretary; Josephus Huffman, Tyler. The chapter has twenty-seven members and applications for several more. Its financial condition is good, and it dispenses charity with a liberal hand.

Bentonville Lodge No. 37, K. of P., was organized in June, 1887, with sixteen members. Its present officers are F. E. Gilmore, P. C.; E. H. Looney, C. C.; J. W. Taliaferro, V. C.; C. C. Huffman, Prelate; S. H. Claypool, K. of R. S.; T. T. Blake, M. F.; W. B. Deming, M. E.; J. D. Bryan, M. A.; present membership about thirty.

Benton Lodge No. 33, I. O. O. F., was organized under a warrant or dispensation dated November 25, 1870, granted to H. S. Coleman, T. K. Blake, Leonard West, J. O. Alexander and J. W. Simmons. The present officers are R. B. Lawson, N. G.; G. W. Hurley, V. G.; Lewis M. Dailey, Secretary; George M. Bates, Treasurer. The membership of the lodge is about fifty, and its financial condition is good, having money at interest. Nearly three-fourths of its membership have been acquired within the last year.

Burnside Post No. 4, G. A. R., was organized in June, 1887. B. F. Hobbs was the first Post Commander, and still holds that office. The other officers are M. Starbuck, S. V.; A. H. Gingrich, J. V.; George Bill, Adjutant. This post has about thirty-five members now in good standing.

The Masonic Hall and the Methodist Episcopal Church, South, a large two-story brick building erected in 1869, was built conjointly by the church and the Masons, the church occupying the first and the Masons the second story. The building cost $3,000. All of the above mentioned societies except the G. A. R. meet in the Masonic hall.

The Bentonville Press.—The *Advance*, a Democratic newspaper, was established early in the seventies, and was published for a number of years, frequently changing hands, and was finally sold to the founder of the *Bentonian*, and consolidated therewith.

The *Bentonian*, also a Democratic paper, was established in the fall of 1881 by S. D. McReynolds, with S. M. Wamack as editor. McReynolds continued its publication until October,

1885, when he sold it to J. B. Thompson. The latter then changed the name of the paper to the Benton County *Journal*. Soon thereafter W. M. Bumbarger bought a half interest, and in the fall of 1886 became sole proprietor of the paper, and in July, 1887, he sold it to S. M. Dailey, who still continues its publication. The *Journal* is an eight-column folio, well printed and ably edited in the interest of Benton County. In politics it is stanchly Democratic.

The Benton County *Democrat* was established in January, 1885, by John W. Corley, who continued its publication about one year, and then sold it to J. B. Thompson, who published it about the same length of time, and then sold it to H. A. Cook. The latter published it a few months, and until July, 1888, when he sold it Hurley & Stevenson, two young and energetic men, who are now publishing it. It is located in the new Peoples Bank building, and has one of the most convenient and commodious offices in the State. It is also neatly printed and well edited, and is Democratic in politics. Both of the Bentonville papers have a large circulation, and both do a good business.

BLOOMFIELD.

The village of Bloomfield lies on Round Prairie, six miles north of Siloam Springs. It was surveyed and platted by David Chandler for G. W. Mitchell, its original proprietor. It contains a large public square surrounded with lots. Dr. J. H. Neagle built the first house in the village. It stands at the northeast corner of the public square. R. B. Mitchell opened the first store, and has continued in business ever since. The post-office was established the next year after the town was laid out, and R. B. Wilson was made postmaster, and still holds the office. Following Wilson, several parties opened stores, but soon left. Following is the present business of the village: General stores, R. B. Wilson, W. I. Richardson; drugs and groceries, Mitchell & Bro.; hotel, David Chandler; blacksmith, J. Johnson; woodwork, J. E. Stewart; physician, J. R. Floyd. The Masonic hall building was put up in 1871 by the Masons. The lodge hall is in the second story, and the lower room is used by all religious demoninations that choose to have it. The Rogers Academy is a fine two-story brick building, with seating capacity for 150 pupils. Prof. A. B. Marbury is principal of this school. He teaches all branches ordinarily taught in high-schools, and also the public school in connection with his school.

Bloomfield Lodge No. 243, A. F. & A. M., was chartered in 1871, and William Kellum was the first W. M. The present membership of the lodge is from forty-five to fifty, and the officers are Z. T. Mitchell, W. M.; William Parker, S. W.; James Peek, J. W. This has always been a prosperous lodge. It is out of debt and has money on hand.

The Bloomfield Steam Roller Mills are located three-fourths of a mile south of the village. These mills have just undergone repairs, have had the roller process apparatus put in, and are thus prepared to make the best of flour.

ELDORADO.

This town was extensively laid out early in the eighties, occupying nearly all of the southeast quarter of Section 31, Town 20 north, Range 33 west, being seventeen miles west of Bentonville on a straight line. There being good springs there, it was established for a watering place or summer resort, and for a short time it had a business boom, but now it contains only one small country store.

CHEROKEE CITY.

The village of Cherokee City is situated in Section 26, Town 19, Range 34, about three-fourths of a mile from the Indian Territory line. It was surveyed by David Chandler in 1880, for himself, James Ingle and M. D. Cunningham, the original proprietors. Before the war there was a place kept on the opposite side of the branch at Cherokee City, called "Hog Eye," where whisky was kept to sell to the Indians. Cherokee City was built up in 1881 and 1882, by a "boom" it acquired as a summer resort. Like several other places, it has some excellent springs of good water. It was built in a great hurry, to accommodate its guests who resorted there in 1881 and 1882, consequently the houses are small and of a temporary character. W. D. Cunningham opened the first general store in the place. The directory of business at present is as follows: General stores, J. M.

Tucker, Crawford Bros; drugs, J. M. Norris, Eurial Farmin; furniture, Mr. Baxter; blacksmiths, A. E. Funk, —— Cook; hotel, Cherokee House, by Samuel Haag; physician, Dr. O. M. Dodson; churches, Baptist, Christian, Methodist Episcopal, South, Congregational. The population of the place is about 200. T. A. Fleener has an orchard of 2,200 apple trees and many other kinds of fruit, adjoining the village.

CITY OF ROGERS.

The original town of Rogers was surveyed and laid out in March, 1881, by John P. Hely, a land surveyor and civil engineer, for Benjamin F. Sikes, the original proprietor. It comprises parts of the southeast quarter of the northeast quarter of Section 12, Town 19, Range 30, and the west half of the west half of Section 7, Town 19, Range 29. The bearings and courses of the town were surveyed on a magnetic variation of seven degrees east. The plat contains fifteen blocks, with twelve lots each, one tier of blocks being east of the railroad, and two west thereof. The lots are fifty feet north and south, by 140 feet east and west, and all streets are eighty feet wide except Arkansas and Douglas, which are fifty feet each. The town is situated on the St. Louis & San Francisco Railroad, at the junction of the Bentonville Railway. The first addition to Rogers was laid out the same year by the original proprietor, and it comprises tracts of land adjoining the first plat on every side thereof. This addition contains in all nineteen blocks, subdivided into lots. It was surveyed by D. W. German.

J. Wade Sikes' Park Addition to Rogers, embracing the southeast quarter of the southeast quarter of Section 12, Town 19, Range 30, was surveyed and laid out the same year. It lies southwest of the original plat, and contains sixteen blocks, subdivided into large residence lots, some being 150x238 feet, some 150 feet square, and some 150x245 feet. It contains the most desirable residence lots.

Reuben Wallace's Addition to Rogers was laid out in 1882. It lies northeast of the old plat, and contains seven blocks of twelve lots each, and two blocks of six lots each, all lots being 50x140 feet in size.

The Electric Springs Plat, adjoining Wallace's Addition on the northeast, was laid out in September, 1881. It contains forty-five blocks surrounding the springs, all being laid out in the most ornamental style, for residence lots.

Rogers' Cemetery, containing five acres, was laid out in November, 1882.

Enough land at Rogers has been surveyed into town lots to make a large city.

Rogers was incorporated on the 28th day of May, 1881, and in June following an election was held for town officials." In evidence of the fact that the people have always been fortunate in the selection of their officers, Rogers is entirely out of debt, and its paper is at par and has been from the first year. But few young towns can say as much.

When the site of Rogers was chosen, in 1881, it contained nothing but a dilapidated pole cabin. When the St. Louis & San Francisco Railway was making its way through the county, a number of farmers, with a view to their future interests, secured the amount demanded by the company's right of way agent, some $600, and secured the location of the depot where it now stands. The parties who contributed this amount may truly be called the founders of Rogers. Their names are H. B. Horsley, George E. Wilson, Clark Brixey, Ben T. Oakley, N. S. Horsley, J. R. Swafford, Maj. S. S. Horsley, W. B. Horsley and, possibly, others. B. F. Sikes donated to the railroad company one-half of sixty acres in the original town, and the depot grounds and the right of way. He lived on the land first platted, and was therefore the first resident of the town. The first house built after the town was projected was put up by John Cox, and a saloon was opened therein. The next house was erected by Lowry and Scroggins, and a grocery and the post-office were located therein. Then followed the "Rogers House," and a number of business houses and dwellings too numerous to mention in detail. The town was named in honor of Capt. C. W. Rogers, who was at that time general manager of the St. Louis & San Francisco Railway, and a good friend of the town. The natural advantages of the place attracted the attention of enterprising men, and before the trains actually got to running there were several business houses in successful operation.

The following is a directory of the first business of Rogers, as it existed a short time after the town was established: C. C. Davis, clothing; George Raupp, furniture; J. L. Merritt, restaurant; W. A. Miller, dry goods; Huffman & Wade, hotel; H. L. & S. T. Stokes, livery stable; Pratt & Gibbs and J. H. Rackerby, hardware; John Cox, A. Greenstreet, Capt. Blue, saloons; Scroggins & Lowry, Stokes and Bowman, groceries; Van Winkle & Blackburn, wholesale lumber merchants; Huffman & Williams, McCubbins & Peck, produce and commission merchants; J. W. Brite, Berryhill & Durham, Mitchell & Dunagin, J. Beasley, general merchandise.

The following, pertaining to the period before the railroad was completed to Rogers, but after it was decided that a depot would be erected there, is an extract from the pen of Maj. A. J. Allen, who wrote a history of the town when it was a year old: "The months of March and April were extremely cold and stormy, as the winter months preceding them had been. We had no railroad and no telegraph line. The wagon roads, most of the time, were entirely impassable. It was impossible to get lumber, and all building operations were delayed in consequence of bad roads. But few people were here then, and they took hotel lodgings in the forest during the night, and kept themselves busy during the day by foraging for subsistence and building huge fires by which to keep warm.

"One man, who had waited patiently and long for good weather and lumber, opened up a business house in the top of an oak tree. The huge oak had been felled to the ground, and he took his wagon body off the wheels, and placed it lengthwise on the trunk of the tree. He then, like a good Southern man with Yankee principles, stuck up a sign with six letters, and spread out his goods for sale; and, judging from the number of people who daily gathered about his place of business, we conclude that he did a good thriving business. He said he would open the first business house in Rogers, and he kept his word."

During the seven years of the existence of Rogers it has grown to be a thriving and prosperous little city of from 1,500 to 1,800 inhabitants. The following is its present business directory, to wit: Bank of Rogers, W. R. Felker, banker; dry goods, clothing and notions, Finch Brothers, C. A. Nelson, W. A. Miller, H. L. Stroud; groceries, Caywood & Son, J. A. Smith, W. L. Watkins, W. R. Cady, Nance & Oakley, C. Livesay, Williams & Saunders, Osborn & Garnett, Z. H. McCubbins, Kimble Bros.; hardware, C. L. Gibbs, Dyer Brothers; drugs, I. V. Davis, C. L. Alexander, J. E. Applegate, Dr. R. D. Cogswell; restaurants, L. J. Merritt, William Story, W. W. Reynolds; confectioner, A. Bucklin; furniture, George Raupp, W. H. Dwyer; millinery, Miss Alice M. Roberts, Mrs. L. Horsley, Mrs. C. A. Wickes; harness and saddles, Morgan & Stewart; general second-hand store, Joseph Milligan; livery, James M. Vandover, Oakley & McSpadden; bakery, B. F. Woodruff; butchers, C. Juhne, S. Fleek; barbers, K. T. Heflin, W. A. Patterson; hotels, Brown House, Rogers Hotel; boot and shoe maker, F. Duval; watchmakers and jewelers, W. H. Dwyer, J. E. Applegate; painters, James Neal, Charles Clark; blacksmiths and wheel-wrights, Jeffreys & Duff, Robertson & Duff; steam roller mills, Rogers Milling Company; fruit evaporator, D. Wing & Brother; canning and packing factory, Rogers Canning and Packing Company; Arkansas Lime Works, C. A. Wickes; cider and jelly plant.

Lumber yards, J. A. C. Blackburn, W. H. Fowler; mineral waters, ginger ale, etc., King & Co.; water supply works, Rogers Lime & Water Works Company; contractors and builders, W. H. Fowler, R. C. Copp, H. Nelson, J. B. Mills; attorneys, E. R. Morgan, Ed. Finch; insurance agents, Duckworth & Bixler, J. W. Price, Z. H. McCubbin; real estate agents, Duckworth & Bixler, J. W. Price; physicians, H. Weems, R. D. Cogswell, P. C Pennington, J. C. Freeland, E. N. Stearns; dentists, — Reynolds, R. F. Stringer; churches, Congregational, Methodist Episcopal, Methodist Episcopal, South, Baptist, Cumberland Presbyterian, Christian; Rogers Academy, principal, J. W. Scroggs; Miss Mary G. Webb, J. R. Williams, Elta Scroggs, Hettie C. Tryon, assistants. This was the faculty for the school year closed. Societies, Rogers Lodge No. 460, A. F. & A. M., Rogers Lodge No. 89, I. O. O. F., Rogers Encampment No. 14, George H. Thomas Post No. 29, G. A. R.

The manufacturing industries of Rogers deserve especial mention. It is claimed that the Rogers Flouring Mills are the best and most extensive in the State of Arkansas, and that they are doing an extensive business, running both day and night. D. Wing & Bro.'s evaporating plant was the first one established in the State. Their lead in the industry dates from 1882. The capacity is 450 bushels of apples, or 250 bushels of peaches, per day. The evaporator used by them is the Alden patent, and their parer the Wizard machine. During the working months they employ an average of sixty hands, many of whom are women. The canning and packing company was organized with a capital stock of $12,000, and next to the milling company its business is probably the most valuable single enterprise in Rogers. It has extensive buildings, and has the advantage of a long season for operations, as it cans all kinds of fruits (small fruits included) as well as vegetables. It employs a great many hands.

Business Transactions in 1887.—Four dry goods, clothing and notions, $60,000; seven groceriers, $46,000; two hardware and implements, $23,000; three drugs and medicine, $15,000; one harness and saddlery, $2,000; one newspaper and job printing, $4,100; two butchers, $3,400; one variety store, $3,000; three millinery and ladies' furnishing, $4,000; one furniture and undertaking, $5,000; two hotels, $5,500; one barber, $1,500; one lumber, sash, doors, etc., $16,000; contracting and building, $28,000; produce, hides and furs, $45,000; grain and grain products, $123,300; live stock, $44,500; 374 carloads ties, $18,000; 11,125 barrels apples shipped, $22,500; 15,000 bushels potatoes shipped, $6,000; evaporated fruit transactions, $60,000; miscellaneous, $20,000—total, $565,600. Bank transactions and loans, $663,872. Grand total, $1,239,472.

Carload Shipments.—Total carloads forwarded, 737, divided as follows: flour, 123; wheat, 13; potatoes, 15; apples, 51; dried fruit, 13; eggs, 10; live stock, 89; ties, 374; miscellaneous, 49.

The Press.—The Rogers *New Era* was established in the fall of 1881, and has ever since been controlled by its present proprietors, Graham & Mason. It is a six-column quarto, neatly printed and well edited. It is Democratic in politics, and is the oldest paper now being published in the county. The publishers of this work are under obligations to it for much of the history of Rogers.

The Rogers *Republican*, a five-column quarto, was established in April, 1888, the first number being published on the 26th day of that month, by its present proprietors, Warner & Honeywell. It is also a neatly printed paper and well edited. In politics it is Republican, and has done much to organize the Republican party in Benton County.

The Rogers papers are both well patronized by local advertisers, which speaks well for the town.

GARFIELD.

This is a station on the St. Louis & San Francisco Railroad, in Section 32, Township 21 north, Range 28 west, containing about 200 inhabitants. The first store existing at this place was opened in 1881 by A. Blansett, and the next year another was opened by A. Peel. Following this a drug store was opened by Thomas R. Marshall. In July, 1883, the village was surveyed into lots and named Garfield. Following is a directory of its present business: General stores, A. Peel, G. P. Rogers & Son, J. A. Wilks; hardware, L. Ellison & Co.; groceries, J. W. Cundiff; confectionery, H. Wilks; post-office, jewelry, etc., A. J. Wilks; hotel, J. N. Wilks; drugs and jewelry, M. J. Walters. Also two blacksmith shops, a barber shop, the Arkansas Lime Works, the fruit evaporator of D. D. Ames and the lumber yard of A. L. Ricketts. The Arkansas Lime Works Company manufacture 200 barrels of lime per day, make their own barrels and employ about seventy-five men. The fruit evaporator has capacity for from 100 to 150 bushels of apples per day, and when running the proprietor employs about fifteen hands. Garfield has a frame schoolhouse and Masonic hall combined, the school-room being in the lower story and the hall in the upper, built recently, costing $800. Fruits, timber, railroad ties and fence posts are shipped in great quantities from this place. There are no church buildings. Baptists and Christians worship alternately in the school-room.

LOWELL.

Lowell is a station on the St. Louis & San Francisco Railroad, located six miles south of Rogers. It was laid out in 1881 by J. R. McClure. J. W. Main built the first house in the place, and opened the first business—a grocery. Next, M. B. Hathaway erected the building now occupied by J. W. Williams, and opened a general store therein. The business at this writing consists of two general stores, kept respectively by J. W. Williams and F. H. Rizer; a drug and grocery store, by Green Bros.; a grocery, by R. H. Odell; confections, by J. Plummer, and a blacksmith shop, by Daniel Wann. Also J. W. Williams and F. H. Rizer each have a fruit evaporator and grain warehouse. Grains, fruits, poultry, timber and railroad ties are extensively shipped from this place. The village contains a brick school-house and Masonic hall combined, and built conjointly by the Masons and public school board, the school-room being in the first story and the hall in the second. This building was erected in 1885.

Lowell Lodge No. 424, A. F. & A. M., was chartered in 1886, and it has now thirty-two members. The principal officers are J. F. Archer, W. M.; J. N. Tuttle, S. W., and J. W. Packer, J. W.

The Missionary Baptists, Methodists, South, and Christians worship in the school-room.

MAYSVILLE.

The village of Maysville, one of the oldest in the county, is situated on the State and Indian Territory line, twenty-one miles west and one and a-half miles north of Bentonville. An Englishman by the name of Tigret opened the first store in Maysville, in 1839. His most profitable trade was selling whisky to the Indians. He continued in business about ten years, and then returned to his native country, where he died. The second merchant in the place was a Jew, who did business about three years. Early in the forties Maysville contained six or seven stores, all of which did a thriving business, getting much of their trade from the Indians. The place continued to have this number of stores most of the time until the Civil War broke out. Then business was nearly wholly suspended or destroyed, and it has never regained its former magnitude. The Missouri, Kansas & Texas Railroad, built through the Indian Nation, has cut off much of the trade formerly given to Maysville. It is claimed by old settlers that in 1846 Maysville was larger than Bentonville. The village lies entirely on the east side of the line, and all the business houses face toward the "Nation." The "line" is the main street, with the business on one side of it only.

Northwestern Lodge No. 36, A. F. & A. M., was organized at Maysville about the year 1850, prospered for many years, and suspended about ten years ago.

Directory of Maysville.—Dry goods, Freeman & Dumas, Henry Coats, Mrs. E. J. Tinnin (these also kept groceries); groceries and hardware, Thomas Keith; groceries, Samuel Ward, M. Harmon; harness and saddler, Isaac Harrouff; hotel, Line House, by Alex. McDonald; grist-mill, Spencer & Taylor; post-office, Mrs. Mary Linch; physicians, C. F. Baker, E. N. Freeman, J. L. Larue, A. B. Bills. The town has a Union Church and a public school-house. Maysville is surrounded with a good country, and should it get a railroad, as contemplated, it will make an important trading point.

NEBO.

This is a small village, containing two or three business houses, located on the line between Sections 12 and 13, in Township 20 north, Range 33 west. A post of the G. A. R., No. 62, was organized at this place August 29, 1888, with Robert Green as commander, and M. J. Anderson, adjutant.

SPRINGTOWN.

This beautiful village is located on Flint Creek, eighteen miles southwest from Bentonville. It derives its name from its famous spring, which flows from the foot of a bank in the valley not more than fifteen feet high. The village lies just west of the spring, at the foot of the southern bluff of Flint Creek Valley. The hills beyond the valley, covered with their native forests, present cheerful scenery. Charles Kincheloe built the first house where Springtown is located, about the year 1841, and Isaac Dial built the next one close by the spring, and it is still standing. Soon thereafter a Mr. Yarberry built the next house, it being where Frank Wasson now lives. No business, however, was established at Springtown until 1868, when Manning Richardson opened the first store in the place, and built the first house in the town proper. Marion Seaburn was the next merchant, and Thomason & Northcut the next, neither of whom remain. The town was surveyed and laid out in lots in 1871. It lies in the southeast corner of Section 6, Township 18, Range 32, and is laid out on a bearing of south $59\frac{1}{2}$ degrees west.

The following is its present business directory: General merchandise, W. D. Wasson, McGaugh Bros.; hardware, drugs and groceries, W. Collins & Co.; drugs, Sewell & Enterkine; hotel, J. L. Allen; steam grist and saw-mill, Mitchell & Loy; blacksmiths, Collins & Holland, Collins & Brown; boot and shoemakers, R. D. Morland, A. T .Moodey; post and telephone office, William J. Collins; physicians, N. Sewell, James Hall, T. H. Roughton; churches, Baptist, Methodist Episcopal, Methodist Episcopal, South. The Methodist Episcopal society has not as yet erected a church building. The village also contains a school-house and lodge hall combined, the school-room being in the first story and the hall in the second.

Societies.—Springtown Lodge No. 222, A.F.& A. M.,was chartered about the year 1868, and has now about thirty-five members. The principal officers are W. E. Garrett, W. M.; J. T. Chastine, S. W.; R. J. McGaugh, J. W.

Springtown Chapter No. 70, R. A. Masons, was chartered about the year 1873, and has now thirty members. This was the first chapter organized in Benton County. The present officers are J. F. Mitchell, High Priest; J. T. Chastine, King; Isaac January, Scribe. Both of these societies are in good financial condition, and both prosper in the work laid down on the Masonic trestle-board

SILOAM CITY.

This city is situated on Sager's Creek, in Hico Township, twenty-eight miles southwest from Bentonville, and has a population of about 1,500. It is within two miles of the western and six miles of the southern line of the county. Hico, which may be properly called a residence suburb of Siloam City, is a very old place for this country. Col. D. Gunter settled where he now resides, in Hico, in 1844, before the place had even become a village. About that time, or perhaps a little later, a post-office named Hico was established at a point about two miles from the present Hico. This office was soon thereafter moved to the village that now bears its name, and Hico became a trading point, especially for the Indians, who patronized it to a considerable extent. It continued to be the leading place in that corner of the county until Siloam City was established, which drew away nearly all of its business except that of its flouring mills, and left it only a residence suburb.

That which led to the origin of Siloam City is its natural springs of pure, health-giving waters. In 1879 it was discovered that these waters contained medicinal qualities, and preparations were at once begun for the establishment of a summer resort. On the 24th of June, 1880, the first anniversary of the place was celebrated by a large and interesting meeting of the citizens of that vicinity. In March, 1880, J. V. Hargroves laid out the original plat of Siloam City, embracing parts of the northeast quarter and of the northwest of Section 6, in Township 17 north, Range 33 west. The following November East Siloam was laid out by Logan Teague. This addition contains the "college grounds and park," and a large number of lots. Couches' addition was the next one laid out, and in April, 1881, the additions of J. H. Beauchamp, T. R. Carles and William C. Tate were laid out. Johnson's addition was surveyed and laid out in November following. In January, 1882, " C. D. Gunter's Addition No. 1 to the town of Hico" and " S. G. Rogers' Addition to Hico and East Siloam " were laid out. At the same time, or soon thereafter, Gunter's second addition to Hico was laid out. By the foregoing it will be seen that the real estate owners in that vicinity intended to be ready at all times to accommodate persons desiring to purchase lots.

As soon as the first plat of Siloam City was surveyed buildings began to be erected and the town began a rapid growth. John D. Hargrove opened the first business, a general store, on Main Street. The place rapidly gained a reputation as a sumner resort, and that fact, coupled with the prospects of the early completion of a railroad through it, induced many people to immigrate thereto. In 1880, the first year of its existence as a town, it was incorporated as such, and the influx of immigrants was so rapid that in 1881 it had acquired a population of over 3,000. It was then incorporated as a city of the second class. During the rapid increase of population it was impossible to build houses fast enough to supply the demand, consequently for a time many of the new-comers had to camp out in their wagons or in tents. To supply the demand for houses "the sound of the hammer" was heard both day and night, and the whole town as it now stands, with the exception of a few buildings, was built in the first two or three years of its existence. After the "boom" ceased many who had gone there for the purpose of going into business discovered that the place was overdone, that the prospect for a railroad was not encouraging, and consequently moved away. Those also who went there in the summer of 1881, to get relief from the excessive heat and drouth of that year, returned to their respective homes, and the large population (being chiefly transient), on which the city obtained its charter, has dwindled away until it is now only about one-half of what it then was. Fortunately, however, Siloam City is situated in the midst of a good agricultural country, which will sustain it as a good, substantial trading place, even though it remains deprived of railroad facilities. The citizens still have hopes for a railroad, and when these hopes are realized, if ever, Siloam City will make a large and flourishing town, with a large and permanent population. The exceedingly pure water of its many springs, and the magnificent natural scenery surrounding it, and its healthy location, make it a most desirable place to live.

This place is commonly called "Siloam Springs," but the name given it on its first recorded plat is "Siloam City."

Siloam City is in fair financial condition, having a debt of only about $700. The city officers are D. R. Hammer, mayor; William H. Cravens, recorder, and Charles E. Copeland, marshal. The city is divided into three wards, and has two aldermen in each.

Sales Transactions in 1887.—Seven general merchants, $76,-000; three grocers, $22,500; two hardware, $6,500; three druggists, $7,100; two furniture, $8,500; one saddlery and harness, $8,000; two lumber dealers, $6,500; two newspapers and job printing, $2,900; two milliners and dressmakers, $1,400; one bed spring and mattress factory, $1,600; two watch-makers and jewelers, $1,600; three wheel-wrights and blacksmiths, $4,200; grain products, $18,000; live stock, $15,500; hides and furs, $2,100; 18,000 pounds wool, $3,600; 31,000 pounds dried fruit, $2,170; 53,000 dozen eggs, $5,300; 1,000 dozen quails, $2,000; 17,000 dozen pigeons, $6,800; deer, turkey and ducks, $930;

hotels, $2,900; butcher, $4,000; livery and transfer, $6,500; miscellaneous, $2,500—total, $220,100.

Present Directory of Siloam City.—Bank of Siloam, R. S. Morris, cashier; Z. T. Conley, assistant cashier.—General merchandise, Ewing & Gilbreath, Jacob Nathan, Crane Bros., R. S. Gibson, W. W. Brown, C. W. Hinds & Co., J. H. Chitty, R. G. Ravenscraft; groceries, Parker & Mason, R. D. Jordan, J. V. Tracy, Morris & Graves, C. B. Randall, Mrs. A. Bottoms; drugs, R. B. Pegues & Co., D. W. Atkinson & Co., W. F. Brooks & Co.; hardware, R. E. Henry, W. A. Griffin, Wyatt & Bartell; furniture, M. O. Hicks; harness and saddles, J. P. Carl; watch-makers and jewelers, N. L. Lindsay, H. J. Hancock; photograph gallery, B. M. Rakestraw; boot and shoemakers, A. H. Budd, P. R. Stanfield, J. F. Nethery, J. Eslinger; wheel-wrights, E. B. Rosson, Paul Williams; cabinet-maker, L. L. Goacher; carpenters, H. Jack, C. B. Randall, H. Mark, W. M. Jones, W. H. Hancock, O. C. Davis; blacksmiths, McNair Bros., Bruner & Daniels, H. M. Martin; Hico Roller Mills, Gunter & Late; evaporating factory, W. O. Morris; wool carding mills, J. H. Chitty; furniture factory, Chamberlain & Woodmansee; bed spring and mattress factory, L. M. Prowse; Distillery No. 129, C. E. Noyes; steam saw and planing mills, Hinds, Wisner & Ragsdale, Suttle & Bruner; physicians, J. T. Clegg, J. F. Runyan, G. W. Jackson; dentist, J. A. Doss; attorneys, A. T. Rose, E. D. Feno, J. H. Trader; real estate, D. Shafer, Z. Abernathy, Rose & Davis; hotels, Ewing House, J. M. Ewing, proprietor; Fountain House, A. J. Davis, proprietor; butchers, Tolbert & Spencer; livery, Breedlove & Cresswell, M. N. Donaldson, I. S. Davis; churches, Methodist Episcopal, Methodist Episcopal, South, Cumberland Presbyterian, Congregational, Missionary Baptist, Society of Friends, Christian; high-school—faculty last school year, principal, H. J. Blake; assistants, Misses Annie Egy and Gertie Backus, E. S. Gibbs.

Societies.—Key Lodge No. 7, A. F. & A. M., at Hico, was chartered long before the Civil War. At the beginning of the war its charter was taken to Texas, and kept by a lady who returned it after the war closed. The present principal officers are Felix Miller, W. M.; Dr. J. F. Clegg, S. W.; Frank Carl, J. W. It has a small membership.

Advance Lodge No. 435, A. F. & A. M., was chartered in 1887. Present officers, E. T. Smith, W. M.; G. W. Mead, S. W.; Rev. E. S. Gibbs, J. W. It has about thirty-five members, and is prospering. Among its charter members were W. H. Hancock, D. R. Hammer, G. W. Mead, A. J. Norris, J. H. Walker, D. B. Swallow, Levi Davis, J. J. Preece and R. P. Pegues.

Calumet Lodge No. 5, American Protective League, was chartered in the spring of 1886, with ten members. It now has thirty-seven members in good standing. Its officers are F. M. Reager, ruler; J. Van Butler, financial secretary; T. T. Chamberlain, recording secretary; S. A. Broyles, treasurer. It is progressing satisfactorily.

Agricultural Wheel, No. 984, was chartered in the fall of 1885, and has now about thirty members.

Streeter Union Labor Club was organized August 3, 1888, with thirty members. John H. Chitty, president; C. B. Randall, vice-president; A. J. Egy, secretary; J. B. Newbury, treasurer.

Siloam Springs Lodge No. 91, I. O. O. F., was chartered in 1882, with C. B. Randall, A. J. Egy, John H. Chitty, T. J. Patton, J. B. Newbury, John A. Denny and others as charter members. Present officers, A. G. Wilkinson, N. G.; C. B. Randall, V. G.; A. J. Egy, Sec.; W. F. Brooks, Treas. It has from thirty to forty members, and is in a prosperous condition.

Curtis Post No. 9, G. A. R., named after Gen. Curtis, of Pea Ridge fame, was chartered in 1884, and has had since its organization 109 members. Lewis Simmons is Post Commander, and E. D. Feno, Post Adjutant.

The Siloam Press.—The first paper published in Siloam City was the *Sun*, established in 1880, by Thomas Gallagher. In 1881 it was changed to the *Dispatch*, continued about a year, and then suspended. The *Globe* was established in 1881, by D. O. Bell, who published it about one year only. The *Arkansas Herald*, an eight-column folio, was established in 1882, by S. Abernathy, who published it two years, and then transferred it to Messrs. Grammer & Dameron, who published it one year, and then J. B. Dameron became sole manager of the paper, and continues to publish it. It has a good circulation, and is Democratic in politics. The *Locomotive*, a six-column quarto, was established in December, 1886, at Springdale, Ark., by H. Milton Butler and J. Van Butler, and was moved by the latter to Siloam Springs in August, 1887, where it continues to be published; J. Van Butler is sole proprietor. The paper is independent in politics, and has also a good circulation. The Siloam papers are well printed and edited, and receive liberal support from local advertisers.

SULPHUR SPRINGS.

This delightful summer resort is beautifully situated in the vale of Butler Creek, on Section 23, Township 21 north, Range 33 west, and on the line of the survey of the Kansas City, Fort Smith & Southern Railroad, now graded to Split-Log, in Missouri. It was surveyed and laid out in December, 1885, by S. B. Robertson, for the proprietors, Hibler & Cox. Lyons' addition thereto was laid out in May, 1887, and the whole village was re-surveyed in July of that year, by Mr. Robertson, for Charles Hibler and John Black. The group of springs at this place " includes one white sulphur, one potash sulphur, one magnesia, one chalybeate, one nitre, and one intermittent freestone spring, and is distant by highway northwest from Bentonville eighteen miles; from Split-Log, Mo., sixteen miles; from the Missouri State line, one and one-half miles, and from the line of the Indian Territory, eight and one-half miles." The village, surrounding the main group of springs, lies on a gently inclining plane, with a gravelly soil, and the natural scenery in every direction is "romantic and wild," like that usually seen from the valleys of a mountainous country. The village is in the heart of a region of cavernous limestone caves, there being fifteen caves within the radius of five miles. An elevated site, just south of the village and springs and overlooking the same, has been selected for the erection of a commodious hotel. The promenade grounds reserved around the springs contain several acres, beautifully ornamented and shaded with natural forest trees, some of which are gigantic in size. Of the five vales, which form a junction at this place, three of them open toward the southward, and the place is protected from the chilling winds of winter by a semi-circular mountain ridge rising high above it.

The flow of the mineral springs is sufficient to supply 10,000 people. The supply of water for domestic use, the source of which are springs near at hand, is collectively 700,000 gallons per day. The largest of the springs producing this supply is about one and a half miles southeast of the village, and over 100 feet above it. A good hotel, with adjacent cottages for the accommodation of guests, is now in operation, under the able management of Mr. Charles Hibler and his lady. An excellent bath-house has just been completed. A first-class livery stable stands near the pleasure grounds, the proprietors of which are always ready to furnish rigs for pleasure drives.

The village also contains a post-office, stores, a school-house, and a number of residences, and deserves especial mention as being the neatest and most cleanly kept village or town in Benton County. The approaches to the village are by hack line from Bentonville; by same from Southwest City, Mo., ten miles; and from Split-Log, Mo., sixteen miles, and it is confidently expected that this will soon be improved by railroad communication north and south.

There is no doubt about the waters at Sulphur Springs containing medicinal qualities, as every person that has used them can readily testify. The white sulphur spring is the most noted, and contains the greatest amount of curative qualities. With or without a railroad, this place is bound to remain a favorite resort for invalids and pleasure seekers.

The Benton County *Bulletin*, published at Sulphur Springs, was established at Bentonville in July, 1888, by its present editor and proprietor, John R. Huffman, and was moved to Sulphur Springs early in September following. It is a four-column quarto, is neatly printed, and labors in the interest of Republican principles.

VANWINKLE MILLS.

This very lively place is situated on Section 22, Township 19 north, Range 28 west, and is worthy of especial mention on account of its being the headquarters of the native lumber industry of Benton and other counties. Peter Vanwinkle erected the first saw-mill at this place in 1858, and ran it until some time during the war, when it was burned, it is said, by

Confederate bushwhackers to prevent its being used by the Federal armies. It was rebuilt in 1866 and run until 1882, when it passed into the hands of J. A. C. Blackburn, son-in-law of its original proprietor. Mr. Blackburn has made some improvements, and continues the business on an extensive scale. The mills are inclosed in a building 70x90 feet in size, two stories high, and all covered with an iron roof. The power consists of a 150-horse power engine, with a 22x30 inch cylinder, and a balance wheel twenty feet in diameter and weighing 20,000 pounds. The steam capacity, equal to 200-horse power, consists of three boilers twenty-four feet in length and forty-two inches in diameter, with four twelve inch flues in each. The smoke stack is five feet in diameter and sixty feet high. The machinery consists of one circular saw, two planers, three cut-off saws, two rip saws, one resawing machine for making bevel siding, one shingle machine, one scroll saw, two moulding machines, one tenanting machine, one mortising machine, one automatic emory wheel for grinding planer bits, one lathe for turning iron and one for turning wood.

Mr. Blackburn has also another mill at Rock House, in Madison County; capacity, 20,000 feet per day, with all machinery for preparing the lumber ready for the builder's use. He also has in his employ two portable mills, one in Madison County and one in Benton County, four miles east of the home mill, cutting lumber for him by the thousand feet. The capital invested in this enterprise, including mills, machinery, teams, wagons, lands, etc., is about $60,000. The immense amount of lumber manufactured by Mr. Blackburn is all sold in home markets—in Benton, Madison and Washington Counties. He employs fifty hands, about twenty in Madison and thirty in Benton County, and he owns 17,000 acres of land, principally in these counties, 16,500 of it being timbered and the balance being farm land.

WAR EAGLE MILLS.

This little village, consisting of the War Eagle Roller Mills, a large general store, blacksmith shop, and other industries, together with a small number of residences, is located in the beautiful and romantic valley of War Eagle Creek, in the southeast part of Benton County. Sylvanus Blackburn built the first mills at this place, consisting of a saw-mill and grist-mill, in 1848. These mills were used for a number of years, and until a second grist-mill, four stories high, was erected. This mill was burned during the war by order of a Confederate general, as claimed by Mr. Blackburn. The present mills were built about 1872. They are now operated by James K. P. Stringfield, who does an extensive business. This is one of the best water powers in Arkansas.

There are a few post hamlets, containing a post-office and store, etc., in the county not herein named. There is a telephone line extending from Rogers *via* Bentonville and Springtown to Siloam Springs.

EDUCATION AND LITERATURE.

For many years after the formation of the State of Arkansas her educational facilities were of the most meager kind, and although many improvements have been made in the past, it may truthfully be said that in this respect she is still far behind many of her sister States, though perhaps fully on a par with those having had the same opportunities. But few of the children of the early settlers of Benton County enjoyed the benefit of schools, even of the poorest class, while the great majority of them were, on account of the very few schools and the great distance to them, almost entirely deprived of educational facilities. The only schools taught in those days were subscription schools, and those were taught only in neighborhoods sufficiently settled to maintain them. With but few exceptions the early teachers were very illiterate, being able only to read, write and "cipher." And frequently they would contract to teach "'rithmetic" only to the "rule of three." Subsequently, when villages became established, or neighborhoods became thickly settled, a few select schools or academies were established therein by men well quali- fied to teach, but, on account of the tuition necessarily charged, none but the more wealthy classes could avail themselves of these privileges, so upon the whole the children of the poor had to be reared with but little education farther than what could be imparted to them by their parents.

The pioneer schools were always taught in the old-fashioned log cabin school-house, with its puncheon floor and stone fire-place, with stick and mud chimney, and with seats made of split logs, the flat side being hewed smooth with an ax or broad-ax. The early school-teachers who taught in the War Eagle neighborhood were James Martin, Moses Dutton, Alfred Laws, Holland Hines and Thomas Macon. The latter is said to have been well educated, while the education of the others was not up to the standard required of teachers at the present. In 1840 a school was taught in a log school-house in the neighborhood of the settlement of Walter Thornberry, in the southern part of the county, by a young man who also professed to be a Christian minister. W. W. Burgess, now of Springtown, was one of his pupils, and he relates the following rather ridiculous incident. He did not like his teacher, and did not believe that he was what he professed to be, a Christian man, and while he (Burgess) behaved at school, and respected the young man as a teacher, he did not feel constrained to respect him as a preacher. So, on one Sunday when the young man was to preach in the school-house, young Burgess saddled an ox and rode it to church, at the same time wearing upon his head a raw coon-skin for a cap. After service he again mounted the ox and escorted a young lady to her home—she having attended the service on horseback—and took dinner with her. Mr. Burgess delights to relate this incident, but declines to give the lady's name for publication.

About the year 1842 a Mr. Holsten, or Holstein, taught the first school in the vicinity of the present town of Siloam Springs. He taught in "a little cabin," and some white children from the Indian Territory attended his school. Among these may be mentioned Mrs. Cal. D. Gunter, of Hico. In 1844 or 1845 a school and church combined was built in Maysville, that being then the largest town in the county. This house is not standing now. The Shelton Academy, at Pea Ridge, was erected about the year 1851, and Prof. Lockhart taught the first school therein. He was succeeded by other teachers, and the academy was kept up until about the year 1858, when it was abandoned, and the building turned into a store-room. In 1853 and 1854 J. Wade Sikes, now one of the proprietors of Rogers, taught school near Bentonville.   His patrons boarded him and paid him $15 per month for his services.   After this he taught the Shelton Academy at Pea Ridge for two years, where he had about forty pupils in attendance.   Upon the approach of the Civil War the few schools that were being taught in Benton County were closed, and none were opened again until some time after the war.

The Free School System.—In the constitution of 1836, under which the State of Arkansas was admitted into the Union, under Article VII, is found the following general provision pertaining to education, viz.:

" Knowledge and learning, generally diffused through a community, being essential to the preservation of a free government, and diffusing the opportunities and advantages of education through the various parts of the State being highly conducive to this end, it shall be the duty of the General Assembly to provide by law for the improvement of such lands as are or hereafter may be granted by the United States to this State for the use of schools, and to apply any funds which may be raised from such lands, or from any other source, to the establishment of the object for which they are or may be intended.   The General Assembly shall from time to time pass such laws as shall be calculated to encourage intellectual, scientific and agricultural improvement, by allowing rewards and immunities for the promotion and improvement of arts, science, commerce, manufactures and natural history, countenance and encourage the principles of humanity; industry and morality."

This reads well, but it makes no provision for a system of free schools wherein the children of the poor can be educated along with those of the rich.   It was the ruling opinion in Arkansas, as it was in all slave States, that every man should educate his own children, and that no man should be taxed to educate another's children; consequently the framers of the first constitution of the State did not provide for the inauguration of a system of free schools, and following it the General Assembly did not " from time to time pass such laws as should be calculated to encourage intellectual, scientific and agricultural improvement," etc.   But with the abolition of slavery the way was opened for the subsequent inauguration of a method or system whereby "knowledge and learning, * * * being essential to the preservation of a free government," might be generally diffused throughout the State.

The constitution of Arkansas, made in 1864, during the continuance of the late war, contains under Article VIII an exact copy of the aforesaid provision pertaining to education found in the constitution of 1836. It also contains a few other general provisions which may be considered to be in the general line of education, but says not a word about "free schools." Passing on to the constitution of Arkansas made and adopted in 1868, under Article IX is found nine sections pertaining to education, the first and seventh of which reads as follows, to-wit:

SECTION 1. A general diffusion of knowledge and intelligence among all classes being essential to the preservation of the rights and liberties of the people, *the general assembly shall establish and maintain a system of free schools* for the gratuitous instruction of all persons in this State between the ages of five and twenty-one years, and the funds appropriated for the support of common schools shall be distributed to the several counties, in proportion to the number of children and youths therein between the ages of five and twenty-one years, in such manner as shall be prescribed by law, but no religious or other sect or sects shall ever have any exclusive right to, or control of, any part of the school funds of this State. * * *

SECTION 7. In case the public school fund shall be insufficient to sustain a free school at least three months in every year in each school district in this State, the general assembly shall provide by law for raising such deficiency by levying such tax upon all taxable property in each county, township or school district, as may be deemed proper.

The other seven sections of the ninth article of this constitution defined what should constitute the common-school fund, and how the income therefrom should be distributed, and how taxes should be levied and collected for the building of school-houses, etc., etc. Here, then, is found, under the constitution of 1868, the first provisions for the inauguration of the free school system of the State of Arkansas. In accordance therewith laws were subsequently passed creating the system. Much prejudice existed throughout the State against this constitution and the party in power that adopted it. Education for the masses, however, having obtained a foothold, will itself in the course of time remove all prejudice from it, at least all that can be of injury to

BENTON COUNTY, ARKANSAS - BIOGRAPHICAL AND HISTORICAL MEMOIRS 113

****

it. In evidence of the removal of this prejudice the XIVth article of the present constitution of the State of Arkansas, made and adopted in 1874 by the political party that was then and has ever since been in power, is here inserted in full:

SECTION 1. Intelligence and virtue being the safeguards of liberty and the bulwark of a free and good government, *the State shall ever maintain a general, suitable and efficient system of free schools* whereby all persons in the State between the ages of six and twenty-one years may receive gratuitous instruction.*

SECTION. 2. No money or property belonging to the public school fund, or this State for the benefit of schools or universities, shall ever be used for any other than for the respective purposes to which it belongs.

SECTION 3. The general assembly shall provide by general laws for the support of common schools by taxes, which shall never exceed, in any one year, two mills on the dollar, on the taxable property of the State, and by an annual *per capita* tax of one dollar, to be assessed on every male inhabitant of this State, over the age of twenty-one years. Provided, the general assembly may, by general law, authorize school districts to levy, by a vote of the qualified electors of such district, a tax not to exceed five mills on the dollar in any one year for school purposes. Provided, further, that no such tax shall be appropriated to any other purpose, nor to any other district than that for which it was levied.

SECTION 4. The supervision of public schools, and the execution of the laws regulating the same, shall be vested in and confided to such officers as may be provided for by the general assembly.

Two mills on the dollar, the authorized State levy, equals 20 cents on the hundred dollars, and five mills on the dollar, the authorized school district levy, equals 50 cents on each $100; consequently the maximum authorized levy for school purposes is 70 cents on each $100 of taxable property. It must be conceded that this is a liberal provision for the support of the schools, and under the wise and liberal provisions of the constitution, laws have been passed fully providing for the operation and enforcement of a system of free schools for the masses, both white and black.

In the county of Benton the territory has been subdivided into 126 common and four special school districts, making 130 in all. Under the law, schools have to be maintained, where maintained at all, not less than three months in the year, and as much longer as the funds arising from the amount of tax levied will sustain them. In some districts in Benton County the people levy only a two-mill tax, in others more, and in some the full

*Italics by compiler.

amount allowed, five mills; consequently the school terms vary in length, many of them being more than three months, especially in the towns and villages.

The following, from the last biennial report of the State superintendent of public instruction, is a "statement of the public school funds of Benton County for the year ending June 30, 1886."

AMOUNT RECEIVED.

From common school fund (State)	$10,029 18
From district tax	7,338 51
From poll tax	4,023 84
From sale or lease of sixteenth sections	4,122 00
From other sources	105 97
Total	$25,619 50

AMOUNT EXPENDED.

For teachers' salaries	$10,967 80
For building and repairing	2,463 02
For treasurer's commission	311 80
For other purposes	407 40
Total	$14,150 02

BALANCE IN COUNTY TREASURY UNEXPENDED.

In litigation	$ 7,589 18
Of district fund	3,880 30
Total	$11,469 48

According to the late circular report of the State superintendent of public instruction, showing the amount of school funds in the State treasury ready for distribution on the 13th of August of the present year (1888), there were for the whole State the amount of $287,714.10, and of this amount Benton County gets as her distributive share the sum of $8,380.51. Now to this amount must be added the aggregate amount derived from the local levies made in each separate school district within the county.

The Sixteenth Sections.—When the State of Arkansas was organized Congress donated to it the sixteenth section of land in each Congressional township for the support of common schools, providing that these lands should be sold or leased, and that the annual income from the leased lands or from the amount of principal for which such lands were sold should accrue to and belong to the inhabitants of the township in which the lands were located. Afterward the State enacted laws to carry out the provisions of the donation. The county court was authorized to lease these lands, when in its judgment it was best to do so, and to collect the annual income. Provision was also made for the sale of the school lands. Under these provisions the most of these lands in Benton County were sold, and the money received for them was loaned in small sums to individual borrowers. But from the public records of Benton County it cannot be ascertained how much money was received from the sale of these lands, nor what has become of the amount of money that was received. It is known that much of the school funds belonging to and controlled by the several counties of the State was lost during and on account of the Civil War. A subsequent law required the balance not lost in each county to be paid over to a State board of school fund commissioners, by whom it is now controlled. The county of Benton has no school funds under its control at interest. It, however, gets its share of the annual income derived from the permanent school funds managed by the State officers. There is only one colored school in Benton County, and that is located at Bentonville, the colored population being insufficient in number to compose a school at any other place in the county.

Pea Ridge Academy.—This institution of learning was established in 1874 by Prof. J. R. Roberts. Its first session was opened in Buttram's Chapel, two and one-half miles east of the present academy buildings, and there the school was continued five years. Then, after a cessation of one year, the school was reopened at its present location, where the first academy building was erected in 1880. This building was 24x40 feet in size and two stories in height, with a school room and cloak room in each story. The school was chartered as an academy with a full course of instruction in 1884. In 1887 and 1888 an additional building, 50x60 feet in size and two stories in height, was added to the former, making the whole building as it now stands contain seven school rooms and a sufficient number of cloak rooms, the whole having a capacity for the comfortable seating of 250 students. The building is constructed of brick, and in its construction convenience, safety and ventilation were studied, rather than showy architecture. The academy is located on Pea Ridge, an elevated plateau of country nine miles northeast from Bentonville, in Benton County, Ark., and five miles northwest from Avoca, a station on the St. Louis & San Francisco Railroad. From the latter place it has a daily mail, and a tri-weekly one from Neosho, Mo. The healthfulness of the location is unexcelled, while the morals of the community are proverbial. There are in close proximity two dry goods stores and one drug store; five churches within two miles of the school, and two Sunday-schools within 100 yards of it. Eleven graduates have gone out into the world to testify of the character of the school since it was chartered as an academy. A good library of valuable books is connected with it.

Board of Trustees: J. R. Roberts, president; J. A. Steward, secretary; S. B. Smith, Dr. H. H. Patterson, John Hall and P. W. Roberts, of Pea Ridge, Ark.; also George T. Lincoln and R. J. Laughlin, of Bentonville, Ark.; J. D. James, of Alma, Ark., and W. B. Dean, of Wills Point, Tex.

Faculty: J. R. Roberts, A. M., principal; J. A. Steward, principal intermediate department; Miss Nannie Roberts, principal primary department; J. W. Osborn and P. S. Jones, assistants; Miss Lillie Dale, instruction in instrumental music; T. A. Coffelt, M. D., lectures on anatomy, etc.

Benton County may well be proud of this institution, with its successful operation, and eminent satisfaction given.

Bentonville Public and High School.—The public school building of Bentonville is located in a beautiful grove of natural forest trees, about one-half mile southwest of the court-house. It is a large two-story brick building, containing seven school-rooms, besides the necessary halls and cloak-rooms. It was constructed in 1872, but was afterward burned down, and was rebuilt in 1881. The first session of the present school year commenced September 3, and at this writing, September 10, 1888, 326 pupils have been enrolled in attendance, and more are yet expected to come in. The faculty consists of Prof. William Stephens, principal; Prof. J. D. Partelow, Miss Laura Schwab,

Miss Lou Taliaferro, Miss Flora Cotton, Miss Georgia Nesbit and Miss Ida Trotter. The number of pupils already enrolled is exceedingly large for such a small corps of teachers.

The Rogers Academy.—This is a handsome structure, three stories high, built of brick, and would be a credit to any country. It was erected in 1884–85 by the American Home Missionary Society and the people of Rogers, and has generally been and is now under the control of the Congregational Church and the citizens of Rogers, the former having five trustees and the latter four on the school board. The public free school is taught in connection with the academy. The first session of the present school year began September 5. Following is the faculty: Principal, J. W. Scroggs, academic department; grammar school department, Miss Mary G. Webb; intermediate department, Mr. J. R. Williams; primary department, Miss Ella W. Scroggs; music and drawing, Mrs. F. W. Hormon.

The Arkansas Traveler.—Who has not read and been greatly amused with the account of the "Arkansas Travelers?" Perhaps but few people are aware that some one in Benton County was connected with the authorship and preparation of that funny and interesting article. The reputed author of the "Arkansas Traveler" was Col. Sandy Faulkner, of Little Rock, and the individual who drew the illustrations which accompanied and formed a part of the article was Edward Washburn, a son of Rev. Ceaphas Washburn, a Presbyterian minister, who lived in Benton County, about six miles southwest of Bentonville, on the farm now occupied by L. B. Mallory. It is related by good authority that the author of that article in his travels actually met with and saw such a scene as he therein describes, the old backwoodsman with his fiddle, the rude log cabin, the wife and untutored children, etc. That article has been read throughout America, and perhaps in foreign countries, and many people believe that it has been a great injury to the State of Arkansas by creating the impression abroad that the family therein described was a fair sample of the people generally, which of course was not the case.

CHRISTIANITY.

The real pioneer settlers of a new country, those who select a wild and lonely spot away out on the frontier, and erect a rude habitation thereon, where they intend to make their future home, and where they do in fact remain and endure the privations incident to the settlement of a new country, and subdue the forest and prepare the soil for cultivation, and thus open up and make way for others to follow, are, as a rule, God-fearing and Christian men. The first real and permanent settlers of Benton County were no exception to this rule. Coeval with the first settlements the voice of the Christian minister was heard, pointing out to the pioneers the way to eternal life. And, as was the case in nearly all the settlements west of the Mississippi near this latitude, the Methodist Episcopal, Cumberland Presbyterians and Baptists were the pioneer churches in this county. The early ministers of these and other denominations preached in the cabin dwellings of the early settlers before any church edifices were erected, and members of all denominations then met together to worship. The settlers being so scattered there were not enough at any one place of the same denomination to form an organization until several years after the settlement of the county began. The services were generally conducted by ministers who traveled great distances to perform their labors, and who generally worked in the capacity of missionaries, receiving for their support the small contributions that the people were able to give them.

Methodist Episcopal Church.—In a very early day, probably early in the thirties, Rev. James Mayfield organized a church of this denomination in the vicinity of War Eagle Mills. Prior to 1839 Rev. Walter Thornberry organized a Methodist church at his residence in the southern part of the county, in the vicinity of Wager's Mills. Rev. Swaggerty was a pioneer minister of this denomination in Benton County, laboring during the thirties, and perhaps later. Martin and Walter, sons of Walter Thornberry, Sr., both became Methodist preachers. Other Methodist churches were established in the county in an early day, and when the separation took place, in 1844–45, nearly all the members thereof united with the Methodist Episcopal Church,

South, thus leaving the original church without an organization in the county, and so it remained until 1882, when Rev. O. R. Brant, formerly of Eureka Springs, organized a society under a brush arbor at Rogers, with seven members, three or four of whom belonged to his own family. About the same time an organization of the church was effected at Siloam Springs. Since that time all the societies of the Methodist Episcopal Church in the county have been organized, and all belong to the Rogers District of the Arkansas Conference, with Elder Mattox presiding. The county is divided into stations and circuits as follows: Rogers' station includes one monthly appointment at Springdale in Washington County; Rev. H. H. Scroggs, who lives at Rogers, is the station preacher. The Bentonville station includes one monthly appointment at Cave Springs, and Rev. William Buck, residing at Bentonville, is the station minister. The Siloam Springs station includes only the city of Siloam Springs, and the present station minister is Rev. J. M. Jackson. The Mason Valley circuit consists of appointments at the following places: Springtown, Harmony, Moter's Chapel and Dripping Springs; Rev. John Welch is the preacher on this circuit. War Eagle Mills circuit consists of War Eagle Mills, Hickory Creek and Silver Springs; Rev. La Fayette Mason is the minister on this circuit. The Wheeler circuit, in Washington County, has one or two appointments in Benton County.

After organizing the church at Rogers, Rev. Brant remained and preached three years, and was succeeded by Rev. Mattox, who also preached three years. The church edifice at this place was erected in 1884, and the one at Bentonville in 1887–88. The church at Bentonville was organized in June, 1887. The aggregate membership of the Methodist Episcopal Church in Benton County is about 370.

Cumberland Presbyterian Church.—The first organization of this denomination in Benton County was formed about the year 1830, near the present site of Bentonville, being some distance east thereof. The second one was organized at Pea Ridge, and about the same time or a little later one was organized at Maysville. Revs. Andrew and John Buchanan, ministers of this denomination, were pioneer preachers in Benton County during the thirties, and are claimed to have been the first religious workers in the territory of the county. They were great workers in the cause of Christianity. Up to the time of the outbreak of the Civil War Rev. John Buchanan had preached in every county of Arkansas then organized. Following are the names of the several churches of this denomination now existing in Benton County, together with the names of the pastors thereof: Bentonville, Rev. F. T. Charlton; Woods, two miles east of Bentonville, Pea Ridge and Rogers, Rev. Peter Carnahan; Maysville, Rev. Johns; Siloam, Rev. J. D. Rush. The aggregate membership of these churches is about 500 or upward. Outside of these organizations there is a number of members of this denomination within the county.

Baptist Church.—The first Baptist society organized in Benton County was the one known now as "Twelve Corners." It was organized in 1842, in the log cabin residence of William Reddick, at the place where the famous Elkhorn tavern now stands. It was organized by Elders J. F. Mitchell and Charles B. Whiteley, the latter of whom resided in what is now Carroll County. Several years before that time Elder Whiteley had organized a church on War Eagle Creek, a short distance south of the Benton County line. He, like many other men, had certain peculiarities, one of which was a desire to preach his own funeral sermon. About a year before he died he announced to the public that if he lived to reach the age of fifty years he would then preach his own funeral sermon; and if he did not reach that age he had a man selected to preach the sermon at his death. He lived to the desired age and preached his own funeral sermon in Prairie Township, in Carroll County, near where he lived. After the sermon he gave a public dinner at his house, to which he invited all his friends. Many partook of his hospitality, and joined in the exercises of this pleasant and joyful occasion.

As time passed and settlements increased more Baptist churches were organized throughout the county. The Mount Zion Baptist Association was organized in Carroll County in 1840, and when churches of this denomination were organized in Benton County they joined the association. In 1886 the churches of Benton County, formerly belonging to this association, formed the Benton County Baptist Association. The first session of this association was held at Corner Springs Baptist Church, in the western part of the county; the second session at Pleasant Hill Baptist Church, near Rogers, and the third and last one was held in the Baptist Church at Siloam Springs, in September of the present year (1888). This church has become very strong, and in numbers is the strongest one in the county. According to the published minutes of the second session of the Benton County Baptist Association (those of the third session not being published yet), there were the following named churches of that denomination in Benton County, with pastors' names annexed, and a total membership of 1,971, to wit: Bentonville, I. R. Hall and J. B. Stark; Bloomington, W. F. Green; Butler Creek, G. W. Setser; Bethesda, I. R. Hall; Corner Springs, Joseph Setser; Elm Springs, J. C. Robertson; Flint Creek, Joseph Setser; Honey Creek, E. J. Hogan; Illinois, E. S. Gibbs; Mount Pleasant, G. W. Setser; Mount Enterprise, same; Mason Valley, L. Hine; Maysville, — Nelson; New Prospect, G. P. Rodgers; Pleasant Grove, I. R. Hall; Pleasant Site, A. J. Maxwell; Pleasant Hill, J. Dunagin; Pea Ridge, A. J. Maxwell; Rogers, J. Dunagin; Siloam, A. J. Estes; Southern Grove, S. S. Graham; Spring Creek, J. C. Robertson; Springtown, same; Spavinaw, ——— ; Sulphur Springs, J. W. West; Temperance Hill, I. R. Hall; Twelve Corners, W. R. Mahuren; Wager's Mill, J. C. Robertson; Walnut Hill, ——— ; Cherokee City, L. Hine; Lone Valley, S. B. Ford; thirty-one in all.

Methodist Episcopal Church, South.—This church, after its organization in 1844-45, continued to grow in strength, and now it has twenty-four separate organizations, and a membership of 1,600 in the county of Benton. The several organizations form an integral part of the Fayetteville District of the Arkansas Conference, of which Rev. James A. Peebles is the present presiding elder. The church of this denomination at Bentonville has been made a "station," and Rev. T. J. Reynolds is the present station minister. Another "station" is composed of the churches at Rogers, in Benton County, and Springdale, in Washington County, and Rev. B. C. Matthews, of Springdale, the station minister, preaches alternately at these places. The Bentonville Circuit lies northeast of the city of Bentonville, comprising the Pea Ridge country. It consists of Tuck's, Buttram's, Hileman's and Post Oak chapels; Rev. W. M. Baldwin is the rider on this circuit. The Clifta Mission lies east of the Bentonville Circuit and east of the St. Louis & San Francisco Railroad; Rev. R. P. Hardcastle is the minister of this mission. The Center Point Circuit lies south of Bentonville, and consists of the churches known as Center Point, Oakley's Chapel and Hebron; Alex. Matthis is the circuit preacher. The Siloam Circuit lies in the southwestern part of Benton County, and is composed of the church at Siloam Springs, and at Cincinnati, in Washington County, and other country churches; Rev. J. H. Meyers is the circuit minister. The Bloomfield Circuit lies in the west central portion of the county, and consists of the churches at Bloomfield and Maysville and some country churches. Between this and the Bentonville Circuit is a large tract of country not included in any circuit, but in which the church does missionary work. The value of the church property belonging to the Methodist Episcopal Church, South, in Benton County, is reported at $10,500. There are twenty-one local preachers of this denomination in the county. The number of Sunday-schools is sixteen, with 960 scholars belonging to them. The church has occasionally held camp-meetings at Buttram's Chapel, and is making arrangements to hold annual camp-meetings there hereafter. The membership of this church is fairly increasing, and the several organizations are doing good work.

Christian Church.—Elder Larkin Scott, now of Bentonville, settled near the Osage Springs in 1856, and upon inquiry found only one organization of the Christian Church in Benton County; and that one was located on Spavinaw Creek, about sixteen miles west of Bentonville. The preacher in charge was Elder Goodnight. The following year, upon solicitation, this elder organized a society of the Christian denomination at the house of Mr. Scott, where they continued to worship until the outbreak of the Civil War. Up to this time no other organizations of this church existed in Benton County, and the first one organized after the war closed was the one at Bentonville, which was organized in the fall of 1865, principally through the instrumentality of Larkin

Scott, who was elected as elder thereof, and preached his first discourse in February following. Since that time a large number of organizations of the Christian Church has been formed in the county, of which the following is a list of their names or localities, together with the names of the elders preaching at each, so far as they are supplied: Bentonville, E. T. Russell; Maysville, S. R. Beaman; Rogers, Lowell and Wire Springs, Larkin Scott; Pea Ridge, Prof. J. R. Roberts; Oak Grove and Antioch, W. S. Herman; Nebo, J. C. Lawson; Gordon Hollow, Bloomfield and Cherokee City, no regular preacher; Robinson, John Leonard; Siloam Springs, —— Marshall; Mason Valley, Dr. G. W. Robinson; Brightwater, John Nantz; Roller's Ridge, no regular preacher; church north of Pea Ridge Academy, M. L. Banks; head of Sugar Creek, Elder Inman. This makes nineteen church organizations of this denomination within the county, all of which have been organized since the Civil War closed. Estimating the average membership of all of these organizations at forty-five, the aggregate would be 855 members, which is believed to be a fair estimate.

In May, 1887, Elder Larkin Scott, at the age of seventy, baptized and took into church fellowship "Uncle Dick" Bennett, whose age, according to best information, was one hundred and nine years. Mr. Bennett had never made a profession of religion, and at the age of one hundred and nine years he concluded that it was time to prepare for death. He voted the Democratic ticket at the last election (September, 1888), and still lives at this writing.

Presbyterian Church.—Of this denomination there never has been but one organization in Benton County. It was organized about 1844–45 at the head waters of the Osage, six miles southwest of Bentonville, by Rev. Cephas Washburn, who resided there, and was missionary, by appointment, for the Cherokee Indians. He preached there about six years, until the church was discontinued at that place. It was reorganized at Bentonville about 1852 by Rev. Joshua F. Green, of Little Rock, and Rev. W. K. Marshall, of Van Buren, Ark., and Rev. A. W. Morrison, of Bentonville. The latter served as pastor of the church until he was killed, during the war, while returning from mill.

On February 5, 1870, the church was again reorganized, this time by Rev. C. M. Richards, an evangelist under the Arkansas Presbytery, assisted by Rev. W. A. Sample. Rev. Richards remained and preached until his death, which occurred August 27, 1872. The congregation was without a pastor until July 1, 1873, when Rev. D. C. Boggs took charge as stated supply, and still stands in that relation to it. The present membership of the church numbers fifty-eight, and they are scattered throughout the county. The Sabbath-school has a fair average attendance, and is kept up throughout the year. A. W. Dinsmore is the superintendent. The fine brick edifice of this denomination was erected in 1877.

The Congregationalists have a church at Rogers, and also at Siloam Springs, and the Society of Friends have a church at the latter place. There may be a few organizations of other denominations, not herein mentioned, in the county.

The churches of all denominations in the towns and villages sustain Sunday-schools throughout the year, while most of them in the country have their Sunday-schools during the summer months.

BIOGRAPHICAL APPENDIX.

BENTON COUNTY.

David Adams. Prominent among the progressive and successful farmers of Benton County, Ark., may be mentioned Mr. Adams, who was born and reared in Coles County, Ill., and came to Arkansas in 1886, purchasing the farm of 550 acres on which he now lives. Three hundred acres of the land are situated in the Osage Valley, and his residence is pleasantly situated on a high hill. He was born June 26, 1849, and his first presidential vote was cast for Gen. Grant, who was then running for his second term. He is a member of the I.O.O.F., and May, 1873, was married to Miss Hannah Harris, who was born and reared in Illinois. Their union has been blessed in the birth of three children: Grace, Jefferson and Fannie. Mr. Adams is a son of John J. and Nancy C. (Dryden) Adams, who were of English descent, and came from Tennessee to Illinois in 1830, assisting in the early settlement of that State. The father was a soldier in the Black Hawk and Mexican wars and the Civil War, and died in 1878. He was first married to Martha Gammil, by whom he had seven children: William E. (deceased), Elizabeth, wife of Rufus Brown; Eliza, wife of Dr. Reel, of Oakland, Ill.; Martha, wife of Thomas West; Margaret, wife of John Grimes, and John, who died during the late war, at Pocahontas, Ark. After the mother's death the father married Nancy C. Dryden, who became the mother of one child, David.

G. L. Alexander, druggist, Rogers, Ark., and one of the prominent citizens of Benton County, was born in Elbert County, Ga., in 1838. His father, Elijah Alexander, was born in Northfield, Mass., and when a young man immigrated to Georgia, where he met and married Miss Savannah Wilhight, and by her became the father of four children, G. L. Alexander being the eldest of their children. The father was a farmer by occupation, and died near Independence, Mo., on a steamboat while on his way to California; his wife in 1864, while in Georgia. G. L. Alexander was reared and educated in Georgia, and when the great Civil War broke out joined the Confederate army, and was a member of Longstreet's corps. He was quite severely wounded, and while home on furlough his mother died. After recovering from his wound he rejoined his command and served until the close of the war. He rose to the rank of first lieutenant, and afterward, for distinguished service at the battle of Fussell's Mills, he was promoted to the rank of captain, and served in this capacity with Company C, Fifteenth Georgia Regiment. Mr. Alexander has a number of interesting relics of the war in his possession, among which is a pistol with which he shot his way through a Federal regiment at the battle of Gettysburg. Two of his brothers were also Confederate soldiers, and the following are some of the battles in which they participated: Fredericksburg, Yorktown, Williamsburg, Richmond, Malvern Hill, second Manassas, Gordonville, Wilderness, Spottsylvania and numerous others of lesser note. Mr. Alexander has been married three times. The first time to Miss Emma Trenchard, who died after four years of married life. He was next married in Kansas to a Miss Early, a New York lady, and after her death was married, in Arkansas, to Miss Hattie Camden. While in Georgia Mr. Alexander dealt in cotton and other articles of merchandise, and after moving to Kansas followed various occupations for twelve years. In 1881 he came to Rogers, Ark., and engaged in the drug business, and by his honesty, energy and efforts to please has a large and paying trade. He is a stanch Democrat.

Gustavus H. Alexander, storekeeper and gauger at Siloam Springs, Ark., was born in Cumberland County, Ky., January 20, 1856, son of Joseph H. and America (Baker) Alexander. The father was born in the same county, and was a tiller of the soil. He received his final summons in 1865, in his native county, where he had passed his entire life. The mother was born in the same county, is still living there, and is fifty-four years of age. Their son, Gustavus H. Alexander, was educated at Alexander College, Burksville, Ky., also Columbia College, Adair County, Ky.; remained in his native county until sixteen years of age, when he moved to Fort Smith, Ark., where he worked on a farm and traded a great deal. He was in the United States police service for one year, and then deputy constable in Upper Township, Fort Smith. After moving to this county he was made marshal of Siloam Springs in 1884, and was afterward appointed storekeeper and gauger. He owns some property in Siloam Springs. He chose for his companion in life, October 16, 1884, Miss Susan M. Barton, who died September 8, 1885. She was of religious faith, but a member of no church. Mr. Alexander is a member of the Methodist Episcopal Church, is a member of the I. O. O. F., K. of H., and in his political views has been a Democrat all his life.

Elijah L. Allen is one of the successful farmers of Benton County, Ark., and is also engaged in grist-milling. He is of French descent, and was born in Northern Georgia July 25, 1833. His father, Matthew Allen, was born in South Carolina in 1807, and in October, 1852, left Georgia and came to Arkansas, where he died October 11, 1862. He was married to Lucinda Vaughter, who died in Georgia in 1848, having borne nine children: James (deceased); Amanda E., wife of W. E. Smith; Elijah L.; Martha J., who became the wife of Rev. Isom Hall and died in 1854; William C. (deceased); Lindsay M., who died during the late war; Catherine (deceased wife of W. P. Henderson); Hiram S., living in Arkansas, and an infant, deceased. Elijah L. Allen came to Arkansas when nineteen years of age, and for twenty-seven years was a resident of Conway County. Since that time he has resided on his present farm of 120 acres. In 1856 he married Louisa Jones, a native of Tennessee, who died in May, 1863, leaving five children: Sarah C. (Mrs. Solomon Glenn), William A. (deceased), Mary M. (Mrs. J. A. Matthews), Lindsay A. and Laura J. (Mrs. James H. Willis). Ellen A. Townsend was married to Mr. Allen September 28, 1865, and by him became the mother of seven children: Georgia A. (Mrs. F. C. Grimsley), Hiram R., Elijah H., Isom (deceased), Fannie (deceased), T. J. (deceased), and Hattie (deceased). Mrs. Allen died August 15, 1880, and two years later Mr. Allen married Mrs. Amelia C. Willis. In 1862 Mr. Allen enlisted in the Union army, and after honorable service was discharged July 9, 1865. He was at Prairie Grove, Helena, the evacuation of Little Rock and in the Camden raid. He supports the principles of the Republican party, and his first presidential vote was cast for Fremont. He is a member of the Missionary Baptist Church, and belongs to the Masonic fraternity and the G. A. R. His wife belongs to the Methodist Church.

John Barnhouse Allensworth, merchant and postmaster at Decatur, Ark., was born in Springfield, Ohio, March 15, 1839, and is a son of Rootan and Eliza (Barnhouse) Allensworth, both of whom were born in the "Buckeye State." The father was an artisan and builder, and a member of the Presbyterian Church. John B. Allensworth grew to manhood in Harrison County, Ohio. He received his primary education in the common schools, and afterward completed his education in the McCannahan High-school at New Jefferson. He was married in Ohio, in October, 1859, and in 1860 removed to Martin County, Ind., where he met with good success as a farmer. Five years later he moved to Southern Illinois, and in 1876 to Texas, where he farmed with excellent results. He came to Benton County, Ark., in 1879, and here has since resided. About 1883 he engaged in the mercantile business at Decatur, and has a stock valued at $1,600. His wife's maiden name was Elizabeth Knouff, a daughter of John and Susan Knouff, the former of whom was a soldier in the War of 1812. To Mr. and Mrs. Allensworth ten children were born, five of whom are living: Charles C., James M., George I., John B. and Eliza J. Mr. Allensworth's paternal ancestors were of Scotch descent, and his maternal ancestors of Pennsylvania-Dutch origin. His mother was a member of the Methodist Church, and his wife was raised a Lutheran.

Walter Alley, son of David and Nancy (Ross) Alley, was born in Washington County, Mo., February 29, 1835. The father was born in Tennessee, and came to Missouri when a young man. He was here married, and here passed the remainder of his days engaged in merchandising. He died in 1861. The mother was born in Kentucky, and died in Missouri when her son Walter was quite young. The latter remained with his parents until grown, and then married Miss Elizabeth Mahan; she bore him three children, named Martha, Nancy and George W. After marriage they settled on a farm in Oregon County, Mo., where they remained until 1863, and then moved to Polk County, of the same State, where they remained three years. From there they went to Benton County, on the Illinois River, and have since lived in this vicinity. He has 155 acres under cultivation, and 320 acres in all. Mr. Walter Alley took, for his second wife, Miss Mary Carter, and one child was born to this marriage, Thomas, who is living on the river bottom farm. Mr. Alley took for his third wife Mrs. Frances (Embree) Lee, and following named children were born to this marriage: Elizabeth, William, David (deceased), Willie (deceased), Ross, Laura, Joseph, Luella and Walter. During the late war Mr. Alley was sworn in but not mustered into the Union service, having been rejected on account of being a cripple before mustering. He is a Republican in his political views, and a public-spirited and enterprising citizen. His church preference and former affiliation was with the Missionary Baptist Church, his wife being a member of the same.

D. D. Ames, who is the acknowledged fruit king of Arkansas, was born in Ohio July 14, 1840, and is a son of Lyman and Celinda Ames, who were born in the "Nutmeg" State. They became residents of Ohio in 1832, and there died only a few years ago. D. D. Ames was reared in his native State and is, by natural proclivities, a horticulturist. He was married in Ohio to Miss Emma Rinehart, and by her became the father of eight children: Emma, Alice, Burton, Walter, Ernest, Gracie, Freddie and Bessie. Mr. Ames came to Arkansas the 1st of May, 1883, with only 25 cents in money, but, with that determination, energy and intelligence which has ever characterized his actions, set to work to rebuild his fallen fortunes. He first became a traveling agent for a nursery, and his success in that capacity was exceptionally good. As soon as he had acquired sufficient means he leased seventeen acres of land of Albert Peel, and put it all in orchard and small fruits. The first crop on five acres of strawberries cleared Mr. Ames $500, and the first crop on an acre and a half of raspberries cleared $525. The enterprise had been ridiculed by the people near his home, but at this juncture their eyes began to be opened, and they began to follow his example. About this time Mr. Ames purchased eighty acres of land at Van-Buren, and the first year put in twenty-two acres of small fruit, on which he has realized a large amount of money. He is now the owner of 130 acres of land, and has sixty-four acres in small fruits, which is the admiration and wonder of all who see it. Mr. Ames took for his second wife Miss Frona Callis, a member of one of the prominent and highly respected families of the county. Although quite young she is an exemplary wife and mother. They have one child, Nellie Don. Mr. Ames is a stanch Democrat.

O. I. Anderson, a prosperous farmer residing near Bentonville, Ark., was born in Lawrence County, Ala., July 5, 1831, being a son of Hugh A. and Mary A. (Anderson) Anderson. Col. Hugh A. Anderson was born at Logan Station, Ky., June 10, 1782, and was captain in the War of 1812. He moved to Alabama in 1818, and in 1836 located in Benton County, Ark. He was married January 11, 1810, and his wife died September 30, 1860. They were the parents of eight children: Louisa Ann, deceased wife of Robert W. Mecklin; Elizabeth H., deceased, first the wife of Albert Peel and afterward the wife of Judge Hiram Davis; James J., deceased; William W., deceased; Mary Jane, the deceased wife of Nathan M. Moran; Catherine, the deceased wife of A. W. Dinsmore; Hugh Allen, deceased, and Oliver I. Our subject came to Benton County, Ark., with his parents in 1836, and was married in 1856 to Mary Kelleam, a native of Arkansas, by whom he became the father of nine children: William, a farmer living in Benton County; Robert P., a stockman in Colorado; Mary Kate, wife of William Crum, a farmer of Washington County; O. P., a stockman of Idaho Territory; Bettie E., James Hugh, Nancy L., Amy Pearl and Annie W. The mother of these children died July 12, 1878, and October 13, 1880, Mr. Anderson was married to Margaret A. Stites. She was born in Missouri and reared in Texas. Mr. Anderson served in the Confederate army during the late war, and was a participant in the battle of Pea Ridge. By industry and good management Mr.

Anderson has become the owner of 683 acres of land; in his political views he is a Democrat, casting his first presidential vote for Taylor. He is also a member of the Masonic fraternity.

John C. Arthur, member of the firm of Lincoln & Arthur, dealers in clothing and gents' furnishing goods, of Bentonville, Ark., was born in Macon County, Mo., in 1840, and is the son of Lilburn Q. and Letitia G. (Saunders) Arthur, and grandson of James C. Arthur. Lilburn Q. was born in Bedford County, Va., September 26, 1814, and was a farmer, blacksmith, gunsmith and wheelwright by trade, and, in short, was a natural genius. He moved with his father to Pulaski County, Ky., when seventeen years old, was married here, and in 1839 moved to Macon County, Mo., where he passed the remainder of his life. He died January 1, 1871. The last six years of his life he was engaged in the practice of medicine. Letitia G. (Saunders) Arthur was born in Kentucky, February 24, 1821, and died March 25, 1855, in Jasper County, Mo., she and her husband having moved there in 1853. Mr. Arthur was twice married, and was the father of sixteen children, ten by the first marriage and six by the second, seven living by the first marriage and four by the second. John C. Arthur was the eldest child by the first marriage. He attained his growth on the farm, and his education was sadly neglected; what education he received was by his own efforts and self study. He remained at home until twenty-two years of age, and at the breaking out of the late Civil War he enlisted in the Union army, Company A, Twenty-seventh Missouri Infantry Volunteers, and was in the siege of Vicksburg, Jackson, Miss., Missionary Ridge, Lookout Mountain, Atlanta, and was with Gen. Sherman in his march to the sea. He went to Richmond and back to Washington, D. C., in the grand review. He was neither captured nor wounded during the war, and received his discharge at St. Louis. October 8, 1866, he married Miss Mary E. Dodson, who was born in Macon County, Mo., in 1846, and who became the mother of three children: Sallie, wife of W. H. Johnson, William A. and Perry W. After the war Mr. Arthur located near his birthplace and engaged in farming, which he continued until 1886, when he came to Bentonville, Ark., and with George T. Lincoln formed a partnership in the present business. Mr. Arthur was the owner of 300 acres of land in Macon County, and was one of the best citizens. The firm of Lincoln & Arthur have the only clothing and gents' furnishing store in Bentonville, and they have a large trade, having won the confidence and esteem of the community by their fair dealing. Mr. Arthur and family are members of the Cumberland Presbyterian Church, and he is a Democrat in politics. He was justice of peace while in Macon County, and was also township trustee for eighteen months, resigning that office when coming to Arkansas.

Dr. C. F. Baker, a successful practicing physician of Maysville, was born in Franklin Parish, La., March 25, 1836, son of William and Sarah (Howe) Baker. William Baker was born either in Maryland or Virginia, but no positive information has been obtained as to what State he was born in. He was married in Virginia, and was also a practicing physician and a graduate of the University of Philadelphia. After receiving his diploma he returned to Virginia, and there began the practice of his profession. He continued there for a number of years, and then left for Franklin Parish, in Louisiana, where he practiced for a number of years. He then began the establishment of the Medical and Surgical Institute at Cincinnati, but had not completed the same at the time of his death. After his death Mrs. Baker was instrumental in seeing it completed, the State also taking an active part, making a large endowment, and when the work was completed Dr. A. H. Baker was made president of the institution, and professor of surgery, which positions he held until his death. Sarah (Howe) Baker was married in Virginia, also received a good education and was an accomplished musician. She is now living in Franklin Parish, La., and is ninety-two years of age. She was the mother of eight children, four now living. Dr. C. F. Baker was reared principally in Franklin Parish, La., and was educated under private tuition until fourteen years of age, when he went to Schenectady, N. Y., and there entered Union College or the University of New York. He remained there as a student for about two years, and then went to Oxford, Ohio, where he took a short course, after which he entered the Ohio Medical College and took one course of lectures. From there he went to Indianapolis, where he attended the medical department of the Asbury University, from which he graduated. He then went to Cincinnati and attended the Medical and Surgical Institute, where the degree of Doctor of Medicine was conferred at the annual commencement of this institute, and afterward having the degree conferred by a regular course of study. Dr. Baker, after finishing his medical studies, went with a number of gentlemen to Fort Smith, and organized a company for the building of the Northwestern Border Railroad, but on account of the breaking out of the war was never able to carry their plan into execution. He then returned and enlisted in Company C, Third Louisiana Regiment, but remained with that company but a short time, when, under the orders of Gen. McCullough, he started for the Indian Territory, where he organized a company of Cherokee and white scouts, and rejoined Gen. McCullough in Benton County, at Camp Walker. He was then transferred, and did duty for Gen. Price on Cow Spring Prairie under special orders. After his duties as scout had been accomplished in Missouri, he rejoined his regular command, marched to Fort Wilson Creek, and there participated in that bloody battle. He then went to Lexington with Gen. Price again under special orders, being at the capture of that city. He then returned to Springfield, and there went into winter quarters, remaining only a short time, being forced to evacuate before Gen. Curtis' army. He then went down and participated in the Pea Ridge battle, after which his army retreated to the Arkansas River and continued on down south until they reached Memphis, Tenn., where they remained a short time. From there they went to Corinth, Miss., and participated in that battle, thence to Tupelo. Dr. Baker was then ordered back to Little Rock, from there to Fort Smith, and then joined Gen. Raines. He then went to the Indian Territory, and was on general duty, after which he went to Missouri, and then drifted into Louisiana, where he was on post duty at Alexander. He was paroled at Shreveport. Dr. Baker then went to New Orleans, but returned home and subsequently went to Mississippi, and afterward to St. Louis and then to Canada, being there during the Fenian invasion, and was on military duty. He participated in the capture of Fort Erie, after which he received orders from Gen. Barry to withdraw from the British territory. Dr. Baker then returned to the United States, settled at Bentonville, but his professional work was after his location at Maysville, which was in 1867. Since that time he has been thoroughly identified with his profession. The Doctor is a member of the Masonic fraternity and is politically a people's man, being now allied with the Union Labor party, but formerly being a strong Democrat, never having voted any other ticket.

Jabez B. Banks, farmer, Benton County, Ark., was born in Alabama in 1825, and is a son of Thomas and Susannah (Jarvix) Banks, who were born July 12, 1784, and February 29, 1799, respectively. The former was a native of Virginia, and at an early day immigrated to Alabama, where he was married and resided until 1837, at which time he and his family moved to Arkansas. They were the parents of twelve children, who lived to be grown; Lydia, who became the wife of Daniel Perkins, a farmer and tanner, and died in Oregon; Verlinder, wife of Jesse Kincannon, a farmer residing in Wise County, Texas; Simon P., deceased; Reziah J., a farmer of Texas; Samuel A., deceased; Elizabeth, the wife of James S. Doggett, a Methodist minister residing in California; Tirzah, deceased; Hilkiah, a farmer of Oregon; Jabez B., farming on the old homestead; Susan Margaret, wife of Frederick Green, residing in Texas; Rhoda, residing in Texas and the wife of Lowry Davis; and Sebins, a farmer of Oregon. Jabez B. came to Arkansas at the age of twelve years, and after attaining man's estate was married to Sarah Sherrod, a native of Tennessee. The following are their children: Nancy E. (deceased), Benjamin F., Martha C. (deceased), David F., Thomas Arthur, Kilkiah Wesley (deceased), Susan Verlinda, wife of John McClusky; Margaret, wife of Wiley B. Johnson; George Lafayette and Henry Jordan (deceased). Mrs. Banks died in 1860, and in 1861 Mr. Banks married Elizabeth Gamble, and by her became the father of four children: Jabez Jefferson, Samuel Green, John Reziah and Sarah F. Mr. Banks is a Democrat in politics, and is the owner of 200 acres of valuable land, seventy-five acres being under cultivation. He is a Mason, and he and wife are members of the Methodist Episcopal Church, South.

Tompkins Coleman Barney, furniture dealer of Bentonville, whose birth occurred in Woodford County, Ill., in 1845, is the son of Harlow and Amy (Wolf) Barney. Harlow Barney was born in Luzerne County, Penn., in 1800, was of Irish descent, and was a physician and surgeon by profession. He graduated from the New York Medical College, and when still a young man went to

Ohio and there followed teaching, and also continued the study of medicine. In 1824 he married Miss Amy Wolf, who was born in Newark, Licking Co., Ohio, March 3, 1809. About 1844 they moved to Woodford County, Ill., and here lived for some time at Lacon and Spring Bay, and here Dr. Barney devoted his entire attention to the practice of medicine. His wife was of Scotch descent, and died in 1855, just three months previous to the death of her husband. They were the parents of nine children, four now living: Carey, farmer in Monroe County, Mo.; Allen, in the Rocky Mountains; Tompkins C., and Wirth W., who is a painter and contractor in Bentonville, Ark. Tompkins C. Barney was but ten years old when his parents died, and he was taken to Richland County, Ohio, and reared by his mother's sister, Mrs. Phœbe A. Coleman, and remained with his aunt until seventeen years of age. About this time the war broke out, and young Barney donned his blue uniform and enlisted in Company D, Seventy-seventh Regiment Illinois Infantry, under Col. D. P. Greer. He was in the battle of Arkansas Post, Champion Hill, Black River Bridge, siege of Vicksburg, Red River campaign, siege and capture of Mobile. He was discharged at Springfield, Ill., at the close of the war. He then located at Bolivar, Polk Co., Mo., and invested in one-half interest in the Bolivar *Sentinel*. This interest he sold out in 1867 and went into Kansas, where he assisted in the survey of that State west of Wichita, and one year later returned to Bolivar, Mo. Here, in 1868, he married Miss Cornelia Evans, who was born in Polk County, Mo., in 1849. They have four children: Margaret, Frank, Lillard and Gracie. Soon after his marriage Mr. Barney moved to Quincy, Ill., and hired as baggage and express agent on the Chicago, Burlington & Quincy Railroad from Quincy to Louisiana, Mo. In 1878 he returned to Southwestern Missouri, and worked in the woolen mills at Springfield for two years. He then went to Eureka Springs and clerked in the Southern Hotel a short time. He afterward became manager, and occupied this position eighteen months. August, 1886, he moved to Bentonville, Ark., and established himself in the furniture business, which he has since continued. He is a Republican in politics; is a member of the K. of P.; Mrs. Barney is a member of the Baptist Church.

Benjamin S. Beach is one of the enterprising and intelligent young business men of Benton County, Ark., and has a large general merchandise store at Osage Mills. He is a native of Benton County, and was born February 8, 1855, and was educated in the common schools. Besides his store he is postmaster at Osage Mills, and is the owner of forty acres of land. He is a Democrat, and Tilden received his first presidential vote. He is a Mason, and a member of the Missionary Baptist Church. In 1880 he was married to Miss Sallie Simmons, who died in 1882, having borne one child, John E. She was born in Tennessee in 1858, and came to Arkansas when quite small. Mr. Beach is a son of Elam J. and Rachel J. (Gambill) Beach. The father was born in Georgia, and came to Arkansas when a young man, and was married in 1853 to Miss Gambill, who was born in Tennessee January 3, 1835. She came with her parents to Arkansas when about six years of age, and she and Mr. Beach became the parents of the following family: Benjamin S.; Mollie, wife of J. W. Livesay; Ella, wife of T. J. Simmons (Mrs. Simmons is now a widow, her husband having died in 1877); Alice, deceased; Sallie, Nettie, Robert Lee and Rosa. The father was a soldier in the Confederate army during the late war, and in 1863 was taken prisoner and kept at Fort Delaware until the cessation of hostilities. He died in 1883.

Dr. A. R. Bills, son of Pascal W. and Drusilla (Barlow) Bills, was born June 12, 1850, in Bourbon County, Ky. The father was born in the same county, and there grew to manhood. He was well educated, having attended Millersburgh Academy of Kentucky, but never completed his course. While in that State he taught school for a number of years, and afterward graduated at Bryant & Stratton's Commercial College. He then kept books for Waide, Extine & Co., wholesale druggists of Cincinnati, for two years, after which he went to New Orleans and kept books in that city for some time. He had traveled quite extensively, going through Louisiana, Arkansas, Mississippi and Tennessee as collecting agent. Mr. Bills then returned to Kentucky, and was married to Miss Drusilla Barlow August 23, 1849. To them were born seven children, six now living: Alvin R., Mrs. Ann Eliza Rheinhordt, John H., Mrs. Mary L. Burney, Mrs. Lillie O. Bird, Laura and Mary (deceased). After marriage Mr. Bills taught school, and in connection carried on farming in Bourbon County, Ky., until 1854, when he removed to Cass County, Mo., settled about three miles from

****

Lone Jack, and there he has since lived. His wife was also born and reared in Bourbon County, Ky., and like her husband received a good education, being educated at North Middleton. Alvin W. Bills, grandfather of Dr. A. R. Bills, was born in North Carolina in 1806, but immigrated to Tennessee with his parents when but a lad. He was there educated, and was a classmate of James K. Polk. After graduation he began the study of medicine at Lexington, Ky., graduated from the Transylvanian College, and then followed his profession in that State until his death, which occurred in 1848. His wife, the grandmother of Dr. A. R. Bills, Mary N. (Simms) Bills, was born in Culpeper County, Va., and when about twelve or fourteen years of age removed to Kentucky, and was there afterward married. The maternal grandparents, Alvin W. and Mary (Fisher) Barlow, were both natives of Kentucky, and the grandfather was a soldier in the War of 1812. Dr. A. R. Bills remained at home until ten years of age, and was then placed in school, where he remained until the breaking out of the war. During that eventful period he remained at home and made himself generally useful around the farm, carrying provisions to the army. After the close of hostilities he returned to his books and entered the school at Lone Jack, Mo., where he remained from 1866 to 1867. He then began teaching, and this continued for eight years in the public schools of Jackson, Cass, Lafayette and Johnson Counties, Mo., teaching ten months out of each year, and in three years had taught thirty-three months. During that time Dr. Bills began the study of medicine, teaching himself, but under the preceptorship of Dr. Andrew O'Conner. He took one course of lectures at the College of Physicians and Surgeons in Kansas, and then took one course at the Medical Department of the University of Kansas City, graduating in March, 1882. Dr. Bills then removed to Maysville, Ark., and began the practice of his profession. Here he has since lived, and has built up a large and successful practice. He became a member of the County and State Medical Societies shortly after removing to Maysville, and has since retained his membership. November 7, 1871, he married Miss Johanna Jones, a native of Scott County, Ky., and the daughter of Joseph and Rachel A. Jones. To this marriage were born three children: Ethelyne, John Warren and Beulah. The doctor is a stanch Democrat in politics, is a member of the Masonic fraternity, and he and wife are members of the Christian Church.

John Black, clerk of the county court of Benton County, Ark., is a native of Warren County, Tenn., born in 1831, son of Alexander and Mary (Smith) Black, and grandson of Samuel Black. Alexander Black was born in Kentucky, was of Scotch-Irish descent, and a merchant by occupation. When a small boy he went to McMinnville, Tenn., and here in later years followed merchandising. He died in East Tennessee in 1856. His wife was born in Roane County, and was of Scotch-Irish descent also. To their marriage were born seven children, all of whom lived to be grown: Samuel (deceased), John, Dr. Thomas, Mrs. Mary L. Mason, Robert, Alexander and Marawether Smith Black. John Black was educated in McMinnville, Tenn., and at the age of nineteen began the study of law. He soon entered the law department of Cumberland University at Lebanon, Tenn., and here remained fifteen months. In 1851 he was admitted to the bar, and the year following he immigrated to Carroll County, Ark., located at Carrollton, where he entered upon his practice. July 10, 1855, he married Miss Sophia A. Greenwood, who was born in Georgia in 1837. She bore him six children: Alexander G. (deputy clerk of Benton County), Kittie, John S., Mary L. (widow of William Tinnin, deceased), Carrie (wife of Clinton Crouch) and Hugh D. In 1856 he was appointed agent of the Poney Indians of Nebraska, and held that position for two years. During the war his sympathies were with the Confederate States, and in 1862 he enlisted in Company F, Thirty-fourth Regiment Arkansas Infantry. He was in service in Arkansas, Louisiana and Texas for about three and a half years. He surrendered at Fort Smith, Ark., and after peace had been declared he returned to his home and to his practice. This he continued until 1869 or 1870, when he was appointed county attorney. In 1872 he was appointed clerk of Benton County, and was clerk of the county court, probate court and recorder, it being the best office in the State. From 1876 to 1880 he was re-elected to the same office. In 1882 the office was divided, and Mr. Black was clerk of the county court, and was re-elected in 1884 and 1886. He now holds that position. Mr. Black is one of the old and much respected citizens of Benton County, is a man of much public spirit and a man of good character. He has been in public office for the past eighteen years, and during that time has escaped without a stain or blot upon his public or private life. He is a member of the Masonic fraternity, Royal Arch and Council Degree, and he and Mrs. Black are members of the Cumberland Presbyterian Church.

J. A. C. Blackburn, who is the recognized "lumber king" of Northwestern Arkansas, was born in War Eagle Township, Benton Co., Ark., in 1841, and is a son of Rev. Sylvanus and Catherine Blackburn, both of whom were born in 1809, in Georgia and North Carolina, respectively. They became residents of Arkansas in 1832, and are still living. J. A. C. Blackburn is their sixth child, and his boyhood days were spent in assisting his father in the grist-mill. In 1861 he joined the Confederate army, and was a faithful soldier for four years, and in 1865 returned to Arkansas; here he engaged in the peaceful pursuit of farming, succeeded in accumulating some money, which, in partnership with his father, he invested in a general mercantile store, and at the end of six months bought his father's interest. Here he remained from 1867 till 1873, and then moved his stock of goods to War Eagle and erected the mills at that place, and also continued to carry on merchandising. He continued in the saw and grist milling business at War Eagle until 1884, when he succeeded Peter Van Winkle as proprietor of the Van Winkle Saw and Planing Mills. He has been so successful in the management of these mills that he has often been called the "lumber king" of Northwestern Arkansas. His principal mill is situated nine miles east of Rogers. The engine is 150-horse power, the cylinder 22x30 inches and the balance wheel is twenty feet in diameter and weighs 20,000 pounds. He has three large boilers, each twenty-four feet long and forty-two inches in diameter, with four 12-inch flues, and has one circular saw, two rip saws, three cut-off saws, one gang lath machine, one shingle machine, two planers, two moulding machines, one scroll saw, one mortising machine and one automatic emery wheel. He has another mill in Madison County, which is twenty-five horse power, with a capacity of 20,000 feet of lumber per day. Besides this he has two other mills cutting lumber for him by the thousand. He handles 3,000,000 feet of lumber per annum, and owns in connection with his mills 15,000 acres of fine timber lands. There has not been an enterprise started in Benton County in which he has not taken a deep interest, and in the majority of cases become a heavy stockholder, the Stock Bank, Fair Association, Roller Mills and Water Works being some of the enterprises in which he has been interested. He was first married to Miss Ellen Van Winkle, who died November 10, 1884, having borne three children: Carrie, Lucy M. and Laura May. Mrs. Belle Harris, widow of Mack Harris and daughter of C. Petross, became his second wife. Mr. Blackburn is a Democrat and an A. F. & A. M. of the highest order, and belongs to the Knights of Honor.

Thomas K. Blake, merchant, and one of the old and influential citizens of Bentonville, Ark., is a native of Roane County, Tenn., born 1813, and the son of Thomas and Elizabeth (Owen) Blake. Thomas Blake was born in Georgia, and was of English origin. He went to North Carolina when a young man, and from there to Tennessee in 1799. He was a speculator in lands, and did a great deal of trading. He was the owner of a number of mills, and was a good business man. His wife was born in Alabama, and died in 1829. She was the mother of seven children, Thomas K. being the only one now living. He remained at home until after his mother's death, and then went to Alabama, where he lived among his mother's people a number of years, and worked at machinery in various kinds of mills. In 1836 he married Miss Clara Chitty, who was born in North Carolina in 1819, and seven children were born to this union: Jesse C., in Whitesburgh, Tex.; Missouri E., wife of J. E. Russell; Larkin L., in the Chickasaw Nation; William A., killed in the battle of Pea Ridge; Paulina J., deceased; Thomas T., an extensive lumber merchant at Bentonville, Ark., John Y. F., in New Mexico, a United States officer, and a graduate of West Point with the rank of first lieutenant, and Clara F., wife of F. W. Derrickson. Thomas K. Blake resided in Alabama until 1841, when he immigrated to Polk County, Mo., and in 1859 he went to Denton County, Tex. In 1868 he became a citizen of Bentonville, Ark. While in Missouri he was the owner of two woolen mills, and while in the Lone Star State he was engaged in merchandising, dealt in stock and was also engaged in milling. After coming to Bentonville he and Josiah Claypool erected a flouring-mill, and they were also the proprietors of two mercantile establishments in Bentonville. Previous to the erection of the grist-mill, Mr. Blake erected a woolen-mill, and afterward he and Mr. Claypool became partners in this mill, and it was attached to the grist-mill. Mr. Blake and Mr. Claypool were partners for about three years, when they sold the mills; each took a store, and after this each man did business on his own responsibility. Mr. Blake also erected a lumber mill in Carroll County, and was the proprietor of it for one year, when he moved it to Huntsville, Ark., and converted it into a flouring-mill, which he turned over to his sons, Larkin L. and Thomas T. Mr. Blake followed merchandising in Bentonville for about fifteen years, and was successful in his business transactions. He erected the Western Hotel, and the large block occupied by L. J. Laughlin. He has also erected a large number of private dwellings and other business houses in Bentonville, and has been of much benefit to that city. Although starting with little or no means, Mr. Blake has, by attending strictly to the business on hand, and by his honesty, become one of the solid, substantial merchants of Bentonville. For the past five years he has lived a retired life. He lost his wife in 1859. Mr. Blake is a Democrat in politics, and is a member of the Masonic fraternity, and also a member of the I. O. O. F. He was proprietor of the Western Hotel for six years, and followed merchandising at the same time. While residing in Texas he had 137 horses stolen from him by the Indians, and he thinks he will yet get pay for them from the United States Government.

M. R. Blevins, son of Allen and Clara (Owens) Blevins, was born in Bradley County, Tenn., May, 1837. The father was born in Sullivan County, Tenn., received a common-school education here, and was here married. He afterward moved to Bradley County while the Indians were still there, and assisted in banding them together to take them to the reservation set apart for them. Mr. Blevins continued to live in Tennessee until 1851, when he immigrated to Independence County, Ark., where he died the same year. His wife, Clara Blevins, was born in North Carolina, her parents leaving that State when she was but a small girl. She was married to Mr. Blevins in Meigs County, and became the mother of eleven children, seven now living: John, Michael R., Gideon T., Mrs. Lorinda Tunnel, Mrs. Malinda Millsap, Mrs. Myra Teal and Mrs. Mary Wood. Those deceased are William, Allen, Catherine and an infant. M. R. Blevins was but twelve years of age when his parents moved to Arkansas, and his father dying soon after, the support of the family was largely dependent upon his efforts. He only received a common-school education, and remained with his mother until twenty-one years of age, when he married Miss Elizabeth Wakefield, daughter of William and Jane Wakefield, who were originally from Mason County, Tenn. This union, which has been a long and happy one, was blessed by the birth of eleven children, nine now living: Allen, James, Charles, Mike, Robert, Mrs. Amanda Copeheart, Mattie, Clara and Ida. The two children deceased were named Florence and Annie May. Mr. and Mrs. Blevins live on the farm that they first settled, and raised their first crop with the aid of a yoke of cattle. During the war Mr. Blevins enlisted in Company A, First Cherokee Volunteer Cavalry, Confederate Army, and was in the battles of Honey Springs, Fort Wayne, Newtonia and others of less importance. During his absence Mrs. Blevins carried on the farm, doing the greater part of the work herself, and often went a distance of forty miles to mill. She was energetic and determined and kept her family from want. Returning home after his term of service had expired, he and twenty-three others, including his captain, took a trip through Old and New Mexico and into Colorado, where they remained until the close of the war. He then came home and resumed farming and stock raising, and handled cattle for about eighteen years. He has now an excellent farm of 340 acres, 140 under cultivation, and has good buildings on the same. It was largely through Mr. Blevins' influence and efforts that the district school building was erected, and his children are all blessed with a good common-school education. Mr. Blevins is a strong Democrat, politically, and cast his first presidential vote for Breckenridge. He is a member of the Masonic fraternity, and his wife is a member of the Baptist Church.

Samuel Box, farmer, machine agent and postmaster at Hico Post-office, was born near Bolivar, in Polk County, Mo., March 1, 1845, and is the son of William P. and Hannah (Cantwell) Box. William P. Box was born near Knoxville, Tenn., August 1, 1825. His parents were born in the Carolinas, and on his father's side the family is of Dutch descent, and Scotch on the mother's side. William P. Box was educated in the common schools of Tennessee, and in 1842 he removed with his parents to Polk County, Mo., and here married Mrs. H. Slagle, in 1844. They were among the early pioneers of Polk County, Mo. In 1863 he and family removed to Cooper County, Mo., and in 1870 they moved from there to Benton County, Ark. Mr. Box is still living, and is residing near Hico Post-office. Mrs. Box was born in Jackson County, Ohio, August 9, 1820. Her parents were natives of Ohio, and of Scotch descent. Mrs. Box was the mother of two children by a previous marriage with John Slagle. They were named as follows: John and Conrad. By her union with Mr. Box she became the mother of four children: Samuel, Thomas (deceased), Pleasant and Joseph. Samuel Box, the eldest child born to the second marriage, enlisted in the Confederate service, October 11, 1864, at Boonville, Mo., in Company C (Capt. Norman's) Third Regiment Missouri Volunteer Cavalry, Col. Smith commanding, and remained until the close of the war. He was in the engagements at Sedalia, Lexington, Independence, Westport, Fort Scott and Newtonia. He was in Shelby's brigade until the close of hostilities, and refusing to accept the terms of surrender he left the United States, and took refuge in Old Mexico; was present at the burial of the Confederate flag at Eagle Pass, Texas, July 4, 1865, in commemoration of which Col. A. W. Stayback, who was present also, composed a touching poem. From here Mr. Box went to California, via Monterey, Saltillo, Buena Vista, Durango and Mazatlan, Mexico, remaining only a short time, when he went to Jackson County, Ore. He resided here less than two years, and returned to Booneville, Mo. Here he lived over two years, and then moved to Benton County, Ark., where he was married August 19, 1879, to Mrs. Mollie E. (Comer) Neill, the daughter of John B. and Caroline (Estes) Comer, formerly of Gallatin, Daviess Co., Mo. Mr. Comer is yet living, but Mrs. Comer died in 1882. Mrs. Box is the mother of one child by her first husband, Arthur Neill, and three children by her second husband, Mr. Box. They are named as follows: Fred, Effa and Vard. Mr. Box is a Democrat politically, and his first presidential vote was cast for S. J. Tilden in 1876. Mr. Box is the owner of 180 acres of land and some good town property; he was justice of the peace for two years, and was also notary public, and postmaster for eleven years. He is a member of the K. of H. and American Protective League. He has traveled extensively in the United States, Old Mexico, Central America and South America. He has always taken an active part in local politics; is not a member of any church, but a strong believer in the bible, and holds to the faith and doctrines of the Missionary Baptists; he takes a great interest in schools and education, and the upbuilding of good society, and is a warm supporter and defender of the temperance cause, but above all the highest ambition of his life is to see his children grow up to be sober, religious and useful men and women.

Pinkney A. Bozarth, farmer, was born in Howard County, Mo., November 13, 1823, son of Jonathan and Cyntha (Gross) Bozarth. The father was born in Virginia, April 21, 1780; was a successful farmer, and at the age of nineteen married his first wife, Miss Nancy Alexander. They then moved to Christian County, Ky., and from there to Howard County, Mo., in 1818, where they purchased 400 acres of land. The father died in 1856. His second marriage was with Miss Gross, a native of Kentucky, born 1811. She was married in Missouri to Mr. Bozarth, and after his death she moved to Collins County, Texas, where she died in 1885. She was of Scotch descent, a member of the Christian Church, and an energetic, persevering woman. Their family consisted of six children: Lucinda, Pinkney A., Elnora, Jonathan, Benjamin and Elizabeth. Pinkney A. Bozarth received an ordinary education, and at the age of twenty-seven, married Miss Helen M. Terrell. He immigrated to California in 1850, followed mining for one year and then returned, but in 1861 moved to Collins County, Texas, where he engaged in farming. In 1863 he volunteered in Col. Stone's regiment, Confederate army, Texas cavalry, and served through the war. He was in the battles of Mansfield, Pleasant Hill and Fort Donelson, also other battles. In 1866 Mr. Bozarth and family moved to Benton County, Ark., and here the wife died in 1871. She was born near Louisville, Ky., October 28, 1830, was a member of the Christian Church, and was the mother of these children: Jonathan R., Alice, Cornelia, Emma, William F., Willis L., Mollie A., Cynthia R. The members of this family now deceased are Alice, Cornelia, Emma and Cynthia. Mr. Bozarth took for his second wife Mrs. Polly A. Berry, a native of Wilson County, Tenn., born October 8, 1858, and was married in after years to Mr. Arnold Berry. One child, James

Berry, was the result of that marriage. She moved to Benton County, Ark., Febuary 15, 1873, and in May of the same year married Mr. Bozarth. Her parents, Redden and Polly (Farrington) Fields, were natives of Tennessee. [For further particulars of parents see sketch of John A. Fields.] Mr. Bozarth is a Democrat in politics, and is an excellent citizen of the county.

J. Wesley Breedlove, liveryman of Siloam Springs, Ark., was born in Miller County, Mo., July 20, 1866, being a son of Clay and Amelia (Reed) Breedlove. The former was born in Illinois, near St. Louis, Mo., January 8, 1834, and afterward moved to that city, where he was principally reared. He was married in Miller County, Mo., in 1855, and in 1874 located in the Choctaw Nation, where he still resides. During the late war he enlisted under Gen. Price in the Confederate service, but owing to being accidentally wounded in the hand in 1863, he was compelled to give up soldiering for a time. His grandfather came from Wales and settled in Virginia, where the father of Clay B. was born. The latter moved to Indiana, thence to Illinois, and afterward settled in Boone County, Ark., where he yet resides, at a very advanced age. The wife of Clay B. was born in Miller County, Mo., May 10, 1827, and died in the Choctaw Nation in May, 1885. Her father was born in Ireland, and after locating in the United States, in Pennsylvania, came to Miller County, Mo., and reared a large family of children. The following are the children born to Mr. Breedlove and wife: J. Wesley, Rachel (deceased), James H., William A., Robert T. and Sallie M. J. Wesley Breedlove was educated in Richland Institute, Pulaski County, Mo., and made his home with his father until he was twenty-two years of age, at which time he was married to Amanda Burness, a native of Illinois. She died in 1882, leaving three children: Edward Clay, Clara Eugenia, and William Newton (deceased). In 1883 Mr. Breedlove was married to Mrs. M. J. Steele, who was born in Montgomery County, Mo., January 30, 1853. By her first husband she became the mother of one child, Arthur L. Steele. She has three children by Mr. Breedlove: Inez A., Clara Alice (deceased) and Mary I. Mr. Breedlove went with his father to the Choctaw Nation in 1874, and there married both his wives. He followed the occupations of farming, stock-raising and teaching in the Nation, and in 1885 came to Arkansas and ran a hack line from Siloam Springs to Bentonville, and afterward engaged in the livery business, which he has made very successful. He has a fine stable, centrally located, and has done a good business financially. He is a Democrat in politics, but owing to his roving life has never had a chance to vote. He is a member of the board of alderman of Siloam Springs, and he and wife are members of the Christian Church.

James J. Britt was born in Carroll County, Tenn., February 12, 1837, son of James J. and Winneford (Hilliard) Britt. The father was born, reared and married in North Carolina, but afterward moved to Tennessee, where he died in 1836. He was a farmer and merchant. The mother was born near Knoxville, N. C., and died in 1867 in Texas. She had married again, and had moved to several different places. James J. Britt was the youngest of five children of his father's family that lived to be grown. He was partly reared in Carroll County, Tenn., and at the age of twelve moved to Washita County, Ark., and from there to Barry County, Mo., where he remained three years. From there he came to Benton County, Ark., in 1853, where he settled to farming, and has continued this occupation ever since except two years in Texas, just after the war closed. During the war he served in Company H, First Arkansas Cavalry, Confederate States Army, where he remained until 1863, when he was wounded at the Prairie Grove battle by a gunshot in the leg, which still causes him considerable trouble. Since the war Mr. Britt has devoted his time exclusively to farming. He was married, in 1857, to Miss Mary Ann Sager, a native of Benton County, Ark., and to them were born eleven children, eight now living: John F., James A., Sarah B., Willmina L., Eddie L., Albert and Addie (twins) and Ida A. Mr. Britt was justice of the peace of the township six years, and was a deputy sheriff of the county two years. He is a Democrat in politics; his wife is a member of the Methodist Episcopal Church, South. He is the owner of 200 acres of land, 120 under cultivation.

William F. Brooks, pharmacist, of Siloam Springs, Ark., is a North Carolinian, and was born in 1838. He left the paternal roof at the age of fourteen years, and went to Georgia, where he began fighting the battle of life for himself. He soon after went to Chattanooga, Tenn., and began working in a commission house, where he remained two years, and then began steamboating on the Tennessee River, afterward becoming p ilot. He then spent about five years at home, and was married in Mississippi to Mary Jane Smith, who was born and reared in Knoxville, Tenn. After his marriage he went to Illinois, and there remained from 1857 to 1868. At the latter date he moved to Bentonville, Ark., where he has been engaged in various occupatious, but the most of his attention has been given to the furniture business. Since about 1879 he has been a resident of Siloam Springs, and since 1886 has been engaged in the drug business. Mr. Brooks is a Democrat, a member of the I. O. O. F., and he and wife are members of the Baptist Church. His parents, Thomas F. and Mahala Brooks, were born in North Carolina, the former in 1785, and the latter about 1786, and died in 1885 and 1880, respectively. The father was a farmer and of Irish descent, his father being an Irishman who helped to fight for American independence. Mr. and Mrs. Brooks became the parents of fifteen children: George W., Isaac, Eliza (wife of Bluford Baxter), Lawrence, William F., Lucinda (the deceased wife of Peter Clark), Riley M., Margaret (wife of William Lavin), James N., Abner, Jane, Joel, Calvin, Richard W. and Amanda.

Amos A. Brown, a farmer of Benton County, Ark., was born on the 2d of February, 1820, and located on his present fine farm of 260 acres in 1852. He has lived a quiet, uneventful life, but has always taken a deep interest in matters pertaining to the welfare of the county in which he resides. He has 130 acres of land under cultivation, and is in a prosperous condition, financially. Mr. Brown votes the Democratic ticket, and his first vote for President, as far as he recollects, was for James K. Polk. He is a member of the Missionary Baptist Church. His parents, Alfred and Narcissus (Belk) Brown, were married in their native State, North Carolina, and immigrated to Tennessee in 1832, and from Tennessee to North Carolina in 1834. In 1851 they left North Carolina and arrived in Benton County in 1852. Their children were as follows: Elvira, Darling (deceased), James, Amos A., Arra A., Asoph (deceased), Alfred (deceased), Harriet, J. M. and John W. The paternal grandfather was an Englishman, and came to America at a very early day, locating in North Carolina.

Charles W. Brown, member of the firm of Smart & Brown, proprietors of the livery, feed and sale stable of Bentonville, was born in Warren County, Ohio. in 1847; son of William C. and Martha E. (McBay) Brown. The father was also born in Warren County, Ohio, in 1811, and was a farmer and stock dealer by occupation. He moved to Shelby County, Ohio, in 1861, and there died in 1874. The mother was born near Harrisburg, Penn., and died in 1873. They were the parents of seven children: Charles W.; Ellen, at home; Margaret, wife of Daniel Vandamark, of Shelby County, Ohio; Joseph, who was conductor on a train and was killed while coupling a car; Martha, a teacher in Sidney, Ohio; John, a railroad conductor, and Ida, a teacher by profession in Sidney, Ohio. Charles W. was reared on his father's farm, and in March, 1864, he enlisted in the Eighth Ohio Battery, Light Artillery, and was in service until the close of the war, being discharged at Cincinnati, Ohio. He served in Mississippi, and was on garrison duty. After the war Mr. Brown operated a threshing machine for fourteen years. In the spring of 1885 he went to Kinsley, Kas., and was engaged in a stock and ranch business. In 1886 he became a resident of Bentonville, Ark., and he and E. F. Henry speculated in real estate. They owned Clark's second addition, sold numerous lots, and met with good success. In June, 1887, Mr. Brown and L. P. Smart became partners in the livery and feed stable, and have since continued at this business. Mr. Brown brought the first full-blooded Norman horse to Benton County, and he and Mr. Henry brought the first Galloway cattle ever in the county.

John G. Brown, son of Joseph and Sarah (Green) Brown, was born January 21, 1848, in Watauga County, N. C. The father was also born in the same county, is now living, and is engaged in tilling the soil on the same farm that he first settled. During the late war he enlisted in Company D, First North Carolina Volunteer Cavalry, served through the entire war and participated in many battles—Petersburg, Willis Church, Manassas, Bull Run, Gettysburg, Richmond, Stony Creek, Bellefield and a number of others. He was captured near Petersburg three days before Lee's surrender, and imprisoned at Point Lookout, where he was kept for three months, and then paroled. Sarah (Green) Brown was also born in Watauga County, N. C., and by her marriage with Mr. Brown became the mother of seven children, four now living: C. E., Mrs. Harriet E. Clowson, Julia A. and John G. Those deceased were named Susanna,

James and Mrs. Mary L. Yonce. The parents of these children are sixty-four and sixty years of age, respectively. John G. Brown received a common-school education before the breaking out of the war, and after that eventful period. At the age of nineteen he left the home of his youth, turned his face westward, and finally settled in Northern Missouri, where he remained for fourteen years. He married Amelia E. Watson, daughter of Abner and Mary (Emmons) Watson, of Chariton County, Mo. This union resulted in the birth of three children: Rosa A., Joseph Abner and James O. Mr. Brown left Missouri and moved to his old home in North Carolina, where he remained for about two years. He then moved to Bentonville, Ark., where he worked at the carpenter's trade, and after a two years' residence in that city, moved to his present farm, where he has since lived. Like his father, Mr. Brown enlisted in the Confederate army, Company D, First North Carolina Volunteer Cavalry, and served a part of the last year. He took part in some skirmishes, but no actual battles. He was wounded, and was disabled for about a year. Mrs. Brown is a member of the Missionary Baptist Church.

Lorenzo D. Brown is a well-to-do farmer of Benton County, Ark., and was born in Alabama in the year 1842. He is a son of S. P. and Grace A. (Muldeo) Brown, the former of whom was born in the "Palmetto State," and was a planter by occupation. He moved from his native State to Alabama at a very early day, and from there to Texas in 1859, settling in Collins County, where he remained seven years. He then returned to Alabama, where he died in 1878. Lorenzo D. Brown was educated in the common schools of Alabama, and remained with his parents until he reached manhood. At the breaking out of the war of 1861 he joined the Confederate service, enlisting in Company D, Sixth Texas Cavalry, and after serving one and a half years returned home, and soon after re-enlisted in Company I, Second Texas Partisan Rangers, commanded by Capt. White, and served until the close of the war. While in Louisiana he was taken prisoner, but soon after succeeded in effecting his escape, and returned to his command. He received his discharge at Hempstead, Tex., and returned to his home in Collins County, that State, and resumed farming. In 1884 he came to Benton County, Ark., and purchased his present farm, which consists of 120 acres of very fair land. He was married in 1864 to Miss Mary J. Carson, of Titus County, Tex., and by her has a family of seven children: Horace P., Frank C., Albert L., Lora V., Gracie, Robert and Corrie. Mrs. Brown is a member of the Cumberland Presbyterian Church.

Thomas Gilbert Brown, a prominent farmer, stock raiser and fruit grower of Benton County, Ark., was born in Wayne County, N. Y., June 30, 1827, and is a son of Jesse and Sally (Taylor) Brown. The father was a farmer, born on Long Island in 1804, and afterward became a well-to-do farmer, stock raiser and saw-mill owner of York State. He was a member of the Baptist Church, and died in Fulton County, Ind., in 1846. His father, Thomas Brown, was a farmer and a native of France, being a schoolmate of the Marquis de La Fayette, of Revolutionary fame. Sally (Taylor) Brown was born in New York in 1806, a daughter of Jacob Taylor, and a Methodist in her religious views. Thomas Gilbert Brown, her son, was taken by his parents to Indiana at the age of thirteen years, where he received his education and grew to manhood. He was married in 1849 to Nancy Jane Lewis, who was born in Indiana in 1831, and died in that State in 1855. Two children were born to this union: Sarah Alice, wife of William Fuller, and Leander, residing in Cherokee City. Mr. Brown was married to his second wife, Nancy M. Elliott, in 1855, and by her became the father of eight children: Rebecca A. (wife of A. N. Cherry), Jay W., Ida Belle (wife of B. Evans), Amy Dell (wife of John Ingalls). Ruth Jane, Ulysses Grant, Lillian and John E. In 1858 Mr. Brown went to Minnesota, where he resided until 1860, and then went to Washington County, Kas. While residing in this place, in 1862, the Indians made a raid on his stock, and took all that he had. He then returned to Indiana, but only remained a short time, when he went to Nebraska, taking up the first homestead claim in Jones County. They were troubled a great deal by the Indians at first, and Leander, the eldest son, was often posted as sentry on the top of their house, to watch for their approach. Mr. Brown made his home in Nebraska for twelve years, and then located in Benton County, Ark., where he has since resided. He has a good farm of fifty-five acres, all under cultivation, and an orchard of over 2,000 trees. He is a man who commands the respect and esteem of all who know him, and he and family worship in the Congregational Church. While in New York Mr. Brown's father resided about a mile and a half from the Mormon prophet, Joseph Smith, and assisted him in digging up the plates from which the Book of Mormon is supposed to have been written.

Daniel Lanning Bruner, a well-to-do farmer and stock raiser of Benton County, Ark., was born in Monroe County, Ind., August 1, 1841, and is a son of Elias and Matilda (Williams) Bruner, and grandson of Jacob Bruner. The latter was born in Germany, and was a hatter by trade, but also owned and managed a farm. Elias Bruner was born in Shenandoah County, Va., in 1797, and, like his father, was a farmer and hatter by occupation. He was a member of the Methodist Episcopal Church, South, and died in Benton County, Ark., April 10, 1871. His wife was born in Tennessee in 1807, and died in Benton County, Ark., October 25, 1874. Daniel Lanning Bruner was taken to Cumberland County, Ill., at the age of nine years, and the next year was removed to Cole County. He was taken to Texas in 1853, and was there reared to manhood. All the schooling he received was obtained while he was a small boy in Indiana and Illinois, reading and writing being the extent of his scholastic attainments. Since that time he has improved his education very much by private study, and he is an extensive and thoughtful reader. He located in Benton County, Ark., in 1868, and was here married two years later to Miss Penelope Litteral, who was born in Tennessee in October, 1843, a daughter of James Litteral, a farmer. In March, 1862, Mr. Bruner enlisted in the Confederate army, in Company I, Fifteenth Texas Volunteer Infantry, and served until the cessation of hostilities. He was in a number of hotly contested battles, but was never wounded. He was sergeant of his company, and after the war returned home, broken down in health from hardships and exposure. By industry and good management he is now the owner of a good farm of 120 acres. He is a Master Mason, and he and family worship in the Methodist Episcopal Church, South. His children were as follows: Mary Ellen, James B., Lucinda E., Walter Lee, Cora Edna, Reumira and Daniel Clinton; the latter of whom died September 18, 1888.

John H. and James P. Burns, grocery merchants of Bentonville, Ark., were born in Bedford County, Tenn., in 1830 and 1838, respectively. They are the sons of Thomas P. and Mary Ann (Knott) Burns, and the grandsons of John Burns, who was a native of Ireland, coming to the United States when a young man; was a soldier in the Revolutionary War, and drew a pension for services rendered. He located in North Carolina, but afterward located in Bedford County, Tenn., where he died about 1836. Thomas P. Burns was born in the State of North Carolina in 1793, and was of Irish descent. He died in 1838. Mary Ann (Knott) Burns was born in Bedford County, Tenn., and died in 1870 at the age of sixty-three. She was the mother of five children, three of whom are now living: William, who resides in Bell County, Tex., engaged in farming; John H. and James P. The father of these children died when they were quite small, and, after his death, the mother continued to keep house, and keep her children together on the farm. In 1860 she and her three children moved to Benton County, Ark., purchased a farm five miles southwest of the county seat, and here John H. and James P. remained with their mother until her death. They followed farming until 1881, when they established a grocery store in Bentonville, and this they have since continued. They carry a first-class stock of goods, and are men of good business ability, are strictly honest, and are good citizens. In 1871 John H. married Miss Mary Elizabeth Simpson, a native of Alabama, born in 1838, and the daughter of James Simpson. Mrs. Burns died in 1875, and in 1877 he married Miss Harriet E. Campbell, who was born in Logan County, Ky., and who is the daughter of James M. Campbell. James P. married, in 1878, Miss Sarah Emaline Jackson, daughter of Haley Jackson. They have five children: Mary E., Margaret G., Edna A., James H. and Ida. In politics the brothers are both Democrats. They are both Masons, and both are members of the Methodist Episcopal Church, South, of which John H. is steward and James P. trustee. In 1862 the brothers enlisted in Company F, Confederate army, under Capt. Miser. John H. was in the battle of Helena, Jenkins' Ferry, and was captured and retained about twenty days. He was discharged at Washington, Ark., after the surrender. James P. was in the battle of Prairie Grove, and was afterward transferred to the commissary department, and was there from August, 1862, until the close of the war. He was wounded quite severely in the battle of Prairie Grove.

J. Van Butler, editor and proprietor of *The Locomotive* at Siloam Springs, is a native of Gordon County, Ga., born January 22, 1866, son of James F. and Mary F. S. (Watts) Butler, and grandson of Absolom Butler, who was born in South Carolina, was of English parentage, and was a relative of Gov. P. Butler, of the last named State. James F. Butler was born in Pendleton District, S. C., November, 1821, but grew to manhood in Gordon County, Ga., where he married and where he lived until 1868, when he engaged in merchandising at Fairmount, Ga., and followed this occupation at that place for ten years. At the last mentioned date he moved to Benton County and located where he now lives, six miles east of Siloam Springs, where he is exclusively engaged in agricultural pursuits. He is the owner of 160 acres of land, ninety under cultivation. His wife, Mrs. Mary F. S. (Watts) Butler, was born in Rabun County, Ga., March 20, 1826, was reared there, and is still living. Their son, J. Van Butler, has acquired his education, outside of six months' schooling, by private personal study. He remained at home until twenty years of age (1886), and then entered the *Corner Stone* office, where he remained but a short time. Then he and a brother purchased a printing office at Springdale, and he did the mechanical work of that paper, *The Locomotive*, which was issued from December 25, 1886, and was continued until May, 1887. They then sold out and removed to Siloam Springs, where they established this paper August 26, 1887, which is independent in politics. Mr. Butler is a member of the Protective League, and is financial secretary of the lodge at this place.

LeRoy B. Camden was born in Coffee County, Tenn.. in 1836, and is a son of LeRoy S. and Odelia (Payne) Camden, who were born in Rockbridge County, Va., and Georgia, in 1799 and 1808, respectively. John Camden, the grandfather of our subject, was born and reared in Virginia. In 1811 he moved to Tennessee and purchased a large tract of land near Hillsboro. He held the office of justice of the peace for over thirty years, and was one of the early pioneers of Coffee County. His son, LeRoy S., was married in Tennessee, and in 1846 moved to Lawrence County, Mo., where he purchased 320 acres of land, and died in 1877. He was captain of the Mustering Guards in Coffee County for five years. His wife died in 1888. LeRoy B. Camden is the sixth of her ten children, and was reared to manhood on a farm in Lawrence County. April 14, 1861, he was married to Miss Dorinda Bennett, who was born in Pulaski County, Mo., in 1842, and by her became the father of nine children: Hattie, wife of G. L. Alexander; LeRoy T., Richard, John, Sarah (deceased), Mary, Andrew, Eva and Effie. Mrs. Camden is a daughter of Richard Bennett, who is the oldest man in Benton County, having attained his one hundred and seventh year. Mr. Camden resided in Lawrence County until 1875, with the exception of about three years, and then removed to Cook County, Tex., and a year later came to Benton County, Ark., and speculated in cattle for three years. In 1878 he purchased 130 acres of land in the county, which he has since increased to 180 acres. In 1885 he erected a large two-story frame dwelling house at a cost of $1,200. He is a Democrat in his political views, and his first presidential vote was cast for Breckinridge in 1860.

Rev. Peter Carnahan, who resides one mile east of Bentonville, Ark., is a native of Washington County, Ark., born in 1838 at Cane Hill. He is a son of Samuel and Mary (Pyeatt) Carnahan and grandson of Rev. John Carnahan, who was a South Carolinian, a Cumberland Presbyterian minister and an immigrant to Tennessee in 1800. Eleven years later he moved to Arkansas Post, and a year later went to Pulaski County. He was the first Protestant minister in the State of Arkansas. His son, Samuel, was born in South Carolina in 1794, and made his home with his father until 1827, when he moved to Cane Hill, Ark., where he passed the remainder of his days. During the time he was living at Crystal Hill his father moved back to Tennessee, but after Samuel moved to Cane Hill his father made his home with him. Samuel Carnahan died in 1867. He was the owner of 500 acres of land at the time of his death. His wife was of French descent, born in South Carolina in 1797, and died in 1879. She was a daughter of Jacob Pyeatt, and became the mother of twelve children, nine of whom are living, Peter Carnahan, our subject, being the eleventh child. He was reared on his father's farm, and was attending the Cane Hill College when the war broke out, and he immediately espoused the cause of the Confederacy, serving as third lieutenant of Capt. Buchanan's company. In 1862 he enlisted in Company B, Thirty-fourth Arkansas Regiment of Infantry, and was elected

second lieutenant of the same, and after the battle of Prairie Grove was promoted to adjutant, holding the latter position until the close of the war. He
participated in the battles of Oak Hill, Prairie Grove and Jenkins' Ferry. After
the war he returned home and farmed on the old homestead until 1870. He was
ordained a minister of the Cumberland Presbyterian Church in 1866, and was
given charge of a church at Pleasant Hill and one at Cincinnati, Ark. In 1870
he was called to Bentonville to take charge of the church at that point, and was
pastor of the same for fourteen years. During this time he also had charge of
the Mt. Vernon congregation, on Pea Ridge, which charge he still retains. In
1884 the Bentonville congregation was divided, and Rev. Carnahan took charge
of the new congregation, known as Wood's congregation, the church being
about two miles east of Bentonville. In June, 1862, Mr. Carnahan was married
to Martha J., daughter of Rev. John Buchanan, one of the pioneer Cumberland
Presbyterian ministers of Washington County, Ark., and by her became the
father of six children: Stella (wife of D. C. Lewis), Otho, Edgar, John Hurley,
Harry Pyeatt and Earl. He has a good farm of ninety-four acres, and is a
Democrat and an Ancient member of the Masonic fraternity. He is noted for
his many Christian virtues, and the fact that he has been eighteen years the
pastor of the same two congregations speaks volumes in his praise.

I. J. Cawood, of the grocery firm of Cawood & Son, at Rogers, Ark., was
born in Tennessee in 1861, and is a son of W. H. and R. J. (Sharp) Cawood, who
were born in Tennessee in 1835 and 1839, respectively. I. J. Cawood is the
second of their six children, and was reared and married in his native State, his
wife's maiden name being Esther Sharp. In 1881 he and wife moved to Kansas,
and here his parents also came a short time after. At the end of one year they
came to Arkansas and located in Benton County, where they purchased land and
followed agricultural pursuits for about seven years, after which they engaged
in the grocery business at Rogers. They are doing a good business, and their
trade is increasing rapidly. The Cawood family own an excellent farm of 120
acres in Benton County. I. J. Cawood and wife are the parents of three children: Charley P., Jesse and Otto. Mr. Cawood is a young man of fine business
qualifications, and in his political views is a Republican. He belongs to the
I. O. O. F. and A. F. & A. M. fraternities.

Hon. David Chandler is one of the old and highly esteemed citizens of
Benton County, Ark. He was born in Burke (now McDowd) County, N. C.,
October 3, 1804, and there grew to manhood. He was educated in the common
schools, and received a supplemental education in a college at Morgantown. In
1846 he immigrated to Bloomfield, Ark., and began tilling the soil, entering 320
acres of land. In August, 1846, he was elected county surveyor, and in 1850
was elected to the State Legislature, was re-elected in 1872, and was in the
famous Brooks and Baxter call session of 1874. He has been a notary public for
twelve years, and holds that office at the present time. He was married to Eliza
Fagan, a daughter of Col. John Fagan, who was a soldier in the War of 1812.
She was born December 4, 1812, and died in Arkansas in 1871. Three sons and
two daughters blessed their union: J. Elizabeth, wife of Dr. J. H. Neagle, residing
in Paris, Tex., is the only one from home. Mr. Chandler has the confidence
and esteem of all who know him, and although nearly eighty-four years of age
is in excellent health, both bodily and mentally. March 28, 1878, he was married to his second wife, Mrs. M. A. (Martin) Pearson, who was born and grew to
womanhood in Monroe County, Tenn. Her first husband was William Pearson,
who died in Cedar County, Mo., in 1866. Mrs. Chandler is a member of the
Cumberland Presbyterian Church, and her husband belongs to the Masonic and
I. O. O. F. fraternities. His parents, John and Elizabeth (Oustatt) Chandler,
were born in Randolph and Burke Counties, N. C., respectively, and died in
their native State, the former December 21, 1839, in his "seventies."

Francis M. Clanton is one of the prominent and prosperous young farmers
and a blacksmith of Benton County, Ark., and was born in 1859, being a son of
Ed and Nancy Clanton. The father was a farmer, and was highly esteemed as
a man and citizen; he died in 1861. His wife is still living, and is now sixty-
two years old. Francis M. Clanton was reared and educated in Benton County,
Ark., and after attaining manhood was united in marriage to Miss Delilah A.
Roller, their union being blessed in the birth of five children; Jacob E.,
Sophronia, Mary, Ada and Ella. Mr. Clanton is a strong supporter of Christian-
ity, and formerly belonged to the Missionary Baptist, but is now an advocate

of Bible holiness, believing and teaching that all who are born again are members of the church of God, and this membership being retained by obedience is sufficient to give an abundant entrance into the kingdom of heaven.

William R. Clark, farmer and dealer in fresh meats, of Bentonville, Ark., was born in that city in 1846, and is the son of James W. and Jane M. (Dickson) Clark. James W. Clark was born in Giles County, Tenn., in 1825; was of Scotch descent, and a saddle and harness maker by trade. In 1842 he located in Benton County, Ark., and commenced working at his trade in Bentonville, establishing the first business of the kind in town. He carried this on until his death, which occurred in 1879. He was married about 1844, and soon after commenced keeping hotel. In 1849 he erected a hotel known as Clark Hotel, and is yet known by that name, and operated this up to the time of his death. Gen. Sigel made this hotel his headquarters previous to and during the fight of Pea Ridge. Mr. Clark was an honest man, and a consistent member of the Methodist Episcopal Church for many years. James W. Clark donated six acres of land for the public school buildings of Bentonville, and upon this they are now standing. He was very charitable in all his acts. His wife, who is yet living, was born in Bedford County, Tenn., in 1828, and is the daughter of Maj. John B. Dickson. She is the mother of nine children, six now living: William R., Pierce, Charles T., Oscar P., Carson E. and Belle (wife of Joseph Peel). William R. was educated in Bentonville, and after reaching his majority commenced gardening, raising small fruit and vegetables. He was at Eureka Springs two years. He afterward turned his attention to farming, and followed this until 1884, when he commenced the butchering business. He continued this occupation until May, 1884, when he sold out. Mr. Clark now expects to return to raising small fruits and vegetables again. He is the owner of ten acres adjoining Bentonville, also seventy acres a short distance from Bentonville, and eighty acres near Royar. He was in the army two years (Confederate States Army) and was in Capt. C. C. Waters' company. He was in the fights at Fayetteville, Cabin Creek and Prairie Grove. In 1866 he married Miss Martha Elzey, daughter of Benjamin Elzey, and a native of Benton County, Ark., born in 1848. They have eight children: Albert M., Arthur, Mabel, Robert, Bessie, Minnie E., Charles and William. Mr. Clark is a Democrat in politics, was marshal of Bentonville several years and deputy sheriff of Benton County four years. He is a member of the I. O. O. F., and he and wife are members of the Methodist Episcopal Church, South.

Dr. Joseph T. Clegg, physician, of Siloam Springs, Ark., was born in Jefferson County, in the same State, on the 21st of February, 1850, and is of English descent; both of his grandfathers were English, and were soldiers in the Revolutionary War. His father, Thomas W. Clegg, was born in North Carolina May 19, 1803, and was there reared and educated. He was married to Rebecca Lasater, a daughter of William Lasater, of North Carolina, and in 1848 removed to Jefferson County, Ark., where he died in 1877. His wife died in 1872. She was the mother of seven children: Josiah Q., Bennett L., James B. and John L. were all Confederate soldiers, and the three elder died during the war, Bennett L., being killed at the battle Murfreesboro; Cornelia B. P. (Stanfield) is deceased; Catherine E. is wife of William C. Cleveland. Dr. Joseph T. Clegg was educated in the common schools and also by private tutors, and remained on the farm with his parents until he entered the medical department of the University of Nashville in 1871, and was graduated in 1873. He located at Red Bluff, Ark., where he practiced medicine for four years, and then came to Siloam Springs, Ark., where he has since been a successful practitioner. He took a post-graduate course in the College for Medical Practitioners, at St. Louis, Mo., in 1884, and also the post-graduate course in the Medical College Hospital, of New York City, in 1888. He is a member of the drug firm of R. P. Peques & Co. He is a member of the State Medical Society of Arkansas, and of the Benton County Medical Society. The Doctor was married, in 1875, to Ida Daugherty. of Jefferson County, Ark., who died in 1879, leaving two children: Moses D. and Ida Neill. In 1882 Dr. Clegg married his second wife, Ada B. Fagan, a daughter of Maj. J. W. Fagan. She was born in Benton County in 1858, and is the mother of two children: Chester B. and Ethel E. (deceased). The Doctor is a Democrat in his political views, and cast his first vote for Tilden for the presidency. He is a Mason.

Thomas Clifton, who is one of the enterprising citizens of Eldorado Township, was born in Scott County, Ill., December 9, 1853, and is the son of John and Nancy (Clifton) Clifton. The grandparents Clifton on both sides were natives of Delaware. John Clifton was also born in Delaware, and grew to manhood in that State. His parents dying while he was still quite young, a guardian was appointed, who gave him very meager advantages for an education. When leaving his old home he first went to Ohio, and from that State soon after to Indiana, and subsequently going from that State to Illinois. Later he moved to Kansas, where he remained for about twenty years, but afterward came to Benton County, Ark., and here died in 1885. Nancy (Clifton) Clifton, was born in Delaware, and was a cousin of Mr. Clifton. To them were born eleven children, eight now living: Mary, Julia A., John W., Isabel, Nancy, Benonia, Sarah and Thomas. Those deceased were named James, Ellen and Charles. Thomas Clifton, subject of this sketch, remained with his father until the latter's death, taking care of both parents in their old age. When a boy he received but a common-school education, and continued to work on the farm until his marriage, which occurred in 1874, with Miss Eliza Jackson, daughter of Abel and Martha Jackson, and a native of Illinois. To this union were born five children, four now living: John Franklin, William Andrew, Charles Thomas and Nancy Jane. The one deceased was named Benonia. After his marriage Mr. Clifton continued to live with his parents, and moved with them to Arkansas. The mother died in Kansas, and the father married his second wife in that State, and moved with her to Arkansas, where she now lives. The father died on the farm his son has since occupied. Thomas Clifton is now the owner of 129 acres of land, eighty under cultivation. He is a strong Republican in his political views; never has voted any other ticket. He is a strong advocate of the public school system, doing what his circumstances would permit in that direction, and he and Mrs. Clifton are members of the Methodist Episcopal Church, South.

Rev. Wyatt Coffelt, minister of the Methodist Episcopal Church, South, and also farmer and stock raiser of Benton County, Ark., was born in Knox County, Ky., February 3, 1812, and resided in his native State until he was fifteen years of age, when he was taken to Monroe County, Tenn., by his parents, Jacob and Susanna (Wyatt) Coffelt, who were born in Greenbriar County, Va., in 1782 and 1786, respectively. Jacob Coffelt was a son of Philip Coffelt, who was of German birth, and served under Col. Washington in the French and Indian War at Braddock's defeat. He also served through the Revolutionary War. His wife, Ellen (Ryan) Coffelt, was captured by the Shawnee Indians during the French and Indian War, and after eleven weeks' captivity succeeded in effecting her escape. She was born in Ireland, and came with her parents to America at the age of five years. Jacob Coffelt was a farmer, and died in 1827, and his widow in 1864. They were members of the Baptist Church. The mother's father, Samuel Wyatt, also served in the French and Indian War and the Revolutionary War. Rev. Wyatt Coffelt was reared, educated and married in Monroe County, Tenn., and there learned the saddler's trade. His wife's maiden name was Jane Sligar, a daughter of Adam and Catherine (Brown) Sligar. This wife died January 20, 1887, having borne fourteen children, six of whom are living, and September 11, 1887, he married his second wife, Mrs. Louisa C. Sooter. His children were as follows: Louisa J., wife of N. C. Curry; Nancy A., the deceased wife of J. C. Anderson; Nicy A., wife of E. A. Torbuss; Thomas W., who was waylaid, murdered and robbed by some cut-throats in Texas; Enas J., James A., Theo. A. and Robert Lee; four died in infancy, and one, a son, died at the age of fourteen years. Mr. Coffelt worked at his trade for twenty-two years, and in 1850 moved to Missouri, and there resided until 1854, when he became a missionary among the Cherokee and Creek Indians, with whom he labored for eight years. In 1860 he moved his family to Benton County, Ark., but he remained in the Indian Territory until the fall of 1861, when they took refuge in the South until the close of the war, and then returned to Benton County. He began life with very small means, and met with many reverses, but is now in comfortable circumstances financially. He has an exceptionally fine orchard, and ships his fruit to all parts of the United States. His fruit took the first premium of $50 and the second premium of $15 at Springdale, Ark., and again took the first premium, $25, this fall, 1888, at Rogers, Ark.

Judge Samuel A. Cordell, county and probate judge of Benton County,

Ark., is a native of Cedar County, Iowa, born November 3, 1854; son of Jacob A. and Margaretta (Singrey) Cordell. The father was born near Chambersburg, Franklin Co., Penn., December 2, 1817, was of German descent, and a carpenter by trade. He was married in his native State, and here resided until his wife's death in 1849. He then moved to Morrow County, Ohio, where he married Margaretta Singrey in 1854, moved to Cedar County, Iowa, where the subject of this sketch was born. The following year he moved to Noble County, Ind., and in 1860 to Andrew County, Mo., and in 1864 moved to Nodaway County, Mo., where he resided until 1871, when he moved to Benton County, Ark., and in June, 1888, went to Los Angeles, Cal., where he now resides. The mother was born August 12, 1828, in Morrow County, Ohio, and was of Swiss origin. She died September 30, 1882. Their family consisted of six children, four now living. Judge Samuel A. Cordell received his education in the district schools of Benton County, was reared on a farm, and there remained until twenty-three years of age. He then engaged in teaching, and followed the teacher's profession for nine terms, all in Benton County. During his teaching he took up the study of law, his preceptor being Hon. Samuel W. Peel, now a member of Congress from the Fifth Congressional District of Arkansas. October, 1879, Judge Cordell was admitted to the bar, and immediately entered upon his practice at Eureka Springs. At the end of five months he returned to Benton County, and located at Rogers. July 22, 1880, Judge Cordell married Miss Rosa Spencer, who was a native of the State of Ohio. She died January 18, 1882, and November 4, 1883, the Judge married Miss Alice King, *nee* Sikes, daughter of B. F. Sikes, and a native of Bedford County, Tenn. In 1886 Judge Cordell moved to Bentonville, where he has since resided. In 1886 he was elected county and probate judge of Benton County, and re-elected in 1888. He was city attorney of Eureka a short time, and was also city attorney of Rogers one year. He is a Democrat in politics, casting his first presidential vote for S. J. Tilden, in 1876, and he and Mrs. Cordell are members of the Methodist Episcopal Church, South, he being one of the stewards of the same.

James T. Craig, retired merchant, Bentonville, Ark., was born in Ray County, Tenn., December 22, 1818, and is one of the oldest and most respected citizens of the county. He is the son of Samuel and Jane (Henderson) Craig, natives of Pennsylvania and North Carolina, respectively, the former born in 1781 and the latter in 1790. They were married in North Carolina, whither the father had immigrated when a young man, and after marriage they moved to Ray County, Tenn. Here the mother died in 1827. The father moved to Cane Hill, Washington Co., Ark., in 1848, and there died two years later. He followed the occupation of a farmer, and was also a teacher by profession. He was the father of only two children who lived to be grown—James T. the only one now living. Samuel Craig's father was a native of Scotland, and after coming to the United States settled in Pennsylvania. He was a soldier in the Revolutionary War. James T. Craig was only eight years old when his mother died, and at that age was taken by one of the neighbors, with whom he lived for a few years, and did what work a small boy could do on the farm. At the age of fifteen he began working at the tailor's trade in Pikesville, Tenn., where he remained one year. He then worked in a store for some time, and in 1838 went to Lynchburg, Ala., where he resumed clerking. He worked for James Lyle, and in a letter of commendation written by the latter, dated Lychburgh, DeKalb Co., Ala., February 11, 1838, and which is now in the possession of James T. Craig, are the following words: "With the bearer, James T. Craig, I have been acquainted with more than twelve months, the greater part of which time he has done business in my store. As a young man of honest principle, virtuous, and business habits and amiable disposition, he is surpassed by none and equalled by few. I therefore confidently commend him as a salesman and clerk to any who wish to employ a person in the above line of business. [Signed] James Lyle." Immediately after the above was written Mr. Craig went to Fort Smith, Ark., and clerked there for one year, but his permanent location was at Fort Gibson, where he acted as salesman for a year. The following year he purchased a stock of goods and began merchandising on his own responsibility. In 1846 he married Miss Samantha Reagan, who was born in Tennessee in 1827, and who died in 1848. The same year Mr. Craig moved his stock of goods to Cane Hill, Ark. In April, 1850, he disposed of his goods, and with the determination of obtaining his share of the hidden wealth in California, turned his face westward, and after a long, perilous journey over the vast plains that stretched between, reached that State. He remained in the mining regions from August until May of the following year, and not meeting with very good success he returned via the Isthmus, and resumed his former business in Cincinnati, Ark. June 12, 1851, he married Miss Elizabeth A. Russell, a native of Ray County, Tenn., born August 20, 1830. To them were born three children: Charles R., Edward A. and George M. Charles R. was born in 1854, and is in the real estate business at Bentonville; is also engaged in the mercantile establishment of Craig & Sons. March 27, 1876, he married Miss Lottie Redding, on the anniversary of her twentieth birthday, and to them have been born five children: James R., Carrie M., Eddie M., Ethel and an infant daughter. Edward A. Craig was born in Bentonville, Ark., in 1860, and is a member of the firm of James T. Craig & Sons. January 14, 1884, he married Miss Wincie McDaniel, who bore him two children: Bessie and John. George M. was born at Cane Hill, Ark., in 1862, and is also a member of the above mentioned firm. September 14, 1886, he married Miss Jennie A. Taliaferro, and is the father of one child, Annie B. In February, 1852, James T. Craig became a resident of Bentonville, Ark., and engaged in merchandising, continuing the same until the breaking out of the late war. He then returned to Cane Hill and engaged in farming, which occupation he continued until 1871, when he again returned to Bentonville and resumed merchandising. In 1882 he turned his business over to his sons. Mr. Craig is now seventy years of age, and lives a quiet, retired life. During his active life he lived and acted the characteristics set forth by his employer, James Lyle, in his commendation. Mr. Craig is the oldest merchant in Bentonville, and he has met with good success. He erected the first two-story business houses ever built in Bentonville. He is Democratic in his political views, and he and wife are members of the Cumberland Presbyterian Church.

James E. Crane. The Crane family was first represented in the United States by three brothers, who came from England and settled in New England, the great-grandfather of our subject being one of the brothers. The grandfather of James E. Crane was Elihu Crane, who was born in Massachusetts February 8, 1763, and was a soldier in the Revolutionary War. He moved with his family to Erie County, Penn., at an early day, being one of the first settlers of that region. His son, Elihu Crane, the father of James E., was born in 1791, at Stockbridge, Mass., and when only four years of age was taken with his parents to Erie County, Penn. He was a soldier in the War of 1812 and 1814. He assisted his father in tilling the soil, and January 31, 1827, was married to Nancy Carlin, who was of Irish descent, born in Crawford County, Penn., September 5, 1806. She died in 1886 and he in 1875. The following were their children: James E., Wealthy (wife of J. J. Ticknor), Adonijah, Abiather, Nancy (wife of George N. Sawdy), John (deceased) and Joel. James E. Crane was born in Erie County, Penn., January 14, 1829, and was educated at an academy at Albion, Penn. He followed various occupations, but was principally engaged in farming. He was married in Lockport, Erie Co, Penn., December 29, 1852, to Emily Leach, a native of Pennsylvania, born April 19, 1835, and their union has been blessed in the birth of ten children: Ella L., wife of V. D. Billiang; Wealthy, wife of Walter Robley; George, deceased; Mary I., wife of Henry Robley; Ulysses G., James L., Emily J., John C., Clara L. and Milo T. In 1862 Mr. Crane enlisted in the Union army, and was commanded at various times by Burnside, Hooker and Meade, and served as sergeant for one year. He resided in Pennsylvania until 1876, when he and family moved to Kansas, where he tilled the soil until 1887, and then came to Siloam Springs, Ark. He cast his first presidential vote for Gen. Scott, and in his political views is a Republican.

William J. Curry, M. D., was born in Shelby County, Ill., January 30, 1851, and is a son of John W. and Catherine (Bennett) Curry, both of whom were born in Tennessee. The father was reared to manhood in his native State, and then removed to Illinois with his parents, where he married Miss Bennett, and by her became the father of eight children: William J and George living, and Lafayette, Mary E., James R., Pierce, Annie and Ella deceased. The father is still living in Illinois, and is engaged in farming and stock raising. His wife died in April, 1874. Dr. William J. Curry was educated at Decatur, Ill., and at the Louisville Medical College, from which institution he was graduated in 1875. In 1877 he came to Benton County, Ark., and the following year was

****

married to Emma Neal, who was born in Tennessee, and came to Arkansas, when quite young, with her parents. George, Ethel, John, Eulala and Donnie are their children. The Doctor is a Republican in politics, and is a member of the Masonic fraternity. He owns considerable property in the town of Lowell, and is deeply interested in all enterprises calculated to benefit his county. He has arisen to prominence in his profession, and is one of the first physicians of the county.

S. M. Dailey, editor and proprietor of Benton County *Journal*, of Bentonville, was born in Franklin County, Ind., in 1834, son of James and Mary A. (Miller) Dailey. The father was born in New Jersey in 1787; was of Irish descent, and a farmer by occupation. He was married in his native State, and about 1823 immigrated to Franklin County, Ind., where he passed the remainder of his life. He died in 1849. The mother was born in New Jersey in 1791, and was of German extraction. She died in 1841. Of the ten children born to her marriage, S. M. Dailey was the youngest. He was educated in Bluffton, Ind., and at the age of seventeen began teaching, which occupation he followed for several years in Wells, Adams and Allen Counties, teaching in all thirteen terms. He met with good success, and was school examiner for four years. In 1859 he was elected recorder of Wells County, served four years, and in 1867 he was elected auditor of the same county, and held the position until 1871. Mr. Dailey was residing in Bluffton all this time, and was a member of the city council one year. For several years Mr. Dailey followed merchandising in Bluffton, Ind., and then moved to Arkansas City, Kas. In September, of the same year, he became a citizen of Bentonville, and here engaged in the grain and produce business, which he continued for one year. He then purchased the Benton County *Journal*, and has since been proprietor and editor. In 1867 he married Miss Lucinda Merriman, a native of Wayne County, Ohio, born in 1839, and to them have been born eight children, five now living: Mrs. Mary E. Fulton, Lewis M., Laura A., Forrest W. and Emma J. In politics Mr. Dailey has been a life-long Democrat, casting his first presidential vote for James Buchanan, in 1856. Mr. Dailey is a man held in high esteem by all who know him, and edits a newspaper full of valuable thoughts and sentiments. The *Journal* is one of the ablest edited papers of Benton County, and has a circulation of 1,400, being the largest in the county. Mr. Dailey deals out straight Democratic doctrine, and wavers neither to the right or to the left from what he believes to be right. He is a member of the I. O. O. F., being a member of Grand Lodge and Grand Encampment. He has devoted much study to this great and growing benevolent order, has been a hard working member, ever ready to fill any station where he can be of most benefit to the order. He is at present District Deputy Grand Master of his lodge, and Grand Marshal of the Grand Encampment of Arkansas.

James B. Dameron, editor and proprietor of the Arkansas *Heraid*, at Siloam Springs, was born in Chariton County, Mo., August 10, 1861, to the matrimonial union of James and Mary A. (Moore) Dameron. James Dameron is the son of Jesse Dameron, and was born in Madison County, Ky., in 1817. He moved with his parents to Chariton County, Mo., in 1835, and two years later participated in the Seminole War. In 1839 he returned to Chariton County, Mo., and in 1841 chose for his life's companion, Miss Mary A. Moore, who was born in Chariton County in 1823. This union was blessed by the birth of eleven children, who are named as follows: Missouri (deceased), Gazella (wife of J. K. Robinson), Sarah (widow of Hiram Shipp), John, Susan (wife of Richard Ford), Jennie (wife of John Wilkinson), Frank, Mollie, James B., Lida E. and Nannie. The parents are now living in Siloam Springs, and are respected citizens. Their son, James B., moved with his parents to Cherokee County, Kas., in 1874, and went with them to Washington County, Ark., in 1876, where he attended the State University at Fayetteville. He came to Hico, Benton Co., Ark., in 1878, and after remaining here one year went to Colorado, and was in that State three years. He then returned to Siloam Springs, Benton County, engaged in the *Herald* office in 1882, and took charge as editor and proprietor in 1884. May 2, 1888, he married Miss May Jarrett, daughter of Mr. and Mrs. J. T. Jarrett, former an early settler and prominent farmer of Cherokee County, Kas. Politically Mr. Dameron is a Democrat, and his paper advocates the principles of that party. He is a member of the K. of H. and American Protection League; he and his wife are members of the Missionary Baptist Church.

146   BENTON COUNTY, ARKANSAS - BIOGRAPHICAL AND HISTORICAL MEMOIRS

****

Andrew Baker Davis, a farmer and stock raiser of Benton County, Ark., and a native of Nashville, Tenn., was born on the 14th of January, 1838, and is a son of Elijah and Rebecca (Fletcher) Davis, and grandson of Eli Davis. The latter was born in the "Old Dominion," and was an eminent educator of that State, and also of Tennessee, whither he had moved at an early day. His death occurred in the State of his adoption. His son Elijah was born in Hancock County, Tenn., May 14, 1807, and received his education under the able instruction of his father. He was an eminent mathematician, and his name became well known in the colleges and educated communities of the United States. He attained a very high degree of excellence as a teacher, and followed his profession at different times in Virginia, Tennessee, Indiana, Missouri and Arkansas. He was always a strong anti-slavery man, a Whig in politics, a firm believer in the teachings of the Bible, and temperate and consistent in his habits. In fact, he may be said to belong to the great army of self-made men for which America is famous. He became a resident of Arkansas in 1841, and for many years was one of the progressive, energetic and prominent citizens and educators of Benton County. Many of the leading citizens of Benton, Washington and adjoining counties tell with pride of having been under his instruction. His death occurred on the 19th of October, 1884. He was a consistent member of the Baptist Church, and was of Welsh descent. His wife was born in Hancock County, Tenn., in 1814, and died in Montague County, Tex., in 1867. She was a member of an old American family and the daughter of James Fletcher. Andrew Baker Davis, whose name heads this sketch, grew to manhood in Washington and Madison Counties, Ark., and received an excellent education under his father's instruction. His youthful days were spent in farming and stock raising, and he has made that his chief calling through life. At the early age of nineteen years he was married to Miss Evaline Hock, who was born in Madison County, Ark., March 25, 1837, a daughter of Jesse and Elizabeth (Homsley) Hock, who were originally from Tennessee, and of German and Welsh descent, and by her became the father of twelve children, ten of whom are living: James O., a lawyer of Johnson County, Tex.; William J., a stockman of Washington Territory; John C., a farmer residing in the Cherokee Nation; Abraham Lincoln, residing in Benton County; Cleopatra Anne Bolyn, Mary Elizabeth, Martha Albertine, Rebecca Druscilla, Ben Frank and Sydney Emmet. At the breaking out of the war Mr. Davis enlisted in the Eighteenth Regiment Arkansas Volunteers, United States Army, and served until the cessation of hostilities. He escaped without receiving any wounds, but was captured by the enemy at Cherokee City; was soon after paroled and sent back to Barry County, Mo., with about twenty of his comrades. He soon after went to Montague County, Tex., where his only brother, Charles O. Davis, had raised a company of 100 men, and had with great difficulty made his way to the Union army, and afterward served as chief of scouts in Gen. Blount's army. Charles O. Davis was a lawyer by profession, and died in Montague County, Tex., in 1867. Andrew B. Davis returned to Madison County, Ark., after the war, and has since lived in that and Benton Counties. His labors through life have met with a fair degree of success, and he is now the owner of a good farm and a pleasant and comfortable home. He has been enabled to educate his children, and is himself a man of good education and sound judgment. He is a member of the Masonic fraternity, and is one of the few men who had the courage to assert his principles, living as he did in a disloyal section.

Goldsmith Chandler Davis, a prominent nurseryman and fruit grower of Osage Township, Benton Co., Ark., was born in the "Hoosier" State in 1844, and is a son of Benjamin F. and Ruth J. (Chandler) Davis, who are of Welsh and Irish-English descent, respectively. The father was born in Ohio in 1820, and was married in his native State. After residing alternately in Ohio and Indiana until 1853 he moved to St. Paul, Minn., where he was engaged in merchandising one year. The following eleven years he kept hotel in Scott County, and was also engaged in farming and running a lime kiln, supplying the city of St. Paul with its lime for several years. In 1867 be became a citizen of Bentonville, Ark., where he kept a hotel, and was also postmaster for about eight years. In 1878 he immigrated to Los Angeles County, Cal., and has since been engaged in raising oranges, grapes and small fruits. His wife was born in Ohio in 1830, and is a descendant of Oliver Goldsmith, the poet. She is the mother of five children: Goldsmith C.; Phoebe, wife or R. C.

BENTON COUNTY, ARKANSAS - BIOGRAPHICAL AND HISTORICAL MEMOIRS   147

****

Brown; Rose A., Nannie and Benjamin F. Goldsmith C. was educated in the public schools of Minnesota, and came to Arkansas with his parents. His father owned a farm of eighty acres near Bentonville, and the mother in the spring of 1869 planted a pint of apple seeds, which Goldsmith C. grafted in the spring of 1870. He gradually increased his stock until the cold winter of 1880–81, when all his trees were killed. He immediately set to work with renewed energy, and purchased eighty acres of land where his house now stands, and. without paying a dollar down, began setting out trees. He now has the largest nursery in the county, if not in the State, and is the owner of 640 acres of good land. His orchard consists of 20,000 trees, and his nursery stock comprises 1,000,000 trees from one to four years old. He is doing a highly satisfactory business, and his trees are shipped to nearly every State in the Union. In 1875 he was married to Miss Sallie West, a daughter of A. A. West, of Carroll County, Ark. She was born in Alabama in 1856, and is the mother of five children: Betsey Trotwood, Benjamin Franklin, Catherine, Lou Duskey and John Chandler.

Dr. William R. Davis, of Bentonville, Ark., was born in Montgomery County, Ky., in 1832, and is the son of Col. Josiah Davis and Patsy Chandler (Smith) Davis, and the grandson of James Davis, who was a soldier of the Revolutionary War. Col. Josiah Davis was born in Fayette County, Ky., in 1797, and was of Irish-Welsh extraction. His grandfather immigrated to the United States from Ireland with a flail upon his shoulder, and hired to a Welshman in Maryland to thresh his wheat, fell in love with his daughter and married her. Col. Josiah Davis was a colonel in the Home Militia, and had three older brothers in the War of 1812, two of whom were killed in running the gauntlet at the battle of River Raisin. The Colonel was a farmer and politician. He was a member of the State Legislature two terms, and was one of the influential and prominent men of his locality. He was a man of eminent ability, and a warm personal friend of Henry Clay. He died of pneumonia in 1847. His wife was of English extraction, and was born in Fayette County, Ky., in 1805. She died in 1862. She was the mother of twelve children, six sons and six daughters, four of whom are now living. Dr. W. R. Davis was the sixth child born to his parents. He received his literary education at country schools, finishing up at Sylvan Academy, near Lexington, Ky., and at the age of twenty years commenced the study of medicine, his preceptor being Dr. John A. Hannah, of Mt. Sterling, Ky. In 1852 he entered the Ohio Medical College, of Cincinnati, Ohio, and during the winter of 1853–54 attended a partial course at Louisville Medical College, graduating in the spring of 1855 at Transylvania Medical College, Lexington, Ky., and at once began the practice of his profession in the county of Clarke, afterward removing to Lewisport, Hancock Co., Ky., where he commanded a leading practice for ten years, during which period, in the year 1858, he was married to Miss Harriet A. Echols, of Wheeling, Va., who was born in 1837. Three children were born to this union before the death of his wife, which occurred in 1864. Only one is now living, Samuel E. Davis, attorney at law in Bentonville. In 1866 Dr. Davis, then a widower, removed to North Middleton, Bourbon Co., Ky., and in 1868 he married Miss Mary F. Seamands, who was born in Bourbon County in 1843, and who has since borne him seven children, to wit: Mary A., Preston S., Josiah, William R., Winfield C., Patsy C. and Eleanor A., all of whom are living. In 1876 Dr. Davis received a diploma from Louisville Medical College, and in same year commenced business in Winfield, Cowley Co., Kas., where for nine years he continued to enjoy a large and lucrative practice, acting a part of the time as local surgeon for the Atchison, Topeka & Santa Fe Railroad; was a member of the Southern Kansas Medical Society; was for one year vice-president of same, and also member of the Kansas State Medical Association. He spent a year with his family at Vinita, Indian Territory, during which period he was local surgeon for the Missouri Pacific and M., K. & T. Railroads. In 1886 he became a citizen of Bentonville, Ark. Dr. Davis is a Democrat in politics, is stockholder and director in the People's Bank, also director and stockholder in the Bentonville Evaporating and Canning Company. Dr. Davis has always commanded a large practice as well as the confidence and esteem of his acquaintances, and is a man of public spirit and progressive ideas. He has been one of the leading men in making Bentonville what she now is, having aided largely in securing enterprises of value and worth to the town, and has in conjunction with Mr. Dunn laid off and platted a forty-acre addition, known as Dunn & Davis' addition. During the short time he has been here he has erected a number of houses, and now owns a large number of lots in the city. He is agent for the Jarvis-Conklin Mortgage Trust Company, Kansas City, Mo. Dr. Davis is a member of the Christian Church, a Mason, and belongs to the I. O. U. W.; also, before moving west, was a member of district and State medical societies in his native State, Kentucky.

William B. Deming, real estate dealer and speculator of Bentonville, was born in Harrison County, Ohio, September 21, 1849, son of Lot and Frances E. (Urkuhart) Deming, and grandson of George Deming, who was a native of Weathersfield, Conn., and at an early date moved to Harrison County, Ohio. Lot Deming was born in Harrison County, Ohio, in 1823, and soon after his marriage moved to Tuscarawas County, Ohio, where he followed school-teaching for many years, and afterward devoted his time to farming. In the spring of 1870 he moved to Dickinson County, Kas., and in October, 1883, removed to Bentonville, where he now resides. His wife, Frances E. (Urkuhart) Deming, was born in Harrison County, Ohio, in 1828, and is of Scotch descent. Her grandmother lived to be one hundred years old. Mrs. Deming is now sixty years old and has not a gray hair in her head. She is the mother of the following named children: James W., William B., Newton A., Johnston G. (deceased), M. Edwin, George and Anna (twins) and Mollie. William B. was educated in the public schools of his native State and county. He remained at home until twenty years of age and worked on the farm. In 1869 he went to Dickinson County, Kan., and settled on a government tract of eighty acres, where he followed farming. In 1875 he married Miss Jennie Hart, who was a native of Stark County, Ill., born 1847, and who became the mother of two children: Earl and Daisy. Mr. Deming followed farming in Kansas until 1883, when he moved to Bentonville, Ark., and bought 152 acres of land adjoining the town. By December of the same year he had laid off 120 lots, known as Deming's Addition. He made a second addition of lots in April, 1887, known as Deming's Second Addition. In July, 1888, he donated two acres for the erection of a school building, which illustrates his benevolent spirit and enterprise. He has been dealing in real estate outside of his own land for a part of four years. September, 1887, the Arkansas Tobacco Company was organized in Bentonville, and Mr. Deming is a stockholder and president of the company. He is a thorough advocate of temperance and sobriety, and while a resident of Kansas took an active part in prohibition and local politics. He is rather independent in his political views, but inclines somewhat to Republican principles. Mr. Deming has a fine residence, and is one of the substantial citizens of the county. He is a member of the K. P., and a charter member in Bentonville. He is a regular attendant at the Christian Church, of which his wife is a member.

Ezekiel John Alcorn Dickson, one of Benton County's (Ark.) oldest and most highly esteemed citizens, was born in Rutherford County, Tenn., March 21, 1813, and is of Scotch-Irish descent. He is a son of Ezekiel Dickson, who was born in Lincoln County, N. C., in 1782, and in 1802 was married to Mary McKissick, and the following year moved to Tennessee, where he resided until the spring of 1836, when he located in Benton County, Ark., and in 1841 settled on the farm now owned by his son, Ezekiel J. A. Dickson. He died on the 14th of May, 1858. His wife was born in 1780, also in Lincoln County, N. C. She was a daughter of Daniel McKissick, a Revolutionary soldier, who was for many years clerk of Lincoln County, N. C. He died in 1818 in Bedford County, Tenn. Mrs. Dickson died June 2, 1853, having borne nine children, two of whom are living: Ezekiel J. A. and Mary E., widow of William R. Ogden. The paternal grandfather of our subject was Gen. Joseph Dickson, who was a native of Pennsylvania, born about 1750. He was a soldier in the Revolutionary War, and died in 1825 in Rutherford County, Tenn. Ezekiel J. A. Dickson was reared on a farm, and in 1835 left his native State and immigrated to Arkansas with his uncle, Joseph McKissick, and located on a farm about eight miles west of Bentonville. November 26, 1840, he was married to Sophia Jane Morrison, who was born in Bedford County, Tenn., in 1820, and a daughter of Andrew and Jane (Robinson) Morrison, and their union was blessed in the birth of seven children: Isabella Emily, widow of R. P. Lynn; James Milton, who died in 1862 at the age of eighteen years; Margaret Adaline, wife of Dr. E. P. Hansard; Caledonia Wilson, wife of T. J. Vaughn; Nannie Eliza, wife of John W. Williams; Mary Harris, wife of J. M. Wier, and Robert A., who died in 1880 at the age of twenty-five years. Mr. Dickson located on his present farm in 1847.

He owns 770 acres at the present time, but at one time owned 990 acres. He is one of the oldest citizens of Benton County, Ark., having been a resident of the same for fifty-three years, and in politics has always been a firm believer and supporter of Democratic principles. He was school commissioner of Benton County for eight years, and was justice of the peace for six years. He is a Royal Arch Mason, and he and wife have long been members of the Presbyterian Church.

J. Alvin Dickson, farmer and nurseryman, three miles southeast of Bentonville, is a native of Benton County, Ark., born in 1845, and is the son of James A. and Mary A. (Wood) Dickson, and grandson of Maj. John B. Dickson, who immigrated to Madison County, Ark., about 1830, and two years later moved to Benton County, of the same State; he was circuit clerk, ex-officio recorder of Benton County, and a member of the State Legislature. He was in the War of 1812, was in the battle of New Orleans, and was shot in the leg. He was one of the first settlers of Benton County. About 1851 he moved to the Lone Star State, and there died in 1879 at the age of eighty-four years. His son, James A., was born in Bedford County, Tenn., in 1819, and was but a boy when his parents moved to Benton County. June, 1844, he married Miss Mary A. Woods, who was born in Marshall County, Tenn., in 1820, and who was the daughter of Samuel Woods. She is the mother of five children: J. Alvin; Sarah, wife of James Black; Charlotta E.; Belle, wife of Frank Kindley, and Dwight. After marriage Mr. Dickson located four miles southeast of Bentonville, and in 1846 moved to Osage Springs, and from there to Bentonville in 1849. Here he followed merchandising until 1866, when he moved three and a half miles southeast of Bentonville, and there he now resides. J. Alvin Dickson was educated in Bentonville, and served two years in the late Rebellion. He was in Company G, Second Arkansas Cavalry, and was in the fight at Marks' Mill, Jenkins' Mill, Pine Bluff, and in numerous other skirmishes. After the war he was in a drug store in Bentonville, Ark., and in 1877 he married Miss Lillie Woolsey, daughter of Henry B. Woolsey, and a native of Benton County, Ark., born in 1860. This union was blessed by the birth of five children: Eva, Mettie, Jewell, Gertrude and an infant son. Mr. Dickson is the owner of 200 acres of land, on which he located directly after his marriage. In 1881 he became a partner with his father-in-law in the nursery business. He is a Democrat in politics, and he and wife are members of the Cumberland Presbyterian Church.

Joseph S. Dickson, farmer, of Bentonville, was born three-fourths of a mile from where he now lives, in Benton County, Ark., June 20, 1839, son of Joseph and Mary (Hare) Dickson, and grandson of Robert Dickson, who was a native of Lincoln County, N. C., born in 1772. Robert moved to Rutherford County, Tenn., about 1826, from there to Carroll County, W. Tenn., 1831, and later to Northwest Arkansas, where he entered land and resided where Bentonville now stands. He was not very well pleased with the country, and accordingly the following year returned to Carroll County, Tenn., but in 1835 again came to Arkansas, and here passed his last days, dying in 1848. He was one of the first white men to make a permanent settlement in Northwest Arkansas. He lived in Benton County several years before the county was organized, and even before the State was admitted, the entire country being then in its infancy. Robert Dickson and Esther Moore were married March 23, 1796, and their children were Joseph, born February 9, 1797; Margaret, born December 15, 1799; Ephraim, born January 5, 1802; Isabella, born March 22, 1804; Robert, born March 22, 1807; Elizabeth, born June 6, 1809; Polly, born September 2, 1811; John W., born November 3, 1813; Ezekiel K., born August 9, 1816; Sally S., born January 15, 1819; Martha M., born November 15, 1821. Joseph was born, as above related, February 9, 1797, and was brought by his parents to Rutherford County, Tenn., when a mere boy, and moved with them to Carroll County, Tenn., in 1826, and to Arkansas with them in 1831. He settled near his father, and owned a portion of the land where Bentonville now stands, or the first addition of the town. He was one of the active spirits who assisted in the organization of the county, and was one of the first settlers. May 30, 1821, he married Mary Hare, who was born in North Carolina April 8, 1805, and died in 1867. She was the mother of eleven children, as follows: Frances Ann, born March 6, 1822; Margaret, born September 23, 1823; Martha, born September 6, 1825; Sarah Priscilla, born February 8, 1828; Mary Jane, born September 1, 1829; Robert B., born January 2, 1832; Nancy, born October 6, 1834; John E., born February

3, 1837; Joseph, born June 20, 1839; Ephraim H., born January 28, 1843; William G., born May 28, 1845. Of this family the following named have died: Margaret, in 1824; Sarah Priscilla, in 1828; Frances Ann, 1844; Joseph, October 2, 1845; Mary Jane, October 23, 1846; Martha, June 13, 1861; William G., November 25, 1862; Robert B., July 26, 1863; Mary, March 11, 1867. Frances Ann's funeral text was Thess. IV., 13, 14; Joseph's funeral text was I. Cor. XV., 55, 56, 57; Mary Jane's funeral text was II. Cor. IV., 17, by Rev. B. H. Pierson; Mary Dickson's and Martha Maxwell's, Robert and William G. Dickson's funeral texts were Phil. I., 21, by Rev. S. H. Buchanan. Joseph S. attained his growth on a farm, and August, 1862, he enlisted in Capt. Jefferson's company, Arkansas Cavalry, and in three weeks was transferred to Company F, Thirty-fourth Regiment Arkansas Infantry. He was in the fight at Saline, Little Rock, Helena, and surrendered at Fort Smith June, 1865. November 7, 1868, he married Miss Sarah C. Pickens, a native of Tennessee, born September 9, 1846, and this union resulted in the birth of the following named children: William A., born March 31, 1870; Myrtie E., born November 8, 1872; Charlie C., born December 8, 1874; Pearl B., born June 13, 1877; Eva L., born October 22, 1878; Alva E., born July 2, 1882. Of this family there have died: Pearl B., at the age of seven months; Myrtie E., January 1, 1884. Funerals preached by the Revs. Peter Carnahan and F. T. Charlton. Mrs. Sarah C. Dickson died April 10, 1884, and in July of the same year Mr. Dickson married Miss Nancy A. Gould, daughter of John and Jane Gould, who were born in 1800 and 1809, respectively. Both were natives of Tennessee, and moved to Benton County, Ark., in 1859, where both are now living. They have been married sixty years. Mr. Dickson is the owner of 160 acres of land, and also has a general store at Brightwater. He has succeeded well in his business, and is an honest, enterprising citizen. He is a Democrat in politics, and he and wife are members of the Cumberland Presbyterian Church.

Capt. John A. Dienst is a well-to-do farmer, residing near Siloam Springs, Ark. His birth occurred in Tuscarawas County, Ohio, November 24, 1824, and he was there educated and reared to manhood. He is one of six children born to John P. and Mary E. (Keller) Dienst, who were born in Westphalia, Germany, April 27, 1786, and September 26, 1790, respectively. The father was educated in the schools of the "Fatherland," and was reared to manhood on a farm. He was married in 1817, and immigrated to America in 1819, settling near York, Penn. He resided there six months, and then located in Tuscarawas County, Ohio, where he died in 1846. His wife died in 1850. The following are their children: Mary E. (wife of John Heter), Anna (deceased), Sarah (deceased), John A., Benjamin and Lydia (deceased). John A. was married in 1847 to Anna E. Oehler, who was born in Wurtemburg, Germany, February 19, 1828, and came to America with her parents when she was three years old, settling in Ohio. She and Mr. Dienst became the parents of seven children: Rufus and Louis C. (deceased), Henry, and Eugene, Ira, Laura and Oliver (deceased). In 1853 Mr. Dienst moved to the present site of Leavenworth City, Kas., but in 1854 moved to Benton County, Ark., and in 1862 enlisted in the Federal army, Company F, First Arkansas Cavalry, under the command of Col. Harrison, and participated in the engagements at Fayetteville, Enterprise, Mo., East Mount, Ark., and others. In August, 1865, he returned home. He located his family in Washington County after the war, and there he continued to reside until 1881, when he located at Siloam Springs, and in September, 1887, moved to his farm near town. He supports the principles of the Republican party, and belongs to the Masonic fraternity. He and wife are members of the Moravian Church.

Jacob S. Dobkins, son of Hugh and Hannah (Neely) Dobkins, was born in Arkansas May 1, 1843. The father was born in Virginia, but immigrated to Tennessee when young, and, although receiving a limited education, he was a man of more than ordinary ability. He was quite a successful farmer, and after coming to Arkansas was the owner of 320 acres of land. Hannah (Neely) Dobkins, the mother, was born in Tennessee, and here married Mr. Dobkins, by whom she had eight children, six now living: Mrs. Sarah J. Wakefield, Mrs. Margaret A. Newell, Robert, Mrs. Nancy McPhail, Mrs. Melvina Tucker and Jacob S. The two deceased were named James and Alexander. Shortly after his marriage Mr. Dobkins moved to Missouri, where he made his first start in life, and where he often worked hard all day for a peck of meal, which he carried home on his shoulder after night. He remained in Missouri for about ten years, rented land, and then moved to Arkansas, where he rented land for one year. He then went to California, making the trip overland, and was away from home eighteen months, being engaged in mining the greater part of the time. After returning to Arkansas he purchased the farm that he had rented, and where he spent the greater part of his life, selling out a short time before his death, and moving to Cherokee City. He here died in 1882. The mother died three years later. The paternal grandfather of our subject was of English descent, and the maternal grandparents were both of Irish extraction. Jacob S. Dobkins received a fair common-school education, and remained with his parents until twenty-seven years of age. He enlisted in Company H, Fifth Texas Partisan Rangers, Confederate army, and served for two years. During that time he was almost exclusively on frontier duty in the Chocktaw and Cherokee Nations, was in many skirmishes, but no actual battle. After the war Mr. Dobkins went to California, where he remained six months, when he returned home and resumed work on the farm. In 1869 he married Miss Nancy McPhail, daughter of Daniel and Elizabeth McPhail, the father of Scottish descent and a native of Kentucky, and the mother a native of Tennessee. Grandfather McPhail was born in the highlands of Scotland, and the grandmother was of English descent. To Mr. and Mrs. Dobkins were born four children, all now living: Kate, Hugh, James and Maud. After his marriage Mr. Dobkins purchased his present farm, where he has since lived, and where he now has 103 acres. He has a good home, and is surrounded by every comfort. In 1886 Mr. Dobkins was elected justice of the peace, and he and Mrs. Dobkins are members of the Cumberland Presbyterian Church. He is a member of the Masonic lodge, and is Democratic in politics, casting his first vote for McClellan and his last for Grover Cleveland.

Matthew N. Donaldson, liveryman, of Siloam Springs, Ark., was born in East Tennessee, March 13, 1844, and was reared in Illinois, whither his parents had moved in 1857. He attended the common country schools, and in August, 1865, united his fortunes with those of Eliza Marlowe, who was born and reared in Illinois, her birth occurring in 1849. Six children blessed their union: Missouri C. (wife of R. L. Allen), Martha L. (wife of Wilson Weaver), Alexander B. (deceased), Mary K., Minnie C. and Eliza Myrtle. After his marriage Mr. Donaldson moved to what is now known as Cherokee County, Kas., and, with the exception of two years spent in Missouri, resided here until 1880, at which time he came to Siloam Springs, and at the end of two years went into the livery business. He has an excellent stable in a good location, and well supplied with horses and carriages. He is prospering financially, and besides this property is the owner of the Mount Olive House, a boarding-house, which is located just above Twin Springs. He is a Democrat, and has been a member of the I. O. O. F. since 1865, having filled all the important offices connected with the lodge. He is also a member of the K. of H. His parents, Lorenzo Dow and Margaret A. (Newman) Donaldson, were born in Tennessee in 1806 and 1811, respectively. The father was reared on a farm sixteen miles from Knoxville, and was a farmer and stock dealer the greater portion of his life. After residing in Indiana a few years he returned to Tennessee, and in 1857 located in Washington County, Ill., and in 1866 went to Cherokee County, Kas., and there died October 25, 1886. He was a cousin of Andrew Jackson's wife, and a son of William Donaldson, who was an Irishman, and a graduate of a college in Northern Ireland. He immigrated to America before the War of 1812, and assisted in that struggle, being with Gen. Jackson at New Orleans. Our subject's mother died on the 8th of January, 1887. She and husband were the parents of eleven children: Catherine (killed by a cyclone in Southern Illinois in 1860), William, David (deceased), Jesse D., Elizabeth (wife of George W. Mathews), Lorenzo L., Matthew N., Martha Jane (deceased), Margaret Ann (wife of James Brown), Eliza (wife of Philip Keelerman), and Sophronia N. (deceased).

Charles Dorkens is a native of the "Old North State," born in 1822, and is a son of Benjamin H. and Fannie (Mack) Dorkens, the former of whom was born in Virginia, and removed with his parents to North Carolina at a very early day, where he met and was united in marriage to Miss ————. He followed the occupation of farming all his life, and died in 1853 at a good old age. Charles Dorkens was educated in his native State, and assisted his father on the farm until he attained manhood. In 1856 he concluded to seek his fortune in the West, and immigrated to Benton County, Ark., and located on a farm near Garfield, but in 1873 moved to Texas, and remained in that State for six years. He then returned to Arkansas, where he has since resided, purchasing his present home of eighty acres in 1879. He was married in 1853 to Miss Callie Sabine, of Benton County, Ark., and their union has resulted in the birth of three children: Jennie S., John W. and Thomas P. Mr. and Mrs. Dorkens are members of the Baptist Church. In 1864 he joined the Confederate army, enlisting in Maj. Brown's battalion of cavalry, and served until peace was declared He was in a number of engagements, and after receiving his discharge returned home, and has since been engaged in the peaceful pursuit of farming.

J. W. Duckworth is a member of the real estate, loan and insurance company of Duckworth & Bixler, of Rogers, Ark. Mr. Duckworth was born in Benton County, Ark., in 1850, and is a son of J. P. and Nancy (Alexander) Duckworth, who were born in Missouri and Kentucky, respectively. They are at present residing in Rogers, and eight of their nine children are living. Their son, J. W., was reared and educated in his native State, and after reaching a suitable age spent some time in pedagoguing. He took an irregular course in the Springdale Academy, and then went to Jackson, Tenn., where he took a course in Greek and the mental and moral sciences. Owing to ill health he concluded to travel for some time, and in his wanderings visited many of the principal points of interest, and the large cities of the United States. His health finally returned, and in 1877 he settled down in Rogers, Ark., and engaged in his present business. He is one of the stockholders in the canning and packing factory at Rogers, and is one of the enterprising and public-spirited citizens of the county. In 1875 he was united in marriage with Miss Arizona Sikes, who was born in Benton County in 1858, and is the mother of two children, Charley R. and Siddie. Mr. and Mrs. Duckworth are members of the Baptist Church; he is a Democrat, and a member of the A. F. & A. M.

Hon. J. Dunagin, a minister of the Missionary Baptist Church, of Benton County, Ark., was born in Georgia in 1825, and is a son of Hiram and Mary (Rush) Dunagin, both of whom were Georgians, born in 1800 and 1803, respectively. The father died in Missouri in 1844, while on the way to Arkansas, and his widow came on to this State with her family, and after living in Benton County for about six years she went to Texas, where she died in 1882. Hon. J. Dunagin is the third of her eleven children, and until nineteen years of age he was a resident of Georgia. At that time he came to Arkansas with his mother, and, as he was the oldest of the family, the duty of caring for his mother and brothers and sisters fell mainly on his shoulders. He was of a very studious turn of mind, and, although the educational advantages of that day were of the very poorest kind and his labors quite heavy, he succeeded in obtaining a practical education. On the 4th of July, 1847, he was united in marriage to Miss Susan Caveness, a native of Tennessee, whose parents came to Arkansas while it was still a territory. She was born in 1830, and became the mother of nine children: Sarah (wife of Thomas Stokes), Rebecca (wife of J. Tuck), John R., Amanda (wife of F. M. Seamster), Minerva (wife of Dr. J. W. Underwood), Mary T. (wife of Thomas Threet), W. D., Mattie and Robert. Mr. Dunagin became a member of the church the year before he was married, and soon after began preaching, being ordained in 1849. He has been actively engaged in ministerial work up to the present time, with the exception of two years, which were spent in trying to regain his failing health. He is now the regular pastor at Rogers and Pleasant Hill Churches. He is still a devoted student, and spends much of his time in his library. He was a member of the State Legislature for nine years, and was a member of that body when the question of secession came up, and strenuously opposed that measure, and is a Democrat. He owns a good farm on the watershed of the Ozark Mountains.

J. R. Dunagin, merchant at Avoca, Ark., was born in Benton County in 1852, and is a son of Rev. J. Dunagin, also of Benton County. He was reared on a farm, and after attending the common schools finished his education in the Arkansas State University. He then returned home, and after teaching the "young idea" for about three months, gave up that calling and engaged in mercantile pursuits as a clerk for Dunagin & Mitchell, at Rogers. After a time he came to Avoca and engaged in the grocery business in partnership with F. M. Seamster, but after a short time purchased Mr. Seamster's interest, and is now the sole proprietor. Besides his stock of groceries, he carries a large line of boots

****

and shoes, and is doing a thriving business. He began his business career with a small capital, but has built up a good trade, and has largely increased his stock of goods. He is a stanch supporter of Democratic principles, and is a member of the Baptist Church. In 1873 his marriage with Miss Sarah J. Stokes was consummated, and their union has resulted in the birth of two children: Albert and Annie. Mrs. Dunagin was born in Tennessee in 1849.

Benjamin F. Dunn, member of the firm of B. F. Dunn & Co., of Bentonville, Ark., and real estate agent, is a native of Giles County, Va., born in 1841, son of Martin and Mary (Pine) Dunn. Martin Dunn was born in Virginia in 1793, was of Irish origin and a farmer by occupation. In 1846 he immigrated to Buchanan County, Mo., where he died one year later. Mary (Pine) Dunn was born in Virginia in 1795 and died in 1848. They were the parents of ten children, Benjamin F. being the only one now living. He was the youngest, and only six years old when his father died, and seven when his mother died. At the age of ten he was taken by B. A. Dickson, with whom he lived until he was twenty-one years of age. He received a limited education in the district schools, and at the breaking out of the war he enlisted in Company A, First Missouri Cavalry, Confederate army, and was in the battles of Carthage, Wilson Creek, Dry Wood, Lexington, Champion Hill and siege of Vicksburg. In October, 1862, he was captured at home and held a prisoner at St. Louis until February of the next year, when he was exchanged. He was afterward captured at Vicksburg and taken to Indianapolis, where he was retained eleven months. He was then discharged and returned home. He was slightly wounded three different times. In 1865 he went to Richardson County, Neb., and there remained until 1870, when he became a citizen of Benton County, Ark., and began clerking in a store in the western part of the county. In 1872 he began teaching, and followed this profession for one term. In January, 1873, he was appointed deputy sheriff, and served three years. In the same year he married Miss Mary J. Smith, who was born in Benton County, Ark., in 1845, and who is the daughter of H. C. Smith. To this union were born two children, Mary Bennie and Elijah Frank, twins. In 1876 Mr. Dunn was elected treasurer of Benton County, and re-elected in 1878. In 1880 he was elected clerk of the circuit court and *ex-officio* recorder. He was re-elected in 1882, and in 1884 was again elected to the same position. He was in office continuously for ten years, and filled the official position with credit and ability. He is a lifelong Democrat in politics; is a Royal Arch Mason, a member of the I. O. O. F., and he and wife are members of the Christian Church. Mr. Dunn is secretary of the Benton County Emigration Bureau, and is a stockholder in the People's Bank at Bentonville.

Hiram A. Elam is the son of James and Marinda (Sharp) Elam, and grandson of Louallen and Polly (Eans) Elam, and great-grandson of Richard Elam. The latter emigrated from Scotland to the United States with his two brothers, John A. and Samuel, and is supposed to have settled in Virginia. Louallen Elam was born in Campbell County, Va., in 1780, and in 1817 immigrated to Butler County, Ky., thence to Clark County, Ill., in 1825. Here Louallen Elam died in 1835. He was a soldier in the War of 1812. His wife was born in Amelia County, Va., in 1783 and died in 1850. The following are their children who are living: James, Susan, Elizabeth, Alfred, Nancy and William. James Elam was eight years old when his parents moved to Kentucky, and sixteen years of age when they located in Illinois. He was born in Campbell County, Va., February 25, 1809, and in 1832 was married to Miss Sharp, a daughter of Levi and Margaret (Coffee) Sharp, who were natives of North Carolina. Mrs. Elam was born in that State in 1811, and at the age of three years was taken by her parents to Clark County, Ill., where she afterward met and married Mr. Elam. Seven of their children lived to be grown: Mary J., wife of J. Y. Black; John, Alfred M., Louisa, wife of H. T. Cork; Hiram A. and Margaret, widow of John F. Owen. Henry died in 1887 at the age of fifty years. Mr. Elam resided in the State of Illinois until 1866, when he located in Benton County, Ark., where he has since resided. He is one of the oldest citizens of the county, and he and wife have celebrated their golden wedding. He is a Republican in politics, and was a Whig previous to the war. He has been successful in all his business transactions, and has accumulated a comfortable competency. He is highly esteemed and commands the respect of all. Hiram A. Elam was married, April 6, 1879, to Miss Palestine M. Baxley, a native of Benton County, born in 1860. She is the mother of six children: Era Earl, James E., Myrtie, Marinda, Etta and Lou Allen. Mr. Elam cast his first presidential vote for Grant, and is a Republican in politics. He was born in Clark County, Ill., October 1, 1848, and was educated in the common schools of his native State, and also received two years' instruction at a college located in Marshall, Ill. From 1868 to 1870 he was deputy sheriff of his county, and was at one time United States Marshal. In 1870 he was clerk of the board of registration. He owns an excellent farm of eighty acres, on which is a spring which affords the clearest and coldest of water. It bursts forth from the ground a convenient distance from his residence and supplies water to a number of neighboring farms.

Hon. Samuel N. Elliott, ex-county judge of Benton County, is a resident of Bentonville, and a native of Rutherford County, Tenn., born where the battle of Stone River was fought, December 22, 1823. He is the son of James and Adaline (Bowman) Elliott, the former a native of Orange County, N. C., born in 1796, of Quaker descent, and a mill-wright, farmer, general mechanic, etc., by trade. He was a genius, and a successful business man. At the age of fourteen he left his native State and went to Rutherford County, Tenn., where he married and where passed the remainder of his life. He died in 1841. He was a soldier in the War of 1812, and was at the battle of New Orleans. His wife, Adaline Bowman, was born in North Carolina, in 1802, and died in Murfreesboro, Tenn., in 1885. Her father, Samuel Bowman, was a soldier in the Revolutionary War, as was also several of her uncles. She was the mother of nine children, Hon. Samuel N. Elliott being the second child. He was educated in the country schools, at Clinton College in Smith County, Tenn., one year, and was three years at the Transylvania University at Lexington, Ky., graduating from the law department of the last named institution in the spring of 1845. In 1848 he married Miss Jane K. Brack, a native of Trumbull County, Ohio, born in 1825. Six children were born to this marriage: Charles D., superintendent of three silver mines in New Mexico; Harry W., in New Mexico, and the owner of silver mines, attorney at law and a very successful business man; David J., in California; Clarissa H., deceased; Adaline B., wife of J. B. Woods, of Benton County, Ark., and Pearl, a graduate of Dr. Price's school, at Nashville, Tenn. After his marriage Judge Elliott went to Seguin, Gaudalupe Co., Tex., where he resided until the war broke out, and practiced law with success, Gov. Ireland being his opponent in many a law case. In February, 1862, Judge Elliott enlisted in Company K, Eighth Regiment Texas Infantry, and was elected third lieutenant. He was in the bombardment of Corpus Christi, Fort Esperanza and other skirmishes, remaining in service until the close of hostilities. He was judge advocate of court martial at Sabine Pass for three months, and surrendered at Pelican Spit in May, 1865. In 1866 he was in the North, and for and during the years 1867 and 1868 was in Bryan, Tex. In May, 1869, he became a resident of Bentonville, Ark., and resumed the practice of law. He was justice of the peace for several years, and in 1876 he was elected county judge, which position he held for eight years. When he first entered the office the county was $18,000 in debt, and at the end of six years Judge Elliott had paid the entire principal and interest, leaving the county out of debt, for which act the people of Benton County will hold him in grateful remembrance. In 1882 Judge Elliott went to California, purchased an orange grove, and at the end of nine months traded it for a farm near Fayetteville, Washington Co., Ark. Before the war he was an old line Whig, and in 1861 was a candidate for a seat in secession of Texas convention, but was defeated by Gov. Ireland. He is a Democrat politically, and in religion is an independent free thinker. Mrs. Elliott is a member of the old school Presbyterian Church.

James Enterkine, analytic chemist and druggist, of Springtown, Ark., was born in Glasgow, Scotland, on the 1st of May, 1864, and was reared and educated in his native land. He attended the Jaynefield British Government Academy, taking a classical course, and graduated from that institution. At the age of seventeen years he entered the Belleviewdaur Hospital, where he studied chemistry and pharmacy under Prof. Noble, the great chemist of Glasgow, and completed his course at the end of two years. On June 6, 1883, he sailed for the United States, and went almost directly to Eureka, Kas., where he has an uncle by the name of Joseph Enterkine. He had an interest in a drug store at that place until 1886, and during the winter of that year and 1887 and 1887–88, he took two courses in the National Institute of Pharmacy on

Dearborn Street, Chicago, Ill. He came to Springtown, Ark., in February, 1888, and engaged in the drug business in partnership with Dr. N. Sewell, and is the junior member of that firm. Mr. Enterkine has had to make his own way in the world, and has been exceptionally successful in accumulating property. He is now worth about $4,000, all of which he has made by his own energy and good management, and, as he is a young man, his future prospects are very bright. His parents are John and Ellen (Smilie) Enterkine, both of whom were born and reared in Scotland. The father was a woolen manufacturer and designer, and was connected with the firm of Lord Napier & Co., woolen manufacturers, of Glasgow, Scotland. The father died in July, 1888, the mother October 14, 1888.

Stephen Thomas Fair, the subject of this sketch, a farmer and teacher residing near Center Point Church House, near the "McKisick Spring," in Benton County, Ark., is the second son of Ellis and Nancy H. Fair, was born in Sullivan County, East Tenn., in the year 1836, and came to Arkansas in the year 1859. His father, Ellis Fair, was born at Cheraw, S. C., in the year 1805, and there received an education common to those of that time and place. He immigrated from there to East Tennessee, and in the year 1832 was married to Miss Nancy Hamilton Easley, daughter of Stephen and Hannah Easley, of Sullivan County, E. Tenn., and to them were born nine children, to wit: Mary Ann, Harvey Cummins, Stephen Thomas, Edwin Franklin, John Dickson, George Fanning, Joseph Asbery, Sarah Edna, and Nathan Easley. Two of these children, to wit, Harvey Cummins and John Dickson, died in childhood, and one of them, viz., Mary Ann, who became consort of Mr. W. C. Sellars, of Benton County, Ark., died in the year 1871, leaving an infant son, Robert Lee, who in a few months also died, and its remains were interred by those of its mother in Bethel Cemetery, on Spavinaw. During the Mexican War the father of these children volunteered, but his company was not called into service. In the year 1859 these parents, in order to secure good homes for their children, sold out in Tennessee, and with their family immigrated to Benton County, Ark., bought lands and were prospering at the breaking out of the Civil War, in which, though opposed to the war, the five sons, before its close, became members of the army of "The Lost Cause," the father, mother and daughters remaining on the farm and managing to raise and retain enough of its products to support and clothe themselves, notwithstanding they were frequently robbed of everything that could be carried away by lawless bands of plunderers, who made it their primary object to scour the country for individual booty. On the 7th day of May, 1864, the father, on returning from his labor, was met by an enraged posse of "Pin Indians," and, notwithstanding his age and inoffensive life, was by them cruelly murdered. The mother and her two daughters, assisted by the good women of the neighborhood, managed to make a rude coffin and to bury his remains in the yard near the residence, where it rested till after the close of the cruel war, when it was disinterred and suitably re-interred in Bethel Cemetery, the Rev. Martin Thornsberry conducting the funeral services from the text: "Be ye, also, ready." This funeral was largely attended, and it is believed by all who are acquainted with Mr. Fair that at the last day, on the resurrection morning, his remains will, at the sounding of the first trumpet, come forth to life immortal. Edwin F., the third son, married Miss Sarah Jane, daughter of Dr. Samuel and Mrs. Mahala Martin; is a successful farmer and a Methodist class leader; resides in Scott County, Ark., and has ten children, to wit: John, George, Maud, Lewis, Albert, Samuel, Nancy, Ellis, Ann and ——. George F. married Miss Martha Elizabeth Beard, of Yell County, Ark., is an itinerant minister of the Methodist Episcopal Church, South, and resides at Sipe Springs, Comanche County, Tex. The names of their children are Nancy R., Mary E., Emma B., Ellis N., Floyd and Ennis Lee. Joseph A. married Miss Martha Ann Russell, of Benton County, Ark.; is a successful farmer and a local minister of the Methodist Episcopal Church, South; resides in Benton County, Ark.; has nine children, to wit: Elija Ellis, Harvey Dickson, Lovic Pierce, Joseph Clark, Sarah Altha, Commodore Vanderbilt, Wiley Cicero, Hugh Lancing and Oma Pear. Sarah E. married Mr. Wiley C. Sitton, of Georgia, and resides in Benton County, Ark. They have no children. The mother, Nancy H. Fair, now seventy-six years of age, lives with this, her youngest, daughter. Mr. Sitton is a successful farmer, and is now serving his second term as justice of the peace of Decatur Township. Nathan E., the youngest son, married Miss Amanda Hamilton, of Yell County, Ark., is a minister of the Methodist Episcopal Church, South, and teacher in Belleville Academy, Yell County, Ark. They have five children, to wit: Laura, Loula, Minnie, Grace and Pearl. Stephen T. was educated in the common schools of Sullivan County and at Jefferson Academy, in Blountville, E. Tenn. After leaving the Academy he taught several terms in the public schools of his native county, and then came to Benton County, Ark., where he resumed the business of teaching, in which he continued till in the summer of 1861, when he joined the Fourteenth Arkansas Regiment, Confederate States Army, in which he served, first as teamster, second as commissary-sergeant, third as forage master, fourth as wagon-master, and after the battle of Pea Ridge, fifth as hospital steward, until, overcome by fatigue and exposure, he was left by his command at the point of death, near Little Rock, Ark. After partly regaining his health, he returned to his home in Benton, where he remained about two months, and then joined General Standwatie's Indian command, under Maj. Joel Bryant. In this command he served, first as company clerk, second as quartermaster-sergeant, and third as adjutant of Col. William Penn Adair's Second Cherokee Regiment, Confederate States Army. He was in the battles of Sherley Ford, Newtonia, Fort Wayne, Honey Springs, Mazzard Prairie and a number of other minor engagements. At the time of the surrender of the Confederate States army his command was at Boggy Depot, I. T., from which place he went to Northwest Texas, where he remained about a year, and then returned to Benton County and resumed the business of teaching. On the 22d day of March, 1868, at Center Point Church, Benton County, Ark., in the presence of a large congregation, he was united in the bonds of matrimony with Miss Agnes Julia Ann Womack, the Rev. Martin Thornsberry officiating. Mrs. Fair is the daughter of Mr. Richard and Mrs. Matilda Lee Womack, who moved from Wilson County, Tenn., in the year 1855. She was born in Wilson County, Tenn., in 1851. There have been born to Mr. and Mrs. Fair ten children, to wit: first, William Wallace, who died in infancy; second, Mary Ann; third, an infant son, deceased, without name; fourth, Ellis Hamilton; fifth, Richard Lee; sixth, Martha Edna; seventh, Stephen Thomas; eighth, Cora Ethel; ninth, Emma Vivian; tenth, Edwin Claudia. Mr. Fair still follows teaching in the public schools of the county, holds a first grade certificate, and when not employed as teacher works upon and manages his farm. He is secretary of the Benton County Sunday-school Association, a member of the Methodist Episcopal Church, South, member of Bentonville Lodge No. 56, A. F. & A. M., justice of the peace of Osage Township, in which capacity he is now serving his fourth term; is Democratic in his political views, and is true to his honest convictions, but opposed to bigotry and ultraism in all things.

William R. Felker. Among the prominent and highly esteemed citizens of Benton County, Ark., may be mentioned Mr. Felker, who is proprietor of the Bank of Rogers, Ark. His birth occurred in Barry County, Mo., in 1855, and he is a son of Stephen and Eliza (Dougherty) Felker, who were native Tennesseeans, and farmers by occupation, and are now residents of Barry County. William R. Felker spent the healthy, happy and busy life of the farmer's boy, and received his early education in the common schools of Barry County. In 1874 he began life for himself by clerking in a store in Barry County, and being a young man of energy and honesty, he soon purchased a half interest in the store. He remained in the mercantile business in Washburn, Mo., until 1881, and then sold out. After traveling in the West for some time, he returned home and located in Barton County, Mo., where he loaned money and speculated in various kinds of merchandise for about two years. In 1883 he became a resident of Rogers, Ark., where he engaged in the banking business, in which he has been quite successful.

Dr. James W. Fergus may be mentioned as one of the prosperous and successful physicians of Benton County, Ark. He was born in Miami County, Ohio, October 29, 1852, and is a son of Samuel and Malissa J. (Woodward) Fergus, who were natives, respectively, of Ohio and Illinois. The father is of Scotch descent, a farmer by occupation, and was a soldier in the Union army during the late war. He now resides in Ashland, Ore. From 1860 until 1866, they resided in Iowa, and at the latter date moved to Jasper County, Mo. Their son, James W., was reared and received his education, first attending the common schools, and then the high-school at Peirce City, Mo. He received his medical education in the Joplin Medical College, at Joplin, Mo., graduating from that institution as an M. D. in March, 1883. He first began practicing at Bloomington, Benton Co., Ark., and in 1879 removed to Elm Springs, and the same year located in Robinson, Ark., where he has since resided. He has a large and increasing practice, and consequently is doing well financially. In the latter part of 1878 he was married to Elmira Smith, born in Newton County, Mo., in 1854, a daughter of Howell Smith, a prominent Methodist minister, born in Tennessee, and their union was blessed in the birth of five children: Elbert, James, Franklin, Carrie and William. Dr. Fergus is a Master Mason, and he and wife attend the Methodist Church.

John A. Fields was born in Wilson County, Tenn., September 29, 1833, son of Redden and Polly (Farrington) Fields, grandson of David and Mary (Jarmon) Fields, and grandson of John and Easter (Charlin) Farrington. The father, Redden Fields, was born in Wilson County, Tenn., June 3, 1803, and was a farmer by occupation. At the age of twenty-three he married Miss Polly Farrington, and afterward moved to Benton County, Ark. (1857). A year later he moved to Hickory County, Mo., and in 1862 he went to Southern Iowa, where he practiced as veterinary surgeon. In 1866 he moved to Illinois, and from there in 1873 to Henry County, Tenn., where he still continued working at his profession. He was a member of the Baptist Church, and a Democrat in politics. His wife was also born in Wilson County, Tenn., in 1804, and died October 29, 1849. They were the parents of six children: Amanda M., Paralee, David C., John A., Polly A. and Joel H. The paternal grandparents of our subject were both natives of North Carolina, and both born in the year 1768. They died in 1828 and 1842, respectively. The maternal grandparents were natives of South Carolina, and both were born in the year 1771, and the maternal grandfather died in the year 1861. John A. Fields, subject of this sketch, received a fair education in Wilson County, Tenn., and in 1853 moved to Benton County, Ark., where he engaged in the stock business and farming. At the breaking out of the war he joined Gen. Standwatie's command, Arkansas Cavalry, but in 1862 joined Col. Thompson's regiment, Second Arkansas Cavalry, and was made lieutenant of the same, remaining in service until the close of the war. He was at the battles of Neosho, Fayetteville, Ft. Gibson and many other battles. In 1867 he married Miss Mary L. Smith, daughter of William and Mary (Townsend) Smith, natives of Tennessee and Vermont, born in 1818 and 1816, respectively. Mrs. Fields was born in Bradley County, Tenn., December 7, 1848, and by her marriage became the mother of three children: Charles L., Mary E. and Bessie L. Mr. Fields is a Democrat in politics, as were also his father and grandfather; is the owner of 230 acres of land, and he and wife are members of the Methodist Episcopal Church, South.

Dr. James R. Floyd was born near Alexandria, Smith Co., Tenn., September 20, 1860, and is a son of John W. and Eliza J. (Snodgrass) Floyd, who were also natives of Tennessee. The father was a merchant until the beginning of the war, when he enlisted in the Confederate army and served until the close of the war, when he came to Arkansas and engaged in farming. Our subject's paternal grandfather was William Floyd, and his maternal grandfather was James Snodgrass. Both his parents were members of the Methodist Episcopal Church, South. Dr. James R. Floyd was educated in the Bentonville high-school, and took a special course, preparatory to the study of medicine, in the Arkansas State University at Fayetteville, Ark. In 1885–86 he attended the Memphis Hospital Medical College, and was graduated from that institution in 1887. The following article is quoted from the Mississippi Valley *Medical Monthly*: "To J. R. Floyd, of Bentonville, Ark., fell the honor of valedictorian, and the class certainly felt proud of their choice while hearing his valedictory. In phraseology and manner of delivery rare excellence was displayed." Dr. Floyd practiced for a short time with Dr. Hurley, of Bentonville, and then located at Bloomfield, where he has been successfully engaged in practicing his profession for over a year. He is a young man of ability and energy, and has bright prospects for future success.

John H. Ford is one of the oldest native residents and farmers of Benton County, Ark., and was born in 1835. His early educational advantages were exceedingly limited, owing to the fact that there were no schools in the county until he was almost grown, and he then picked up what education he could. In 1853 he lost his father, and he was compelled to work very hard in order to support his mother and her younger children. In 1862 he enlisted in the Federal army, in Company F, Seventy-second Arkansas Regiment, and after serving eleven months went to Springfield, Mo., where he remained until the close of the war. He was in a number of battles and skirmishes, but was so fortunate as to escape without being wounded. He has been engaged in farming all his life, and is now the owner of 240 acres of land, a portion of which he inherited from his father and the rest he had homesteaded. This is one of the most desirable farms in the county, and is under fine cultivation. In 1859 he was married to Miss Elizabeth Lee, who is a native of Benton County, and by her became the father of ten children, eight of whom are living: James A., Mary A., wife of G. W. Reddenck; Polly, wife of T. L. Howell; John W., Delilah, Lee, Joe and Tom. Mr. Ford is a member of the Masonic fraternity, and in his political views supports the principles of the Republican party. His father, Richard Ford, was born in North Carolina, and was a farmer by occupation. He came to Arkansas in 1834, the country abounding in wild game of all kinds at that time. It was a common occurrence to shoot a deer near the door or a wild turkey in a tree in the yard. Panthers and bears were also numerous, and as there were very few settlements at that time, but little attention was given to farming, the most of the settler's time being spent in hunting. The father was one of the first grand jurors of Benton County, and died in 1853. His wife's maiden name was Isabella Logan.

William H. Fry was born in Schuylkill County, Penn., in 1850, and is a son of Henry and Rebecca Van Reed (High) Fry, and grandson of Conrad Fry. Henry Fry was born in Dauphin County, Penn., in 1823, and was there reared and married. About 1848 he began merchandising at Pottsville, Penn., and afterward followed the same calling at Reading, and at the same time was engaged in oil refining and in the milling business. He was a very successful business man, and died in 1872. The last four years of his life he was unable to carry on an extensive business, owing to ill health. His wife was born in Berks County, Penn., in 1827, and is yet living. William H. Fry is the eldest of her five children. He was educated at Reading, and at the Tremont Seminary, at Norristown, Penn., the Kutztown Normal, and took a course in the Commercial Business College at Philadelphia. He clerked in a store in Reading for one year, and in 1873 went to Larned, Kas., where he was engaged in merchandising for five years. Owing to ill health he then abandoned the business and purchased a farm of 400 acres near the town, but sold out in 1887, and came to Benton County, and purchased 102 acres of land east of Bentonville, where he has since made his home. His farm is in a very fine state of cultivation, and he is doing well. In June, 1887, he became a director and stockholder of the People's Bank, at Bentonville, and still retains that position. He is a Republican in politics and his first presidential vote was cast for Grant. He is a Knight Templar Mason. In 1877, he was married to Miss Posie Bowman, a daughter of Jacob and Letitia (Fry) Bowman. Mrs. Fry was born in Greene County, Ill., in 1855, and is the mother of three children: Clara M., Harry R. and Alice B.

C. L. Gibbs, a prosperous hardware merchant of Rogers, Benton Co., Ark., is the fourth of nine children born to Lucas and Electta Gibbs, and was born in the "Bay State" in 1844. His father was reared in Ware, Mass., and was a farmer. C. L. Gibbs, whose name heads this sketch, was reared and educated in Massachusetts, and at the age of twenty-four years resolved to seek his fortune in the West, and first located in Des Moines, Iowa, where he was engaged in the real estate business, in the employ of a railroad company, for several years. He next located in Concordia, Kas., being one of the first settlers of the town, and was engaged in the drug business in that place for twelve years. Here he was married to Mary W. Pratt, a daughter of Dr. Pratt, of Virginia, and Bryce, Virgie and Lettie are their children. The wife died June 18, 1883. In 1880 Mr. Gibbs sold his stock of drugs in Concordia, and moved to Arkansas, being the first man to locate in Rogers, where he has since been a successful hardware merchant. He is a member of the Presbyterian Church, a Republican in politics, and secretary of the Masonic lodge. Mr. Gibbs is always ready to do all in his power to help build up all public enterprises in the town he resides in.

Robert C. Gibbs was born in Callaway County, Mo., April 15, 1832, son of Samuel C. and Charlotta (Kenney) Gibbs. The father was born in Scott County,

Ky., in 1800, was of English descent, and a cousin of Gen. Gibbs, of New Orleans battle fame. He immigrated to Callaway County, Mo., in 1829, and lived there until 1875, when he moved to Audrain, of the same State, and there remained until August, 1880. He was a cabinet-maker by trade, but followed agricultural pursuits most of his life. He was a member of the Old School Baptist Church, as was also his wife, who was born in Scott County, Ky., in 1802, and died in Missouri in 1841. Julius Gibbs, father of Samuel C., was a Virginian by birth, and a pioneer settler of Kentucky, who lived in a block-house. Of the nine children born to Samuel C. Gibbs and wife, Robert C. was the fifth. He was reared on a farm in his native county, and remained with his parents until the age of sixteen, when he was apprenticed to the carpenter's trade, and followed this twenty-eight years. He also owned a farm in Audrain County, and moved to the same in 1853, where he remained until 1881, when he located on his present farm, three miles east of Siloam Springs, which consists of 150 acres, 130 under cultivation, and has since followed farming and stock raising. He was married April 19, 1855, to Miss Sarah E. Kenyon, a native of Pennsylvania, born February 13, 1829, and eight children have been born to them: Infant (deceased), Edgar S., Martha B., Robert O. (deceased), Edward T., Addie (deceased), Annie E. and Herbert E. Mr. Gibbs and wife, and all but the youngest child, are members of the Missionary Baptist Church, of which he is trustee, and the eldest son is a preacher. Politically Mr. Gibbs is a Democrat, and he is a member of the Masonic fraternity. He takes a great interest in public improvements and educational matters, and is a valuable citizen of his community. He was moderator of the Springtown Baptist Association in 1885, and was appointed by Gov. Hughes a member of the Equalization Board of Benton County, in 1886. Mrs. Gibbs' mother, Mrs. Eliza Kenyon, is now living with her son-in-law, Mr. Gibbs, and is over eighty years of age. The Kenyon family has long been noted for zeal in religious matters.

Isaac B. Gilmore, vice-president of the People's Bank of Bentonville, Ark., is a native of McLean County, Ill., born Febuary 23, 1835, and the son of James and Mary (Bradley) Gilmore. The father was born in Pickaway County, Ohio, in 1803, was of Irish descent and a farmer and stock trader by occupation. He resided in his native county and State until 1834, when he immigrated to McLean County, Ill., and here died in 1865. He was a great stock trader, and many times drove cattle through to New York on horseback. His wife, Mary (Bradley) Gilmore, was born in Georgia in 1808 and died in 1875. She was the mother of five sons and five daughters, six of whom are now living. Isaac B. was reared on a farm, and his school advantages were very limited. At the age of six years he went to school all one winter bare-footed, and, as there were no free schools, and his parents were poor, at the age of twenty-six he could not write his name. He was a Union man during the war, and August 7, 1862, he enlisted in Company E, Ninety-fourth Regiment, Illinois Volunteer Infantry, and participated in the following battles: Perry Grove, Vicksburg, Marganzie Bend, Yazoo, Brownsville, Ft. Morgan, Mobile campaign, and others. Mr. Gilmore was first sergeant of his company, and was discharged at Springfield, Ill., August 9, 1865. Previous to the war, in 1860, he married Miss Kate Kane, a native of Bartholomew County, Ind., born in 1842. To them were born seven children: Frank B., cashier of the People's Bank; Vernor S., druggist; John G., Leonard, George, Floy and Birdie. After the war Mr. Gilmore resided in his native State and county until 1869, when he moved to Lawrence County, Mo. On account of the failing health of his wife, Mr. Gilmore returned to his birthplace in 1874, and here resided for three years. He then moved to Caldwell, Kas., and was engaged in the livery business, trading in stock and in farming. For five years he was vice-president of the Exchange Bank of Caldwell. In July, 1887, he became a resident of Bentonville, Ark., purchased a lot and organized the People's Bank at that place, and was elected vice-president. For the past five years Mr. Gilmore has been dealing in stock and real estate and has met with good success. He is a Republican in politics, casting his first presidential ticket for John C. Fremont, and is a member of the G. A. R., Burnside Post No. 4, Bentonville, Ark., being chaplain of the post. He and his wife are members of the Christian Church, he being a member for twenty-eight years, and deacon of the same most of that time.

William E. Gould, of Benton County, Ark., was born in Blount County, Tenn., in 1828, and is a son of John and Jane (Ritchie) Gould, who were born in Tennessee in 1800 and 1809, respectively. The father has always followed the occupation of farming, and in 1859 came to Benton County, Ark. He owns a good farm of 160 acres, and although eighty-eight years of age, has a very retentive memory, remembering with remarkable accuracy facts which occurred seventy-five and eighty years ago. He has been a life-long Democrat, his first presidential vote being cast for Gen. Jackson in 1824. He is well versed in the political history of the United States. He and wife have lived a happy wedded life of sixty-one years, and their children and friends celebrated their diamond wedding in 1887. Both have been earnest and consistent members of the Cumberland Presbyterian Church for over forty-seven years. On the day they were married they resolved that neither would ever drink intoxicating liquors as a beverage, and have faithfully kept their pledge. Seven of their children lived to be grown: William E., Samuel, who died in 1879, at the age of forty-nine years; Levi C.; David N.; Nancy Ann, wife of J. S. Dickson; Narcissa J., wife of Charles Johnson, and Letitia, wife of John Huffman. John Gould's parents were Samuel and Polly (Jackson) Gould, who were born in Ireland and Virginia, in 1766 and 1776, respectively. Samuel Gould immigrated to the United States in 1784, with his father, Robert Gould, who settled in Pennsylvania, but shortly after moved to Tennessee. Samuel was married in 1797, and died in 1835. He was a soldier in the War of 1812. His wife was a daughter of John Jackson, who was born in Ireland, and was a soldier in the Revolutionary War. She died in Henry County, Tenn., in 1842, having borne six children, John being the only one living. William E. Gould served in the late war in Cabbel's brigade, enlisting in 1862, and was at the battles of Prairie Grove, Mark's Mill, Poison Spring, and was with Price on his raid through Missouri. In 1867 he was united in marriage to Miss Elizabeth Patton, who was born in Sevier County in 1842. Seven children have blessed their union: Laura, William E., Robert P., Marcus L., John R., Essie A. and Pearlie C. Mr. Gould was elected to the State Legislature the first session after the war, and served his constituents faithfully and well. He is an indefatigable temperance worker, and a thorough Christian and gentleman. He has been ruling elder in the Cumberland Presbyterian Church for twenty-four years, and has been Sunday-school superintendent for six years.

Graham & Mason. Among the ably edited newspapers of Northwestern Arkansas worthy of especial mention is the Rogers *New Era*, which was established in 1881 by the above named gentlemen, the first issue of their journal being on the 10th of September of that year. James H. Graham, the senior editor, was born in the "Old Dominion" in 1833, and was educated at Crawfordsville, Ind. He has been an active newspaper man ever since 1855, and by profession is a lawyer as well as a journalist. He was married in Illinois to Mrs. Elvina J. Mason, *nee* Falkenburg, the mother of F. A. Mason, of the Rogers *New Era*. To Mr. Graham she has borne three children, two of whom are living: Fannie J. and Flora E. Mr. Graham is a stanch Democrat, and he and wife are members of the Methodist Episcopal Church, South. F. A. Mason was born in the State of New York in 1852, and has been a journalist nearly all his life. He was married in Missouri to Miss Hattie Acres, who has borne him eight children, seven now living: Oscar H., Edgar F., Wesley A., Don A., Robbie R., Nellie and Alice. Mr. Mason is a Democrat.

Sebe Graham is a farmer residing ten miles southeast of Bentonville, Ark., and is a native of the county, born January 24, 1844. His parents, Ellis and Rebecca (Graham) Graham, were born in Kentucky and Illinois, respectively. The former's birth occurred about 1803. He came with his parents to Arkansas when quite young and located on White River. He and wife became the parents of two children: Charity, married to William H. Lewis, a farmer living in Benton County, and Sebe. The latter was reared in his native county, and at the breaking out of the war enlisted in the Confederate army, being then but sixteen years of age. He participated in the battles of Wilson's Creek, Pea Ridge, Prairie Grove, Newtonia and many other engagements of minor importance. After he was honorably discharged at the close of the war he returned home and engaged in farming, and by industry and good management is now the owner of 1,400 acres of land, 1,000 of which is under cultivation. In 1873 he was united in matrimony to Susan E. White, a native of Benton County, Ark., and their union has resulted in the birth of seven children: Albert, Rebecca, Emlis, Joseph, Lucinda A., James Ellis and Millard J.

William B. Gray is a native of Fort Scott, Kas., born October 14, 1862, and is the son of Lee and Catherine (Schoeler) Gray. The father was born in Washington County, Penn., lived there until grown, and there received a good education. When not attending school he clerked in his father's store. He left that State in 1858. and settled in Jasper County, Mo. Catherine (Schoeler) Gray was born in Knox County, Ohio, and there lived until fifteen or sixteen years of age, when her parents immigrated to Jasper County, Mo. She was also well educated, and after coming to Missouri devoted her time to teaching school, which she continued until the breaking out of the war (1861), when she married Mr. Gray. She died December 8, 1862, leaving one child, William B. Mr. Gray had, previous to his wife's death, immigrated to Kansas, and in that State followed farming for some time. He here married his second wife, Mrs. Welch, and by her became the father of five children: Tussie, Jesse, Wesley, Leslie and Maud, all now living. After a few years of farmer's life Mr. Gray ventured into the newspaper business, which he followed for about a year, when he again returned to farm life. Since then he has lived on his farm three miles from Fort Scott, Kas. William B. Gray, after his mother's death, was taken by his grandparents, and was by them reared. From the age of seven to fourteen he was in the school-room, after which time he was put to work on the farm in the summer, but attended school in the winter until eighteen years of age. He then began the battle of life for himself by renting land of his uncle and in following agricultural pursuits. August 4, 1883, he married Miss Eliza Myers, daughter of Noah and Mary Myers, of Jasper County, Mo., but natives of Indiana. They moved from the last named State to Jasper County, Mo., where Mrs. Gray was born. She bore her husband two children, one now living, Isaac M. The one deceased was named Lee B. Since coming to Benton County Mr. Gray has been engaged in farming and stock raising, and although a young man has a farm of 160 acres, eighty being under cultivation, and his prospects are bright for a happy and prosperous future. Since coming to Arkansas he has rented his own land, and has been living on his grandfather's farm, acting as his agent. He is a strong Republican in his political views, yet has never voted for a presidential candidate.

Elisha Green, ex-lumber merchant and contractor, of Bentonville, Ark., is a native of Watauga County, N. C., born in 1828, son of Amos and Sena (Estes) Green, and a great-grandson of Richard Green, who was a native of New Jersey, was a soldier in the Revolutionary War, and a distant relative of Senator James Green, of the State of Missouri. Amos Green was born in Watauga County, N. C., in 1804, was of English descent and a farmer by occupation. He died in 1871. His wife, Sena Estes, was born in 1807, and is also a native of Watauga County, N. C. She is yet living, and is the mother of nine children: Myra (deceased), Elisha, Lot (deceased), Elijah, Loana (widow of Henry Henry), John E., Joseph and Benjamin (twins), and Polly (wife of C. D. Herman). Elisha was reared on a farm and remained and assisted his parents until twenty-one years of age. In 1848 he married Miss Elizabeth Brown, who was born in Watauga County, N. C., in 1828, and who bore him two children: Mary (deceased) and Henry (also deceased). In 1861 Mr. Green enlisted in Company D, First North Carolina Cavalry (Confederate States Army), and was in the second Manassas, Antietam, Fredericksburg, Gettysburg, and also participated in numerous skirmishes. He was captured at the battle of Malvern Hill, and was taken to Governor's Island, and two weeks later to Delaware Bay, where he remained three weeks and was then exchanged. He surrendered at Appomattox Court House with Gen. Lee, in Stuart's cavalry. In 1867 he moved to Chariton County, Mo., and worked at the carpenter's trade for several years in that county. In 1882 he moved to Bentonville, Ark., and here contracted for four years. He erected many of the prominent business houses and upward of twenty dwelling houses, also erected a number of buildings in other counties. In 1886 he purchased the lumber yard of L. Ketchum, in Bentonville, and was proprietor of the same until February, 1888, when he sold to J. A. C. Blackburn. Mr. Green is now engaged in erecting two brick business blocks, having resumed contracting since selling the lumber yard. Previous to the war Mr. Green was a Whig, but since that event he has been a Democrat in his political views. His first vote for President was cast for Fillmore, in 1852. He was deputy sheriff of his native county for many years, and was coroner for two years. He was justice of the peace for thirteen years in Chariton County, Mo., and is a member of the Masonic fraternity.

Judge Alfred Burton Greenwood. Prominent among the old and much respected citizens of Benton County, Ark., stands the name of Judge Alfred Burton Greenwood, who was born in Franklin County, Ga., in 1811, son of Hugh B. and Elizabeth (Ingram) Greenwood. The father was born in North Carolina. was of Irish descent, and a carpenter and cabinet-maker by trade. He went to Virginia when a young man, was there married, and soon after immigrated to Franklin County, Ga. Later he moved to Lawrenceville, Ga., where he died, August, 1825. Mrs. Elizabeth (Ingram) Greenwood was born in Mecklenburg, Va., and died in 1838. They were the parents of five children, the subject of this sketch being the eldest. He was educated at Lawrenceville. Ga., and at the age of eighteen became a disciple of Blackstone, his preceptor being William Izzard, and was admitted to the bar at Monroe, Ga., in 1832. He immediately located at Decatur, De Kalb Co., Ga., and there continued until 1838, when he immigated to Bentonville, Ark., where he located, and where he resumed his practice. In 1833 Judge Greenwood married Miss Sarah A. Hilburn, who was born in Union District, S. C., in 1819, and twelve children were the result of this union, eight of whom lived to maturity: Mrs. Mary Hollingsworth, Mrs. Sophia A. Black, George (deceased), Mrs. Georgia A. Arrington (widow of John A. Arrington), John, Mrs. Sarah A. (widow of V. M. Lassater), Alfred W., and William (deceased). In 1846 Judge Greenwood was elected by the State Legislature as prosecuting attorney, and represented ten counties in Northwest Arkansas. In 1848 he was elected to the same office by the people, and re-elected in 1850. In 1852 he was elected circuit judge of the Fourth Judicial Circuit of the State of Arkansas, which composed ten counties, or the same he represented as prosecuting attorney. In 1853 he resigned as circuit judge, and was nominated to Congress from the First Congressional District, which comprised all territory north of Arkansas River, or about thirty counties, there being but two districts at that time in the State. Soon after his nomination Judge Greenwood threw up his judgeship and entered the canvass. At the November election he was elected by a majority of about 10,000. He was re-elected in 1854 and 1856, and served in all six years. In 1858 Judge Greenwood was appointed by President Buchanan as commissioner of Indian affairs, and held the office during the remainder of Buchanan's administration. While commissioner of Indian affairs the Secretary of the Interior, Jacob Thompson, resigned, and Judge Greenwood was tendered the position, but declined to accept the office. During the war he was appointed by Jefferson Davis Confederate tax collector of the State of Arkansas, and during the month of December, 1864, he collected over $2,000,000, being located at Washington, Hempstead Co., Ark. Since the war the Judge has devoted his time and attention to the practice of law. He is the oldest resident citizen of Benton County, and the oldest member of the Benton County bar. He came to this county when the county seat contained only thirty people, and during his residence here has witnessed its growth and development. He was continuously in office for over twenty years, and during all that time his official as well as private life was above reproach, thus forcibly illustrating his marked ability as an able and efficient public officer. He is a Democrat in politics, and has gained a national reputation, being one of the most influential men in Northwest Arkansas. September, 1884, Judge Greenwood lost his wife, and since then his two daughters, Mrs. Lassater and Mrs. Arrington, have been making their home with him. During his congressional career he served with Vice-president Hendricks, Charles Sumner, John Scott Harrison, father of ex-Senator Benjamin Harrison, John C. Breckenridge, etc. He is a charter member of the Masonic fraternity, and is a member of the Methodist Episcopal Church, South, of which he was a steward for several years.

Lucien E. Griggs was born in Butler County, Ohio, in 1852, and is a son of J. A. and Eliza Griggs, who were natives of the "Green Mountain State." The mother died in 1854, leaving one child, but the father is still living, and resides in Kansas. Lucien E. Griggs was reared principally in Illinois, and from early boyhood was engaged in the saw-mill business, and was also engaged in manufacturing railroad ties. He was married while in Illinois to Eurene Dyer, who was born in Illinois in 1856, and by her is the father of three children: Sadie, Lulu and Eddie L. E. Mr. Griggs became a resident of Dakota in 18—, and after a residence there of two years, came to Arkansas and purchased his present home and engaged in the railroad tie business. Mr. Griggs has a fine orchard of apple and peach trees, and during their season has large quantities of raspberries and strawberries. Mrs. Griggs is a granddaughter of V. Dyer, of Chicago, Ill.

C. D. Gunter, post-office Hico. Among the old and time-honored citizens of Benton County, Ark., stands the name of C. D. Gunter, who was born in Middle Tennessee, March 30, 1818. He is a son of John and Lavina (Thomasson) Gunter. The father was born near Pleasant Gardens, N. C., and was of Dutch descent. He moved to Tennessee, was there married and there remained until 1825, when he went to Alabama. He died in this State in 1854. The mother was born in Tennessee, and died several years previous to her husband. They were the parents of ten children: Telitha T. (deceased), Augustus, now living at Bridgeport, Ala.; William T. (deceased), C. D., Louisa (deceased), Edith (deceased), Col. Thomas M., lawyer and ex-congressman of Fayetteville; Milton D. (deceased), Pearl H. (deceased), and an infant unnamed. C. D. Gunter was reared to farm life, and received a meager education in Alabama. In the autumn of 1839 Mr. Gunter left Alabama and traveled through Missouri, Arkansas and Texas, but finally settled in Benton County, Ark., where he now lives. In 1845 he married Miss Nancy Ward, who was born in Georgia, and immigrated to the Cherokee Nation when a child. Here she grew to womanhood. She is of Cherokee descent on her father's side, and her mother was a native of South Carolina. Mr. and Mrs. Gunter became the parents of nine living children: Ann Eliza, wife of Gaither Chandler; Lavina, wife of L. L. Duckworth; Lucy Jane, wife of Dr. Fortner; John T., farmer and liveryman; Amanda O., wife of David Mars; Lula, wife of William Curtis; Anna, wife of Samuel Frazier; Nancy, Augusta and Cal. Dean. During the late war Mr. Gunter espoused the cause of the Confederacy and enlisted in the Arkansas troops under Gen. Pierce. He was afterward under the command of Gen. Hindman. He was in the engagement at Oak Hill, besides numerous skirmishes. Mr. Gunter is Democratic in his political views, and his first presidential vote was cast for Van Buren. He is a member of the Masonic order. He is the owner of between 900 and 1,000 acres of land situated around Siloam Springs.

Rev. Isom R. Hall, pastor of Pleasant Grove and Shady Grove Churches, in Benton and Washington Counties, respectively, and senior member of the lumber firm of Hall, Guthrie & Co., of Bentonville, is a native of Dawson County, Ga., born 1835, and the son of Isom and Nancy (Arnold) Hall. Isom Hall, Sr., was born in North Carolina in 1804, and was a Missionary Baptist minister and a farmer by occupation. When but a lad he moved to South Carolina with his father, John Hall, and here grew to manhood. He was here married, and in 1826 he moved to Georgia, and from there in 1851 to Conway County, Ark. He died in 1886, having followed his ministerial duties the principal part of his life. His wife, Mrs. Nancy (Arnold) Hall, was born in South Carolina in 1814, and died in 1852. She was the mother of ten children, two now living. Isom Hall, Jr., was educated in Georgia and Arkansas, coming to the last named State with his mother's parents in 1851. In 1859 he married Miss Sarah J. Hankins, a native of Tennessee, Roane County, born 1842, and the daughter of Joseph and Cassandra (Jones) Hall. After marriage Mr. and Mrs. Hall located in Conway County, Ark., and in 1874 they moved to Benton County, and located five miles south of the county seat, where they purchased 240 acres of land. Here they remained until the spring of 1888, when he removed to Bentonville, and is living there at the present time. Mr. Hall is now the owner of 360 acres. He was one of the organizers of the People's Bank, of Bentonville, and is one of the stockholders and one of the directors of the same. June 15, 1888, he and G. W. Guthrie bought the lumber yard of J. A. C. Blackburn, in Bentonville, and they now have the lumber trade of the town. They carry a large stock, and are meeting with good success. Rev. Hall entered the ministry in 1871. He advocated the Missionary doctrine, and had charge of four churches in Benton County up to the present year, when he resigned two of them. During his time he has married and baptized as many people as any other minister of his knowledge. He studied medicine from 1859 to 1865. He is a thorough Christian and an excellent citizen. He is a member of the Masonic fraternity.

David R. Hammer, mayor of Siloam Springs, Ark., was born in Champaign County, Ill., March 10, 1840, and is a son of Daniel and Polly Ann (Childers) Hammer. The former was born in Tennessee in 1807, and was reared and educated in Ohio. He learned the cooper's trade after he was grown, and moved to Illinois, where he was married about 1830. He removed to Iowa about 1849 and

****

followed the occupations of farming and coopering. He died in Des Moines about 1869. His wife was born in Ohio, and died in 1843, having borne five children : Nancy Jane (deceased), Elizabeth A., Polly Ann, David R. and Charity A., wife of William M. Moore. After his wife's death Mr. Hammer married Mrs. Mary A. (Shepherd) Littler. She was born in 1807 in Ohio, and became the mother of five children by her first husband, and one by Mr. Hammer: John J., a minister living in Wisconsin, David, Laban (deceased), Henry, Anna (deceased) and Martha J. Hammer, the wife of R. E. Barrickman. David R. Hammer was taken to Iowa when he was about seven years of age, and was educated in the common schools of that State. He was married in Warren County, February 18, 1860, to Phoebe A. Smith, a native of Belmont, Ohio, born November 27, 1840. Her grandparents were Georgians, and located in Ohio during the early history of that State. Mrs. Hammer is the mother of one child, Alkanzer H., who is a barber, living in Siloam Springs. In 1861 Mr. Hammer enlisted in the Union army in Company B, Tenth Iowa Infantry, and after serving nine months was discharged on account of disability. He lived in Iowa until 1887, when he moved to Western Texas, where he was engaged in merchandising for two years; then went to Kansas, remaining the same length of time. Since that time he was engaged in merchandising in Siloam Springs for one year, and is now engaged in the real estate business. He has been elected mayor three different times. He is a Republican and Mason.

Hon. David H. Hammons, senator of the Twenty-fourth Senatorial District, which comprises Benton and Madison Counties, of the State of Arkansas, and a successful physician, is a native of Cooper County, Mo., born in 1836, son of Harbard and Elizabeth (Plemmons) Hammons, and grandson of George W. Hammons. Harbard Hammons was a native of Warren County, Tenn., of Scotch descent, and was a farmer by occupation. He immigrated to Cooper County, Mo., with his father when a young man; was married here, but afterward settled in Newton County, of the same State. He died near California, Mo., in 1840, at the age of thirty-eight. Elizabeth (Plemmons) Hammons was a native of North Carolina, born in 1804, and was of German-Irish descent. She died in 1849. Their family consisted of seven children, David H. being the fifth. He received the rudiments of an education in the common schools of Carroll County, but received the greater part of his education by private instruction, under the tutorship of Prof. George W. Pattison. At the age of seventeen Mr. Hammons began teaching, and followed this profession for about five years. About 1858 he began the study of law, and in 1861 was admitted to the bar at Carrollton, Mo., his preceptor being Hon. B. D. Lucas. In the spring of 1859 he, in company with his two brothers and a cousin, went to Pike's Peak on a mining excursion, but he returned in the fall, and in the May following married Miss Fanny Lucas, daughter of 'Squire B. D. Lucas, who was a native of North Carolina. This union resulted in the birth of four children, one living, May. Mrs. Hammons died in 1872, and in 1873 Mr. Hammons married Mrs. Sallie Hamnett, nee Lowry, daughter of Thomas Lowry, and a native of Kentucky. Two children were born to this marriage, Lena and David H. After being admitted to the bar Mr. Hammons immediately began practicing at DeWitt, and at the breaking out of the war he enlisted for six months in the State service, and at the end of that time re-enlisted for six months longer. April, 1862, he enlisted in Company H, Sixth Regiment Missouri Infantry, Confederate army, and was in service until the surrender. He was in the battles of Carthage, Wilson Creek, Dry Wood, Lexington, Pea Ridge, siege and subsequent battle of Corinth, Iuka, Grand Gulf, Fort Gibson, Champion Hills, Big Black, and was also in the Georgia campaign. He was captured near Vicksburg, but was retained only two days, and at the battle of Pea Ridge he was slightly wounded. He enlisted as a private, but was promoted from rank to rank until he became captain of his company, receiving the last-named rank after the battle of Franklin. After this battle he was taken sick, and was left at Tuscumbia, Tenn., where he remained until after hostilities had ceased. He then located in Carroll County, Mo., and the next year went to Bedford, Livingston County, where he began the practice of medicine, having studied the same after the war, and where he continued to practice medicine, owing to the fact that the law prohibited all attorneys who had served in the Confederate army from practicing or holding office. About 1876 Capt. Hammons graduated as an M. D. from St. Louis Medical College, and practiced for about four years more. As soon as the law was repealed regarding his attorneyship, he again took up the practice of law. In 1875 he went to Chariton County, Mo., and farmed here until 1880, but in 1878 he was elected to the Legislature from the last named county. He removed to Bentonville, Ark., in 1880, and since then has devoted his time and attention to his profession, the law. In 1886 he was elected State senator, and served on judiciary committee and circuit and inferior courts, on education, county and county lines, claims, etc. He is a member of the Masonic fraternity, having taken nine degrees, Royal Arch Council Degree, and he, his wife and eldest daughter are members of the Methodist Episcopal Church, South.

James Haney, builder and contractor, of Bentonville, was born in the Kings County, Ireland, in 1837, and is the son of Thomas and Mary (Madden) Haney. Thomas Haney was born in 1807, and was a farmer by occupation. He died in Middleton, Lancashire, England, in 1884, having moved there in 1845. His wife, Mary Madden, was born in 1819, and died in 1883. They were the parents of nine children, James Haney being the third child. He was educated in England, and at the age of thirteen became errand boy in a cotton mill. After a short time he was put to spinning cotton, but worked at this but a short time, the work not being to his liking. After about a year and a half he left it, and commenced working at the brick, stone and carpenter's trade; this he followed for about three and a half years, as an apprentice, and then ran away. He did not return for a year, and when he did he was arrested and given the choice of returning to his trade or going to jail. He chose the former, and worked three and a half years longer. He then joined the Trades and Benevolent Union at Manchester, and served in every capacity except corresponding secretary. He was bank trustee of the society in 1860, but resigned this position, and immigrated to the United States. During the war he was in various States of the Union, and after peace was declared and business began to assume its original condition, Mr. Haney settled in St. Louis, and worked at his trade. In 1869 he went to Springfield, Mo., and in 1871 he became a citizen of Bentonville, Ark., where he has since resided. He has erected the largest number of the best business houses in the town, and has succeeded well at his business. When he first came to Bentonville he had $7 in money, but by his honesty and close attention to business he has accumulated a good property. In 1885 he erected a good business block, and in 1887 he put up the second one; both blocks belong to him. Mr. Haney is a skillful workman, and a man who has been of much use to the city of Bentonville. In 1859 he married Miss Mary Adams, who was born in County Mayo, Ireland, in 1841, and who became the mother of nine children: John, who is living in Kansas City, and is a brick mason by trade; Eliza; Thomas F., who is a brick mason in Carthage, Mo.; William W., cadet at West Point; Charles D., Kate, Ada, James A. and George. Mr. Haney was a member of the city council of Bentonville for a year; was also street commissioner for five or six years; is a Democrat in politics; is a member of the I. O. O. F., and he and wife are members of the Roman Catholic Church.

Raphiel W. Hansard, photographer, of Bentonville, was born in Knox County, Tenn., in 1838, son of Samuel H. and Armenia L. (Weir) Hansard, and grandson of William Hansard, who was a native of Virginia, was a farmer and miller by occupation, owning a mill on Bull Run Creek, and was a soldier in the Revolutionary War. He died in 1845 at the age of eighty-three years. Samuel H. was born in Knox County, Tenn., and was a tiller of the soil. He moved to Polk County, Mo., in 1846, and in a few years moved to Cedar County, where he was killed in his own house by the State Militia, in 1863. His wife, Armenia L. Weir, was born in Knox County, Tenn., in 1816, and was of French-Irish extraction. Her death occurred in 1864. She was the mother of eleven children, nine of whom are now living. Raphiel W. Hansard was but a small boy when his parents moved to Missouri, and was educated in the schools of that State. He attained his growth on the farm, and at the age of twenty years commenced teaching and followed that occupation for five terms in Missouri and two terms in Arkansas. April, 1861, he enlisted in Company A, Third Regiment Missouri Cavalry, under Gen. Price, in the State Guards. In 1862, while at Cane Hill, he enlisted in Jackman's company, but later he enlisted in Company C, Third Regiment Cavalry, under Gen. Shelby. He was in the battles of Wilson's Creek, Dry Wood, Lexington, Marks' Mill and a great many skirmishes. He surrendered at Shreveport, La., June, 1865. He entered as a private, but in 1863 he was made third lieutenant of Company C. After the war Mr. Hansard located in Lawrence County, Mo., and commenced learning photography in July, 1866, at Verona. He took up the business on his own ingenuity, only being taught how to make a few pictures by his brother, J. W. Hansard. In November, 1866, Mr. Hansard became a resident of Bentonville, established a gallery and has since continued at the business. In 1867 he married Mrs. Sarah C. Railey, *nee* Fergusson, daughter of John N. Fergusson. Mrs. Hansard was born in Marion County, Mo., April 26, 1842, and by her marriage became the mother of three children: Ida L., Armenia May and Author R. Mrs. Hansard has two children by a former marriage: Edward A. Railey and Laura, wife of W. V. Steel. Mr. Hansard is a first-class artist, and was the only one in Bentonville until a year ago. He thoroughly understands the science and art of photography, and makes pictures equal to any outside of Little Rock. He does all kinds of enlarging, and not only has a reputation at home, but abroad as well, as being a first-class artist, but his work speaks for itself. Mr. Hansard was coroner of Benton County two years, was alderman in Bentonville two terms, is a member of the I. O. O. F., is a member of the Cumberland Presbyterian Church, and he is Democratic in his political views.

Edmond Lambeth Hart, an old and highly esteemed citizen of Benton County, Ark., was born in Davidson County, N. C., in 1817, and is a son of Henry and Barbara (Lambeth) Hart. The father was of Scotch-Irish descent, and was born near Newbern, N. C., about 1780, and was a farmer by occupation. He was also a soldier in the War of 1812, and was in the battles of Horse Shoe Bend, Natchez and New Orleans. In 1829 he located in Bedford County, Tenn., and in 1852 immigrated to Christian County, Mo., where he died about seven years later. His wife was born in North Carolina, and died in 1867. She was the mother of ten children, our subject being the eldest in the family. When he was twelve years of age he moved to Tennessee with his parents, and was reared to manhood in that State. As he was the oldest in the family, and his parents were poor, he was compelled to assist in providing for the family, consequently his educational advantages were very limited, three months being the extent of his school days. While in his native State, at the early age of eight years, he worked in a gold mine, and after moving to Tennessee he was employed as a farm laborer, receiving for his services $8 per month. He worked thus for six years, the proceeds of his labor being given to his parents. April 4, 1839, he was married to Nancy Johnson Moore, a daughter of James and Mary (Murray) Moore, who were North Carolinians. Mrs. Hart was born December 20, 1820, in Bedford County, Tenn., and became the mother of ten children: James H., Harriet E., wife of John Dereberry; Jane E., wife of John Lechliter; Councel L.; Mary F., wife of Benjamin Oakley; George W.; Rebecca A., the deceased wife of James Bird; Louis R. K.; Sarah T., wife of George Duckworth, and Robert F. Mr. Hart came to Benton County, Ark., in 1850, where he became one of the wealthy land holders of the county. He now owns 228 acres, besides giving his children eighty acres of land each. He was a Union man during the war, is independent in politics, and is a Master Mason. He and wife have been members of the Christian Church for many years.

Councel Lambeth Hart, farmer and stock trader of Benton County, Ark., was born in Bedford County, Tenn., in 1848, and is a son of Edmond L. Hart, whose sketch precedes this. At the age of twelve years he was taken to Benton County, Ark., and was here reared to manhood. In 1873 he was married to Miss Nancy E. Caldwell, a daughter of Joshua and Sarah (Alexander) Caldwell. Mrs. Hart was born in Benton County in 1857, and is the mother of eight children: John P., Mary A., Cora B., Evaline, Harden, Jennie May, Edmond L. and Jesse Lambeth. In 1873 Mr. Hart located on his present farm, and in 1882 erected a frame dwelling house at a cost of $973. He is now the owner of 200 acres of land, and for the past fourteen years he has been engaged in stock-dealing. He at first bought and sold stock on commission, but for several years past he has been buying and selling on his own account, shipping to St. Louis. Mr. Hart has bought and sold more stock than any other man in Benton County, and is an excellent judge of stock of all kinds. He is a Democrat in politics, and is a member of the Masonic fraternity. At the present time he is deputy sheriff under F. P. Galbraith.

Capt. T. T. Hays, a prosperous farmer of Benton County, Ark., is a son of John and Lydia (Sims) Hays, who were Virginians and early immigrants to Tennessee. After moving to Alabama and residing there a short time they returned to Tennessee, where the father died. He was a soldier in the War of 1812. The mother's death occurred in Arkansas. Capt. T. T. Hays was born in Alabama in 1825, and was reared in Tennessee. He was married in the latter State to Mary E. Hutchinson, and their union resulted in the birth of seven children: William A., James P., Sarah E., Martha J., Thomas J., Virgil and Maurice. The Captain removed with his family to Arkansas in 1860, and the following May organized the first infantry company in Benton County. After that company was disbanded he organized a company of cavalry for the Confederate service, and served as its captain until he was disabled by inflammatory rheumatism. At the time of Lee's surrender he was at Marshall, Tex., and after peace was declared he returned to Arkansas, purchased his present farm of 160 acres, and has since been engaged in tilling the soil. Besides this farm he owns a number of lots in Bright Water. He is a member of the Christian Church, and supports the principles of the Democratic party.

Kenneth M. Head, of Batie Township, Benton Co., Ark., and son of Joseph and Elizabeth (Nix) Head, was born June 15, 1839, in Rutherford County, N. C. Joseph Head was also a native of the same county, and was a millwright, a carpenter and a cabinet-maker by trade. As a millwright he was considered by all as an expert, and although owning a farm in North Carolina, he left that for his sons to manage, and devoted his time to his trade. He built some of the most extensive grist and saw mills in that country. January 5, 1855, he moved to Arkansas. His wife, Mrs. Elizabeth (Nix) Head, was also born in Rutherford County, N. C., was married in 1827, and became the mother of nine children, six now living: Anderson, of North Carolina; Kenneth M., Mrs. Hester Davis, Mrs. Maria Strain, Harvey M. and Joseph. Those deceased were named Amanda, Alphia and Baylis. Mr. Head, as before stated, moved to Arkansas in 1855, settled in Washington County, and there remained until 1862, when he was taken prisoner by the United States troops and sent to Springfield, where he died the same year. The mother continued to live on the old place until 1882, when she, too, passed away at the age of seventy-two. Philip Head, grandfather of Kenneth M., was born and reared in Pennsylvania, and there married Miss Mary Tanner, grandmother of Kenneth M. A remarkable incident is connected with the life of the grandmother. After her marriage and coming to North Carolina she pulled up a walnut sprout and set it out in the yard. Years passed by and it became a large tree. Two years before her death the tree was struck by lightning, and at her request was made into a coffin, in which she was buried two years later. She was then in her eighty-second year. The grandparents Nix were both of Irish descent, and the grandfather was ninety-two years of age when he died. Kenneth Head was but fourteen years of age when he left North Carolina for Arkansas, and received his entire education in the former State, never attending school after coming to Arkansas. They made the trip overland from North Carolina to Arkansas, and were two months and five days on the journey. They settled in Washington County, and began clearing a farm. The nearest church or school was five miles distant, consequently his educational advantages were rather meager. At the breaking out of the late war Mr. Head enlisted in Company K, Twenty-second Arkansas Confederate troops, under Col. King, and during his service was in several battles: Prairie Grove, Helena, Jenkins' Ferry, and surrendered at Fort Smith. He returned home after the war and remained with his mother, being the whole support of the family until December, 13, 1868, when he married Miss Cannie Mullins, daughter of Leland and Millie Mullins, who were natives of Kentucky and South Carolina, respectively. Her father was fifteen years old before he had a hat. Cannie Mullins was born in Lawrence County, Mo., and moved to Madison County, Ark., where she married Mr. Head. To their union were born seven children, five now living: Fannie C., Sarah, Martha, Joseph and Walter. The two deceased were named Mary and Julia Cleveland. Mr. Head continued to live in Washington County, Ark., until about 1883, when he moved to Benton County, of the same State, here purchased a farm of 200 acres, 100 under cultivation, and here he has since made his home. He is a member of the Masonic fraternity, and is a Democrat in politics, having cast his first presidential vote for Breckinridge, and his last for Grover Cleveland. Mrs. Head at heart is a Methodist, but still has never connected herself with any church, yet living a true Christian life. Mr. Head believes strongly in the Quaker faith.

John G. Heath (deceased) was a farmer three-fourths of a mile from Siloam

Springs, Hico Township, and was born in Cable County, W. Va., February 14, 1829, a son of Richard B. and Sarah (Jordan) Heath. The father was a native Virginian, born in 1803, and his father, Israel Heath, was of English descent, his mother of Scotch-Irish. The father was a soldier in the War of 1812. Richard H. Heath was reared and educated in the common schools of Virginia, and was married in 1823 to Miss Sarah Jordan. He dealt in stock until 1836, when he moved with his family to Warsaw, Benton Co., Mo. After remaining in this county for about four years he moved to Dade County, where he engaged in merchandising and farming. He lived here for about three years, and then moved to Red River County, Tex. At the end of one year he left here, and made his home in Cass County, where he remained eleven years engaged in farming. In 1853 he removed to Hill County, where he spent the remainder of his life. He died in 1873. His wife was born about 1808 in Virginia, and her parents were also native Virginians. Mrs. Heath died in 1875. They were the parents of thirteen children: James (deceased), America, John G. (deceased), Webster, Frederick, Spencer, Daniel, George W., Thomas, Peter (deceased), Fannie (deceased), Mattie (deceased) and Elizabeth (deceased). John G. Heath, the subject of this sketch, lived on a farm in Virginia until eight years old, and in 1850 went to California, where he remained three years. In 1854 he married Miss Sarah Kilgore, who was born in Virginia in 1839, her parents being natives of the same State. To them were born six children: Walter (a farmer), Ada (wife of J. E. Porter, a farmer), Alice (wife of J. T. Gunter), an infant that died unnamed, William Henry and Jennie. In 1856 Mr. Heath moved to Bosque County, Tex., and in 1863 he enlisted in the Confederate service, and remained until the close of hostilities. He was stationed on the frontier of Texas, under command of Capt. Whiteside, Col. McCord's regiment. In 1866 he removed with his family to Benton County, Ark., where he resided up to his decease, which occurred at 4 o'clock in the afternoon of November 15, 1888, caused by Bright's disease and consumption. There were but four or five families on Lindsay's Prairie when he first came to this county. Mr. Heath was the owner of 420 acres of land, besides town property in Siloam Springs. In politics he was a Democrat, and cast his first presidential vote for Buchanan. He was a prominent and influential citizen, and was interested in everything pertaining to the development and prosperity of his section of the county and State.

A. T. Hedges, of Batie Township, was born in Bartholomew County, Ind., February 16, 1826, and is the son of Samuel M. and Martha (Mitchell) Hedges. The father was born in the District of Columbia, and lived there until a man. He was reared on a farm, educated in the common schools, and his first wife was a Miss Browner, who bore him two children, one now living, Merideth B. Hedges. The one deceased was named Robert. The mother of these children died in Virginia, and Mr. Hedges then married Martha Griffith, and by her became the father of five children, only one, Ambrose T., now living. Ignatius, Elizabeth and Mary K. and another are deceased. At the time of her marriage with Mr. Hedges Mrs. Griffith was a widow and the mother of one child, Henry J., who was educated at West Point, and after graduation received a lieutenant's commission. While in the service during the Rebellion he was drowned at Rock Island, where he was buried by the Government. After his second marriage S. M. Hedges immigrated to Kentucky, leaving his comfortable home in the east for one of privation and hardship in that wild and unsettled west. Here he remained for seven or eight years, and then moved to Bartholomew County, Ind., where he purchased land, and there remained until A. T. was about twelve years old. They then moved to Missouri, where they remained for about six years, and then started for Texas, but on the way stopped for a short time in Benton County, Ark. They continued their journey to Texas, and were in that State before it was admitted into the Union. They did not tarry long in this State, but in 1844 returned to Benton County, Ark., and here the father died in 1867. The mother had died previously while the family were living in Missouri. Their son, A. T. Hedges, at the time of coming to Arkansas was eighteen years of age, and until that time lived with his parents, although depending on his own work and his own resources for a means of living. He secured a fair education, and in 1853 he married Miss Eliza J. Denton, daughter of John Denton, who was from Missouri. Two children were born to this union, one now living, Child S., and Elenora M. After his marriage Mr. Hedges continued to make his home on the old farm, where he has lived for forty-four years. He was among the few first white settlers of the county, and the Indians were still quite numerous. There was a school and church building in the neighborhood, but little attention was paid to either, school being taught on the subscription plan. During the war Mr. Hedges enlisted in Capt. Hendren's company of volunteers, in the Indian brigade, under Col. Standwatie, and served from 1863 until the close of the war in the Confederate service. He was in the Fayette fight and numerous other encounters. Mr. Hedges is a member of the Masonic fraternity, of which he has been a member for thirty-five years, being one of the oldest in this section of the country. He has ever taken an interest in all public affairs, such as schools, churches, etc., and politically is a strong Democrat, always voting the Democratic ticket, for Pierce and the same ticket down to Grover Cleveland. His only son, Child Hedges, has always lived with his father, and was educated in the common schools. At the age of twenty-seven he married Cynthia A. Torbutt, daughter of J. O. Torbutt, of Benton County, Ark. To this marriage have been born three children, two now living, Maud and Parra. The one deceased was named Grover Cleveland. Since his marriage Mr. Hedges has lived on the home place, engaged in agricultural pursuits and in stock raising. He, like his father, is a Democrat in politics. He and his father are the owners of 700 acres of land, 500 under cultivation.

Anderson Herman was born in Pennsylvania October 22, 1839, and is a son of Daniel and Nancy (Wirts) Herman, who were also born in the "Keystone State." The father's birth occurred about 1804, and in the autumn of 1855 he went to Illinois, and there died in 1880. His wife also died in Illinois, in December, 1887. They were the parents of twelve children: Henry, John, Harriet (wife of Lucius Flory), William, Anderson, Sarah (wife of Norman Pringle), Alexander (deceased), Abner, Margaret (deceased), Winfield Scott, and two children who died in infancy. Anderson Herman went to Illinois with his parents in 1855, and made his home there until January, 1888, when he came to Arkansas and purchased 200 acres of land in Benton County. His farm is finely situated, and is well cultivated. Mr. Herman is a Democrat politically, and is a member of the I. O. O. F. Mr. Herman was married in 1863 to Miss Louisa Sturgis, who was born in Illinois. Seven children have blessed their union: John William (married, and living in Arkansas), Charles Henry (at home), Mary Alice (married to William A. Deardoff, a farmer living in Illinois), James (deceased), Albert, Leonard and Tilden.

Robert A. Hickman, hardware merchant, of Bentonville, Ark., and a member of the firm of Hickman & Maxwell, was born in Monroe County, Tenn., in 1839, and is the son of James and Ann (Daniels) Hickman. The father was born in East Tennessee in 1801, and was a carpenter by trade, but in connection also followed farming. He immigrated to Benton County, Ark., in 1857, and located on Pea Ridge. He bought 440 acres for $4,500, and later entered 200 acres more and purchased forty acres. Still later he purchased 283 acres, making in all 963 acres. He died in 1875. He was a successful business man. His wife, Ann Daniels, was born in Monroe County, Tenn., in 1806, and died in 1868. She was the mother of eleven children, seven of whom are now living, Robert A. being the sixth child. He was reared on a farm, and educated in the schools of Tennessee and Arkansas. He remained at home with his parents until the breaking out of the late war, and June 3, 1861, he enlisted in the State service and served three months in Capt. Hays' company. In September he enlisted in Company F, Fifteenth Regiment Arkansas Infantry, or the "Northwest Fifteenth Regiment," and was in the fights at Pea Ridge, Corinth, Iuka, Port Hudson, Champion Hills, and at the Black River fight was captured and retained for five days, when he escaped and returned to his command after it surrendered. He was paroled at Little Rock. He was in the fight at Marks' Mill and was in service until June, 1865. At the battle of Corinth, Miss., he was shot in the leg and wounded slightly. December, 1866, he married Miss Virginia A. Evans, who was born in Bedford County, Tenn., in 1841, and who became the mother of one child, Myrtie. Mr. Hickman followed farming near his old home until 1882, and was the owner of 163 acres of land. He then moved to Bentonville.

Hezekiah Highfill, farmer and stock raiser, was born in McNairy County, Tenn., May 2, 1834, and is a son of James and Martha P. (Jackson) Highfill, both of whom were born in McNairy County, Tenn., the former in 1813, the latter in 1814. They were married in April, 1833; died in Oregon County, Mo., in 1875 and 1870, respectively. James Highfill was a farmer and Missionary Baptist preacher. His father was Bennett Highfill, who came from England with his parents when a child. His parents died soon after their arrival in America, leaving Bennett, Hezekiah and one sister, from whom there is a very extensive relation, as not one Highfill has been found who did not claim to be related to the former ones. Bennett Highfill located in North Carolina, but soon removed to Illinois, and afterward to Tennessee. His wife was Nancy Heron, a native of North Carolina, but of German descent. The maternal grandfather of our subject was Needham Jackson, a native of North Carolina. He was a farmer, a soldier of the War of 1812, and a relative of Gen. Andrew Jackson. At the age of sixteen Hezekiah Highfill was taken by his parents to Dallas County, Mo., where he grew to maturity At the breaking out of the Civil War he enlisted in the Confederate States army, Eighth Missouri Infantry, and was a participant in the battles of Oak Hill, Lexington, Prairie Grove, Little Rock and others, the last being Jenkins' Ferry. He was neither wounded nor captured during his entire service. He first served as orderly sergeant, but was commissioned second lieutenant, and afterward as first lieutenant, all of which positions he filled with integrity and honor. He was surrendered at Shreveport, La., by Gen. Sterling Price. The war being ended, he settled in Franklin County, Mo., without money or friends. He engaged in the occupation of farming, meeting with success. He was married, February 1, 1866, to Mariah S. Mitchell, the daughter of Greenberry Mitchell, a minister of the Missionary Baptist Church. Greenberry Mitchell was born in Tennessee in 1822, married Sarah D. Williams in 1843, and was ordained in 1849. Sarah D. died June 12, 1884, and Mr. Mitchell was next married to Mrs. Almary Pickle, who survives him. He died at Marshfield, Mo., May 27, 1888. Few ministers have done more preaching and work in the corn-field, with greater success for the cause of Christ. He has been known to ride on horseback twenty miles Saturday morning, preach to the church at 11 A. M., at night, and 11 A. M. Sunday, and be at work in the corn-field at home by sunrise Monday morning. By his wife, Mariah, Mr. Highfill has became the father of ten children: Sarah S., Elisha J., Franklin S., Clarence D., Ora A., and Onia F. Sarah was married, November 4, 1888, to Frank Mitchell, of Bloomfield, Ark., who is a son of George Mitchell, of the same place. Mr. Mitchell is not related to the family of his wife's mother. Hezekiah Highfall, the subject of this sketch, now owns 760 acres of good land in Benton County, Ark., to which place he removed in 1869. He has 170 acres in cultivation, well stocked and furnished. He is a Royal Arch Mason, and a man who has the confidence and esteem of all who know him. He is noted for his peaceable disposition, his habits of temperance, and is a zealous Sabbath-school worker. He is a valuable addition to the community in which he resides, always opposing the law of retaliation, believing it to be productive of evil only. As a proof of this he has been known to give his own ration to prisoners, and even pull his shirt off his back, while serving as lieutenant of the guard, and give it to a destitute soldier of the opposing army. In 1878 he was elected assessor of Benton County, afterward clerk of the Springtown Baptist Association, also of the convention that formed the Benton County Baptist Association; has been superintendent of a Sabbath-school in his own school district for several years, and is now president of the West Benton County Sabbath-school Association, in all of which places he has served with marked ability, and honor to himself and credit to constituents. He deems the superintendency of a Sabbath-school the highest position he ever occupied. He will die as he has lived, loved and respected by all who know him, and it is with pleasure that he is considered among the warm friends of the writer, Ethan Allyn.

William G. D. Hinds, lumberman, living at Siloam Springs, was born in Guilford County, N. C., February 5, 1845. He is the son of Dr. John and Rhoda (Webb) Hinds. The father was born in Overton County, Tenn., in 1809, and was of Scotch-Irish descent. Dr. Hinds received his education in Tennessee, and was married in North Carolina in 1841. He was a life-long student and a Cumberland Presbyterian preacher. He attended medical lectures at Lexington, Ky., and became a practicing physician after his marriage. He went to North Carolina in 1841, and remained there until 1856, when he moved to Newton County, Mo. In 1858 he removed with his family to Cane Hill, Washington Co., Ark. He lived here until 1861, when he went to Viney Grove. In July,

1862, he was made prisoner and taken to Springfield, Mo., but the exposure was too much for him, and he died the 26th of the same month. Mrs. Hinds was born in Rockingham County, N. C., in 1817, and lived here until after her marriage. She is still living in Benton County, and is the mother of six living children: Amanda E., wife of R. A. Medearis, a farmer of Washington County; William G. D.; John I. D., Ph. D., professor of chemistry in Cumberland University, Lebanon, Tenn.; Jennie M. K., widow of John Brasel; M. Julia, wife of Prof. J. C. Ryan, and Corder W. William G. D. Hinds came to Arkansas with his parents, and settled on a farm. He was educated at Cane Hill College, and was married March 30, 1872, to Miss Mary D. Pittman. She is a sister of Judge Pittman, of the circuit court, and was born in Washington County, September 27, 1844. Her parents were natives of Tennessee, and moved to Arkansas in 1828. To Mr. and Mrs. Hinds were born five children: John Herbert, Ethel D., Dudley Pittman, Julian Corder and Mary Stella. In July, 1861, Mr. Hinds enlisted in the Confederate army under Gen. McCullough, and after the battle of Pea Ridge he was transferred to Gen. Price's command, and went east to the Mississippi River. He took an active part in the battle of Pea Ridge, and was present at the battles of Corinth and Iuka. He was in cavalry service west of the Mississippi, and was in many skirmishes. After the war he returned to Washington County, Ark., where he engaged in farming, and followed this occupation until he moved to Benton County, Ark., in 1885. He is here engaged in operating a saw, planing and corn mill. Politically a Democrat, his first presidential vote was for S. J. Tilden, in 1876. He is a member of the Masonic fraternity, and he and Mrs. Hinds are members of the Cumberland Presbyterian Church, he being an elder in the same.

Lewis Hine was born in North Carolina, November 14, 1835, and is the son of John and Phœbe (Phillips) Hine. The father, John Hine, familiarly known by his many acquaintances as "Long John," was born in Stokes County, N. C.; was a farmer all his life, and died in his native State in 1844, at the age of fifty-two years. His widow survived him until 1887. They were the parents of ten children: Winfield, Mrs. Regina Weevil, Joseph (deceased), Mrs. Nancy Tugal, Eli, Nathaniel (deceased), Lewis, Mrs. Phœbe J. Chaimlin, and two, Samuel and Ven, who died in infancy. Frederick Hine and Elizabeth Hine, grandparents of our subject, were early settlers of North Carolina. The grandfather was originally from Pennsylvania. The grandmother was of German descent, and was born on the ship that brought her parents to America. Lewis Hine, subject of this sketch, grew to manhood in his native State, and received his education in the common schools. He left home March 6, 1855, and settled in Hendricks County, Ind., where he remained until December of the same year, subsequently settling in Bartholomew County, of the same State. Here he remained for one year engaged in the carriage and buggy making business. December 10, 1856, he married Miss Susan Reed, who was born and reared in Benton County, Ark. Her parents, Thomas and Catherine (Ply) Reed, were natives of North Carolina, and immigrated to Indiana at an early day, being pioneer settlers. The mother was of English descent and the father of German. Their family consisted of twelve children: Lewis T., Rufus W., Edie A. and Eddie A. (twins), Thomas, Mary, Amos, George, infant not named, Ida, Cora and John. After his marriage Mr. Hine remained in Bartholomew County for about ten years, and in 1867 removed to Johnson County, Mo., where he farmed for about four years. He then lived in Dade County for about nine years, and while there was ordained a minister of the Missionary Baptist Church, having professed religion and joined the church in North Carolina. While in Dade County he was engaged in ministerial work in connection with farming. After moving to Benton County, Mo., and from there to Jasper County of the same State, he finally settled in Benton County, Ark., in 1885. The first year he had charge of the missionary work of the State, and was identified with several churches. During the Rebellion he enlisted in Company I, Sixty-ninth Indiana Volunteer Infantry, and during that time was in several engagements, the most important of which being Mumfordsville, Chickamauga, Pine Bluff, Carrion Crow Bayou and Arkansas Post. He was taken prisoner at the first mentioned place, and from there was paroled. During his twenty months' service in the war his family moved to Indiana. Although a strong Democrat in his political views, Mr. Hine cast his maiden vote for Lincoln. He has about 220 acres of land, about 140 under cultivation. He is a member of the

****

Masonic fraternity, and his wife and four children are members of the church.

William H. Hoblit, farmer and stone-mason, was born in Clinton County, Ohio, June 26, 1840, son of Amos and Elizabeth (Shields) Hoblit, and grandson of David Hoblit, who was a native of Kentucky, born in 1792, who served in the War of 1812, was a member of the Baptist Church, and died in 1868. Amos W. Hoblit was born in Clinton County, Ohio, March 18, 1811, was a farmer by occupation, and was married to Miss Shields, also a native of Clinton County, Ohio. She was born in the year 1812, and was a member of the Baptist Church. The following children were born to this union: Martha, Kate, William H. and Marieta. The father of these children afterward married Mrs. Johanna Brandon, who bore him two children, Emma and Eliza. William H. Hoblit moved to Bureau County, Ill., in 1852, and in 1861 he enlisted in the Union army, Company H, of the Twelfth Illinois Volunteer Infantry, and continued in service four years and three months. He was in the battles of Donelson, Shiloh, Corinth, Iuka, Resaca, Dallas, Kenasaw Mountains, Atlanta, Chapel Hill, Jonesboro and Altoona Pass. He was in many other battles, was with Sherman in his march to the sea, and was wounded several times. After the war he moved to Madison County, Iowa, but previous to this had married Miss Ellen Whitworth, a native of Yorkshire, England, born February 6, 1846, and who came to America at the age of six years. She settled with her parents at Toledo, Ohio, but moved from this State to Illinois, where she married Mr. Hoblit in 1866. Mr. Hoblit moved to Iowa, Kansas, Missouri and Nebraska, and in the last named State had the misfortune to lose his wife, March 25, 1886. In 1888 he moved to Benton County, Ark. He is the father of these children: Cora E., Ernest, Abbie, Delbert, Wilson, Nettie and Roy. Mr. Hoblit is a member of the G. A. R., and is one of the enterprising citizens of the county. His maternal great-grandfather, James Shields, was one of the signers of the Declaration of Independence.

Guthridge Lee Holland is a North Carolinian, born March 13, 1844. He is a son of William J. and Sarah (Moore) Holland, who were born in Maryland and North Carolina in 1812 and 1818, respectively. After leaving home the father went to Georgia, thence to North Carolina, and afterward located in Arkansas. Five children were the result of his union with Miss Moore: Martha Jane (deceased), Guthridge L., Thomas M. (a farmer of Benton County, Ark.), Josephine (deceased) and William H., also a farmer of Benton County, Ark. Guthridge L. Holland came to Arkansas with his parents when he was twenty-four years of age. He enlisted in the Confederate army when he was eighteen or nineteen years of age, was in Gen. Robert E. Lee's command the greater part of the time, and was present when Lee surrendered. He resided with his parents until his marriage, in 1873, with Miss Arabella Cook, who was born in Kentucky, January 27, 1850, and to them the following children have been born: Edgar Milton, Robert Leslie, Florence A., William J., Minnie and Charles Otto. Mr. Holland is a Democrat in his political views, and his first presidential vote was cast for Horace Greeley. He owns 300 acres of good land in the valley of Osage Creek, and is one of the progressive and enterprising farmers of Benton County. His wife is a member of the Methodist Church.

Dr. Thomas W. Hurley, a successful practitioner of Bentonville, Ark., is a native of Lawrence County, Ala., born 1834, and the son of Israel W. and Sarah (Bonds) Hurley, who was a native of North Carolina, and who moved to Middle Tennessee at a very early date. Israel W. Hurley was born in Tennessee in 1805, was of Irish descent and a farmer by occupation. He went to Lawrence County, Ala., when a young man, was married there, and afterward moved to Lowndes County, Miss., but in 1858 he moved to Carol Parish, La. He died in 1868. Sarah (Bonds) Hurley was born in Tennessee, was of Scotch descent, and died in 1876 at the age of seventy years. She was the mother of the following children: Dr. Thomas W.; William A., killed at Vicksburg during the Civil War; John W., at Fort Smith, a mechanic by trade; James, killed at Vicksburg during the war; Robert, who is on the old home farm in Louisiana; Sarah, widow of Richard Ingram, and Mary, wife of John Ingram. Dr. Thomas W. is the eldest of this family. He received his literary education at Oxford, Miss., and at the age of seventeen he commenced the study of his chosen profession. In 1854 he entered the Memphis Medical College, at Memphis, Tenn., and attended one year. In 1855 and 1856 he attended the medical department of the University of Louisiana, and in the spring of 1856 he graduated as an M. D.   The same year he located in Noxubee County, Miss., and began practicing, but moved to Calhoun County, Ark., the following year and settled at Hampton, where he resided until 1862.   Previous to this, in 1855, he married Miss Maria L. Neal, who was born in Rising Sun, Ind., April 6, 1834, and who bore him five children: May, wife of Edwin L. Richards, who is residing in San Diego County, Cal.; Augustus W., Charles E., Emma D. and Eva.   In March, 1862, Dr. Hurley enlisted in Barnett's Battalion as volunteer surgeon, and was immediately appointed surgeon of the battalion.   He was in the battle of Shiloh and Farmington, and immediately after the battle was appointed by the war department of the Confederate army a surgeon in the Confederate States army, with headquarters at Memphis.   In 1863 his health failed and he returned home, but was soon appointed as surgeon in the Transmississippi Department, and held this position the remainder of the war.   He surrendered at Jefferson, Texas, after peace was declared, and after the war he located at Dallas, Texas, where he resumed his practice.   In 1868 he became a resident of Bentonville, Ark., and has devoted his time and attention to his profession from that day until the present.   Dr. Hurley is the oldest practitioner in Bentonville, with one exception, having been a resident here for twenty years.   He is an excellent physician, as his many patients now living can testify.   May, 1884, he was elected president of the State Medical Society and served one year.   He is a member of the American Medical Association, State Medical Society of the State of Arkansas, and is a member of the Benton County Medical Society, and is secretary of the same.   He is Democratic in politics, and he and wife are members of the Cumberland Presbyterian Church.

John H. Hust is a well-to-do and prominent citizen of Benton County, Ark., and was born in Montgomery County, Tenn., on the 13th of November, 1832. His parents, William and Elizabeth (Harris) Hust, were North Carolinians.   The father was a man when he removed to Tennessee, and was married in that State to Miss Harris.   He was a soldier in the War of 1812, and was under the immediate command of "Old Hickory" Jackson.   He was a brick-layer by trade, and followed that occupation for many years, but finally engaged in farming.   His wife died in Tennessee at the age of sixty-five years, having borne eleven children: Arthur, deceased; Emily, wife of J. O. Hunt, both deceased; William, deceased; Washington, deceased; William; Mary, wife of W. M. May; Rosanna, deceased; John; Sarah, wife of A. Shelton; Susan W., wife of I. Wilkinson, and Frank, who was killed during the war.   Mr. John H. Hust remained in Tennessee until 1874, and then came to Arkansas, where he has a good farm of 210 acres, on which is erected a fine brick dwelling-house.   In his political views he is a stanch Democrat, and has always voted the straight ticket.   He is also a Mason, and is a member of the Methodist Episcopal Church, South, as is his wife, whose maiden name was Carrie Dixon.   Previous to his marriage with Miss Dixon Mr. Hust was married to Frances Harris, a native of Tennessee, who died about 1860, being the mother of two children: James and Mary, wife of John Kelton.   In 1863 he married his present wife, by whom he is the father of eight children: Luzena, Annie, Harry, Reuben, Esline, Matthew, Arthur and Angie.   Mr. Hust is of German descent, his paternal grandfather having been a native of Germany.

Rev. William A. Inman is a native of Clay County, Ind., born in 1851, and is the son of David L. and Sarah (Poe) Inman.   David L. Inman was born in the "Palmetto" State, and when a very small boy was taken to Indiana, where, after attaining a suitable age, he adopted farming as his calling through life.   He died in his adopted State at the age of forty-four years.   William A. Inman resided in Indiana until he reached manhood, and in 1873 entered Bedford College, where he remained one year.   He then began studying for the ministry, and at the age of twenty-one years entered the pulpit as a local preacher in the Christian Church.   He preached the gospel in Clay County, Ind., until 1880, at which time he came to Arkansas, but at the end of two years removed to Kansas. After remaining there three years he returned to Benton County, Ark., and took charge of the Christian Church at Garfield, and also expounds the gospel at Washburn, Rocky Comfort, and at a church on Sugar Creek, in Missouri.   He has a good little farm of forty acres, which he purchased in 1887, and is devoting it principally to raising fruit.   He was married in 1869 to Miss Armilda C. Duncan, by whom he has four children: Alonzo, Edward, Winfield and James M.   Mr. Inman is a Democrat.

George W. Jackson was born in Middle Tennessee November 24, 1835, and

****

is a son of Haley and Margaret (Johnson) Jackson, who were born in North Carolina and Tennessee in 1810 and 1806, respectively. The father was taken to Tennessee by his father, James Jackson, when he was about six years of age. Here he resided until grown, and then came to Arkansas and remained two years, then returned to Tennessee and married. About 1832 he settled on a farm, and in 1855 took up his permanent abode in Arkansas. His wife died in 1885, the mother of seven children: Louisa J., widow of Madison Mayberry; James H. (deceased), George W., John F. (deceased); M. Elizabeth, wife of William Weatherly; Dawson H. and Margaret S. E., wife of James Burness. George W. Jackson came to Arkansas with his parents, and in 1860 was married to Emeline Weatherly, who was born in Tennessee in 1839, and by her he became the father of ten children: Georgia A., wife of Alonzo Moody: Margaret A., wife of W. B. Sumpter: James T., Mary J., John B., Charles H., Elizabeth E. (deceased), Bertha A., William D. and Robert M. During the war Mr. Jackson espoused the cause of the Confederacy, and enlisted in the First Arkansas Cavalry, serving until the close of hostilities, and being in many battles and skirmishes. He owns 232 acres of fine land near Bentonville. In his political views he is a Democrat.

Nicholas S. Jackson, merchant, was born in Benton County, Ark., March 14, 1845, son of James and Rebecca (Williams) Jackson. James Jackson was born in North Carolina in 1804, received a good common-school education, and after arriving at mature years immigrated with his father to Tennessee, making the journey to that State in wagons. The country was wild and unsettled, and our sturdy adventurers suffered many of the privations incident to those early days in an unsettled country. Rebecca Jackson, the mother, was also a native of North Carolina, and removed to Tennessee when but a young woman. She was afterward married to Mr. Jackson, and bore him fifteen children, six now living: Albert, Dawson, Andrew, Mrs. Laura Curtis, Nicholas and Mrs. Virginia Ludley. The children deceased were named Mary, Zachariah T., Mrs. Elizabeth, Gailbreath, James Mc., Acenith, Conway, Richardson and an infant unnamed. Mr. Jackson followed farming in Tennessee, and afterward emigrated to Benton County, Ark., and was among the first settlers of this county. He was here before the State was admitted into the Union, and when there were a few cabins where Springfield now stands. He was obliged to go forty miles to mill, and all his trading was done at Van Buren and Fort Smith, where he went twice a year. The people of Benton County showed their appreciation of him, after the county had been made, by electing him to represent them at Little Rock as a member of the House of Representatives. He selected the site of his grave, and died on the old homestead. His wife is now living, and is eighty-two years of age. She is strong and vigorous, does her own house-work, and is able to ride horseback. Their son, Nicholas S., was born on the farm where the father spent the greater part of his life, and passed his days, like most children, in the school-room. At a time when his mind should have been almost entirely taken up with his studies the war broke out, and his books were thrown aside. On account of his strong Southern convictions, Mr. Jackson was driven from home, and afterward enlisted in the Confederate service, being engaged in active duty for one year. He enlisted in Company A, Col. Adair's regiment, Cherokee brigade, and during this time of service was in a number of engagements: Fort Smith, Blackburn, Prairie, crossing the Arkansas river on rafts, swimming the horses and charging a fortified troop of negroes, and capturing a number, and Fayetteville being the most important fights, but was in numerous skirmishes. He surrendered at Fayetteville. Mr. Jackson returned home after the war only to find the magnificent property in ruins; houses, fences, etc., being destroyed. Mr. Jackson went to work to repair and rebuild, hauling apples to Texas to buy their meat and bread the first year. He continued to live on the home farm, and was there married to Miss Martha ————, a native of Washington County, Ark., and the daughter of Hugh ————. This union resulted in the birth of ten children, eight now living: Leanora, James H., Arthur, Arkie, Maud, Chester, George and Frank. Those deceased were named Ida and Conway. After marriage Mr. Jackson began farming for himself on the farm given him by his father, and there he continued to live until 1883, when he sold out and went to Bentonville. He there dealt in stock, and was also engaged in shipping grain. He then purchased and operated the mill at Bentonville, being engaged in that business for only a short time. He then engaged in the clothing business, but soon sold out and engaged in the general commission business. This he followed until coming to Maysville, where he formed a partnership with W. D. Dudmon, and again ventured into the general mercantile business. Since that time he has bought out his partner's interest, and now conducts the largest and most extensive establishment in Maysville. Mr. Jackson is a stanch Democrat in politics, never having voted any other ticket; is a member of the Masonic fraternity, and he and Mrs. Jackson are members of the Missionary Baptist Church.

Isaac January, a prosperous farmer and stock raiser, of Benton County, Ark., was born in Warren County, Tenn., June 6, 1827, but grew to manhood in Franklin and Lincoln Counties, where he followed the occupation of farming. In 1847 he enlisted in the Mexican War, and served until the close of that conflict. He then returned home, and in the fall of 1849 removed to Benton County, Ark., where he settled on unimproved land and began making him a home. In March, 1851, he was married to Miss Elizabeth C. Hastings, who was born in Bedford County, Tenn., September 15, 1834, a daughter of Henry C. and Mary D. (Word) Hastings. By industry and good management Mr. and Mrs. January have become the owners of 341 acres of land, and are worthy citizens of the county. During the early part of the late war Mr. January was captain of a company of home guards, but in the fall of 1862, when Arkansas was invaded, he disbanded his company and enlisted in the regular army, but never operated east of the Mississippi River. He was in a number of engagements, but was never wounded. He was captured several times, but was always released after a short time. His parents were Joseph Clark and Martha (Mash) January. They were both born in Tennessee, the former in 1801 and the latter in 1812. Mr. January was a son of Isaac January, and Mrs. January was the daughter of John Mash, a Methodist clergyman. Both parents were members of the Methodist Church. Henry C. and Mary D. (Word) Hastings were born in Tennessee in 1793 and 1800, respectively. The former was a farmer and carpenter by trade, and was a colonel in the War 1812.

Samuel Allen Jefferson was born in Washington County, Ark., in 1838, and is a son of George H. and Elizabeth (Moore) Jefferson, who were born in Virginia and Tennessee in 1802 and 1810, respectively. The mother died in 1883. The father was of German-English descent, and was a young man when he became a resident of Trigg County, Ky. He was married in Bedford County, Tenn., and in 1835 located in Washington County, Ark., and in 1841 came to Benton County. He began keeping hotel in Bentonville in 1842, and in connection with this kept a cabinet-shop. His death occurred in 1846. His wife was a daughter of Samuel Moore, who was a soldier in the War of 1812, and was with Gen. Jackson at the battle of New Orleans. Samuel Allen Jefferson is one of three surviving members of a family of ten children, and was reared and educated in Benton County. In 1862 he was married to Miss Joan Neal, born in Missouri in 1839, a daughter of Daniel Neal, and by her became the father of eleven children: Bartlett A., Georgette (wife of C. C. Huffman), Mary J., William T., Mabel, Pearl, George (deceased), Charles, Pierce (deceased), Minnie and Edna. Mr. Jefferson has a good farm of 160 acres. He is a Democrat in his political views. May 21, 1861, he enlisted in Company B, First Arkansas Cavalry, State troops, and in August of the same year enlisted in Company G, First Arkansas Cavalry, and was in the battles of Pea Ridge, Prairie Grove, Poison Spring, Mansfield and others. At the battle of Oak Hill he was severely wounded in the left thigh, and was obliged to go on crutches for nine months. He served four years, and surrendered at Fort Smith, Ark.

Elbert Jennings, whose birth occurred in Carroll County, Va., October 3, 1859, is the son of Peter A. and Eliza J. (Duncan) Jennings. The father was born in the same State and county, but the latter was then called Pulaski County. He received a fair education, and while growing up learned the tinner's trade, which he followed for a living until coming to Arkansas, which was in 1870. He then rented land for two or three years, and homesteaded the land where he now lives. Mrs. Eliza (Duncan) Jennings, the mother, was born in Pulaski County, Va., there received her education, and was there married to Mr. Jennings, by whom she had two children, both living: Elbert, and Isabella Abercrombie, wife of T. C. Abercrombie, of Benton County, Ark. Peter A. Jennings enlisted in the Confederate army during the Rebellion, and served but a short time on account of disability, being discharged at Richmond. He also had three brothers in the Confederate service, and an uncle on his mother's side, who was wounded several times, but is living. Elbert Jennings was reared principally on the farm, and while in Virginia attended school at odd times, thereby receiving a common-school education. In 1870 he left his native State, and moved with his parents to Arkansas, where he remained with them until 1880. He then went to Bentonville, and worked at Davis' Nursery for about five years. He then returned to his father's farm, and, having by this time a thorough knowledge of the nursery business, started out in the same for himself, putting out about 10,000 trees, and made a success of the same, having at all times a good trade. Business still increasing, he put out 20,000 trees, and the nursery became known as Sulphur Springs Nursery. Mr. Jennings was married March 18, 1888, to Miss Mollie Davis, daughter of W. S. Davis. Mr. Jennings has always voted the Democratic ticket. He is a young man of energy and perseverance, and one who has the confidence of the people.

John Keith was born July 8, 1834, and is the son of William B. and Sarah (May) Keith. The father was born in Tennessee, and received a rather limited education, as did also his wife, who was born in the same State. They were married in that State and became the parents of thirteen children, seven now living: John, Elijah, Mrs. Polly Ballinger, Mrs. Rowena Anderson, Mrs. Isabella Primrose, Thomas and Josephine. The children deceased were named William, Ann, Sarah, Joshua, Martha and James. After his marriage Mr. Keith immigrated to Arkansas and settled on Little River, in the southern part of the State, where they remained but a short time. They then moved to Washington County, Ark., and from there to Benton County of the same State, and later to Missouri, where he remained long enough to raise one crop, when he moved back to Arkansas, settling on the farm two miles north of where Mr. Keith now lives. Here he spent the remainder of his life engaged in farming and blacksmithing. He died about 1856 at the age of fifty-four, and the mother died in 1885 at the age of seventy-five. Mr. May, the maternal grandfather of John Keith, was a soldier in the War of 1812 under Gen. Jackson. John Keith was born in Benton County, Ark., and when a boy the Indians were settled quite thickly in this country, and often came to his father's shop to get work done. Mr. Keith spent his boyhood days on the farm, and received but a meager education on account of the scarcity of schools. At the age of twenty-three he began for himself in the blacksmith business at Maysville, where he remained for about six years. During that time he married Miss Margaret McCall, daughter of James and Elizabeth McCall, and a native of Missouri. This union resulted in the birth of nine children, eight now living: Walter, Mrs. Emma Gillett, Mrs. Martha B. McCall, Hugh, John, Henry, Faunt and Charley. The deceased was named James B. After marriage Mr. Keith left Maysville and moved on a farm a short distance from where he now lives, and shortly after, the war breaking out, he joined a company, but never participated in any battles. By order of Col. Standwatie, he was assigned to a position in the repair department, and worked at the blacksmith trade. Under the command of Hugh Timnen he was at Honey Springs, and in company with another man helped take 100 mules south. He was discharged from duty at Boggy Depot, in the Choctaw Nation, returned to Benton County, Ark., and again engaged in agricultural pursuits. He remained south of Bentonville a short time, and then moved to the southern part of the county, where he remained one year, after which he moved to his present farm, and there he has since remained. He has about 175 acres of land, 100 under cultivation. Mr. Keith had the misfortune to lose his faithful companion December 14, 1876. He is a member of the Cumberland Presbyterian Church, and politically is all that the word Democrat would imply, never having voted any other ticket from the time of his majority down to President Cleveland.

Elijah Keith, son of William B. and Sarah (May) Keith, was born March 19, 1836, in Benton County, Ark. He received a limited education on account of the scarcity of schools, and at the age of ten began on the farm with his parents, where he continued until reaching manhood. At the breaking out of the Rebellion he enlisted in Company G, Third Arkansas, but remained in that company for only a short time. He then enlisted in Company A, First Cherokee Volunteer Cavalry, Confederate service, and was in active duty until the close of the war. During that time he participated in numerous battles and skirmishes, the most important being at Springfield. When the news was received at his station that Lee had surrendered he went to Ft. Smith and was there paroled. He was in Texas a short time, and then returned to his home in Benton County, and began working on the farm. Two years later he married Miss Prudy Anderson, daughter of Arch C. and Emily Anderson, who were formerly from Texas. Mrs. Keith was born in the last named State, and came to Arkansas after the close of the war (1867). To Mr. and Mrs. Keith were born ten children, eight now living: Alma, Lemuel H., Ora, Katie, Minnie, Grace, Stella and Blanche. The two children deceased were named Arthur and Bernice. After marriage Mr. Keith lived on the farm with his parents a short time, and then moved to a piece of timber land one and a fourth miles from where he has since lived, began homesteading a farm of eighty acres, and there remained for five years. He then moved to his present farm, which consists of fifty-eight acres of cleared land and eighty acres of timber land. Mr. Keith is a Democrat in politics, casting his first presidential vote for Hancock. He is a member of the Christian Union Church.

Capt. William Marion Keith. In giving the genealogy of the prominent families of Benton County, Ark., the biographical department of this work would be incomplete without mentioning the Keith family, who first became represented in this county in December, 1866. Gabriel Keith, the great-grandfather of our subject, was a Scotchman, who came to America at an early day and served in a Virginia company in the Revolutionary War. His son William was born in Buncombe County, N.C., and served in the War of 1812 under Jackson, being at the battle of New Orleans. He was a farmer and a minister of the Baptist Church, and at the time of his death, August 28, 1853, was in comfortable circumstances. He was married to Sarah Allen, of Scotch descent, who was born in North Carolina, and died there in 1872 at the age of eighty-five years, and John Keith, the father of Capt. William M. Keith, is their son. John was born in Buncombe County, N. C., October 29, 1814, and followed the occupation of farming throughout life. He was a Mason and a member of the Baptist Church. His death occurred in his native county March 29, 1854. He was married to Elizabeth Edwards, who was born in Washington County, Tenn., September 22, 1815. She is now residing in Benton County, Ark., and is a daughter of Thomas and Elizabeth (Erwin) Edwards, who were born in Virginia and Tennessee, and died in Tennessee in 1850 and 1849 at the ages of seventy-three and seventy-six, respectively. Alfred F., Riley C., James A. and William M. Keith are the brothers of John Keith, and were all soldiers in the Mexican War. William M. was killed at Matamoras, Tex., March 16, 1846. At the age of fifteen years William Marion Keith removed with his father to North Carolina, and grew to manhood in Buncombe County. He was born in Washington County, Tenn., December 29, 1835, and received no educational advantages whatever. At the age of twenty-three years he entered Morris Hill College, being at that time unable to read, and remained in that school from March, 1857, till April, 1861, when he volunteered in the Confederate army in Company B, Sixth North Carolina Volunteers (afterward the Sixteenth North Carolina Volunteers), and entered service as first lieutenant, and afterward was promoted to captain. He operated principally in Virginia, and participated in the battles of the Wilderness, Seven Pines, the seven days fight at Richmond, Cedar Mountain, second battle of Manassas (where he received a dangerous wound, breaking his collar bone, arm, and dislocating his shoulder), Sharpsburg, Harper's Ferry, Fredericksburg, Chancellorsville, Gettysburg, Seminary Hill, siege of Petersburg and Appomattox Court House. He saw Gen. Jackson, who was shot by one of the men in Mr. Keith's brigade, ten minutes after he received his death wound. After the close of the war he returned home and, in 1866, with his wife, who was a Miss Harriet McMahan, born in North Carolina in 1837, and whom he married in 1862, removed to Benton County, Ark., where his wife died September 10, 1868, leaving two children: Aurelius H., who died in the Indian Territory February 16, 1887, at the age of twenty-four years, and Bregetta Valencia, wife of James L. Craig, residing at Eldorado, Ark. After coming to Arkansas Mr. Keith engaged in farming and teaching school, and has continued those occupations almost continuously up to the present time. He is considered one of the first educators of the State, and is a man of native talent and ability. April 11, 1869, he was married to Sarah M. Carl, a native of Benton County, Ark., born May 15, 1843. Her father, Thomas Carl, was born in New York State, March 24, 1802, and is still living, being one of the oldest settlers in the county.

He has numerous descendants: 'eleven children, eighty-nine grandchildren, 100 great-grandchildren and four great-great-grandchildren living. Mr. Keith, by his last marriage, is the father of three children: Harriet Amna, Nancy Elizabeth and Robert E. Lee. In 1879 Mr. Keith represented Benton County in the lower house of the State Legislature, having for his opponent Hon. A. M. Rodgers, one of the most popular men in Benton County. Mr. Keith is an Odd Fellow, a member of the Baptist Church, and a stanch Democrat.

Morgan Kendrick, a well-to-do and worthy farmer of Benton County, Ark., is a son of Obediah and Patsey (Lynch) Kendrick, and was born in Benton County in 1845. His parents were born in Alabama, the father being a farmer throughout life. He enlisted to serve in the Mexican War, but peace was declared before he reached the scene of battle. He removed from Alabama to Benton County, Ark., in 1834, and here died in 1868, leaving thirteen children to fight the battle of life alone. Morgan Kendrick received limited early educational advantages, and remained with his parents until the war broke out, and in 1863 enlisted in Company F, Arkansas Regiment, Confederate States Army, under command of Gen. Hawthorn, and was sent to Louisiana, and after serving about six months was honorably discharged, but continued to remain with the command until peace was declared. He then returned to his old home in Benton County and resumed farming, and the following year was married to Miss Susan Phillips, by whom he became the father of seven children: Lee, Eva E., Anthony, Patsey E., Hugh Middleton, Wallace F. and Amanda B. Mr. Kendrick owns a good farm of 160 acres. Mrs. Kendrick is a member of the Missionary Baptist Church.

Seth Kendrick was born in Alabama in the year 1839, and is a son of Martin and Nancy (Phillips) Kendrick. He secured a common-school education, and remained with his parents until he entered the army in 1861. He enlisted in the Confederate service in Capt. Ironton's company, from Bentonville, Second Arkansas Cavalry, and served until the cessation of hostilities. He was slightly wounded at Atlanta, Ga., and besides this battle was at Corinth, Franklin, Murfreesboro, Nashville and others of less note. After receiving his discharge he returned home, and in 1867 was married to Miss Elizabeth Graham, the following being the children born to their union: Tolitha J., Mary L., Martha A., Sarah C., Adaline, Martin A. and William N. Mr. Kendrick inherited a portion of his father's farm, on which he now resides. It is well improved and very valuable. He, wife and one daughter are members of the Missionary Baptist Church, and he is a Democrat in his political views.

Thomas B. Kendrick is a native of Benton County, Ark., born in 1842, and is a son of Martin and Nancy (Phillips) Kendrick. [See sketch of Lafayette G. Kendrick.] He has always followed the occupation of farming, and owns a farm of eighty acres, a portion of which he inherited from his father's estate, and the rest he purchased. In 1861 he enlisted in the Confederate army in Company F, Fifteenth Arkansas Infantry, and was a participant in the following battles: Corinth, Big Black, Port Hudson and the siege and surrender of Vicksburg. He started home after the battle of Vicksburg, but was taken ill on the way, and it was over a year before he was able to reach his destination. He then resumed the occupation of farming, and has continued the same with fair success up to the present time. He was married, in 1873, to Miss Susan Phillips, of Benton County, and five children have blessed their union: Bettie A. L., Ben. W., Nettie B., Mary J. and Nancy E. Mr. Kendrick and wife are members of the Baptist Church.

Lafayette G. Kendrick, farmer, and native of Benton County, Ark., was born in 1852, and is a son of Martin and Nancy (Phillips) Kendrick. The father was born in Tennessee, and immigrated to Arkansas at a very early day, when the State was almost an unbroken wilderness, and where wild animals of all kinds roamed the woods at pleasure. He settled in Benton County on land which he afterward bought from the Government, but did not live to see the country settled or to improve his farm. His death occurred in 1863. Lafayette G. Kendrick was educated in the common schools of Benton County, and was reared by his mother, with whom he remained asssisting on the farm until he was grown. In 1876 Miss Martha Slayback, a daughter of Anderson Slayback, of Benton County, became his wife, and by her was the father of two children named John H. and Lucy A. After his marriage Mr. Kendrick located on a portion of his father's farm, which he had inherited, and there has since resided.

His little place of twenty acres is finely cultivated, and on it are erected good buildings. He votes the Democratic ticket, His wife is a member of the Christian Church.

Joel Wilson Kimmins, fruit grower, residing near Lowell, Ark., was born in Bedford County, Tenn., October 17, 1856. His father, Benjamin F. Kimmins, was also born in Bedford County, and during the late war served in the Confederate army. About 1852 he was married to Nancy Ann Turrentine, who was of French descent, and died in 1863, leaving three children: Mary Elizabeth, wife of William Simmons, both deceased; Joel W. and William James. In March, 1864, Mr. Kimmins united his fortunes with those of Miss Ann P. Nowlinand; by her he is the father of three children: Susan Melvina, wife of H. T. Mays; Robert Lee, a physician and surgeon in Iredell, Tex., and Minerva Frances. The Kimmins are of Irish descent, the great-grandfather of Joel W. having been a native of Ireland. Joel moved from Tennessee to Izard County, Ark., in 1866, and at the end of seven years started for Texas, but stopped in Benton County, Ark., and since that time has resided there the greater portion of the time. April 15, 1880, he was united in marriage to Nancy Walker, a native of Arkansas, her father being one of the early settlers, and Mattie Elizabeth (deceased), Lucile and an infant are their children. Mr. Kimmins supports the principles of the Democratic party, and cast his first presidential vote for Hancock. He owns forty-five acres of fine land, twenty-six acres being in orchard, and is engaged in shipping raspberries, peaches and apples.

James C. Knott, groceryman, of Bentonville, Ark., was born in Bedford County, Tenn., in 1855, and is the son of John and Harriet (Steel) Knott. The father was born in Bedford County, Tenn., in 1808, and was of Irish origin. He grew to manhood in his native State and county, was married there and there lived until 1859, when he moved to Benton County, Ark., and settled six miles south of the county seat. In 1862 he sold out and moved to Pike County, Ark., but moved from there, in the spring of 1865, to Hempstead County, Ark., where he died in August of the same year. His wife was born in Bedford County, Tenn., in 1815, and after the death of her husband she moved back to Pike County, Ark., and in the spring of 1866 she returned to Benton County, of the same State, bought a farm of 186 acres, five miles southwest of Bentonville, near the former place of residence, and is now living. She is the mother of five children who lived to be grown: Frank, who died in 1886, at the age of forty-five; Bettie, who was born in 1843, and who is now deceased; John, who is salesman for his brother, James C., and who was born in Bedford County, Tenn., in 1848, was twelve years old when his parents came to Arkansas, was reared on a farm, and in 1873 married Miss Mattie Jackson, daughter of J. E. W. Jackson, and a native of Benton County, Ark., born 1855; they are the parents of three children, Arthur, Elma and Virgil; Eliza J., wife of A. W. Hutchinson, who resides in Pike County, Ark., and James C. The last named was but four years old when his parents moved to Benton County, Ark., and was but ten when his father died. At the age of fifteen he left the parental roof, and commenced to fight the battle of life on his own responsibility. He attended school during the winter seasons, for two years in the country schools, and then attended two years at Bentonville. The following three years he clerked for William A. Terry, and in 1877 he engaged in the grocery business for himself at Bentonville. He commenced on a small scale, but by his good business ability and honesty he arose year by year, until he has one of the largest and best stocks of groceries in Bentonville. He has one room 23x102 feet, and an L 20x40 feet. In 1880 he married Miss Ella Peel, a native of Boone County, Ark., born 1857, and the daughter of John W. Peel. They have two children: Ada and Eugene. Mr. Knott is a Democrat in politics.

Reuben J. Laughlin, son of William and Mary Laughlin, was born in Caldwell County, Ky., April 3, 1840. His grandfather, Anthony Laughlin, was a native of Dungannon, Ireland, and immigrated to Charleston, S. C., in 1782, where he married Mary Gill, and in 1803 moved to Kentucky, and there reared a large family. His son William was born in Charleston, S. C., in 1795, and from the age of seven years was reared on a farm. While a lad he learned the tanner's and currier's trade. He was a fine musician, and as a fifer volunteered in Capt. Dodd's company, Maj. Wadlington's battalion, Kentucky Volunteers, in the War of 1812, and got to New Orleans in time to take part in that memorable battle, and the fife that called the troops into action on that morning is now in possession of his son Reuben. At the close of that war he returned to Cald-well County, sunk a tan-yard, and carried on that business in connection with a shoe and harness shop for over fifty years. He was married twice, his first wife being Winifred Margraves, who was also a native of Charleston, S. C., and died in 1819. He married Miss Mary Greer in Hopkinsville, Ky., in 1821. She was born in Alabama in 1805. They were the parents of three children: Abner G., Sarah and Reuben Johnson. They lived to a good old age, and died, he in 1876, she in 1879. Their youngest son, Reuben, after completing his education and working with his brother, who was a watchmaker, went to Louisville and finished his trade. He enlisted in December, 1861, in J. K. Huey's company, afterward Company A, First Kentucky Cavalry, Confederate States Army, and was in the engagements at Fort Donelson, Perryville, Murfreesborough and many severe skirmishes. After he was discharged he went back to Kentucky, and married Miss Phebe A. Herrin, daughter of A. J. and Isabella E. (Harral-son), of Providence, Webster County, and engaged in general merchandising and stemming tobacco in Nebo until 1878, when he went to Louisville and opened a commission warehouse; his health failing in 1881, he came to Benton-ville, and has been merchandising until the fall of 1887, when he sold out, and has since then been devoting his entire time to his trade, keeping a fine stock of clocks, watches, jewelry, silverware, etc. He has three children: William A., Robert E. and Phoebe. He is a Mason, and has taken all the degrees of the Ancient York rite, is Past Grand High Priest of Kentucky, and at present (1888) Worshipful Master of Lodge and High Priest of the chapter. In politics he is a Democrat. He and family are members of the Christian Church,

Flavius J. Lindsey, a resident of Sulphur Springs Township, is the son of Felix G. and Eliza Ann (Northington) Lindsey, and was born near Warsaw, Benton Co., Mo., November 25, 1841. He attended the common schools of his native county, and at the age of sixteen entered the drug store of his uncle, Dr. J. A. Lindsey, who was residing in Bolivar, Polk Co., Mo. He here studied medicine, and had considerable experience with his uncle, becoming familiar with surgical work. At the breaking out of the war he joined the home guards at Bolivar, Mo., Capt. Mitchell's company, who was afterward attached to Gen. Raine's corps. Here he received an appointment of assistant surgeon, Fifth Missouri. During the Wilson's Creek battle he supported Bledsoe's battery, in which was the noted cannon, Sacramento, a relic of the Mexican War. During the Rebellion Dr. Lindsey was in seventy-two engagements. After Gen. Price crossed the Mississippi, Dr. Lindsey joined the Twelfth Texas Cavalry, Com-pany F, commanded by Capt. W. G. Veal, regiment commanded by the noted W. H. Parsons. He served in that command for three year, entering as a private and orderly sergeant. He was afterward appointed by Gen. Holms as a special scout, detailed to make a map of the country immediately surrounding Helena, Ark., at that time occupied by Gen. Curtis. The Doctor did his work so well, and his Texas scouts kept so close around and inside the Union pickets, it was reported that Gen. Curtis said that he expected to wake up some morning and "find a damn Texan in bed with him." Afterward he was made third lieu-tenant, serving in that capacity until the close of the war. He was lieutenant commanding the advance guard most of the time from Mansfield to Yellow Bayou. Dr. Lindsey had many narrow escapes. One of the most noted was opposite Vicksburg, where, in an engagement with the Kansas troops, he cap-tured a horse, but the horse was immediately shot while the Doctor was holding it. After the war the Doctor located at Waxahachie, Ellis Co., Tex., where he served as deputy sheriff under "Charlie Foster." He afterward clerked in a dry goods store a year and a half. In 1869 he moved to Benton County, Ark. November 8, 1871, he married Miss Oma Curtis, daughter of John and Caroline Curtis, who were natives of North Carolina and Kentucky, respectively. Mrs. Lindsey was born near Bentonville, Benton Co., Ark., and by her marriage became the mother of eight children, five of whom are now living, to wit: Olga T., Maggie C., Bertha B., Felix G. C., Flavius K.; those deceased were named Walter S., Ruth E. and one unnamed. The Doctor practiced his profession until 1880, at which time he ventured into the mercantile business at Round Top, one of the most noteworthy places in Benton County. He has charge of the post-office at Round Top. He is a Royal Arch Mason, and a good citizen.

Elbert S. Lindsey was born in Benton County, Mo., March 30, 1849, and is the son of Felix G. and Elizabeth Lindsey. He attended the public schools, but his education was somewhat interrupted by the breaking out of the war, which closed most of the schools. However, he secured a fair education in the graded school at Stockton, and at the age of sixteen began to earn money for himself by herding cattle. He afterward engaged in the lumber business, which he continued for about six months, and by that time had saved enough money to send him to school. He attended two terms of five months each, and by that time was pretty well qualified to teach, which he did. His first school was at Hunters Point, Cedar Co., Mo., where he taught a five-months term. He then taught another term of five months, after which he went to Benton County, Ark., and taught the first public school taught in district No. 7 after the reconstruction. He then returned to Stockton, and took another five-months course, and continued to teach afterward until October, 1874. He then went to McDonald County, Mo., and clerked in a store at Elk Mills for John Streacher for five years, it being a branch house, and Mr. Lindsey having entire control. He then went to Eureka Springs and speculated in real estate for some time, and then returned to Elk Mills and engaged in general merchandising, which he has followed ever since; although he moved to Benton County in 1885 and located at Crump. It was through his efforts that the mail route, now in existence from South West City, Mo., and Bentonville, Ark., was established, and in him the prospect originated and by his industry was at last realized. Mr. Lindsey was married January 5, 1871, to Miss Mary E. Derrick, daughter of Rufus and Martha A. Derrick, of Benton County, Ark. The fruits of this union were five children: Rufus G., Ida L., Thomas W., Elbert M., and Eugene L. Mr. Lindsey is a Democrat in his political views, but refused to vote for Greeley. He is a member of the Masonic fraternity.

George T. Lincoln, member of the clothing firm of Lincoln & Arthur, of Bentonville, Ark., and the son of George and Julia A. (Gaitwood) Lincoln, was born in Clay County, Mo., in 1840. George Lincoln was born in Scott County, Ky., in 1796, was of German descent, and was the son of Thomas Lincoln, who was a native of Virginia, and a first cousin of Abraham Lincoln. George Lincoln was reared in Kentucky, whither his parents had moved at an early day, and in 1821 he immigrated to Clay County, Mo., purchased a farm of 320 acres, which he cultivated, and which to this day is in the possession of his wife, Julia A. (Gaitwood) Lincoln. Mr. Lincoln afterward became the owner of 480 acres. He was a soldier in the War of 1812, and was in the battle of Raisin River. He died in 1852 at Council Bluffs, Iowa, while on his way home from medical treatment at Fort Pier. His wife was born in Scott County, Ky., in 1802, and is of Scotch origin. She now resides on the old home place in Clay County, Mo., and is eighty-six years old. She was the mother of fifteen children, thirteen of whom lived to be grown, and eight of whom are now living: John K., Mrs. Fannie Hockaday (widow of I. N. Hockaday), Lemuel S., Lucy (wife of T. K. Bradley), George T., Charles H., James E. and Julia (wife of John McMichael). George T. was reared on the farm, and remained with his mother until twenty years of age. He was educated at William Jewell College, his mother being one of the original subscribers to the fund of the institution, and graduated in the English course and in mathematics. After reaching his majority he commenced merchandising in Clay County, Mo., and at the end of one year sold out, and returned to farm life. He tilled the soil for about a year, and, the war breaking out, he enlisted in Capt. Jesse Price's company, Confederate States army, John T. Hugh's battalion, in June, 1861. He was in the battles of Lexington, Elk Horn, Corinth, Iuka, second battle of Corinth, Jackson, and afterward a scout under Joe Blackburn, now Senator from Kentucky. He was captured in front of Vicksburg, and retained twenty-nine days in the city. He was slightly wounded at two different times, and was in service four years and two months, surrendering at Grenada, Miss. Previous to the war, in 1860, he married Miss Virginia M. Pryor, who was born in Kentucky in 1844, and to them was born one child, Morton. Mrs. Lincoln died in 1861. After the war Mr. Lincoln located at Nebraska City, Neb., and was in the freighting business until 1870, when he went to the Indian Nation, near Fort Smith, Ark., and followed farming and trading stock for six years, when he returned to his birthplace. In 1875 Mr. Lincoln married Miss Ellen S. Sykes, a native of Alabama, born in 1848, and the daughter of Dr. William T. Sykes. In 1884 Mr. Lincoln moved to Bentonville, Ark., where he established a clothing and furnishing house, his partner being N. S. Jackson. January 20, 1886, the firm of Lincoln & Arthur was established, and this has since continued. They carry a first-class stock of ready-made clothing, gents' furnishing goods, hats, caps, etc. In State and national affairs Mr. Lincoln is Democratic, but in local affairs he is independent. He was a member of the town council of Nebraska, and is a member of the school board of Bentonville, being president of the same. He is a member of the Masonic fraternity, and is Master of the lodge. He and wife are members of the Christian Church.

Capt. Whitfield C. Lefors was born in Scott County, Ky., June 25, 1830, and is a son of Samuel and Margery (Montgomery) Lefors, who were born in North Carolina and Kentucky in 1785 and 1792, and died in Texas and Arkansas in 1849 and 1876, respectively. The father removed with his parents to Kentucky when a child, and there became a successful farmer. His father, Raney Lefors, was born in France, and came to America in his youth, and afterward married Miss Gillispie, of Irish descent. Mrs. Margery (Montgomery) Lefors' father was Henry Montgomery by name, an Irish refugee, who came to America and served in the War of 1812, and died while on his way home after the close of that war. Whitfield C. Lefors moved with his parents to Morgan County, Ill., in 1831, but soon after went to what was then the Territory of Arkansas, and in 1833 became a resident of Green (now Dade) County, Mo. Here he grew to manhood, and received such education as the meager facilities of that day afforded. In his eighteenth year he and his parents immigrated to Texas, where he was married to Miss Martha L. Hale in 1850. She was born in Christian County, Ky., October 29, 1836, and died July 25, 1886, a daughter of Benjamin Hale, a farmer. Mr. Lefors farmed in Texas until October, 1854, when he came to Benton County, Ark., settling on unimproved land, and began the task of opening up a farm. In August, 1863, he enlisted in Company F, Second Arkansas Cavalry, U. S. A., and served in Arkansas, Missouri, Tennessee, Alabama and Mississippi until the close of the war, when he returned to his home and resumed farming. He rose rapidly to the rank of first lieutenant, and afterward acted as captain of his company until the close of the war. In 1868 he was elected sheriff and collector of Benton County, and held that office from March of that year until January, 1873, being afterward appointed county treasurer, which office he held two years. He also served one year as mayor of Bentonville. He resided in Bentonville from 1869 until 1885, but since that time has resided on his farm. He is in comfortable circumstances, and is one of the progressive farmers and worthy citizens of the county. He has seven children living, all of whom have received good educations; their names are Elbridge Gerry, John Henry, Virginia, Elijah Oscar, Capt. Drummer, Lillie and Daisy. He also has seven children dead, whose names are Richard Whitfield, born August 10, 1852, died April 16, 1863; Samuel Green, born January 15, 1854, died August 14, 1854; Benjamin Patten, born December 12, 1855, died March 22, 1857; Fremont, born January 9, 1857, died May 6, 1876; Charles Bingly, born June, 1869, died September 12, 1871; Martha Ellen, born in the fall of 1872, died April 10, 1873; Lucy, born March 25, 1879, died November 15, 1880.

Edgar H. Looney, postmaster at Bentonville, and druggist, is a native of Hart County, Ga., born in 1856, and the son of Morgan H. and Emma M. (Black) Looney. The father was born in Georgia, was of English-Irish lineage, and was a teacher and attorney by profession. He was educated at the State University of Georgia, at Athens, and graduated from the same. For the last forty years he has devoted his time and attention to teaching. He was instrumental in securing the location of the State University of Arkansas at Fayetteville, and was offered a position as teacher. From 1872 to 1875 he was principal of the Bentonville High-school, having 400 pupils in attendance. For the past four years he has resided at Bowman, Elbert Co., Ga., where he is now engaged in teaching, being principal of the high-school. He is also an attorney by profession, is a man of eminent ability, is a first-class criminal lawyer, and one of the leading educators of the South. His wife, Emma M. (Black) Looney, was born in Georgia, and died in 1871. She was the mother of four children: Edgar H., Charles E. (printer and editor, of Georgia), Mirtie and Mortimer B. Edgar H. was educated in Gilmore, Tex., and at the age of seventeen began clerking in a dry goods store at Sulphur Springs, Tex. In 1875 he located at Bentonville, and in March of the same year he married Miss Cora Taliaferro, a native of Bentonville, Ark., and the daughter of C. D. Taliaferro. They are the parents of three children: Charles, Amy and Lowrey. In 1876 Mr. Looney engaged in

BENTON COUNTY, ARKANSAS - BIOGRAPHICAL AND HISTORICAL MEMOIRS 183

****

the dry goods business at Bentonville with W. H. Cloe, and sold out three years later, but soon resumed the same line of business. In 1883 Mr. Looney purchased his partner's share, and has since then conducted the business alone. He is a young man of good business capacity and a first-class citizen. In 1877 he was appointed postmaster at Bentonville, Ark., and served three and a half years. March, 1885, he was re-appointed to the same position. He was treasurer of the city of Bentonville two terms, is a life-long Democrat in politics, is a member of the K. of P. and K. of H., and he and wife are members of the Presbyterian Church.

John C. McAdams, member of the firm of Magruder, McAdams & Co., wagon and carriage manufacturers of Bentonville, Ark., was born in Meigs County, Tenn., in 1844, and is the son of James and Mary (Neal) McAdams. The father was born in East Tennessee in 1825, and was a blacksmith by trade. In 1851 he immigrated to Polk County, Mo., and located at Bolivar. He was a soldier in the Black Hawk War, and while in service was run over by a wagon, which so crippled him that he had to return home. He was also in the late war, and rendered effective service. In 1877 he removed to Berryville, Ark., and there died in July, 1883. His wife, Mary (Neal) McAdams, was born in Virginia in 1824, and was of Irish extraction. She is yet living in Berryville, and is the mother of fourteen children, six of whom are now living. John G. was the eldest of this family, and was seven years old when his parents moved to Missouri. He was in his father's shop a great deal, but did not commence work until seventeen years of age, when he worked with his father about seven years. In 1872 he married Miss Mary S. Wood, who was born in Polk County, Mo., in 1855, and who became the mother of three children: Henry F., John W. and Alfred B. Mrs. McAdams died in 1879, and in March, 1885, Mr. McAdams married Mrs. Rachel (Wood) Gilmore, daughter of John Wood. To this union was born one child, Ethel. Mr. Adams remained in Polk County, Mo., until 1872, when he moved to Monroe County, of the same State, and there resided four years. He next located in Pope County, Ark., and worked at his trade a portion of the time, but for a few months clerked in a store. In 1878 he came to Bentonville, Ark.; he and John K. Putnam became partners, and he carried on his trade for four years. He then sold out and for two years was in the hardware business with the same partner, but soon after bought out his partner and took in B. F. Allison, to whom he sold out four months later. In 1884 Mr. McAdams purchased an interest in the carriage and wagon manufactory with Samuel Magruder and George W. Garrett. They manufacture spring wagons, buggies, and do all kinds of wood-work; also have a general repair shop. Mr. McAdams is a Democrat, is a Mason and an Odd Fellow. Mrs. McAdams is a member of the Cumberland Presbyterian Church.

Joseph G. McAndrew. Prominent among the energetic and prosperous farmers of Benton County, Ark., worthy of special mention is Mr. McAndrew, who was born in Lawrence County, Mo., February 2, 1854. His father, Joseph McAndrew, was born in East Tennessee in 1808. November 17, 1840, his marriage with Miss Malinda Perry took place, and their union was blessed in the birth of nine children: Elizabeth, the wife of J. L. Hagler, and Susan, Alexander, John, George and James, who are deceased; Joseph G., Ida, the wife of Dr. Philo Allen, and Samuel (deceased). The father was previously married, and by his first wife became the father of one son, William, who died soon after the commencement of the late Civil War. His present wife was born in Alabama, and moved to Tennessee when she was quite young. Joseph G. McAndrew was married on the 9th of January, 1878, to Miss Ethel Morrison, who was born in Benton County, Ark., February 5, 1859. Her father, R. A. Morrison, was one of the earliest settlers of Benton County, having come here in 1836. Mrs. McAndrew is the mother of four children: Joseph A., Harley, Emma and Elizabeth. Mr. McAndrew is the possessor of a fine farm of 160 acres, all in a fine state of cultivation. He is a Democrat in his political views, and cast his first presidential vote for Tilden. He has shown his brotherly spirit by becoming a member of the Masonic fraternity, and he and wife, as well as Mr. and Mrs. McAndrew, Sr., are members of the Methodist Episcopal Church, South.

Joseph H. McClinton, ex-sheriff and *ex-officio* collector of Benton County, and also real estate agent of Bentonville, is a native of Richland County, Ohio, born in 1840, and is the son of Hugh and Sarah (Black) McClinton. Hugh McClinton was born near Baltimore, Md., in 1803, was of Scotch-Irish extraction, and was a farmer by occupation.   In 1821 he went to Richland County, Ohio, with his father, John McClinton, who was a native of Ireland, and who immigrated to the United States previous to the Revolutionary War, and served as a soldier in the same. He died in 1846, at about the age of ninety years. Hugh McClinton was married in Richland County, Ohio, and in 1828 moved to Morrow County, of the same State, where he now resides, being eighty-five years of age. His wife, Sarah Black, was born in Washington County, Penn., in 1808, and was of Irish extraction. She died in 1879, and was the mother of seven children: John, James, William (deceased), Joseph H., Elias F., Matthew, and Sarah E., wife of Louis Morton. Joseph H. was educated in his native State, and at the age of twenty began teaching school, and continued this profession six terms. In 1859 he went to Lamar County, Tex., and taught school, and in 1861 he became a resident of Bentonville, Ark. In 1861 he enlisted in Company F, Fifteenth Regiment Arkansas Infantry, and was afterward transferred to Company F, Thirty-fourth Regiment Arkansas Infantry, Confederate States Army, and was elected first lieutenant of the company. He was in the battles of Wilson's Creek, Prairie Grove and Helena. He served until July, 1865, when he surrendered at Fort Smith. He afterward taught three terms of school. In 1867 he hired as salesman to A. W. Dinsmore, and sold goods for five years. In 1872 he went to Galion, Ohio, and he and his brother, James, ran a machine-shop, but at the end of four years sold out and returned to Bentonville, where he resumed his clerkship. In 1878 he was elected sheriff and *ex-officio* collector of Benton County, and in 1880 he was re-elected, serving for four years. He was a good officer and filled the position to the satisfaction of all. In 1881 he married Miss Sallie B. Bryant, a native of LaPorte, Ind., born in 1845. They have one adopted child, Josie, who is eight years old.   In 1886 Mr. McClinton and C. R. Bruce became partners in the real estate, loan and insurance business, and the next year they dealt in real estate exclusively. For the past eight years Mr. McClinton has assisted in collecting the tax of Benton County, in connection with his other business. He is a Democrat in politics; is a Master Mason; his wife is a member of the Presbyterian Church.

Z. H. McCubbins, groceryman, of Rogers, Ark., is one of four children—two of whom are living—born to the marriage of William McCubbins and Thebe Duncan. They were born and married in Tennessee, and about 1834 immigrated to Illinois, where they spent the remainder of their days. Z. H. McCubbins was reared in Illinois, and was there married to Miss Mary F. Clemmons, a native of Illinois and of Kentucky stock. Four children were the result of their union. Those living are Churchill and Orila, wife of Asa Hayes. In 1879 Mr. McCubbins came to Arkansas and spent two years in stock trading, and then moved to Kansas, where he traded in stock and fruit, meeting with fair success in that business. He owns a good ranch in that State, but in 1885 returned to Arkansas and located in Rogers, where he has since been engaged in the grocery business. He is one of the enterprising and thrifty business men of the county, and has a large and lucrative trade. He has assisted materially in building up the town of Rogers, and was one of the first settlers. He and wife are members of the Methodist Episcopal Church, and he is a pronounced Republican. During the late Civil War he joined Company E, One Hundred and Twenty-third Volunteer Mounted Infantry, and served his country faithfully for three years. He was mustered out at Nashville, Tenn., and discharged at Springfield, Ill. He entered the service as second lieutenant, and rose to the rank of first lieutenant and then to captain, serving in the latter capacity for about two and a half years. He is a member of the G. A. R.

H. M. McGaughey. Among the farmers of prominence of Benton County, Ark., deserving of mention is Mr. McGaughey, who was born in Franklin County, Ind., and is the youngest of nine children—five living—born to George and Stella (Byfield) McGaughey. The parents were born in the "Buckeye State" in 1796 and 1798, respectively, and were there married. They afterward became residents of Indiana, and in 1856 moved to Minnesota, where the mother died three years later. The father died in Arkansas in 1883. H. M. McGaughey remained in his native State until nineteen years of age, when he removed with his parents to Minnesota, and was a resident of Goodhue County for thirteen years. He then moved to Cottonwood County, and assisted in its organization, and was chosen its first treasurer. He was the second superintendent of public instruction, and the first legal clerk of the court. In 1878 he was elected to the office of county commissioner, and was chairman of that body for one year. He also held the office of justice of the peace nearly all the time he resided in the county. He was the owner of a fine farm, but after five years, during which his crops were destroyed by grasshoppers, and two seasons unfavorable to agriculture, he determined to seek new fields for his labors, and in 1881 he came to Arkansas, purchased a farm near Rogers, and here has since resided. He also owns some valuable town property. While in Minnesota (1872) he was married to Miss E. A. Shafer, who was born in Indiana in 1852, and by her is the father of two children: Frank and Cora. In 1861 Mr. McGaughey joined Company E, Third Minnesota Infantry; was with the company in the South and through Sibley's first campaign against the Indians in Minnesota, the Third being the first troops on the ground after the outbreak in 1862, and claims the honor of giving the Indians their first defeat, which was at Wood Lake. He was with the regiment through the siege of Vicksburg; was wounded at Helena, Ark., August 7, and remained in hospital till December, when he joined his regiment at Little Rock, Ark. Was on detached service there about six months, when he accepted a commission as first lieutenant Company B, One Hundred and Twelfth United States Infantry. Received his final discharge on account of disability February 13, 1865. He served under Mitchell, Buell, Sibley, Sherman and Steele, and was in a number of hotly contested battles and numerous skirmishes. Our subject is a pronounced Republican in political views, and in religion an Agnostic.

Josiah Wesley McGee, M. D., was born in Lawrence County, Tenn., August 26, 1841, and is the son of James G. and Sarah (Davis) McGee, and grandson of Henry McGee, who was born in Virginia in 1768, was a farmer and a Whig; he was shot by the Indians. The paternal grandmother was a native of New Jersey, was a member of the Baptist Church, and died at the age of one hundred and eight years. The maternal grandfather of the subject of this sketch, John Davis, was a native of North Carolina, a member of the Baptist Church, and a Whig in politics. The maternal grandmother, Rebecca Wakefield, was born in South Carolina, and was also a member of the Baptist Church. James G. McGee, father of our subject, was born in Georgia, not far from Chattanooga, in April, 1806, moved to Lawrence County, Tenn., at the age of twenty, engaged in farming, and two years later married Miss Davis. In 1852 they moved to Hardin County, Tenn., and to Ozark County, Mo., in 1870. The father was the owner of 300 acres of land, was a Whig in politics, afterward a Democrat, was a member of the Baptist Church, and died March 17, 1888. The mother was born in Jackson County, Ind., September 13, 1815, and moved to Lawrence County, Tenn., when about eight years of age. When but fourteen years of age she married Mr. McGee. She was a member of the Methodist Episcopal Church, and became the mother of the following named children: Mary J., Rebecca Ann, John H., William M., Josiah W., James M., Columbus L., Emily J., Thomas H., Solon H., Nancy E. and Jesse J. Josiah W. McGee began farming at an early age, and at the age of twenty-two married Miss Margaret Matthews, a native of Hardin County, Tenn. She was a member of the Congregational Church, and died December 30, 1884. The Doctor after his marriage moved to Wright County, Mo., in 1866, then to Douglas County, same State, in 1868, to Ozark County, Mo., also in 1868, and to Benton County, Ark., in 1879. He studied medicine in 1868, commenced practicing in 1873, and still continues to practice. July 8, 1885, he married Miss Jane Wright, a native of Benton County, Ark., and a member of the Methodist Episcopal Church. She died April 10, 1886. October 5, 1886, Dr. McGee married Miss Harriet W. Buttram, who was also a native of Benton County, Ark., born February 13, 1857, and a member of the Methodist Episcopal Church, South. To the first marriage were born these children: John B., William N., James G., Eugene M., Omar P., Mary E. and George E. By the second marriage one child, Sarah E., was born. Dr. McGee volunteered in Company B, Col. Crew's command, infantry, Confederate army, in 1862, and served one year. He was in the battle of Shiloh. He is a Democrat in his political opinions, is a member of the Masonic fraternity, and also a member of the Methodist Episcopal Church.

Samuel G. McGruder, member of the firm of McGruder, McAdams & Co., manufacturers of wagons and buggies and proprietors of a general repair shop in Bentonville, Ark., is a native of Wheeling, Ohio Co., W. Va., born in 1844, and the son of John W. and Margaret (Porter) McGruder. The father was of Scotch descent, was born in Maryland in 1810, and was a blacksmith by trade. He was married in Virginia, and in 1865 moved to Fayette County, Ohio. He died in 1882. The last part of his life was spent in tilling the soil. His wife, Margaret Porter, was born in Virginia in 1812, and died in 1884. They were the parents of twelve children, Samuel G. being the eighth. At the age of fifteen he commenced learning the wagon-maker's trade, and worked at it until the late war. In 1862 he enlisted in the United States service, Company H, Fifteenth West Virginia Volunteer Infantry, and served three years. He was in the fights at Hatches Run, Petersburg and Appomattox Court House. In the latter part of 1862 he was crippled by rupture, and was in the hospital at Cumberland, Md., for seventeen months. He was at Appomattox Court House when Gen. Lee surrendered, and was within a few feet of him during that ceremony. After the war he went to Ohio, but soon after went to Knox County, Mo., where he farmed for a short time, and then went from there to Wayne County, Iowa, where he worked at his trade, wagon-making, having learned the same at Wheeling, W. Va. He remained in Iowa two years, and then returned to Missouri, located in Chariton County, and soon after commenced working at his trade. In 1879 he became a citizen of Bentonville, and resumed work at his trade, William Haynes being a partner. At the end of three years Mr. Haynes sold to Alexander Smith, and one year later Mr. Smith sold to J. G. McAdams. In 1887 Mr. G. W. Garrett became partner, and since then the firm has been McGruder, McAdams & Co. They manufacture wagons, buggies, spring wagons, and do general repairing. They are good workmen, and their work is warranted to give satisfaction. In 1868 Mr. McGruder married Miss Amanda Hogan, who was born in Adams County, Ill., in 1853, and who became the mother of nine children by her marriage: Laura, Ada, Lillie, Norman, Pearl, James, Malweñ, John and Nellie. Mr. McGruder is a Republican in his political views, casting his first presidential vote for Lincoln in 1864. Mrs. McGruder is a member of the Missionary Baptist Church.

Thomas F. McKennon is one of the wealthy farmers of Benton County, Ark., being the owner of 240 acres of fine farming land, and was born and reared in the county and State in which he now resides, the former event taking place in 1859. His father, W. H. McKennon, was born in Tennessee in 1821, and was there married to Miss Lucretia Bobb, who was also born in that State. Soon after their nuptials were celebrated they came to Arkansas and located in Carroll County, where they became well-to-do farmers. Mr. McKennon died in 1866; his widow is still living, and resides in Clarksville, Ark. Thomas F. McKennon was educated in the common schools of Carroll County, and in the Clarksville Academy, one of the oldest educational institutions in the State, and through life has given the most of his attention to agricultural pursuits. In 1879 he was married to Miss Nannie Morrow, a native of Benton County, born in 1859, and by her is the father of two children, one named Cleva. Mr. McKennon came with his family to Benton County in 1879, and here they have since made their home. He is very public spirited, and has always taken a deep interest in enterprises calculated to benefit the county. He is a member of the Pea Ridge lodge of A. F. & A. M., No. 119, a member of the Presbyterian Church, and votes the Democratic ticket.

J. R. McKinney. Prominent among the old and respected citizens of Hico Township stands the name of J. R. McKinney, who was born in Pickens County, S. C., January 16, 1823, and is the son of John and Elizabeth (Robertson) McKinney, natives of North Carolina and South Carolina, respectively. The father was born in 1789, but was reared from seven years of age in South Carolina. He was married in this State, and here died September, 1873. He had followed agricultural pursuits all his life. The mother was born October 31, 1800, and is still living on the old farm in South Carolina. Of the ten children born to their marriage, nine grew to maturity and six are now living: Hester (Stewart), in South Carolina; Elizabeth E. (Penny), in Benton County; Kittie (Harper), in South Carolina; John H. C., minister and editor, in Indianapolis, Ind.; Josephine (Barron), in South Carolina, and J. R., who was reared in South Carolina, and remained with his parents until grown. He was married in Georgia, and followed agricultural pursuits in this State during the year 1858. In 1869 he moved to Benton County, Ark., and here has followed farming and stock raising. He is the owner of 320 acres of land, about 125 under cultivation. August 26, 1856, he married Miss Mary E. Moseley, a native of Raburn County, Ga., and eleven children were born to them: Lawrence B., Maggie L., Lizzie (wife of Geo. A. Jones), John H., Cornelia, Julia, Robert, Emma, Claburn and two deceased. Mr. McKinney and wife are members of the Methodist Episcopal Church, South. He is a Democrat in politics; is a Master Mason, was clerk of the county and supreme courts in Raburn County, Ga., and takes an active interest in political affairs.

Charles D. McKisick, farmer of Osage Township, is a native of Benton County, Ark., and was born in 1848. He is a son of Alexander and a grandson of James McKisick. The latter removed to Washington County, Ark., at an early day, and held the office of county clerk for several years. His son, Alexander, was born in Bedford County, Tenn., assisted him in the office until his marriage with Miss Serena Kincaid, whose parents were also Tennesseans. He then located on the farm where our subject now resides, and there died in 1865. His widow is living in Hill County, Texas. The following are her children: Mary I., wife of Robert A. Miller; James, who was killed at the battle of Pea Ridge; David C., Charles; Cynthia A., wife of T. T. Stephenson; Alexander H. (deceased), Letitia (deceased) and Robert A. (deceased). Charles D. McKisick was educated in the common schools of Arkansas, and has always remained at the home of his birth, with the exception of three years spent in Texas during the late war. He was married in 1876 to Lydia Callis, who was born and reared in Benton County. Her parents, William H. and Polly Callis, were native Tennesseans, and came to Arkansas at a very early day. Mrs. McKisick was born in 1858, and is the mother of four children: Letitia Bell, James H., Ruth and George D. Mr. McKisick is a Democrat, and owns 107 acres of the original home farm of 360 acres. On his farm is a spring of cold and clear water which flows into the Grand River.

Thomas Alfred McSpadden, farmer, of Benton County, Ark., was born in Monroe County, Tenn., in 1828. His father, Samuel McSpadden, was of Scotch-Irish descent, and was born in Jefferson County, Tenn., in 1790. He was married in that county to Miss Mary Lowry, also a native of Tennessee, and soon afterward moved to Monroe County, where he spent the remainder of his days. He was a soldier in the War of 1812, and was with Jackson at New Orleans. He was a firm supporter of "Old Hickory," and voted for him for the presidency. He was married three times, and by his first wife, Mary Lowry, who died in 1832, he became the father of six sons, only three of whom are living. Thomas Alfred was his fifth child, and was reared on a farm and made his home with his father until over twenty-three years of age. He then went to Lawrence County, Mo., where he purchased 120 acres of land and entered eighty more acres, and began farming on his own responsibility. In 1861 he enlisted in Capt. Lotspiech's company, and was at the battle of Wilson's Creek. While at home on furlough he was captured and taken to Springfield, where he was retained for some time. He served in all about six months. In 1866 he sold his property in Missouri, and became a citizen of Benton County, Ark., his first purchase in real estate amounting to eighty acres, which he has since increased to 194 acres. He is a stanch Democrat in his political views, and is a Master Mason. In 1853 he was married to Miss Elizabeth Williams, who was born in Polk County, Mo., in 1838, and by her is the father of nine children: Frances, the deceased wife of J. D. Douglass; Jennie, wife of S. McSpadden; Belle, wife of Robert Sikes, William B., James, John C., Thomas C., Milton, and Rebecca L., wife of Harry Warbritton. Mr. McSpadden and wife have been members of the Methodist Episcopal Church for about sixteen years.

Rev. John Maddox, presiding elder of the Methodist Episcopal Church at Rogers, Ark., was born in Illinois in 1836, and is a son of Lewis and Elizabeth (Hewitt) Maddox, who were born in Kentucky and Ohio, respectively. They were married in the latter State, and afterward moved to Illinois, thence to Indiana, locating near Terre Haute. The father was a farmer, and died October 22, 1877, the mother's death occurring November 20, 1887. They were the parents of three children, Rev. John H. Maddox being the only one now living. The eldest one, William, was a physician, and died at the age of forty-one years; the youngest died in infancy. The subject of this sketch was educated in the schools of Indiana, and in 1859 joined the Indiana Conference of the Methodist Episcopal Church, located after a few years, and remained a local elder of that church until 1882, when he moved to Kansas. Here he resided until May, 1884, when he came to Arkansas, and in the spring of 1885 joined the Arkansas Conference, and was appointed pastor at Rogers. At the annual conference held at Little Rock, Ark., in February, 1888, he was appointed presiding elder of Rogers District, which position he is ably filling at the present time. Imperfect health hindered him for a number of years from devoting his time to the itinerant ministry. He was married in Illinois, on the 21st of February, 1867, to Miss Kate Woodruff, who was born in Ohio in 1832. Mr. Maddox is a Republican and a strong advocate of the cause of temperance, with which party he is likely to affiliate in the future.

J. Manwaring, of Benton County, Ark., was born June 23, 1847, in Broome County, N. Y., son of George and Sophia L. (Bundy) Manwaring, and grandson of Jabez and Sarah Manwaring, who were natives of Connecticut, but who moved to New York, where they spent the greater part of their lives. The maternal grandparents were also natives of Connecticut. George Manwaring was born in Chenango County, N. Y., and previous to leaving that State was a turner by trade. After coming to Iowa he followed agricultural pursuits. His wife was born in the same county, was well educated and had taught several terms of school. She was married to Mr. Manwaring April 13, 1836, and bore him six children, four now living: Lucius B., Jabez, Louis L. and Mrs. May E. Renicker. Jabez Manwaring, in company with his father and mother, removed to Iowa when eight years of age, and worked on the farm in that State until the death of his father in 1864. He received a good education in the common schools, and continued to operate the farm until 1867, when he removed with his mother to Wheatland, Iowa. He here engaged in the stock business, buying and shipping, which he continued until 1873, when he went to Fort Larned, Kas., took a claim and supplied the fort with wood for a short time. He then engaged in the stock business, remaining in Kansas for about two years. During the winter of 1873 he married Sarah Batterson, daughter of Henry Batterson, and a native of Indiana. Shortly after marriage Mr. Manwaring moved to Edwards County, Kas., followed the stock business again for about eighteen months, and then removed to a ranch in Comanche County, where he began raising stock. In 1879 he moved to Washington County, Ark., but about a year later came to Benton County, Ark., living about three miles north of Maysville, and then purchased the farm where he has since continued to live. He is a Democrat in politics.

Joshua Mason, merchant and postmaster at Mason Valley, Ark., was born in McDowell County, N. C., April 13, 1846, and is a son of John Jefferson and Emily (Gibbs) Mason, the former of whom was born in Alabama. Joshua Mason removed to Benton County, Ark., with his parents in 1858, and was here reared to manhood. He was educated in the common schools and by private study, and in contact with business life he has acquired a good practical education. His early days were spent in following the plow, but he afterward engaged in mercantile pursuits (about 1883), and his efforts in this direction have been followed with good results. His mercantile stock is valued at about $4,000, and his property in the country at about $3,000. All this property he has accumulated by hard work, honest dealing and good management. In September, 1863, he enlisted in the Union service, in Company A, First Arkansas Battery, and served under Capt. Denton D. Stark, his field of action being principally in Arkansas, Indian Territory and Missouri. He belongs to the Masonic lodge of Hazel Valley. He was married to Miss Sally Parker, who was born in Polk County, Mo., and is a daughter of Julia F. Parker, and he and wife worship in the Methodist Episcopal Church, South. Nearly all of Mr. Mason's people are engaged in farming, and are of Irish descent. The father, John Jefferson Mason, was born in Burke County, N. C., July 12, 1809, and is a son of Rev. Michael and Margaret (Hunter) Mason. Michael Mason was born in Pennsylvania, removed to Alabama, and there died in 1824. He was a minister of the Methodist Episcopal Church from early manhood until his death. His wife was born in North Carolina, and died in her native State in 1865. John Jefferson Mason was educated in the old-time subscription schools, and in 1835 was married to Emily Gibbs, who was born in North Carolina on the 22d of September, 1814, a daughter of Joshua and Rebecca (Conley) Gibbs. Mrs. Mason's grandfather, John Gibbs, was a Methodist minister for fifty years or more, and died at the age of eighty years, in North Carolina, in 1853. Mr. and Mrs. Mason became the parents of three sons and three daughters, and in 1857 immigrated to Arkansas, where he entered eighty acres of land and engaged in farming. He and wife are members of the Methodist Episcopal Church, South, and are old and highly honored citizens of the county.

John L. Maxwell, M. D., of Bentonville, Ark., is a native of Jessamine County, Ky., born in 1833, son of Dr. Joseph L. and Sinai N. (Roman) Maxwell, and grandson of John Maxwell, who was a native of Scotland and who at an early date immigrated to the United States. He, John, went to Kentucky with a Mr. Patterson, and they erected the first house where Lexington now stands. Here John Maxwell died, in 1811. His son, Joseph L. Maxwell, was the only son, and was born in Lexington, Ky., about 1801. He was a graduate in both the literary and medical departments of the Transylvania University, at Lexington, Ky., graduating as an M. D. in 1821. He practiced in the town of his birth for a number of years, and afterward moved to Nicholasville, where he resided for a few years. In 1842 he immigrated to Independence, Jackson Co., Mo., and in 1844 moved to Cass County, Mo. He was a soldier in the Mexican War, and enlisted as assistant surgeon in Col. Ralls' regiment, Price's division, and was in service two years, or until the close of the war. He died in 1864 in Independence. He was a physician who stood in the front ranks of his profession, and was one of the highest Masons in the State of Missouri. His wife, Sinai N. Roman, was born in Fayette County, Ky., in 1805, is of German nativity, and is now living, a resident of Kansas City, Mo. She is the mother of nine children, five of whom are now living: Mary S., William R., Sarah, Dr. John L. and Joseph H. Dr. John L. Maxwell received his literary education at Chapel Hill College, Mo., and at the age of twenty years he commenced the study of his chosen profession. In 1853 Dr. J. L. Maxwell entered the medical department of the St. Louis University, now St. Louis Medical College, and in the spring of 1855 graduated as an M.D. He soon after located in Bates County, Mo,, and entered upon the practice of his profession at Johnstown, but soon afterward went to Butler, the county seat. He remained here until the breaking out of the war, and part of the time he edited the *Western Times*. In 1856 he married Miss Alzira C. Simpson, daughter of James M. Simpson, of Harrisonville, Mo., and a native of the Indian Territory, born 1835. To them were born nine children, seven of whom are living: Richard L., Joseph S., William R., Elizabeth A., Robert M., Sinai I. and Charles L. When the war cloud spread over the nation Dr. Maxwell gave up his local work and entered the Confederate army as surgeon. He enlisted in 1861 in Col. T. B. Cummings' regiment, Price's division, was in the battle of Dry Wood, and in many severe skirmishes, among them Carthage and Springfield. He was then moved south, but became sick and was not able for active service. He, however, purchased stock for the army, and rendered other effective service. When peace was declared he surrendered at McKinney, Tex. After the war the Doctor located in Kansas City, established a drug store, and here practiced medicine. In 1871 he moved to Bentonville, Ark., where he has since resided, but. on account of poor health. has not been actively engaged in his profession. Dr. Maxwell has a beautiful home, and is the owner of 120 acres of land adjoining the city of Bentonville. He has been engaged in business in Chicago, Ill., for the past few years, and spends a considerable portion of his time there. He is a Prohibitionist in his political views, and is a good citizen of the county.

Michael Burkhalter Maxwell, farmer and ex-county surveyor of Benton County, Ark., is the oldest of six surviving members of a family of twelve children born to Ebenezer and Martha (Griffin) Maxwell, and was born in Marion County, Tenn., in 1830. The father was of German descent, born in Georgia in 1803, and was a blacksmith, gun-smith and farmer by occupation. When a young man he went to Tennessee with his parents, Thomas and Mary (Campbell) Maxwell, and was married in that State. In 1852 he became a citizen of Benton County, Ark., and entered about 600 acres of land near the county seat. His death occurred about 1871 or 1872. His wife was of English descent, born in South Carolina in 1802, and died in 1874. About the time of her marriage she was living in Greene County, Tenn. Her son, Michael B., was educated at Sam Houston Academy, at Jasper, Tenn., and the University of Tennessee, at Knoxville, but did not graduate at the latter institution owing to failing health. A portion of the time during his academic and collegiate course he was engaged in teaching school, and in 1852 he came to Benton County, and began clerking for James A. Dickson, general merchant, of Bentonville, remaining with him two years. In 1853 he was elected county surveyor to fill a vacancy, and in 1854 was re-elected. He declined a re-nomination in 1856, but was again elected to the office in 1858, and also in 1860 and 1862. From 1866 to 1886 he has held the office with the exception of but a few years. In 1857 he was married to Miss America J. Woods, a daughter of William H. and Mary (Dickson) Woods. Mrs. Maxwell was born in Benton County, Ark., in 1839, and is the mother of nine children: Robert S.; Martha I., widow of George Bone; Mary E., wife of J. R. Woods; John H., Sarah J., Margaret C., Emma M., William C. and Myrtie M. Mr. Maxwell owns 448 acres of land, and has resided on his present farm since 1873. He is very conservative in politics, and has voted both the Republican and Democratic tickets. He is a strong Prohibitionist, and intends [September, 1888,] voting that ticket during the presidential election of 1888. He and his wife have long been members of the Cumberland Presbyterian Church, and all the children are members with the exception of the youngest.

Rev. Andrew J. Maxwell, farmer, is a son of Ebenezer and Martha Jane (Griffin) Maxwell, and was born in East Tennessee in 1840. [For parents' history see sketch of Michael Burkhalter Maxwell.] Andrew J. is one of twelve children, six of whom are living: Michael B., Calvin, Oziras D., Irena (widow of John Deason), Andrew J. and Jane (wife of R. S. Woods). Andrew J. was twelve years old when he was brought to Benton County. His boyhood days were spent in following the plow and in attending the common schools, and in September, 1861, he enlisted in Company F, Fifteenth Regiment "North West" Infantry, participating in the following battles: Pea Ridge, Port Gibson, Vicksburg, Baker's Creek, Shreveport and numerous skirmishes. He was captured at Pea Ridge, and was kept a prisoner at Alton, Ill., for seven months. He was also taken prisoner at Vicksburg, but after five days' captivity succeeded in effecting his escape. After the war he returned home, and August 15, 1865, he was married to Miss Eliza Jane Woods, a daughter of Samuel P. and Eliza G. (Dickson) Woods. Mrs. Maxwell was born in Benton County, Ark., in January, 1846, and became the mother of nine children: Samuel Newton, Thomas Jeremiah, Margaret Emeline, John Smart, Laura Belle, Letitia Ann, Stella Graves, Fred Lee and Charles Calvin. In 1866 Mr. Maxwell purchased his present farm of 153 acres. He became a member of the Cumberland Presbyterian Church in 1860, but united with the Missionary Baptist Church in 1883, and was ordained a minister of that church in the following year. In 1885 he was given charge of the Pea Ridge, Lowell and Pleasant Sight Churches, but in 1887 he gave up preaching in the Lowell Church, retaining charge of the Pea Ridge and Pleasant Sight Churches, and preaching twice a month in each.

William A. Miller. Among the business houses of Rogers, Ark., may be mentioned the general mercantile firm of Mr. Miller, who established his store in the town in 1881, being one of the first residents of the same. He was born in Warren County, Tenn., in 1845, and is a son of Alexander C. and Jane (Miller) Miller, who were born in the "Old North State" and the "Palmetto State," respectively. William A. Miller was educated in his native State, and his boyhood days were spent in assisting his father on the farm. While still living in Tennessee he united his fortunes with those of Miss Clerissa Thomas, who was born in the State in 1848, and their union was blessed in the birth of ten children, as follows: H. H., Hugh J., John F., Charles A., Frank H., Anna M., Mabel C., A. C., Stella E. and Finis E. In 1868 Mr. Miller concluded to seek his fortune in the West, and accordingly located in Lawrence County, Mo., and there followed mercantile pursuits until 1881, when he sold out and came to Rogers, Ark., where he has since been successfully engaged in general merchandising. He is doing well, financially, and has a large and select stock of goods, which is conveniently arranged in his commodious frame business building, which he erected on coming to the town. Mr. Miller is prominently connected with some of the principal manufacturing interests of the town, and is noted for the interest he takes in helping to forward all public enterprises. He has held the office of city treasurer for several successive terms, which he now fills. He supports the principles of the Democratic party, and is a member of the A. F. & A. M.

William Miser, postmaster at Brightwater, Ark., is a native of Benton County, born in 1853, and is a son of G. W. and Jane Miser. The father was born in Tennessee in 1807, and was there reared and married. The mother died in Arkansas in 1840, having borne nine children, and the father was afterward married to Miss Jane Potter, by whom he became the father of eight children, our subject being the fifth. G. W. Miser after coming to Arkansas located on Pea Ridge, where he became one of the leading farmers and stockmen of the county, owning at one time 1,460 acres of land and other valuable property. His death occurred on the 25th of December, 1861. William Miser's boyhood days were spent in following the plow and in attending the common schools. In 1878 he was united in marriage to Miss M. V. Pickens, who was born in Arkansas in 1858. Mr. Miser is the owner of a farm, and has an orchard of 1,300 trees, and is at present engaged in managing the mercantile store of J. S. Dickson, at Bright Water. Mr. Miser is a Democrat, is past master and secretary of Pea Ridge Lodge No. 119, A. F. & A. M., at Brightwater. He is also a Pilgrim Knight and a Chapter Mason. He and wife worship in the Methodist Episco-, pal Church, South.

George W. Miser, farmer and stock raiser, is a native of Benton County, Ark., and was born in 1858, a son of G. W. and Jane (Potter) Miser. [For parents' history see sketch of William Miser.] He has followed agricultural pursuits all his life, and his boyhood days were spent in assisting his father on the farm, and in attending the common schools. In 1879 the nuptials of his marriage with Miss Laura V. Winters were celebrated. She was born in Missouri in 1860, and is a daughter of Joshua Winters, a prosperous farmer and stock raiser of that State. Four children were born to her marriage with Mr. Miser: Jennie E., Mary L., Susan L. and William L. Mr. Miser is one of the enterprising young farmers of the county, and is highly esteemed and respected as a good citizen and neighbor. He is a member of the Methodist Episcopal Church, South, is a Pilgrim Knight in the A. F. & A. M., and votes the Democratic ticket.

Henderson Mitchell, of the firm of Mitchell Bros., druggists, grocers and hardware merchants at Bloomfield, Ark., was born in the town in which he now resides March 17, 1856, and is a son of George Washington and Mary (Londagin) Mitchell, who were born in Tennessee. The father was a farmer, and is now residing at Bloomfield, Ark. He is a son of Nelson and Elizabeth Mitchell. Mrs. Mitchell is a member of the Missionary Baptist Church, and a daughter of John and Susan Londagin. Henderson Mitchell grew to manhood and was educated in Arkansas. He was first educated in the common schools, and at the age of twenty years entered the State University of Arkansas, and graduated from the normal course in 1879. He then engaged in teaching school, and in 1880 went to Durango, LaPlata Co., Colo., where he remained six years, the first three years engaged in freighting, and the three last years had charge of the lumber yard and planing-mill of T. C. Graden & Co. He returned to Arkansas in 1886, and engaged in the drug, grocery and hardware business, his brother Franklin becoming his partner. In 1887 he was married to Miss Ella Douglass, and by her is the father of one child, Emma. Mr. Mitchell began life without means, but his business ventures in the West met with a fair degree of success, and by his own efforts he has placed himself in comfortable circumstances. He belongs to the Masonic fraternity. His wife is a daughter of H. and Emma Douglass, of Benton County.

Roland Mitchell, M. D., is one of the prominent physicians of Benton County, Ark., and was born in Alabama in 1827. His parents, Boswell and Mary Mitchell, were born in the "Palmetto State," but were married in Alabama, where they resided until 1829, when they located in Georgia, and there spent the remainder of their lives. The father's death occurred in 1844 at the age of forty-seven years, and the mother's in 1881 at the age of eighty-seven years. Dr. Mitchell is the fifth of their seven children, and was educated in Georgia. He attended the second course of medical lectures ever delivered in Atlanta, and practiced the medical profession for four years in Tennessee before coming to Arkansas. He became a resident of the latter State in 1860, locating on Pea Ridge at Lee Town, and during the war had charge of the wounded at that place. After the battle of Pea Ridge he went to Fayetteville, Ark., and was appointed assistant-surgeon of the United States army at that point. In June, 1866, he returned to Pea Ridge, and here has since been an active medical practitioner. He is the oldest physician on Pea Ridge, and was a member of the first medical board of Benton County. His first presidential vote was cast for Zachary Taylor, and he is a Master Mason. He was married in Tennessee to Miss Mary P. Lyde, who died in 1872, having borne two children : John and Mary I. His second marriage was with Miss Mary O. Rice, and four children have blessed their union, three of whom are living: Milton, Charles B. and Julia.

Zachariah Mitchell, contractor and brick manufacturer, of Bentonville, Ark., was born in Tippecanoe County, Ind., in 1837, and is a son of James M. and Lucinda (Corbin) Mitchell, who were born in Kentucky and Indiana in 1810 and 1817, respectively. James M. Mitchell was of English and Dutch lineage, and when a child was taken to Ohio, and thence to Tippecanoe County, Ind., where he married Miss Corbin. In 1840 he located in Harrison County, Mo., where his wife, who is of Irish descent, died in 1884. Zachariah Mitchell is the third of eight children, and was only eight years old when his parents moved to Missouri. He grew to manhood on a farm, and in 1857 was married to Miss Martha H. McIntosh, a native of Tennessee, born in 1841. They have six children living: Alice, wife of Thomas Mitchell; William H., James, Charles, Aaron and ——. In 1867 Mr. Mitchell became a citizen of Benton County, Ark. His first investment in real estate was forty acres of land about five miles from the county seat. He sold this land, however, in 1872, and moved to Bentonville, and began working in a brick-yard, and three years later engaged in the manufacture of brick, which has been his business off and on ever since. In 1887 he manufactured 120,000 brick and this year (1888) has made 260,000. He is a Democrat in his political views, and was a strong Union man during the war. He is a Master Mason, and a member of the Methodist Episcopal Church. His wife died in 1887, and in 1886 he was married to Mrs. Martha E. (Gilespie) Lee, who was born is Mississippi, and is a member of the Cumberland Presbyterian Church.

H. Montgomery, one of the old and enterprising citizens of Benton County, Ark., was born in Ste. Genevieve County, Mo., and dates his birth on November 5, 1815; son of William and Margaret (Eads) Montgomery. He lived in his native county until reaching his eleventh year, and was tolerably well advanced in his studies for one of his age. He then went to St. Louis, from there to Sangamon County, Ill., and settled on Sugar Creek, about fifteen miles from Springfield, where he lived for about two years. St. Louis at this time was but a small village, and what is now St. Francois was then Ste. Genevieve. He remained in the last named place about ten months, going from there to Potosi, in Washington Co., Mo. He worked at the blacksmith trade in this county for a year, and from there went to Hempstead County, Ark., and from there in a short time to Clark County, of the same State. Here he remained two or three years dealing in stock, taking mules and horses south, and then selling. While in Missouri failing health caused Mr. Montgomery to be idle for a number of months, and he took a much needed rest. He again went to St. Louis, remained a short time, and then went up the Illinois River to Peoria, and from there soon after to Galena, where he worked in the lead mines for three years. Not meeting with good success he returned to his old occupation of blacksmithing, which he followed for about eight months in Galena. He then returned to St. Louis, Mo., and from there to Arkansas, where he began dealing in stock, driving from that State to Louisiana and Texas. He then went to St. Clair County, Mo., where he purchased land, but did not locate. This land he owned for about seven years, and during this time was stage agent on the line from St. Louis to Cape Girardeau, Mo., which was before railroads, and worked in this capacity for about three years. In 1845 he married Miss Julia White, daughter of John White, of Southwest Missouri. By this union he became the father of two children, both now living: Margaret, wife of William Newberry, and Cora, wife of S. H. Brown. Before his marriage and while in Arkansas Mr. Montgomery spent much of his time traveling, and was over the greater part of Indian Territory and Texas. After marriage he moved to Southwest Missouri and settled in St. Clair County, but from there went to Iowa and then back to Missouri, and then to California, traveling over a large part of the State, and finally returned to Missouri by way of the Isthmus. He was in Madison County of that State during the war, and was taken prisoner nine different times. While in that county he traded in horses and mules, taking them to St. Louis and selling them to supply the Government. After the war Mr. Montgomery went to Greenville, Wayne Co., Mo., and engaged in merchandising. Here he remained for about four years, being burnt out, and then went to Fredrickstown, where he lost his wife in 1860. She was in her forty-second year at the time of her death. Mr. Montgomery's health again failing he took a trip over into Montgomery County, and went down into the Creek Nation, in Indian Territory. After moving around for some time he finally settled in Benton County, Ark., where he has since lived. He is at heart a Christian, but has never connected himself with any organization. Politically he is a stanch Hickory Jackson Democrat. Mr. Montgomery has 120 acres of land, about eighty-five under cultivation.

S. H. Brown, son-in-law of Mr. Montgomery, was born in Macoupin County, Ill., July 27, 1848, and is the son of Daniel T. and Sarah (Olmstead) Brown, both natives of New York State. They were the parents of ten children, four now living: Mrs. Huldah C. Hamilton, Zelina A. and Stephen H.

Those deceased were named Charlotta L., Daniel S., Martin M., Martha L., Sarah J. and Katie M. Mr. Brown worked on the farm during his boyhood, and received a good practical education in the public schools, but later attended McKendry, and finished at the International Business College at Springfield. He then went to Bunker Hill and engaged in the butcher's business for one year. In the fall and summer of 1874 he bought and shipped stock to St. Louis. September 15, 1874, he married Miss Cora Montgomery, daughter of H. Montgomery. She had every advantage for an education, having taken a complete course at Carrollton Institute, at Farmington, Mo., also attended the St. Joseph's Convent in St. Louis, and later attended the school at Bunker Hill. She then married Mr. Brown and became the mother of six children, five now living: Maggie M., Zelma A., William H., Minta B. and Stephen H. The one deceased was named Daniel M. After marriage Mr. Brown farmed for one year in Illinois, and in November, 1875, he started for Maysville, in Benton County, arriving there December 28 of the same year. After remaining there a short time he went to Cow Skin Prairie, rented land one year, and then moved to Benton County, Ark., where he lived for four years, and then went back to Illinois. Here he tarried but ten months, and then returned to Benton County, settled on the farm he first occupied and has remained there ever since. He has 240 acres of land, 160 under cultivation. Mr. Brown has always been a Democrat in politics, and he and Mrs. Brown are members of the Cumberland Presbyterian Church.

Berry P. Morris was born in Rutherford County, N. C., January 5, 1822, and is the son of Dotson and Caroline (Johnson) Morris. The father was probably born in North Carolina, and was reared in that State. He then went to Alabama, where he remained from about 1831 to 1874, and then moved to Little Rock, Ark., where he died at the last mentioned date. He was a farmer by occupation, and a good man. The mother was born in Burke County, N. C., and died in Alabama about 1872; ten children were born to this union, Berry P. being the third child. He was reared from nine years of age to manhood in Alabama, and remained in that State until 1858, when he came to what is now Logan County, Ark., and farmed there for twelve years. From there he went to Sebastian County, Ark., and tilled the soil there until 1885, when he located at Siloam Springs, and here followed his old occupation of farming. He owns two farms three miles from Siloam Springs, 100 acres, fifty-six under cultivation, but he is residing in the town. Mr. Morris also owns some farms in Sebastian County. He was married, at the age of twenty-four, to Miss Laura Ann Shelton, of Alabama, and they became the parents of eight children: Eustacia J., wife of John Darks; Carroll K., deceased; Burrel H., deceased; Fleetwood, in Sebastian County; Elizabeth, wife of Zachariah Ragsdale; Virgil, a merchant in Siloam Springs; Missouri F. and Barclay, who died fifteen years ago, wife of Henry Graves. The mother of these children died November 3, 1884, and Mr. Morris was married April 29, 1885, to Miss Sarah Hill, of Sebastian County; two children were the fruits of this union: Roscoe C., and an infant, Allen B. Mr. Morris was a Democrat before the war, but since then has been a conservative Republican, and is one of the enterprising citizens of the community. He and wife are members of the Christian Church.

Robert S. Morris, banker at Siloam Springs, and son of Joseph and Elizabeth (Griffith) Morris, was born in Monroe County, Ohio, November 23, 1837. The father was born in Virginia, and was a tiller of the soil. He moved to Ohio, where he lived until 1848; one year later he removed to Iowa. During the late war he enlisted in the Graybeard Regiment in Iowa, Union army, and was stationed at St. Louis, Alton and Rock Island at various times during the war. He died in Iowa in 1885. Mrs. Morris was born in Pennsylvania, and moved with her parents to Ohio, where she was married. She died in 1882. Ten children were born to their marriage: Dillon, deceased; Morgan, Mary Ann; Thomas H., an employee in the Pension Bureau at Washington, D. C.; Jane, wife of John B. Morrison, merchant, of Northwestern Kansas; Nancy; Oliver W., farmer near Centerville, Iowa; Rachel, deceased, wife of Abner Harber, of Iola, Kas.; John H., general agent for the Singer Sewing Machine Company at Kirksville, Mo., and Robert S. The last named was reared in a store in Centerville, Iowa, and educated himself at odd times when not at work. In 1862 he enlisted in the Seventeenth Iowa Infantry, and fought in the battles of Pittsburg Landing, the first and second battles of Corinth and Iuka, besides numerous skirmishes. After the war he returned to Centerville, Iowa, and was married in 1865 to Miss Victoria L. Sturgeon, who was born in Ohio in 1845. From this union they have one child, Ollie. Mr. Morris was engaged in shipping stock for four or five years previous to 1882, when he came to Siloam Springs and engaged in banking. He does a prosperous general banking business, and is thoroughly identified with the interests of Siloam Springs and vicinity. He is a member of the Masonic fraternity, is a Republican in politics, having cast his first presidential vote for Abraham Lincoln in 1860; he and Mrs. Morris are members of the Methodist Church.

N. B. Morton, horticulturist, of Benton County, Ark., was born in Henry County, Va., in 1838. His parents, David and Elizabeth (Petty) Morton, were Virginians, and early residents of Southern Missouri, locating in the latter State in 1856, where he followed the occupation of farming. During the Civil War the father was shot by the Missouri State Guards, seventy-two shots being fired at him, and his friends were not permitted to care for his remains at his own home. The mother died in 1878 at the age of sixty-one years. N. B. Morton moved to Tennessee with his parents, and after a residence of twelve years in that State came with them to Missouri. Here he joined the Confederate service, Company A, Fourth Regiment Missouri State Guards, and served over four years. After the close of the war he spent three years in Louisiana, and then returned to Cooper County, Mo., and from there came to Arkansas in 1881, and is the owner of a good farm of 160 acres. His residence is situated at the Electric Springs in Benton County, and he keeps a boarding house, the only one at the Springs. In October, 1865, he was married in Louisiana to Miss Carrie Blackwell, and their union has resulted in the birth of two children: William A. T. and Lewis Napoleon. Mr. Morton and family are members of the Baptist Church.

William M. Murphy is a native of Green County, Ky., where he was born May 5, 1827, and is a son of Philip and Sarah (Hale) Murphy. The former was born in Kentucky, and continued to live there until 1856, when he moved to Texas County, Mo., where he resided until his death, at about eighty years of age. The following were his children: Eliza (deceased), Nancy, Mary Ann (wife of Julius Scaggs), Elizabeth (who married David Scaggs, and is deceased), Henry, James, William M. and Philip (deceased). William M. Murphy was married in 1848 to Miss Lydia Ratliff, of Kentucky, and two years later he and his wife moved to Indiana. Here they lived until 1870, when they moved to Tarrant County, Tex.; five years later he located on his present fertile farm of 587 acres, on Osage Creek. Mr. Murphy affiliates with the Democratic party, and cast his first presidential vote for James Buchanan. He and wife are members of the Baptist Church; they became the parents of the following children: Sarah, wife of David Smith; Alice, wife of Charles Pittman, and James; four children are deceased. The mother of these children died June 20, 1863, and October 24, 1863, Mr. Murphy married Mrs. Catherine James.

W. T. Neal, who has long been a prosperous farmer of Benton County, Ark., was born in Knox County, Tenn., in 1839, and is a son of John A. and Harriet (Comb) Neal, who were also born in Tennessee, and were farmers by occupation. They became residents of Madison County, Ark., in 1853, but the father's death occurred in Washington County, in 1883. W. T. Neal received such education as the schools of his day afforded, and in 1860 concluded to seek his fortunes in the far West, and went to California, where he remained for over nine years. His business enterprises in that State met with good success, and he succeeded in accumulating considerable money. In 1869 he returned to Benton County, Ark., and purchased his present home, which comprises about ninety-seven acres of land with eighty-five acres well improved and under good cultivation. In 1885 he was married to a Mrs. Massey, by whom he is the father of one child, Georgia Pearl. Mr. Neal has shown his fraternal spirit by becoming a member of the Masonic fraternity, and in his political views supports the principles of the Democratic party. His wife is a member of the Methodist Episcopal Church, South.

B. A. Neil, farmer, of Batie Township, and son of John D. and Sallie (Roach) Neil, was born in Bradley County, Tenn., June 20, 1840. The father was born in Marion County, Tenn., December 12, 1810, and there remained until his twenty-third year, when he removed to Bradley County. The country was at that time wild and unsettled, and the few settlers were obliged to band together and erect fortifications to defend themselves from the Indians. The mother was born on the Hiawassa Purchase, in what is now Whitfield County, Ga., and after reaching womanhood moved to Bradley County; was there married to Mr. Neil, and bore him eleven children, nine now living: Benjamin A., Mrs. Elizabeth Knesster, William, Mrs. Sarah Alford, John D., Josephine, Mrs. Martha J. Bair, Mrs. Emily F. Ware and Jennie. James K. and Mary E. are the children deceased. William D. O'Neil emigrated from Ireland to the United States when a boy, and served in both the War of 1812 and the Mexican War. In the former he participated in the battle of Horseshoe Bend, and in the latter in the battle of Buena Vista. After coming to this country he changed his name to "Neil." Sarah (Davis) Neil, the grandmother, was born in Virginia, was thoroughly educated, and was an aunt of Jefferson Davis, the Confederate President. Eliza (Thatch) Roach, the maternal grandmother, was born in Morgan County, Tenn., and was afterward married to David Roach, who was a native of Virginia. B. A. Neil received a common-school education, and when sixteen years of age began work on the E. V. T. & G. Railroad, doing the work of fireman. Afterward he was given an engine, and acted as engineer for four years, at which time he enlisted in Company A, First Tennessee Battalion of Artillery, under Maj. Hugh McClune. His first service, however, was with the Louisiana Zouaves, and he and four others were the only ones who escaped death. At the first battle of Manassas and during the later engagements he was under Gen. Stonewall Jackson, Longstreet's division, the most important battles being Rappahannock, Richmond, Gettysburg, Seven Pines, Chickamauga, Resaca, Ga., the Wilderness and numerous smaller engagements. In 1865 Mr. Neil married Miss Mary M. Breakbill, daughter of Peter and Lea Breakbill. Nine children were the result of this union: Mrs. Mary E. Smith, Mrs. Martha J. Wammack, Benjamin F., William D., Sarah G., George M., John S., Ida B. and Menta Lee. The mother of these children died July 9, 1888. After moving to Missouri Mr. Neil located on Rock Prairie, Lawrence County, and there remained two years. He then went to Texas, but returned to Lawrence County after two years. Here he remained until 1876, when he moved to Sarcoxie, and from there to Arkansas in 1888, settling in Benton County. One year later he again went to Texas, but only remained there ten months, when he returned to Benton County, Ark., and here has since remained. He has ninety acres of good land, all under cultivation. Politically he is a Democrat, never having voted any other ticket.

John A. Nelson, a prominent farmer of Hico Township, was born in Spartanburgh County, S. C., and is the son of James and Annie (Cantrell) Nelson. The mother was born in Spartanburgh County, S. C., and was the daughter of John and Sallie Cantrell. The father was born in the same State, and was of Virginian parentage, a son of John and Creecy Nelson. He moved to Buncombe County, now Henderson County, N. C., at an early date, remained there for thirteen years, and then moved to Lumpkin County, Ga., where he died in 1845. He had followed agricultural pursuits all his life. The mother was born in South Carolina, and died in Georgia in 1864, her death being caused by fright and excitement into which she was thrown by the battle of Altoona Pass, she being on a visit to her sister who lived there. Of the eight children born to this union, six grew to maturity, but all are now deceased with the exception of John A. and a sister. The former was reared on farms in North Carolina and Georgia, and remained with his mother until grown. He then spent three years mining in California, was reasonably successful and returned to his home, and on October 15, 1854, he married Miss Turzah A. Lott, of Forsyth County, Ga., born August 17, 1837, and the daughter of Judge John G. Lott, a prominent citizen of Forsyth County, Ga. To Mr. and Mrs. Nelson were born eleven children: Charles H., James L., John P., Oscar E., Ella E. (deceased), Augusta L. (deceased), Harlow (deceased), Alice (deceased), Emma A., Lula S. and Maggie Lee. After marriage Mr. Nelson farmed until the breaking out of the late war, when he enlisted in the Confederate army, and was in service three years in

Wheeler's Cavalry. He served first as a private, and was afterward made first lieutenant of Company F, of Burke's battalion. After the war he farmed in Georgia until 1866, when he moved to Washington County, Ark., where he remained two years. He then resided near Bentonville one year, and about 1869 he moved to his present property, which is situated five miles northeast of Siloam Springs, and which consists of 160 acres, about eighty under cultivation. Mrs. Nelson died November 30, 1877, and was a consistent member of the Missionary Baptist Church. April 14, 1887, Mr. Nelson took for his second wife Mrs. Annis A Overton, of Washington County, and the daughter of R. M. Huffmaster, an old citizen of Washington County, Ark. He and wife are members of the Missionary Baptist Church, and are excellent citizens. Mr. Nelson has been a Democrat all his life, and takes great interest in public affairs.

Thomas Turner Netherton, a native of Davis County, Mo., was born August 25, 1856, and is the son of Henry and Rachel (King) Netherton. The father was born and reared in Cocke County, Tenn., received a good practical education, followed farming, and, at an early day, immigrated to Missouri. The mother was born in Virginia, but left that State at the age of eleven and immigrated to Missouri, making the journey in wagons. They first settled in Missouri. She was a direct descendant of the famous Daniel Boone on her mother's side. After coming to Missouri she received a fair education and afterward married Mr. Netherton, to whom she bore nine children, eight now living: Daniel and Charles (twins), Sophronia, Boone, Gabrella and Luella (twins), Relda A. and Thomas T. The one deceased was named Branetta. After his marriage Mr. Netherton continued to live in Missouri until after the war (1865), when he moved to Arkansas, settled in Bates County, where he died about one year later. Mrs. Netherton is seventy-six years of age, is strong and vigorous, and, though in direct opposition to her son's will, does considerable work around the house. Thomas T. Netherton, the youngest child, has always continued to live at home, and is engaged in agricultural pursuits. His education was rather neglected, as he assisted largely in supporting the family after the death of his father; and he is now caring for his mother in the evening of her long and useful life In 1884 he married Miss Beatrice R. Rogers, a native of Louisiana, and the daughter of A. M. and M. J. Rogers, of Benton County, Ark. To Mr. and Mrs. Netherton has been born one child, Mabel D. Mr. Netherton is the owner of 186 acres of land, ninety being under cultivation; he is Democratic in politics, and is an excellent citizen. Mrs. Netherton is a member of the Missionary Baptist Church.

James C. Norman, son of Robert and Patsey (Coffee) Norman, was born April 18, 1818, in Bedford County, Tenn., and is a citizen of Benton County, Ark. Robert Norman was a native of North Carolina. When a young man he moved to Tennessee. He was a soldier in the War of 1812, under Gen. Jackson, was at the battle of New Orleans, and received a land warrant of eighty acres for services. Patsey Coffee was a native of Georgia, and immigrated to Tennessee when a young woman. Here she married Mr. Norman, and became the mother of eight children, five of whom are living: James C., William, Poter and Mrs. Eliza Noblett, Mrs. Martha Guthria, Thomas and Mary Butler (deceased) and Elizabeth Craig. Robert Norman married and lived in Middle Tennessee. there raised his children, then moved to Western Tennessee, where he and his wife both died. Grandfather Norman was born in North Carolina, and was of English descent. His wife, Nellie Norman, was also from North Carolina, and immigrated to Tennessee after the death of her husband. Grandfather and Grandmother Coffee were natives of Georgia and the grandmother was of Irish parentage. Grandfather Coffee was a soldier in the Revolutionary War, and was drawing a pension when he died. He was captured and imprisoned, and discovered that his side was victorious by the faces of the British soldiers. Robert Norman, after his marriage, lived on a farm until his children were grown, when he moved to Middle Tennessee, and afterward to Western Tennessee, where he died. The mother died on the old homestead. James C. Norman remained with his father until twenty-one years of age and assisted him on the farm. He received but a common-school education and worked for the neighbors for $10 a month, continuing to hire out until twenty-two years of age. He then married Miss Polly Grammar, a native of Bedford County, Tenn., and to them were born four children, three now living: Milford, William and Mrs. Martha Warsham. The one deceased was named Williamson.

Mrs. Norman died in Tennessee, and Mr. Norman, in 1851, married Miss Sarah J. Gibson, a native of Tennessee, and the daughter of John M. and Martha (Harper) Gibson, both of whom were natives of Tennessee. Grandfather Gibson was of Irish descent, and Grandfather Hooper was a native of North Carolina, and served in the War of 1812. To Mr. and Mrs. Norman were born ten children, four now living: George F, James Mc, Mrs. Amanda H. Carl and Mrs. Dorah F. Sciprey. Those deceased were Nancy A., John M. and four infants unnamed. Mr. Norman immigrated to Missouri in 1854, and resided in Greene County until 1877, when he moved to Benton County, Ark., and settled on his present farm, which consists of 220 acres, 100 under cultivation. He was on home duty at Springfield during the late war, and is a Democrat in his political views. He and Mrs. Norman are members of the Cumberland Presbyterian Church, and are good citizens.

John Milton Norris, druggist, of Cherokee City, Ark., was born in Audrain County, Mo., in November, 1850, and there resided until sixteen years of age, when he went to Montgomery County, Mo., with his parents, and was there reared to manhood. He learned the plasterer's trade, and was a successful contractor in that business for a number of years, but was obliged to give it up after a time owing to the failure of his health. From 1877 to 1878 he was engaged in the livery business in Wellsville, Mo., and from the latter date until 1879 he was a druggist of Edgerton, Kas. From that time until 1886 he was engaged in various occupations in Missouri, Indian Territory, Texas and Kansas, meeting with varying success, and at the latter date located in Cherokee City, Ark., where he has been engaged in selling drugs. He also has a farm near the town, and, although he is a comparatively young man, his business ventures have been in the main successful. He owns a good farm in Kansas, and also some town property in that State. May 6, 1874, he was married in Wellsville, Mo., to Miss Eliza A. Baxter, of Iowa, and their union has been blessed in the birth of the following children: Thomas Harvey, James Monroe, Dellie Callie and one deceased. Mr. Norris was educated in the common schools and the Warrenton College (Missouri), and is a young man well versed in the various topics of the day. He is a son of Thomas and Eliza Ann (Straub) Norris, who were born in Ohio and Kentucky, respectively. The father was a successful farmer, a member of the I. O. O. F., and belonged to the Cumberland Presbyterian Church. Owing to ill treatment during the war his health became very much broken, and he was taken by his son, John Milton, to Southern California, where he was kept three years. His health greatly improved, and he then returned home. He died in Denton County, Tex. at the age of sixty-five years. His wife died at the age of sixty-two years, a member of the Missionary Baptist Church. Their son, Maj. C. J. Norris, died of measles after his return from the army. He was in seventeen hotly contested battles, but was never wounded nor taken prisoner.

Charles E. Noyes, proprietor of Flint Creek Distillery, was born in Saranac, Ionia Co., Mich., April 20, 1854, son of Hiram and Susan (Bowen) Noyes. The father was born in Vermont about 1813, and was of English descent. He moved to Canada when young, and lived there until he went to Michigan in 1850, and thence to Illinois in 1859. In 1876 he went to Texas, and there died one year later. He was a farmer, which occupation he has followed all his life. The mother was born in New York in 1820, and is now living with her son, Charles E., who was one of ten children, eight now living; and is the only one living in this county. At the age of sixteen he began learning the saddlery and harness trade, and then attended commercial college. After finishing he ran a saddlery and harness shop at Lake City, Ill., for about six months, and then clerked in a store for about two years. After this, and while at Sullivan, Ill., he learned telegraphing and book-keeping, and then went to Texas, where he clerked and kept books at Spanish Fort. He left there and moved to Siloam Springs in 1881, and was engaged in the retail liquor business until 1886, when he built his distillery at a cost of $6,000—has wholesale license. For six months he had a trade from his warehouse of 6,000 gallons per six months. He has property in Siloam Springs, and has been one of the most enterprising citizens in giving solid financial aid to public enterprises. He was married in 1882 to Miss Alice McKilberry, a native of Terre Haute, Ind. They have two children: Eugenie Dott, who died at the age of three years, and Edith Dwade, now seventeen months old. Mr. Noyes is a member of the Masonic fraternity, K. of H., and carries a life insurance of $3,000 in the lodges. He is a Democrat in politics.

D. A. Oakley is a member of the grocery firm of Oakley & Nance, of Rogers, Ark., and was born in Bedford County, Tenn., in 1842, and is one of nine children, eight living, born to Haywood and Eliza (Bullock) Oakley, who were natives of the "Old North State." They became residents of Arkansas in 1869, and here the father's death occurred. The mother is still living, and is a resident of Benton County. Their son, D. A. Oakley, came to Arkansas in 1868, and was engaged in tilling the soil until 1882, at which time he purchased property in Rogers, and erected his store building and residence, and was a groceryman of the place for two years. He then sold his stock and returned to the farm, but at the end of three years again came to Rogers, where he has since been engaged in the grocery business, in partnership with R. L. Nance. They are doing a large and paying business, and in connection with their grocery have charge of a warehouse. Mr. Oakley is also a member of the firm of Oakley & McSpadden, liverymen, of Rogers, and besides this property is the owner of two valuable farms near Rogers. He is one of the public-spirited men of the county, and takes an active interest in all enterprises for the public weal. February 27, 1870, he was married to Miss Kittie Brame, who was born in Tennessee in 1846. They have five living children: William, Annie, Oscar, Lula and Edgar. Mrs. Oakley's father, W. S. Brame, is a resident of Tennessee, and is the last male of his race living, and with his death the name will become extinct. Mr. Oakley has been a member of the Methodist Episcopal Church, South ever since he was sixteen years of age, and in his political views supports the principles of the Democratic party. He served in Company D, Confederate States army, under Albert Sidney Johnston, but was wounded at the battle of Murfreesboro, and was never able to rejoin his command.

John H. Pace, a resident of Batie Township, was born in Tennessee, April 18, 1831, and is the son of Christopher S. and Margaret Maria (Woods) Pace. The father was born in Tennessee, and at the age of twenty married Miss Woods, who was in her fifteenth year. To this union were born eleven children, five now living: John H., Mrs. Sarah Walker, Mrs. Margaret S. (Black) Woods, Milton A. and Mrs. Florence Hardy. Those deceased were named William C., Newton B., James O., Thomas J., Alfred and Mrs. Nancy Williams. Christopher S. Pace followed farming the principal part of his life, but in connection ran an old fashioned whip-saw, and also a ferry boat. He moved from Tennessee to Arkansas about 1835, settled three miles south of Bentonville, where he only remained for a year, going from there to Sugar Creek, where he farmed for two or three years. He then moved to different places, but at last settled on the farm where his son, John H., now lives. Here he remained until 1862 or 1863, when he moved to a farm three miles south of Bentonville, where he remained until the close of the war. He then moved to Bentonville, where he continued to live until a year ago, when he returned to the old home place, and there he and his wife have since lived. After coming to Arkansas John H. Pace lived with his father until twenty-eight years of age, and received a fair education during that time. At the age of twenty-two he went to Austin, Tex., driving five yoke of oxen, with a load of apples. Here he remained one year, and while there worked for wages on a farm. He then returned to his home in Arkansas, and there remained until his marriage with Miss Florence L. Hayden, daughter of Clement and Lucy (Fullerton) Hayden, who were natives of Maine and Tennessee, respectively. Miss Hayden was but sixteen years old when she married Mr. Pace, and their union resulted in the birth of seven children, six now living: Mrs. Lura J. Phillips, Elbert Newton, Maggie, Milton, Florence and Olive. The one deceased was named Clemmie. After marriage Mr. Pace lived on his father's farm, where he remained until the breaking out of the war, when Mrs. Pace went to Bentonville, and Mr. Pace enlisted in Company F, Brooks' Regiment, Confederate army. During his time of service he was in only two battles of importance, Prairie Grove and Jenkins' Ferry. He served three years and at the close of the war his company surrendered at Little Rock, and he returned to his home, where he engaged in tilling the soil on his present farm. The country was very sparsely settled when Mr. Pace first moved to Benton County, there being no schools, no churches, and Bentonville only a small hamlet. His father was one of the first grand jurors of the county, and the only one now living. Mr. Pace was constable of his township for two years, and was also deputy sheriff. He is a stanch Democrat in politics, having voted that ticket from his majority down to President Cleveland. He has a farm of 100 acres, fifty-five being under cultivation. Mr. and Mrs. Pace are members of the Cumberland Presbyterian Church.

Hon. H. H. Patterson, Jr., is a son of John H. and Mary S. Patterson, who are Tennesseans by birth, and are among the oldest living settlers of Benton County. H. H. Patterson is a prosperous farmer, and a native of the county in which he resides, and was born on Pea Ridge in 1854. He was reared and educated in Benton County, and after attaining a suitable age engaged in teaching school, and was for many years one of the popular educators of the county. He was elected to the office of justice of the peace when only twenty-one years of age, and with the exception of two years, which he spent in the State Legislature, has held that office up to the present time. In 1882 he was elected on the Democratic ticket to the State Legislature, and was a faithful and efficient representative of his county for two years. He has been a worthy member of the Cumberland Presbyterian Church for sixteen years, and is Past Master in the Masonic lodge. He was married to Miss Dora Rich, and their union resulted in the birth of five children: Katie, Leonard, William, Pearl and John.

Hon. Thomas J. Patton. Prominently identified with the interests of Benton County is the above named gentleman, who was born in Ohio County, Va., February 27, 1822, and is now insurance agent at Siloam Springs. He is the son of William and Anna (Redmond) Patton. The father was born in the north part of Ireland in 1767, and was of Scotch-Irish descent. He was partially brought up on a farm, and after he was old enough he entered a college at Belfast and educated himself for a minister. After graduating he preached for twelve years as a Wesleyan Methodist in Ireland, then immigrating to America he first settled in Kentucky, and afterward went to Ohio County, Va., which is now West Virginia. In 1828 he immigrated to Illinois, and continued to reside there until his death, which occurred about 1843. He was married in Kentucky to Miss Redmon, who was a native born Kentuckian. She was the daughter of George and Henrietta Redmon. Mrs. Patton died in Missouri in 1848, the mother of seven children: Mary (deceased), William D. (deceased), George Washington (deceased), James Christopher Columbus (deceased), Samuel Franklin (deceased), Henrietta (deceased) and Thomas J. The last named received his education in the common schools of Virginia and Illinois. He followed agricultural pursuits in these States, and was married in 1849 to Miss Lucy Ann Gee, in Missouri. Here they remained until after the war. Mrs. Patton's father, Edmon W. Gee, was a soldier under Gen. Jackson in the War of 1812, and helped subdue the Creek Indians. Mr. Patton enlisted in the Confederate army, and served about four years. He was a soldier in Slack's brigade under command of Gen. Price. He was first elected captain of his company, then major, and finally colonel. He was in an engagement at Blue Mills, at which place he commanded, and in the battle of Pea Ridge, in the battle of Corinth and Iuka. He was in a number of minor engagements besides those mentioned. He was a recruiting officer during the latter part of the war, and remained as such until its close. Col. Patton emigrated from Northwest Missouri in 1865, and moved to Prairie Grove, Washington Co., Ark. Here he lived on a farm until 1881, excepting five years spent at Fayetteville, where he removed to educate his children at the State University. He came to Siloam Springs in 1881. Mrs. Patton was born in West Tennessee, near Nashville, in 1835. Her father was a native of Virginia and her mother of South Carolina, and her father was one of the earliest pioneers of Northwest Missouri. Mr. and Mrs. Patton became the parents of five children: Eunice Amanda, wife of James E. Mock, of Prairie Grove, Washington Co., Ark.; Henrietta Frances, deceased; Lucy Alice, Martha Josephine, and Erasmus Manfred (deceased). Lucy Alice and Martha Josephine graduated with honors at the State University in 1880 and 1881. Col. Patton is a member of the Masonic fraternity, and he and wife are members of the Universalist Church. He is a Democrat in politics, and his first presidential vote was cast for James K. Polk. He was a member of the Legislature from Washington County, Ark., during the sessions of 1874 and 1875, and was instrumental in redeeming the credit of Arkansas and in passing laws beneficial to his particular section of the State and of the State at large. During his term of office in the Legislature he introduced a bill, and succeeded in having it passed, which refunded $16,000 to the county of Washington, the money having been erroneously collected before due as interest on bonds issued for building the university of Arkansas at Fayetteville.

Pierce Frank Paul, was born in Upshur County, Tex., October 16, 1861, and is the son of Levi W. and Irena C. (Aldredge) Paul, and grandson of Archibald and Martha (Russell) Paul. The grandparents were natives of Virginia, and were members of the Presbyterian Church. They moved from their native State to Georgia, and from that State to Texas. The father died in 1875, and the mother in 1871. He was a Democrat in his political opinions. The maternal grandparents of the subject of this sketch, Samuel P. and Sarah (Furlow) Aldredge, were born in Morgan and Greene Counties, Ga., in 1812 and 1827, respectively. He was a farmer, also a merchant, was a member of the Masonic fraternity, and a member of the Methodist Episcopal Church. He died June 9, 1888. The grandmother was also a member of the Methodist Episcopal Church, and died in 1844. She was the daughter of David and Sarah Furlow. Levi W. Paul, father of Pierce Frank Paul, was born in Henry County, Ga., April 26, 1828, and engaged in merchandising in 1848, following this business in both North and South Carolina. He moved to Texas in 1856. He was a volunteer in the Confederate army, during the war, was the organizer of one of the first companies in Texas War, was made second lieutenant, and served until the close of hostilities. He was in the battles of Jenkins' Ferry, Pleasant Hill, Mansfield, New Orleans and a great many other battles. He was once wounded. In 1868 he moved to Benton County, Ark., and here followed agricultural pursuits. He was a member of the Masonic fraternity, an elder and one of the founders of the Cumberland Presbyterian Church, and was a Democrat in politics. He died November 27, 1882. The mother was born in Greene County, Ga., March 25, 1838, and was a member of the Ladies Aid Society and also of the Cumberland Presbyterian Church. She was the mother of the following children: James, Pierce F., Hattie M., Leone J., John W., David C. and Sallie A. Paul. Pierce F. Paul moved to Benton County, Ark., in 1868, and attended the high school at Bentonville. He then attended the Trinity University at Tehuacana, Tex., for twenty months, and graduated from the commercial department in 1879, receiving the degree of A. M. He returned to Arkansas in 1880, and engaged in merchandising for five years. He took a general course in the business department of the Kentucky University at Lexington, and graduated, receiving the degree of A. M. He then went to Waxahachie, Tex., and engaged in merchandising, which he continued until 1886, when he moved to Benton County, Ark., and was here married to Miss Etta Burns, October 20, 1887. Mrs. Paul was born in Benton County, Ark., October 20, 1868, was educated at Bentonville High School, and is a member of the Methodist Episcopal Church, South. Mr. Paul has traveled a great deal and has been through sixteen States and Territories, but likes Northwest Arkansas better than any State or Territory visited. He is a Democrat in his political principles.

Albert Peel is one of the representatives of the mercantile interests at Avoca, Ark., and was born in 1837, in Marshall County, Miss. His father, who was also named Albert Peel, was born, reared and married in Alabama, his wife's maiden name being Elizabeth Anderson. His father's name was Hunter Peel, who was cousin of Robert Peel, of England. Hunter lived at Huntsville, Ala., and erected the first water-works in that city. Albert and Elizabeth (Anderson) Peel were farmers by occupation, and became the parents of one son, Albert. When he was about six months old the father died, and the mother immediately moved to Arkansas, locating in what is now Benton County, where she afterward married Hiram Davis. Here Albert Peel was reared, but his education was received in Kentucky. On leaving school he returned to Arkansas, where he has since made his home. Mary K. Anderson became his wife in 1867, and five of their children are living: Albert H., Mary E., Amy K., Prentice E. and Annie A. Mrs. Peel died in 1880, and Mr. Peel took Margaret C. Morrison for his second wife. They have two children: Albert Addison and Eugene Lamar. Mr. Peel is now a widower, his wife having died in 1888. He served four years in the Confederate army, and when peace was declared he returned to Arkansas, and in 1868 began merchandising on Pea Ridge, but at the end of about a year and a half moved his goods to what is now Brightwater, and afterward located and named the town of Avoca. He began life with a very small capital, which, by judicious management, has so rapidly increased that he is now one of the wealthy farmers and merchants of the county. He owns a branch store at Garfield, Ark., a grist and saw mill on Prairie Creek, and about 1,000 acres of land with 140 acres in orchard. He is a Democrat, and a member of the A. F. & A. M.

John W. Peel, one of the old and highly respected citizens of Bentonville, is a native of Livingston County, Ky., born November 7, 1806, and is a son of Richard and Elizabeth (Wilson) Peel, and grandson of Thomas Peel, who was a native of Ireland, and who immigrated to the colonies previous to the Revolutionary War, and was a soldier in the same under Gen. Washington. At an early date, about 1790, he moved to Christian County, Ky., and in 1815 he, with his family, together with fourteen other families, immigrated to Arkansas, and located in what is now Independence County. Here Thomas Peel died. His son, Richard Peel, was a native Virginian, born January 6, 1780, and was but a small boy when his parents moved to Kentucky. He was married in Livingston, Ky., and was one of the fourteen families who immigrated to Arkansas in 1815. In this State he passed his last days, dying in 1864. He was one of the leading spirits of Northeast Arkansas for years, and was judge of the court of common pleas for some time, and was afterward judge of the county and probate court for twelve years. His wife was born in South Carolina in 1797, and was the daughter of John Wilson, who was born in South Carolina three days after his father landed in the United States from Scotland. John Wilson was a colonel in the Revolutionary War, under Gen. Washington. Mrs. Elizabeth Peel died in 1871. She was the mother of twelve children, four of whom are now living, John W. being the eldest. He was thirteen years of age when his parents moved to Arkansas, was there reared on a farm, and remained with his parents until twenty-two years of age. In 1828 he married Miss Elizabeth West, who was born in Rutherford County, Tenn., in 1809. She was the mother of two children, Alice, widow of D. W. Hull, who lived in New York City; Samuel W., a member of the United States Congressional District of Arkansas, and who resided in Bentonville, and is now serving his second term. Mr. Peel removed to Carroll County, Ark., in 1837, and here followed farming and also speculated in lands. In 1848 he was elected county clerk, circuit clerk, ex-officio recorder, and held the office ten years. Mrs. Peel died in 1835, and in 1838 Mr. Peel married Miss Malinda Wilson, a native of Lincoln County, Tenn., born in 1813. They have nine children living: Elizabeth, wife of W. G. Rice; Thomas; Margaret, wife of Judge J. M. Pittman, present judge of the circuit court; John C., attorney-at-law; Alfred M., Joseph H. and Ellen, wife of J. C. Knott. In 1873 Mr. Peel became a resident of Bentonville, Ark., and in 1875, while his wife was on a visit to Fayetteville, she was taken sick and died. Four years later Mr. Peel married Mrs. Elizabeth M. Caldwell, nee Phipps, who died in 1880. Mr. Peel was deputy circuit clerk for two years of Benton County, and for the past thirteen years he has been justice of the peace of Bentonville. Mr. Peel has never been a member of any secret society, church or any other organization. He has been a life-long Democrat, casting his first presidential vote for Van Buren in 1836. He is one of Benton County's eldest citizens, and is a man universally respected. He has a large circle of friends, and is known as "Uncle John" throughout the entire northern part of the State.

Robert M. Philips, a prosperous and well-known citizen of Benton County, Ark., was born in Alabama in 1840, and is descended from James Philips, who was also born in Alabama, and moved to Arkansas in 1842, locating in Benton County, where he lived until his death in 1863. His wife's maiden name was Lucinda White. Robert M. Philips attended the common schools of Benton County, and assisted his parents on the farm until 1861, when he joined Company F, Fifteenth Arkansas Infantry, Confederate States army, and served throughout the war, being a participant in the battles of Elk Horn, Corinth, Big Black and the siege of Vicksburg. After his return home he engaged in farming, and in 1866 was married to Miss Caroline Wingham, by whom he is the father of nine children: George W., Laura L., Mary L., Fannie, Dora, Merta, Wallace, Bettie A. and Johnson. Mr. Philips now owns the old homestead, a valuable farm consisting of eighty-four acres, a portion of which he inherited and the rest being purchased from the heirs. He supports the principles of the Democratic party, and he and wife are members of the Missionary Baptist Church.

Benjamin W. Phillips was born in 1831, in the State of Illinois, and is a son of Mason and Debby (Kendricks) Phillips, who were Virginians by birth, and early residents of Tennessee, where they were married. The father was a pilot on the Tennessee and Mississippi Rivers for a number of years, and in 1831 moved to Illinois, but only remained there a short time, when he came to Arkansas and located on the farm on which Benjamin W. Phillips now resides. He died in 1877, and was the father of seven children. Benjamin W. Phillips was educated in Benton County, and made his parents' house his home until 1853, when he determined to seek his fortune in the West, and accordingly went to California and mined in that State and also in Oregon, British America, Idaho, Montana and Utah. After an absence of twenty years he returned home (in 1873), and has since been engaged in farming, being the owner of 160 acres of fertile and well-improved land. He was married in 1865 to Miss Eliza Creelman, and by her became the father of nine children, seven of whom are living: Jack W., Belle, Frank, Annie, Charlie, Debbie and Myrtle. The mother of these children died in 1884.

Thomas W. and Oscar P. Powell are the sons of Dr. Henry and Mary Anna (Phagan) Powell, and the grandsons of Henry and Elizabeth (Davis) Powell, both of whom are natives of Virginia. The grandfather, after marriage, moved to Tennessee, where he reared his family. He was a tinner and farmer by occupation, and died in Washington County, Tenn. The grandmother died in Greene County, of the same State. Dr. Powell grew to manhood in Washington County, Tenn., and October 25, 1831, he married Miss Mary A. Phagan. After living in that county two years after his marriage he then moved to Jefferson County, and after five years moved from there to Norwood's Prairie, Benton County, where he lived for forty-three years. He died February 17, 1867, having followed the occupation of a farmer and physician the principal part of his life. Mary A. (Phagan) Powell was born in Berks County, N. C., July 17, 1815, and is the daughter of John and Eleanor Phagan, natives of North Carolina, who moved to Benton County, Ark., at an early date, and here passed their last days. To Dr. Powell and wife were born thirteen children, nine of whom lived to be grown, seven married, and five are now living: Ann Eliza, died in infancy; Ellen E., died in infancy; James P., was killed in the war; John C., deceased; Mary C.; Thomas W.; Sarah E., wife of Frank A. Sanders; Henry R.; Samuel W.; Martha E. (deceased); Oscar P. and two infants deceased. Dr. Powell was a preacher in the Methodist Episcopal Church, and was a member of the same at the time of his death. He was a Master Mason, and a Democrat in politics. His surviving wife is a member of the Methodist Episcopal Church, South. Their son, Thomas W. Powell, was born May 22, 1845, near where he now lives in Benton County, Ark. April 14, 1872, he married Miss Susan Wright, daughter of Lewis Wright, and to them were born eight children: Samuel C. (deceased), infant (deceased), James D., Charles T., Bernard P., Mary L., Ellen A. and Anna. During the late war Thomas W. served two years in Capt. Brown's Company, Brooks' Regiment, Confederate army. He is Democrat in politics, is a member of the Masonic fraternity, and he and wife are members of the Christian Church. He is the owner of 153 acres of land, ninety-six in the bottom and sixty-five under cultivation. Oscar P. Powell, the youngest of the thirteen children born to Dr. and Mary A. (Phagan) Powell, is a native of Benton County, Ark., his birth occurring May 5, 1858. He was reared on the farm where he now lives, and has resided there all his life. This farm consists of 177 acres, nearly all bottom land, and ninety acres under cultivation. Oscar P. was married in 1884 to Miss Lee Chesney, daughter of Bird and Margaret Chesney. This union resulted in the birth of two children, Maggie Jay (deceased) and Myrtle. Mr. Powell is a member of the Methodist Episcopal Church, South, and has always been a Democrat in his political views.

Tom Preasley was born in Tennesee in 1830, and at the age of one year was brought to Benton County, Ark., by his parents, Andrew and Sarah Preasley, who were also natives of that State. The father was a farmer, and died in 1832, leaving his wife with a family of small children to support. Tom Preasley was educated in Benton County, and was reared by his mother until he was twelve years of age, when she too died, and he was left to fight the battle of life as best he could. He commenced working on a farm, and has always followed the life of a farmer. He resided on the old homestead in Arkansas until after the war, and then purchased his present place, a farm consisting of 138 acres, well cultivated and with all necessary improvements. In 1861 he enlisted in the Confederate army, in Thompson's company, and served under him and Capt. Campbell until the close of the war. He was in a number of battles and skirmishes, and while on a scouting expedition received a severe wound in the breast. After the close of the war he returned to his home in Benton County, and in 1865 was married to Miss Henrietta Whitehead, by whom he became the father of eight children: James, John, Hunter, Joe, Alex., Austria, Bell and Claud. Mr. Preasley is a Democrat.

Capt. Lewis Puckett is a worthy farmer of Benton County, Ark., and was born in Shelby County, Ill., in 1835, being a son of Elihu and Rebecca (Wilks) Puckett, the former of whom was born in North Carolina in 1809. He was a farmer by occupation, and from his boyhood up to the time of his death, in 1861, led a quiet and uneventful life. Lewis Puckett was educated in Indiana, and made his parents' house his home until his marriage with Miss Eliza J. Zink, which event took place in 1853. The following four children were born to his union with Miss Zink: Elihu Richard, Rebecca, Malissa J. and James. L. The mother of these children died in 1863. In 1862 Mr. Puckett was only twelve days in mustering a company at Terre Haute, and was elected captain of the same, but, after serving until 1864, resigned his commission. He was wounded at Thompson's Station, Tenn., and was there taken prisoner on the 5th of March, 1863, and was sent to Springhill and from one place to another, until he finally arrived at Libby Prison, and was in that hole long enough to learn how long a person could be on the brink of starvation and still live. At the close of the war he returned to his home in Indiana, and opened a store in Clay County, but sold out in 1868 and moved to Illinois, finally locating in Montgomery County, where he was engaged in the hotel business until 1875. At that date he returned to Indiana and began the practice of law in Clay and Sullivan Counties, continuing until 1881, when he concluded to try his fortune a little farther west, and came to Arkansas, where he met and married Mrs. Mary P. Sticley, and settled down to farming. He owns an interest in several mines, which, when fully developed, will be of considerable value. He is a member of the G. A. R. and the Masons and I. O. O. F., and he and wife are members of the Christian Church.

GEORGE RAUPP, GENERAL DEALER IN FURNITURE, AND UNDERTAKER, AT ROGERS, ARK.

Charles W. Rice. In mentioning the names of the prominent and early settlers of Benton County, Ark., the biographical department of this work would be incomplete without a worthy mention of the venerable gentleman whose name heads this sketch. He was born in Roane County, Tenn., in 1813, and is a son of Isaac and Martha Rice. He was reared in his native State, and there made his home until 1859, when he came to Arkansas, and located at Pea Ridge, where he became one of the wealthy farmers and land holders of the county. He has been twice married, the first time to Eliza Haley, who died after having borne five children. His second wife was Juliet C. Rice, by whom he reared a family of fourteen children. Sixteen of his children lived to maturity. He owned 560 acres of fine land which he divided among his children, three of whom are living on the old homestead and caring for himself and wife. T. S. Rice, one of the sons at home, was married to Mamie Butram, by whom he is the father of three children, two being named respectively Walter and Inez. R. M. Rice is the other son at home, and is a young man of twenty years. Harriet is the daughter residing with her parents.

Isaac T. Rice is a representative of one of the old and prominent families of Benton County, Ark., and was born in Hawkins County, Tenn., in 1803. His father, Isaac Rice, was born in Montgomery County, Va., in 1777, and after reaching manhood went to Tennessee, where he was married to Miss Susan Senter, also a native of Virginia, and by her became the father of six children. The father died in 1823. Isaac D. Rice is the fourth of their six children and was reared on a farm in Tennessee. While in that State he was married to Miss Susan K. Senter, and the following are their children: Louesa, Nancy, Mary Jane, John, Susan and Isaac T. Mr. Rice and family immigrated to Arkansas in 1842, and located on a farm in Benton County, where they continued to reside until after the battle of Elkhorn, when they went to Texas and there made their home until peace was concluded. Since that time he has been a resident of Benton County, and is one of its oldest living residents. He makes his home with his son, Isaac T. Rice, near Rogers, and votes the Democratic ticket, although he was previously a Whig. He has long been a member of the Methodist Episcopal Church, South, and during his long and active life his many good deeds have made him beloved and respected by all. His wife died in 1875, at the age of seventy-one years. The son with whom he lives, Rev. Isaac T. Rice, was born in Tennessee in 1836, and was reared and educated in Arkansas. He was married to Miss Mary C. Scruggs, who died in 1869, and by her became the father of three children. He was afterward married to Miss Fannie Arthurs, who bore him two children. He owns a fertile and highly cultivated farm of 190 acres, and is a minister in the Methodist Episcopal Church, South, being ordained in 1867. During the war he served in Company F, Arkansas Volunteers, and was chaplain of Col. King's regiment. He is a Democrat.

Drs. R. S. and T. M. Rice, practicing physicians at Bright Water, Ark., are the sons of Charles and Julia (Cobb) Rice, who are Tennesseans by birth, and who came to Arkansas in 1854, locating on Pea Ridge, where they still reside. They became the parents of thirteen children, twelve of whom are living. Dr. R. S. Rice is their eleventh child, and was born in the State where he now resides in 1863. He was educated at Pea Ridge High School, and read medicine privately for about two years, after which he began taking lectures in the medical college at St. Louis, Mo. After finishing his course of lectures he came to Bright Water and entered into partnership with his brother, who had been practicing here since 1882. In 1884 they purchased their drug store, enlarged their stock, and have since been successfully engaged in selling drugs as well as practicing their profession. Dr. R. S. Rice was married in 1882 to Miss Dorinda Puckett, who was born in Benton County. Dr. T. M. Rice was born in Tennessee in 1854, and removed to Arkansas with his parents. He graduated from the St. Louis Medical College in 1882, and since that time has resided in Bright Water. In 1883 Amelian Johnson became his wife, and is now the mother of two children, Lena and Hugh. These young men have been deservedly successful in the practice of their profession, and have a large and increasing practice. They are stanch Democrats in their political views, and T. M. Rice is a member of Pea Ridge Lodge No. 119, A. F. & A. M.

Simeon B. Riddle, farmer, of Bentonville, Ark. One of the prominent and influential families of Benton County is that of Riddle. There is scarcely a State in the Union in which the name is not found, and always among the very best class of citizens. The gentleman whose name heads this sketch is no exception, and fully maintains the honor and hospitality of this old family. He was born in Meade County, Ky., in 1826, and is a son of George and Nancy S. (Frans) Riddle, who were born in Maryland and Virginia, respectively. The former's birth occurred in 1787, and when a young man he moved to the ''Hoosier'' State, but afterward moved to Hardin County, Ky., where he married, and followed the occupation of farming until his death, which occurred in 1857. His wife was a daughter of John Frans, who was a Virginian, and a captain in the Revolutionary War. Mrs. Riddle died on the 1st of May, 1849, in Buchanan County, Mo. The following are her children: Madison F., Benjamin, John, Arden (deceased), Simeon, Martha (deceased), Tazewell F. and Susan (deceased). Simeon Riddle was married in Hardin County, Ky., on the 1st of February, 1849, to Martha Pauley, who died in 1866, having borne seven children: James M., Mary N., Simeon B., Tazewell F., Martha E. (wife of John Beasley), Theodocia E. (wife of Wilson Finch) and Lydia. October 6, 1867, Mr. Riddle married his second wife, Mrs. Angeline Lockard, who was born in Ray County, Mo., and is a daughter of John H. King. Mrs. Riddle had one child by her first husband, William S. Lockard (deceased), and six children have been born to her union with Mr. Riddle: George H., Mary, Charles E., Susan E., Myrtie and Benjamin F. (deceased). Mr. Riddle left Kentucky in 1849, went to Buchanan County, Mo., and in 1855 went to Clinton County, where he remained three years, then locating in Ray County. In 1862 he enlisted in Company H, Twenty-ninth Missouri Volunteer Infantry, and was in the engagement at Jackson, Miss., the siege of Vicksburg, Lookout Mountain, Missionary Ridge, Resaca, Dallas, Atlanta, Fort McAllister, Kenesaw Mountain, and many others of less note. He returned to Ray County after the war, but moved to Franklin County, thence to Texas, and in 1884 came to Benton County. He owns 120 acres of fertile land in Benton County, and is an Independent Greenbacker in his political views. He is a member of the Christian Church.

Prof. J. R. Roberts is one of six surviving members of a family of ten children born to J.P. and Celia (Rippetoe) Roberts, and was born in Mason County, Mo., in 1849. He was educated at Ozark, Mo., and at Abingdon College, Knox Co., Ill., graduating from the latter institution in 1873. He came to Bentonville soon after, and held the position of assistant in the Bentonville High School for some time, and in 1874 established the high school which is now the Pea Ridge Academy. He is principal of the same, and through his own exertions has erected a handsome brick school building at a cost of $6,000. His school is in a very flourishing condition, the faculty consisting of five teachers, who are well qualified for the work. Prof. Roberts was married in 1876 to Alice Dean, a native of Benton County. She was born in 1859, and is the mother of one child, Josephine, who was born in 1877. Both Prof. Roberts and his wife are members of the Christian Church. The former's father and mother were both born in Jackson County, Tenn., in 1820, and were married about 1840. They located in Greene County, Mo., the same year, but afterward moved to Macon County, where he engaged in agricultural pursuits, and also preached the Gospel, expounding the doctrine of the Christian Church. In 1856 he relocated in Greene County, and in 1872 came to Bentonville, Ark., and here resided until his death in 1887. His father was a native of Wales, and came to America at an early day, settling in Tennessee. His wife is of French descent, and is still living in Benton County. The following are their children who are living: Mary (wife of N. A. Suman), Peter W., J. R., Wealthy (wife of H. C. Collins), Nannie and Martha E. (wife of N. J. Robins.)

Elder Dr. George Washington Robertson is a son of William and grandson of John Robertson. The latter was born in the highlands of Scotland. A tanner by trade, he came to America at an early day, going through the Revolutionary War. He married Sarah Gill, settled in North Carolina, then moved to Kentucky. He was a member of the old Seceder Church of the old Scotch Church. He moved to Missouri and died at the age of one hundred and fourteen. The Doctor's father was born in Barren County, Ky., April 25, 1798; married Mary, daughter of James and Sarah Morris, Pennsylvania Dutch; moved to Missouri in 1827, where he spent the remainder of his days. He was therefore a pioneer of Missouri. The Doctor was born in Cole County, Mo., January 14, 1834. In this early day deer ranged everywhere. Bears were plentiful; turkeys everywhere. His father was a great lover of a gun, and killed wild meats to live on a great part of the first few years of his new home in Missouri. Indians were his neighbors. Fish abounded in great abundance in every stream. His father soon began stock raising and farming—farmed extensively; was a slave-holder, and a great trader. Drove hogs and cattle to St. Louis, a distance of 125 miles. Here our subject was trained in droving, trading and farming, hunting, fishing and sporting. He says he loved a gun and dogs, and many times he spent all night in the woods after his dogs, coon and opossum hunting, and says opossum is the best meat he ever eat. Wishes he was in such a land again. He roved along the banks of the Moreaw picking out large fish. Has stood in the door-yard and shot wild turkey. Killed deer in the field in daylight, as they were tame in early days. His father was an elder in the Christian Church nearly forty years. Died at the age of eighty-four. The Doctor's mother died in 1848, and in the spring of 1850 he went to California, engaged in mining and in mercantile business, and boasts of his greatest success depending on his never drinking or gambling. This, he says, was from his mother's training, a Godly woman. His education was self-made, having poor chances for good schools, but has been an incessant student all his life. He says he has burned out many a midnight candle in his studies. Returning from California he united with the Christian Church. He married Sarah L., daughter of David and Margaret (Leslie) Vanpool. Her father was Dutch and her mother Irish. He was married December 17, 1854. He moved to Texas in 1857, and two years later he was set apart to the work of the ministry in the Christian Church. He then began in a new field, entering on his favorite theme. Soon he was drawn into public discussion, of which he has held seventeen, and says he is proud of his success in each. He has always had advantage of most men in this, as he is hard to confuse; always pleasant, mild in his address, but positive and unwavering, never lost for words, a fluent speaker, with a ready flow of language. He is positively opposed to mixing the world and church. Organs, festivals, lotteries, or anything not Scriptural, he opposes in the church. He has been a regular writer for many religious journals for over twenty-two years, and is now writing and preaching the greater part of his time. He was corresponding editor one year for the *Christian Watchman*, edited by Ashley Johnson, in Knoxville, Tenn. He wrote one little book, of which he sold 800 in one year. He has always had a thirst for literary work. He moved from Texas in 1866, settled in Benton County, Ark., but soon returned to Moniteau County, Mo., read medicine, and attended lectures in the Eclectic Medical Institute, of Cincinnati, Ohio, and entered the practice in 1870. He moved to Southwest Missouri, where he practiced and preached for ten years, and had a very extensive practice. but by overwork he broke down. He here lost his first wife, on the 23d of September, 1874. She had borne him five children: David P., Mary Jane, G. M. (a teacher), W. O. (a preacher) and James N. He was married again to Elizabeth D. Jones (widow), daughter of Dr. Mulkey. In 1881 he moved to his present locality, where he has a pleasant location, and spends most of his time preaching and writing, principally writing on religious subjects, on which he loves to dwell. He says everything he ever engaged in has been successful, but he never got rich, and never desired to. Converts under his preaching number thousands, but he lost his journal and does not remember the number. He says he always tried to be on the right side of everything, and never allow any man to beat him with kindness if he could help it. He is a friend to all worthy enterprises, and does all he can to build up society and extend improvements, and is liberal in his support. He is a strong advocate of good schools, and improvements of the various classes, loves fine stock and good farms, works for good order, and has perfect control of an audience. He says he never has to reprove his audience. He says if you want to be treated like a man act the man yourself; if you want to hold an audience, interest them; if you want to live well, work and make it; if you want good stock, take good care of them; if you want to feel well, keep in a good humor. A man makes himself what he is; to be well thought of, keep good company, and live up to your word.

James Alexander Robinson was born in McNary County, Tenn., December 23, 1829, and is a son of John Brown and Jane McKissick (Dickson) Robinson, and grandson of John Robinson. The latter was of Scotch descent, and was a resident of South Carolina. He served in the Revolutionary War, enlisting in the army at the age of seventeen years; he served until its close and died in Benton County, Ark., in 1842. His wife's name was Abigail Moore. John Brown Robinson was born in Mecklenburg County, N. C., September 14, 1801, and his wife was born in Middle Tennessee in 1805, and died in McNary County in 1835. She was a member of the Presbyterian Church and a daughter of Ezekiel Dickson, who was a farmer, and came from North Carolina to Tennessee. He served in the War of 1812, and was with Jackson at the battle of New Orleans. His death occurred in Benton County, Ark., about 1858, whither he had come in 1836. James Alexander Robinson was reared in Benton County, and educated in the common schools. At the age of twenty-one years he was married to Sarah Jane Yell, who was born in Tennessee on June 16, 1829, and immediately settled down to farming in Benton County. To them were born two children, only one of who is living, Brown Yell, who lives with his father. Mr. Robinson owns a good farm of 325 acres, with 150 under cultivation. He is a Master Mason, and he and wife are members of the Methodist Episcopal Church South. In 1862 he enlisted in the Sixteenth Arkansas Regiment, Confederate States Army, and received his discharge at Baldwin, Miss., in 1863. He was in a number of engagements, but was neither wounded nor captured.

James G. Rodgers, son of Jesse and Martha Rodgers, and great-grandson of Gen. Green, was born in Warren County, Ky., May 8, 1826. His paternal grandfather, Jesse Rodgers, was one of the pioneer settlers of Kentucky, and was a farmer by occupation. He was a Whig in politics. The maternal grandfather, William Jameson, was another early settler of Kentucky, about 1785, and was a farmer by occupation, but was also engaged in the practice of medicine. He was married to Miss Martha Jameson, who was also born in Warren County, Ky., about 1794; after marriage they moved to Sangamon County, Ill., and from there to Rutherford County, Tenn., where the father died October 11, 1834. The mother and two youngest daughters then moved to Haywood County, Tenn., where she died in 1853. The father was a member of the Baptist Church. The mother was a member of the Methodist Episcopal Church. The father was a Whig in politics. Their children were named as follows: Arie E., Martha A., James G. and Sarah E. The third of these children, James G., remained in Rutherford County, Tenn., until he was married to Miss Ruamah E. Sanders, December 22, 1850. He then moved to Cannon County, Tenn., and in 1860 he moved to McDonald County, Mo.; in 1862 he volunteered in Col. Coffee's regiment, Company D, Missouri Cavalry, Confederate States Army, and served until the close; he became the father of these children: Sarah E., Martha M., Jesse E., Annie E., Marshal R., Nancy J., Mary I., Arie L., John W., Lavenia E., William

A.. Minnie V. and James I. After his marriage Mr. Rodgers ran a tan-yard in Tennessee for some time, but has since followed farming. Mr. Rodgers is quite an extensive traveler, having been all over the States of Alabama, Mississippi, Louisiana, South Carolina, Texas, Georgia, Kansas, Missouri and Arkansas, and has been among the following tribes of Indians: Cherokees, Choctaws, Seminoles, Creeks, Paw Paws. He is a Democrat in his political views. Marshal H. Sanders, father of Mrs. Rodgers, was born in Rutherford County, Tenn., in 1803; was a farmer by occupation, a Whig in political views, and a member of the Methodist Episcopal Church. Her mother, Mrs. Sarah Northcut Sanders, was born in the same county as her husband, about November 24, 1801, and died in 1843, leaving these children, Elizie C., Amanda M., Sarah A., Ruamah E., John P., Nancy E., Minerva J. and Martha E.

Mrs. Mary Jane Rodgers, widow of Alexander McQueen Rodgers, was born in Claiborne County, La., March 4, 1838, and is a daughter of Philo and Margaret Ellen (Remer) Alden, who were natives of York State, born July 4, 1800, and July 23, 1808, respectively. The father was a carpenter by trade, and in 1832 went to Louisiana, where he worked at his trade and was also engaged in the milling business. He was a man of public spirit, enterprise and energy, and was filling the office of sheriff at the time of his death, in 1867. His wife was a lady of culture, and was a member of the Baptist Church. She died in Benton County, Ark., July 28, 1868. Mrs. Mary Rodgers grew to womanhood and received her education in Louisiana. In November, 1853, at the age of sixteen years, she was married to Alexander McQueen Rodgers, who was a son of Parmenio and Rachel (Adams) Rodgers, natives, respectively, of North and South Carolina. The father was a school-teacher by occupation, and was a son of Seth Rodgers, who was a soldier of the Revolutionary War. Both Parmenio and Mrs. Rodgers were members of the Old School Presbyterian Church. Alexander McQueen Rodgers was born in Mecklenburg County, N. C., February 20, 1824, and when a young man went to Louisiana, where he met and married Miss Alden. He moved his family to Benton County, Ark., in 1867, and here followed the occupation of farming until his death, May 28, 1886. He commenced life without any property whatever, but by push, energy and good management became blessed with a fair portion of this world's goods long before his death. He was a Mason, and was judge of the police court in Bellevue, La., for two years. After coming to this State he was one of the delegates to assist in framing the Constitution for the State of Arkansas. He was a member of the Missionary Baptist Church. His son, Parmenio Austin Rodgers, was born in Louisiana August 31, 1857, and was educated in the common schools, the Pea Ridge Academy and the Arkansas State University. He entered the latter institution in 1879, took the classical course, and graduated with the degree of A. B. in 1882. Soon after graduating he engaged in teaching in Bloomfield, Ark., and there erected a school building which took the name of the Bloomfield Academy, and became a very successful school under the management of Prof. Rodgers. In May, 1886, shortly after the death of his father, he removed to the old homestead, where he has since been engaged in farming and stock raising. December 29, 1880, he was married to Miss Sallie E. Hall, who was born on Pea Ridge, in Benton County, Ark., August 16, 1862. She was educated in the Pea Ridge High School, and is the mother of three children: Alexander McQueen, Mary Kate and Ida. Prof. Rodgers is a prominent candidate for State representative, and if elected will make a faithful and efficient officer. He is a man of unquestionable intelligence, integrity and refinement, and is highly esteemed and respected by his fellow men. Mrs. Rodger's parents are John and Lavina (Finch) Hall, who were born in Tennessee. They are members of the Missionary Baptist Church, and the father is a well-to-do farmer of Benton County.

Clarkson D. Rogers, proprietor of the Rogers Hotel at Bentonville, Ark., was born near Lawrence, Douglas Co., Kas., in 1859, and is a son of Zeno and Rachel (Griffin) Rogers. The former was born in North Carolina in 1836, and is of English descent. His father was Henry Rogers, who was also a native of North Carolina, and is now living at Clayton, Ind., and is nearly one hundred years of age. He is the father of nine sons and one daughter who lived to be grown, Zeno being the fourth and the only one who is dead. The latter was quite small when his parents moved to Indiana. He was reared to manhood on a farm, and was a school-teacher, book-keeper and surveyor by occupation, serving in the latter capacity for Hendricks County for a number of years. He was

a fine accountant, and was endowed with more than ordinary ability.   His
wife was born in Hamilton County, Ind., in 1839, and is a daughter of Jacob
and Rebecca (Harvey) Griffin, who were born in North Carolina and Virginia,
respectively.   They are now residents of Lee County, Iowa.   Only one child
was born to Mr. and Mrs. Rogers, Clarkson Davis, but after Mr. Rogers' death
the mother married again, and became the mother of a daughter, Cora.   Her
second husband was Josiah Bailey, and they are now residing near Lawrence,
Kas.   Clarkson Davis was only five years old when his father died.   He was
educated in the State University of Kansas, which institution he attended three
years, and then Whittier College of Iowa, which he attended two years, graduating from the former institution in 1882.   He then went to Old Mexico, and
for·eight months was engaged in merchandising; then returned to his old home,
and in 1883 was married to Miss Lucy J. Herndon.   In 1883 he went to Hesper,
Kas., where he farmed and followed merchandising for two years, and then
sold out and became a citizen of Rogers, Ark., becoming proprietor of a hotel
at that place.   This building and all its contents were burned in 1886, and in
March, 1887, he came to Bentonville, and has since been proprietor of the
Rogers Hotel.   He keeps the only first-class hotel in the place.   He is obliging
and courteous, and fully understands his business.   He is a Republican in
politics, and a member of the K. of P.

C. F. Rogers is a native of Walker County, Ga., born June 21, 1841, and is
the son of Hugh and Martha (McWhorter) Rogers.   The father was born in
South Carolina March 7, 1797; was reared in that State, married there, and then
moved to the Cherokee Purchase, of Walker County, Ga.   He moved from there
to Sulphur Springs, Washington Co., Ark., in 1851, then to Prairie Grove in
1852, and is now living with his son, C. F.   He has been a farmer all his life.
The mother was born in South Carolina about 1800, and died at the age of
seventy-three in Washington County, Ark.   C. F. Rogers remained at home
until his marriage to Miss Charlotta Howell in 1859.   She was a native of Washington County, Ark.   Two children were the result of this union: John C. and
Maggie E., wife of B. D. Wilson.   The mother of these children was a member of
the Methodist Episcopal Church, South, and died in 1861.   Mr. Rogers took for
his second wife, February 7, 1869, Miss Amanda Howell, a cousin of his former
wife, and a native of Washington County, Ark.   Eleven children were born to
this union, five deceased: Dora, wife of Henry Daniel; Robert W., Samuel F.,
James W., Myrtle A. and Lawrence H.   This wife died August 7, 1888.   She
was also a member of the Methodist Episcopal Church, South, as is the subject
of this sketch.   During the war Mr. Rogers was in Company E, First Battalion
Arkansas Cavalry, Confederate service, and was in duty all through the war.
He is a Democrat in politics, and has been justice of the peace of his township
for two years.   He moved five miles southeast of Siloam Springs in 1883, and is
the owner of 280 acres of land, 200 under cultivation.

Granville P. Rogers was born in East Tennessee in 1833, and is a son of
John and Eliza (Deckard) Rogers, who were farmers of Tennessee.   Granville
P. was educated in his native State, and up to 1856 assisted his father on the
farm.   At that date he chose the ministry as his calling through life, and at once
engaged in preaching the Gospel, and was a local minister until 1861, when he
was ordained as a minister of the Missionary Baptist Church.   He became a
resident of Arkansas in 1858, and in connection with his ministerial duties followed the occupation of farming on a small scale.   In 1884 he began selling
drugs at Heads Switch, Ark., and later engaged in the same business in the town
of Garfield, and also keeps a stock of general merchandise.   He has a good
trade and is doing well financially.   In 1852 he was married to Miss Eliza
Edens, of Tennessee, and by her is the father of eight children: Hiram, James,
Charley, Robert, Mamie A., Emeline, Vina and Eliza.   Mr. Rogers owns 482
acres of good farming land, besides considerable town property in Garfield.   He
belongs to the Masonic fraternity, and he and all his family are members of the
church.

Dr. Thomas Hopkins Roughton is one of Benton County's oldest citi-
zens, as well as one of its largest real estate holders and prosperous physicians.   He
was born in Warren County, Tenn., in June, 1820, and when a boy of twelve
years of age removed with his parents to Bedford (now Coffee) County, Tenn.,
where he was reared to manhood.   In his twenty-second year he was married to
Harriet Ewell, who was born in Bedford County, Tenn., and died September

BENTON COUNTY, ARKANSAS - BIOGRAPHICAL AND HISTORICAL MEMOIRS   209

****

15, 1883, leaving three out of five children: James Richard, Sarah E., widow of T. H. Harrell, and Polly Adeline, wife of Harvey Davis. After his marriage Dr. Roughton began the study of medicine under Drs. D. Ewell and Stephen Wood, and began practicing that profession in 1848 or 1849, and in 1851 came to Benton County, Ark., where he has since made his home, with the exception of a few years during and subsequent to the war. His practice has secured for him an income of from $1,000 to $2,500 per year, and besides this work he has also been engaged in agricultural pursuits. After serving for about three months in the late war he was released from service, and after some time removed his family to Rush County, Tex., where he made his home until the close of the war. He next moved to Titus, Tex., but at the end of one year purchased a farm of 640 acres in Red River County, Tex., where he spent three years managing his farm and practicing his profession. During this time his health became very poor, and he removed to Benton County, Ark., and here has since made his home. In 1871 he purchased property in Springtown, and also has two good farms in an adjacent county. He belongs to the Masonic fraternity, and is a member of the Methodist Episcopal Church, South. He is a man of undoubted integrity, and is a physician of skill and ability. His parents, James and Nellie (Messick) Roughton, were born in Surry County, N. C., in 1787 and 1791, and died in Tennessee in 1884 and 1842, respectively. The father was a member of the Christian Church, and a son of Josiah Roughton, an Englishman and farmer. Richard Messick was the paternal grandfather. He was also a farmer.

Joseph R. Rutherford. Among the prominent men and enterprising citizens of Ball Township, Benton County, stands the name of the above gentleman, who was born in the Hiawassee Purchase, now East Tennessee, February 24, 1826, and is the son of John M. and Alice (Young) Rutherford. The father was born in North Carolina, and when a young man came to East Tennessee, where he passed the remainder of his days, his death occurring about 1855. The mother died about the beginning of the war. Their son, Joseph R., was reared in the vicinity of his birth, and at about the age of twenty-one he went to Mexico and regularly enlisted in a company of the United States troops in the Mexican War, and is a pensioner of that war. After this eventful struggle he returned to his native county, attended school for some time, and in 1850 married Miss Louisa E. Pearce, of East Tennessee. Four children were the result of this union: Alfred P., farmer; Lewis, farmer; Lenora, wife of Henry Wright, and Mary, wife of Joseph England. The mother of these children died in 1860, and October 2, 1862, Mr. Rutherford married Miss Tennessee P. Snodgrass, who was born in Tennessee and reared in Benton County, Ark. Four children were the fruits of this union: Elizabeth, wife of J. W. Hunton; William McIlroy, farmer; Simmie, wife of Zachary Thomason, and Fannie A., wife of J. P. Farley. After his first marriage Mr. Rutherford farmed for a year, and then moved to Northwestern Missouri, but in 1851 he returned to East Tennessee, and in the fall of that year located in Benton County, Ark., where he has since lived, engaged principally in farming. During the war he was connected with the militia in the Federal service. He commanded the militia in Phagan's attack upon Fayetteville, and there suggested to Gen. Harrison the idea of organizing those of Federal inclinations, yet at home, into companies for mutual protection and for raising crops. Mr. Rutherford was then permitted to raise the first company for that purpose, and his company was known as Company A, Arkansas Home Guard Militia. It was stationed near Ray's Mill, in Washington County, where stockades were made and crops were raised, which saved Northwestern Arkansas from probable starvation during the years 1864–65. During the stay there he was permitted to buy rations of the Government for the general provision of the citizens. In his hands were intrusted the work of investigating and reporting the actual condition of the people and the necessary purchases to meet the emergencies. He sold to those able to buy, and distributed freely to those in urgent need. He paid the Government for these provisions out of his own money, at Government prices, and he sacrificed from his own pocket whatever he gave out. He received the surrender of several Confederate companies, under the instruction of Gen. Harrison, at Union Valley. After the war he sold goods at Cincinnati, Ark., one year, thence going to the farm, where he was elected clerk of Benton County in 1868. While filling this office he purchased a press and published a liberal Republican paper at Bentonville, named the *Traveler*.

In 1873 Mr. Rutherford returned to the farm, where he has remained ever since. He was a dealer and manufacturer in timber, lumber, etc. In 1886 he started his store at his home, and when the post-office at Trident was established he was made postmaster, in March, 1887, and is now occupying that position. He is the owner of about 640 acres of land now, and has deeded about 160 acres to his children. Mr. Rutherford and wife are members of the Christian Church, as was also the first wife. He is a Master Mason, was a Whig before the war, and is now a Republican. Mr. Rutherford is a man whose experience and success is indicated by this sketch and by the general esteem in which he is held by the citizens of the county.

Rev. H. H. Scaggs, pastor of the Methodist Episcopal Church at Rogers, Ark., was born August 11, 1840, in Henry County, Ind. His parents, Samuel Scaggs and Virginia Johnson, were natives of West Virginia. The father was a carpenter by occupation, and in the year 1848 was elected as county clerk in Randolph County, Ind., but only lived a few days after the election. He was a member of the Missionary Baptist Church. The mother died in 1840 and the father in 1848. Our subject was the youngest of five children; was reared and educated in the Hoosier State. After attaining a suitable age he began teaching in the public schools of Indiana and Iowa, following this profession for about four years. In 1864 he entered the Nebraska Conference, first as a supply on Elkhorn Circuit, and was returned the next year; from there was sent to Saltillo charge for one year, and from that to Blue River. Was ordained deacon that year at Plattsmouth, Neb., by Bishop Kingsley. The next year he took a certificate of location and returned to Indiana and supplied the Burlington Circuit one year, in East Lafayette District, Northwest Indiana Conference. Remained two years in Indiana and then went to Columbus, Kas., and engaged in his occupation as a mechanic (jeweler), working through the week and preaching on Sundays. One year he was a supply at Columbus, and after that traveled one year as a supply on Columbus Circuit with another minister. In the spring of 1880, owing to failing health, he went to Eureka Springs, Ark., where he remained until February, 1883, when, being so much improved, he joined the Arkansas Conference and was given charge of the Wheeler Circuit for two years, then the West Fork Circuit, Marble City and Mason Valley. In February, 1888, he was stationed at Rogers, Ark., as pastor of the Methodist Episcopal Church, where he is now at work. Rev. Scaggs has been married twice; first to Lydia R. Ford, of Baltimore. Md., by whom he had five children, three of whom died in infancy. Samuel H. Scaggs, the oldest, is a jeweler by occupation, but is now engaged as a drummer for C. H. Knights & Co., of Chicago, Ill. Allie G. Scaggs married William Carse, and is living in St. Louis, Mo. In 1887 our subject married Miss Lucinda C. Beard, of Frankfort, Ind. Mr. Scaggs is a member of the A. F. & A. M., and in his political views supports the principles of the Republican party.

Elder Larkin Scott, of Bentonville, Ark., was born in Barren County, Ky., in 1818, and is a son of Samuel and Hannah (Phillips) Scott. The father was of Scotch-Irish descent, born in North Carolina, and there resided until his marriage, when he immigrated to Kentucky, and died in Callaway County, of that State, in 1837. He was a farmer. His wife was born in East Tennessee, and died in 1842, having borne eleven children, only two of whom are living. Larkin was the ninth in the family, and was educated in the pioneer schools of Kentucky. April 17, 1836, he was married to Miss Charlotte, daughter of Daniel and Sarah (Caldwell) Kirk, who are Virginians by birth. Mrs. Scott was born in Daviess County, Ky., in 1819, and is the mother of twelve living children: Francis M. (deceased), Margaret A. (wife of M. A. Jenkins), James F., Mary J. (wife of David Hoover), Sarah C. (wife of Frank Carter), Newton B., John W., Celia F. (wife of Larkin Wilson), David P., Martha M. (wife of William Oakley), William T. and Matilda Ellen. Rev. Scott has sixty-seven grandchildren and seven great-grandchildren. In 1840 he left Kentucky and moved to Dade County, Mo., but in 1856 came to Benton County, Ark., and purchased a farm of 200 acres four miles from Bentonville. In February, 1888, he moved to Bentonville, where he expects to pass the remainder of his days. In 1842 he became a member of the Christian Church, and in 1868 was ordained a minister of that denomination. He organized the Antioch Church, and was pastor of the same for about eighteen years. He also organized a congregation at Robinson School-house, and was pastor of that flock for eight years. He is the organizer and pastor of the Wire Spring Church, and is also pastor of the Lowell Church. Elder Scott is the eldest minister in Benton County, where he is widely known as a true Christian gentleman and a useful and upright citizen. His wife has been a member of the Christian Church for fifty-four years. Their youngest child still resides with them. Elder Scott preached his first sermon in a small brick school-house in Bentonville. The house is still standing.

Henry W. Schrader, proprietor of the Eagle Roller Mills of Bentonville, Ark., is a native of the Kingdom of Prussia, born in 1842, and the son of John and Christina (Selmann) Schrader, also natives of Prussia, born in 1794 and 1814, respectively. John Schrader was a wheel-wright by trade. In 1844 he immigrated to the United States and located in Franklin County, Mo., near Washington. Here he followed farming and died in 1879. His wife died in 1868. She was the mother of five children: Mary, Christina, Charlotta, Caroline and Henry W. The last named was only two years old when his parents came to America. He assisted his father on the farm until 1876. In December, 1865, he married Miss Elizabeth Wellmeyer, a native of St. Louis, Mo., born in 1845, and to them were born six children: Josie, Emma (who died in 1877 at the age of nine years and one month, and is resting in Larned Cemetery), William, Clara, Dora and Edward. In 1876 Mr. Schrader moved to Larned, Kas., and for six years was in the livery business. For three years he also speculated in horses and sheep, and for one year he was engaged in the coal and feed business. In July he sold out and moved to Bentonville, Ark., where he purchased the Eagle Roller Mills for $6,500. In October he remodeled it and put in four double set of rollers, at a cost of $3,500, making it a capacity of sixty-five barrels per day, and capable of doing as good work as any mill in Northwestern Arkansas. His brands are "Gilt Edge," "Snow Drift," "Tip Top." Mr. Schrader is an excellent business man, is having a large trade, and is doing a good work. He is rather independent in his political views, but rather favors Democratic principles.

Prof. J. W. Scroggs. Prominent among the educators of Benton County, Ark., stands Prof. Scroggs, who is principal of, and an able instructor in, Rogers Academy, of that county. He is a native of Dade County, Mo., born October 26, 1852, and is the second child born to William L. and Leah C. (Mitchell) Scroggs, who were natives, respectively, of North Carolina and Mississippi. The father was twice married, Miss Mitchell becoming his second wife. She died on the 25th of December, 1883, but he is still living, and resides in Dade County, Mo. Prof. Scroggs spent the healthy, happy and busy life of the farmer's boy, and was educated at the common schools and at Lafayette College, Easton, Penn., in which institution he took a very thorough and extensive course in the languages and sciences, and graduated from the same in 1875. He took the degree of A. B., and the final degree of A. M., and during the close of his collegiate career published a book of college songs, entitled "Songs of Lafayette," on which he realized considerable money. He has also revised Smith's Astronomy, published by Charles H. Whiting, Boston, Mass. The work is intended for a text book. He has written considerable music, one of the most successful pieces being a meditation for the piano, "The River of Life," published by J. M. Russell, Boston, Mass. Another popular piece is the "Honey-Moon Polka," which has been played several times at Rogers Academy commencements. On leaving college his health was somewhat impaired by close application to his studies, and for some time he gave his attention to music, holding conventions in various places in the State of Missouri. He gained in in health so rapidly that in 1878 he took the principalship of the Peirce City Public Schools, and held the position for about two years. He then resigned his position and became principal of the public schools of Vinita, I. T. He built a church there, mostly with his own hands, and also a parsonage, and was the founder of Worcester Academy in that place. He became a minister of the Gospel while in the Territory, but at the end of five years was obliged to seek a more healthy location. He made two tours over the New England States, soliciting money for the academy which he had founded at Vinita, and in 1884 came to Rogers, and in connection with his school acted as pastor of the Congregational Church the first year. Since that time he has given his attention to his school. He has several other books in preparation, which he is finishing as fast as his school duties will permit. August 31, 1878, he was married to Miss Flora Beckwirth, who was born at Pana, Ill., August 24, 1861. They have two children: Maurice and Wendell.

****

Rev. F. M. Seamster was born in Schuyler County, Mo., in 1848, and is a son of Rev. Williamson Seamster, who was born in Virginia in 1817. He was reared in his native State, and afterward went to Kentucky, where he was united in marriage to Miss Susan Rigsbee, a native also of Virginia. They lived in Kentucky until 1837, and then moved to Missouri, where they spent the remainder of their days. The mother's death occurred in 1874, and the father afterward married Mary A. Pendergraff, by whom three children were born to him. He died in 1884. Sixteen children blessed his first marriage. Rev. F. M. Seamster was educated in Missouri, and after coming to Arkansas in 1879 became a minister of the Missionary Baptist Church, and has been actively engaged in that calling up to the present time. He is at the present time pastor of two churches on Pea Ridge, and has done much to further the cause of Christianity. He was married in 1873 to Miss Amanda Dunagan, a daughter of Elder Dunagan, of Rogers, Ark., and by her is the father of five children Carrie L., John William, Cora E., George M. and Robert M. Mr. Seamster is now living at Avoca, where he has a good farm and one of the largest orchards of small fruits in Benton County. He is a Democrat, also a Master Mason.

Mrs. Martha Sellers, the daughter of Clark and Mary Smith, was born October 13, 1840, in Bates County, Mo. The father was born and reared in Pennsylvania, and immigrated from that State to Missouri when quite a young man. He settled in Bates County, purchased land, and devoted his time exclusively to farming and stock raising. The mother was born in Bartholomew County, Ind., and when a young woman emigrated westward with her father. They first settled in Cole County, Mo., but later removed to Bates County, of the same State, and finally settled in Benton County, Ark., where she passed her last days. The father died in Louisiana. Grandfather and Grandmother Smith were from Pennsylvania, and moved to Bates County, Mo., where they were living when they received their final summons. The majority of their children went to California during the gold excitement of 1849. Mrs. Sellers continued to live with her mother and relatives until about seventeen years of age, when she was married to Joel F. Sellers, a native of Warren County, Tenn., who immigrated to Arkansas in 1841. To this union were born seven children, all now living: William C., Hugh A., Robert L., James H., Emma D., Fannie B. and John F. After marriage Mr. and Mrs. Sellers settled on the farm where she is now living, and here Mr. Sellers occupied his time in tilling the soil until his death. Mrs. Sellers is now conducting the farm with the assistance of her sons who are living at home. The farm consists of 240 acres, 140 acres under cultivation. Hugh Sellers, Mrs. Sellers' second son, continued to live with his mother until his marriage. He received a fair education in the common schools, and at the age of twenty-three married Miss Amanda Williams, daughter of John Williams, who is one of the oldest settlers of Benton County, having removed from Missouri to Arkansas when a boy. The daughter was born and reared in Franklin County, Ark., and by her marriage to Mr. Sellers became the mother of one child, David C. Since marriage Mr. Sellers has been engaged in business for himself, and is now occupied in farming in this county. He is a strong Democrat in his political views, not for policy, but from principle and his own honest convictions.

Dr. Newton Sewell, physician and druggist, of Springtown, Ark., is a native of Forsyth County, Ga., born May 24, 1853, and is a son of Aaron J. and Kittie Evaline (Moore) Sewell, who were born in South Carolina and North Carolina, respectively. The father is now residing in Dawson County, Ga., and is a farmer and member of the Baptist Church. He served three years in the Confederate army during the late war, and is a son of Joshua Sewell, a native of Maryland, and of Irish and German descent. The mother died in Georgia. Dr. Newton Sewell received his primary education in the schools of his native county, and afterward entered the Atlanta (Ga.) Medical College, and was graduated as an M. D. from that institution in 1880. He immediately began practicing his profession in Cherokee County, Ga., but in 1886 came to Springtown, Ark., where he has since made his home, and where he has a large and lucrative practice. He ranks among the first physicians of the county, and deserves much credit for his success in life, and his education was obtained through his own unaided efforts. He is a member of the drug firm of Sewell & Enterkin, and belongs to the Masonic fraternity. January 11, 1872, he was married to Miss Matilda C. Pool, and six of their seven children are living:

Elsie Alice, Lenora Theodocia, Laura A. E., Oscar V., Agnes E., Pearl and Maggie Estelle. Mrs. Sewell was born in Forsyth County, Ga., and is a daughter of Dr. M. L. Pool. Dr. Sewell and family attend the Baptist Church.

Thomas Christopher Sheffield, farmer and stock raiser, was born in Henry County, Va., May 24, 1819, and is a son of Leonard and Lucy (Wooten) Sheffield, both of whom were born in the "Old Dominion," where the mother is still living. Leonard Sheffield was a cabinet workman and carriage maker by trade, and was a soldier in the War of 1812. He belonged to the Free Masons, and died in Henry County, Va., in 1839, aged about sixty years. His father, Joseph Sheffield, was born in England, and at an early day came to America, serving in the Revolutionary War. Thomas C. Sheffield was reared and educated in his native county, and at the age of twenty-one years was married to Martha N. Martin, also born in Henry County, September 14, 1821, and a daughter of Stephen and Sally (Fisher) Martin. The father was a farmer and shoemaker, and a son of Joseph Martin, who was a soldier throughout the Revolutionary War, and served as first lieutenant. His wife was born in Virginia and was a daughter of John Fisher, a farmer. After his marriage Thomas Sheffield spent three years as overseer on the plantation of Col. A. B. Staples, in Patrick County, Va. The following year he was overseer in Stokes County, N. C., for David Dalton. He then entered the employ of Sam Hairstin, who owned 1,500 slaves, and was overseer on his plantation for five years. He then served in the same capacity for two years for Robert Matthews, three years with William Poindexter, one year with William Lash, three years with his brother, William A. Sheffield, who owned fifty slaves, then one year with his uncle, Jesse Wooten. At this time he quit overseeing and engaged in farming and tobacco growing, which he made a success. He erected the first tobacco barn in Benton County, Ark. In 1860 he removed to Dallas County, Tex., where he was successfully engaged in farming and stock raising. Since 1866 he has resided in Benton County, Ark. He commenced life without means, but by industry and good management has accumulated considerable property, reared a large family, and has assisted all his children in making a start in life. He has a farm or 200 acres, with 160 under cultivation. His marriage was blessed in the birth of thirteen children, six of whom are living: Lucy, wife of Fred O'Dell; George, Thomas, Mary, wife of William Walker, and Jesse. His sons, Leonard, George and Thomas, were Confederate soldiers in the late war, and during that time Leonard died in Mississippi. Thomas was Kirby Smith's orderly-sergeant.

Thomas E. Sheffield, a prosperous young farmer, stock raiser and merchant at Robinson, Ark., was born at Horse Pasture, Henry Co., Va., February 19, 1846, and is a son of Thomas C. Sheffield, whose sketch is given in this work. He grew to manhood in Dallas County, Tex., and was educated there and in his native State. In the fall of 1863, at the age of seventeen years, he entered the service of Gen. Kirby Smith, at Shreveport, La., and served as his courier until the close of the war. He then returned to Texas, and engaged in farming on his father's homestead. In the spring of 1866 he came to Benton County, Ark., and was here married two years later to Mary E. Walker, who was born in Benton County in December, 1849, and by her became the father of three children: Jesse Thomas, William Leonard and Ellen Joan. Mr. Sheffield's means, when married, did not exceed $500, but by energy and perseverance he has accumulated a fine property. He has a good farm of 307½ acres, and a house and lot in Robinson, besides his stock of general merchandise, which amounts to about $1,800. He is a Master Mason, and he and family are attendants at the Christian Church.

John J. Shores is a Wilkes County North Carolinian, and was born on the 7th of December, 1832. He is a son of William and Polly (Lyon) Shores, and grandson of Simeon Shores. William Shores was married about 1829, and removed to Jackson County, Mo., about 1840. Here he remained one year, and then located in Harrison County, of the same State. At the breaking out of the war he removed to Des Moines, Iowa, where he remained until its close. After residing alternately in Arkansas and Missouri, he died in the latter State October 11, 1875, at the age of sixty-seven years. His wife was born in North Carolina, and died in Benton County, Ark., February 4, 1888. She was a daughter of John and Annie Lyon, and became the mother of seven children: Amanda (deceased), John, Lewis, Mary Ann (wife of John Long), William H. (deceased),

James and Malinda (deceased).   John J. Shores was reared on his father's farm, and made his parents' house his home until he was twenty-seven years of age, and then spent one year in farming and stock raising in Jasper County. While residing in Jasper County, in 1860, he was married to Nancy Jane Davis, the eldest daughter of Anderson and Polly Ann Davis. She was born in Newton County in 1844, and became the mother of twelve children: Malinda, John E., Amanda Evaline, Charles Anderson, Lewis Albert, Maud Elizabeth, Jeptha M., Bessie May and Lucy Jane. Those deceased are Mary Alice, Polly Ann and William Franklin. Mr. Shores came to Benton County in 1866, and owns a fertile farm of 125 acres. During the war he was a Union sympathizer, and since the war has been independent in politics. He and wife worship in the Christian Church.

Rev. J. Wade Sikes is the third of five children born to the marriage of Robert Sikes and Elizabeth Bledsoe, and was born in Perry County, Ala., in 1828. His father was a Tennesseean, born in 1797, and a farmer by occupation. When a young man he went to Alabama, and was there married to Miss Bledsoe, whose people were of Virginia stock. She died in Alabama when her son, J. Wade, was about eight years of age, and after her death the family moved to Tennessee, and thence to Arkansas in 1854, locating on the land on which Rogers now stands. Here the father died in 1856. J. Wade Sikes received a good common school education, but the most of his education has been acquired through self-application. He taught school in Tennessee, and also after locating in Arkansas, and after quitting the school-room engaged in agricultural pursuits, which occupation he followed until 1866, when he was elected to the office of county clerk, and also recorder. The reconstruction period, however, prevented him from filling out his term of office. He then engaged in the practice of law, and also followed the occupation of farming. During the war he was a member of the Second Arkansas Mounted Rifles, and during this time began preaching the gospel, which he continued to do until failing health compelled him to give up this work. He preaches the doctrine of the Baptist Church, and his labors in the cause of Christianity have met with gratifying success. December 25, 1854, he was united in marriage to Miss Almira I. Lee, a native of Missouri. He served about four years in the late war, and in the battle of Atlanta, Ga., lost his left arm.

B. F. Sikes, the original owner of the land on which Rogers, Ark., is now situated, was born in Perry County, Ala., in 1825. He is a son of Robert and Elizabeth (Bledsoe) Sikes, a history of whom is given in the sketch of Rev. J. Wade Sikes. B. F. Sikes is the eldest of their children, and was principally reared in Tennessee, where he was also educated, and afterward taught school. He was an educator in that State for twenty-five years, and in 1873 came to Arkansas and engaged in farming, becoming one of the wealthy agriculturists of the county and the owner of a large amount of real estate. He is now notary public, and gives his attention to the general development of Rogers. He was married, while a resident of Tennessee, to Miss Tabitha Lock, and they have reared a family of nine children: Martha E., Nancy T., Robert R., William W., Pollie M., Almira A., Edward E., Maggie May and Samantha A. Mr. Sikes is a member of the I. O. O. F.

William H. Simpson, son of John and Rachel (Fite) Simpson, was born in Knox County, Tenn., October 26, 1830. The father was a native of Virginia, born in 1785, was reared in that State and came to Tennessee among the pioneer settlers of that State. He lived in Knox and McMinn Counties to the very exceptional age of one hundred and one years, retaining strength of both mind and body up to the last, and could ride on horseback to within a year of his death, which was caused by apoplexy, January, 1886. He was a farmer all his life. The mother was born in North Carolina in 1800, and died in McMinn County, Tenn., in 1860. The father was a member of the Baptist Church eighty-five years, a member of the Masonic fraternity eighty years, and was probably the oldest Mason in the United States at the time of his death. The mother was also a member of the Baptist Church. They reared six children: Margaret, widow of a Mr. Monroe, of Tennessee, living on the old homestead; Andrew J., died during the war; Rebecca, who is living on the old homestead in Tennessee; Julia, wife of W. McKisey, and James M., who also resides on the old homestead in Tennessee. William H. Simpson remained with his parents until twenty-one years of age, and in January, 1855, he married Miss A. J.

Triplett, who was born in Tennessee in 1838, and who bore him seven children: Alexander N., William O., A. Tennessee (deceased), John L., Ollie A., Sterling P. and Maud. After marriage Mr. Simpson ran a wagon-shop in Tennessee for two years, and in 1856 he moved to Texas, where he remained until 1866, when he came to his present farm, which is situated two miles from Siloam Springs, and consists of 280 acres, 220 under cultivation. March 14, 1887, Mr. Simpson had the misfortune to lose his faithful companion. She was a member of the Baptist Church, as is also Mr. Simpson. He is a master Mason, having been a member of that lodge for twenty-eight years, and has always been a Democrat in his political views.

Lewis P. Smart, member of the firm of Smart & Brown, proprietors of the livery and feed stable at Bentonville, Ark., was born in Calhoun County, Ala., in 1857, and is the son of Dr. John and Essie C. (Piles) Smart. [For further particulars of parents see sketch of Dr. John Smart.] Lewis P. Smart came to Bentonville, Ark., with his father in 1872, and received his education in that city. At the age of sixteen he commenced clerking for W. A. Terry, and worked for him five years. In 1881 he was appointed deputy sheriff of Benton County, and served two years. In 1885 he was a candidate for sheriff, with seven opponents, and came out victorious. In the same year he hired to W. A. Terry in the livery stable, and after fifteen months Mr. Smart bought one-half interest. In 1885 Mr. Smart bought the entire stock, and in June, 1887, sold one-half interest to Mr. Brown, and since that date the firm title has been Smart & Co. They keep forty-three horses, two single buggies, sixteen double buggies, and one 'bus to all trains, one transfer wagon, one lumber wagon, a hearse, and keep two stable horses—Percheron Norman, weighs 1,540 pounds, and is eight years old; Denmark, saddle stock, with seven different gaits, weight 1,200 pounds. Their barn is 40x165 feet, extending across one block, with two fronts. Messrs. Smart and Brown have the most extensive and best equipped livery stable in the State outside of Little Rock. They are first-class business men, and attend strictly to the business at hand, and are courteous and obliging. In December, 1887, Mr. Smart married Miss Daisy Perry, who was born in Fort Smith, Ark.

Dr. John Smartt, president of the People's Bank at Bentonville, and also president of the Bentonville Railroad, is a native of McMinnville, Warren Co., Tenn., born in 1820, and the son of George R. and Ethelia (Randolph) Smartt. George R. Smartt was born in Mecklenburg County, N. C., was of Scotch descent and a farmer by occupation. At the age of eight years he removed with his parents to Warren County, Tenn., and in later years married Miss Randolph. He was a member of the Legislature one term, and died in Warren County, Tenn., in 1856. His wife was a native of Tennessee, and died in 1860. She was the mother of nine children, Dr. John Smartt being the third child. The Doctor was reared and grew to manhood on the farm, and received a good education in the Warren County schools. He remained with his parents until twenty-two years of age, and at the age of twenty-four began the study of medicine, his preceptor being Dr. Alfred Payne. In 1846 and 1847 he attended the Lexington Medical College at Lexington, Ky., and in March of the last named year he commenced his practice at McMinnville, Tenn. One year later he went to Oxford, Calhoun Co., Ala., and resuming his practice, remained there until after the late war. In the fall of 1865 he went to Dallas, Texas, and in 1871 he became a resident of Bentonville, Ark. Dr. Smartt has practiced medicine continuously since he entered the profession, or for the past forty-one years, and has met with unusual success in all his work. In November, 1848, he married Miss Essie C. Pyles, a native of South Carolina, born in 1828, and to them were born nine children, five of whom lived to be grown: Mrs. Susan Terry, Athelia, Louis P., Alfred P. and Essie C. In the fall of 1882 the Bentonville Railroad was organized, and Dr. Smartt was elected president of the organization, or company, and he has since held the position. In 1884 he was elected president of the Benton County Medical Examining Board, and has since held the position. In June, 1888, the Bentonville Commercial College was organized, and Dr. Smartt was elected president of the same. He has been a life-long Democrat in politics, casting his first vote for James K. Polk, in 1844. He is a stockholder in the Bentonville Evaporator and Canning Factory, and is vice-president of the same. He and wife are members of the Presbyterian Church, in which he has been elder for twenty years.

Capt. E. T. Smith was born in Belmont County, Ohio, in 1830, and is a son of William and Rebecca (Todd) Smith, who were born in Virginia, in 1798, and Georgia, in 1800. The former was educated in the schools of his native State, and when a young man removed with his parents to Ohio, where he met and married Miss Todd, who had removed to that State when she was a child. Mr. Smith first followed the occupation of farming and then engaged in merchandising, and died in the State of his adoption in 1846. His widow afterward married a Mr. Pierson, who is now deceased, and died in 1875. By Mr. Smith she became the mother of eight children: Thomas, Sabilla (wife of Dr. A. Atkinson), Elisha Todd, Asenath (deceased), Hannah (wife of Elisha Smith), Elwood, William (deceased) and Stephen. Elisha T. Smith, the subject of this biography, was reared on a farm and educated in the common schools and at the Friends' High-school at Mount Pleasant, Ohio. He was married to Miss Lydia Clendenon, who was born in Ohio in 1832. Her father was born in the "Keystone" State and her mother in Georgia. She also attended the Friends' High-school, and by Mr. Smith became the mother of five children: Annie (wife of O. B. Wilson), Rebecca T., Willie (wife of J. D. Mann) and Nettie May (wife of David M. Smith). Ella, the fourth child, is living at home. Mr. Smith was living in Iowa when the war broke out, and he espoused the Union cause, but did not take an active part in the war. In 1858 he was elected clerk of the district court in Iowa, and served in that capacity twelve years, and was then elected to the State senate for four years. After spending one year in the Republic of Mexico, engaged in mining, he located in Stephens County, Texas, and was appointed clerk of the district court, by Judge Fleming, for six years, but before his last term had expired he came to Siloam Springs, Ark., and here has since resided. He is a Republican in politics, and is justice of the peace of Hico Township. He was nominated as a candidate for representative on the Republican ticket in 1888, but declined the nomination. He is interested in the mining lands located in Washington County, Ark., being a member of the Northwestern Arkansas Mining and Smelting Company. He is a member of the Masonic fraternity and the K. of P.

Hiram C. Smith, a resident of Benton County, Ark., and the son of Allison and Louisa (Kates) Smith, was born July 18, 1831, in Benton County, near Osage Creek. The father, Allison Smith, was born in Tennessee, received a limited education in that State, and remained with his father until after his marriage, which occurred in Washington County, Ark., whither he had moved with his parents. After marriage he went to Illinois, and after moving around for some time settled in Washington County, Ark., but moved from there to Benton County, where he died in 1847. Mrs. Louisa Smith was also born in Tennessee, received a common education, and by her marriage to Mr. Smith became the mother of seven children, three now living: Hiram C., William H. and Mrs. Martha E. Weldon. The children who died were named Eliza M., Thomas J., Isaac and D. A. Allison Smith, after coming to Arkansas, with the aid of his wife went vigorously to work at his books, and thus obtained a good education. He was afterward appointed justice of the peace, and held this position two years, occupying that position at the time of his death. Mark and Annie (Allison) Smith, grandparents of Hiram C., were both natives of North Carolina, and were quite well off in this world's goods. The grandparents Kates were natives of Tennessee, and moved from that State to Arkansas. Very little is known of their history prior to that time. Hiram C. Smith, up to his fifteenth year, had never been located very long in any one place, and until that time had received no school advantages, having to work hard on the farm. December 31, 1850, he married Miss Lucy J. Carter, a native of Virginia, and a daughter of John L. and Annie (Gibson) Carter, who were formerly from Virginia. To Mr. and Mrs. Smith were born ten children, eight now living: James M., Serena, Mrs. Mary J. Dunn, Hiram, Clinton, Robert E., Mrs. Annie Peters, Mrs. Maggie Douglas. Henry and John are the children who are deceased. Mr. Smith remained at home tilling the soil until the opening of the late Rebellion, when he enlisted in the Confederate army and served throughout the war, surrendering at Prairie Grove. He was in the following battles: Wilson Creek, Prairie Grove and Fayetteville, and many other minor engagements. During the last named battle his captain and a number of his associates were killed around him. During the war his family had been obliged to move in order to save themselves from being molested or burned out. After the war Mr. Smith returned home, but did not remain long, but went from there to Texas, where he remained for one year. He then returned to the home he had left at the beginning of the war, and here remained for four years. He then moved to the farm upon which he was born, and there remained seventeen years engaged in farming, after which he moved to his present farm. Mr. Smith has been quite fortunate in his business transactions, and is now the owner of 300 acres of good land, 225 under cultivation.

J. H. Snow, a prosperous, respected farmer residing near Garfield, Ark., was born in Illinois in 1836, and is a son of William and Mary Snow. The father is a North Carolinian, and when a small boy was taken to Illinois, where he grew to manhood and married, and was a tiller of the soil until 1842, at which time he moved to Benton County, Ark., and was there engaged in agricultural pursuits until his death, which occurred in 1860. J. H. Snow was reared in Benton County, and received such education as could be attained in the common schools of those days. He resided with his parents until grown, and in 1858 was married to Miss Jane Sutter, who was also a native and resident of Benton County, and their union was blessed in the birth of four children: James H., Ellen T., Mary F. and John L. Mr. Snow has an excellent farm of 120 acres on the White River bottom, about eighty of which are under good cultivation and well improved. He and his wife worship in the Methodist Church.

J. E. Spencer, miller of Batie Township, was born March 10, 1838, in Polk County, Mo., and is the son of William and Nancy (Cordell) Spencer. The father was born in Kentucky. In an early day he went to Fulton County, Ill., remaining seven years, then from there to Polk County, Mo., remaining two years; thence to Cedar County, Mo., where he resided five years; then he returned to Kentucky, and remained there till after the war, then came back to Cass County, Mo.; from there to Bates County, then to Arkansas, and here resided about twelve years, and died. He had received no education, but by his own exertions could both read and write. The mother was born in Alabama, but when a young girl immigrated to Kentucky, where she was afterward married to Mr. Spencer, and bore him thirteen children, nine now living, so far as known. They are named as follows: James, Elizabeth, John E., Fareby, Sampson, William, Nancy J., Mary and Hannah. Those deceased were named, Amelia, Alexander, Mina and William. The grandfather and grandmother Spencer were both native Virginians, and immigrated to Kentucky, being among the pioneer settlers of that State. This was about 100 years ago, and they suffered all the privations and hardships incident to pioneer life. J. E. Spencer has often heard his grandparents speak of making their own gunpowder. His great-grandfather on his mother's side was a soldier in the Revolutionary War, and was severely wounded in the last battle, being almost disemboweled. The maternal grandfather was a native of Germany, and the grandmother a native of Alabama. The latter was a cultured Southern lady, and was the owner of 300 negroes. J. E. Spencer was but two years of age when his parents left Polk County, Mo., and settled in Cedar County of the same State. They remained here five years and then moved to Kentucky, but J. E. received no education, and worked on the farm until nineteen years of age. He then returned to Missouri, settled in Macon County, and there lived for three years, engaged in tilling the soil. From there he went to Ringo County, Iowa, remained but a short time, and was married to Miss Lydia Chambers, daughter of Joel Chambers. One child was born to this union, Eliza A., who is now deceased. At the breaking out of the late Civil War Mr. Spencer enlisted in the Confederate army under Gen. Price; was in Stein's battery, and served faithfully for four years. He was in the battles of Lexington, Blue Mills Landing, Lone Jack and many other smaller engagements. During the war Mr. Spencer was captured, but made his escape; was reported dead by a friend, and when he returned home after the war, found his wife married again. He was married to Miss Mary J. Burch, of Bates County, Mo., whose father was one of the first settlers of North Missouri. Eight children were born to Mr. and Mrs. Spencer, seven now living: George W., Charley R., Emma, Hiram, Ella, Ebb and Emmit Lee. After marriage Mr. Spencer remained in Bates County, Mo., engaged in farming for two years, and then moved to Newton County, where he remained for nine years, working at the carpenter's trade, but also carried on farming. From there he went to Siloam Springs, where he followed carpentering, rail-roading, and was also engaged in mill-wrighting, which he followed until 1887, when he removed to Southwest City, Mo., and here remained two years;

then came to Maysville, Ark., and purchased one-half interest in the mill he is now running. He is doing a good business, and supplies the country for miles around. He is a Mason, a Democrat in politics, and is yet a strong advocate for the lost Southern cause. He assisted in bridging the Mississippi River at Burlington, Iowa, and was and is a first-class carpenter.

Hon. Solomon F. Stahl, cashier of the Benton County Bank, of Bentonville, Ark., is a native of Shelby County, Mo., born February 8, 1851, son of Frederick and Margret (Link) Stahl. The father was born in Economy, Penn., in 1816, was of German descent, a farmer and engineer by occupation. He was a young man when his father, Martin Stahl, moved to Columbiana County, Ohio, and in 1844 Martin Stahl moved to Shelby County, Mo., where he died. He was a farmer by occupation. Frederick Stahl was married in Mahoning County, Ohio, and soon after devoted his time and attention to engineering, at which he has worked the greater portion of his life. In 1844 he moved to Shelby County, Mo., and in 1868 he moved to Aurora Mills, Marion County, Ore., where he now lives. His wife, Margret (Link) Stahl, was born in Columbiana County, Ohio, and died in March, 1852. She was the mother of six children, five of whom lived to be grown: Joseph (deceased), Lydia (deceased), Mrs. Mary Backert, John, Henry M. and Solomon F. The latter received a good common school education, and at the age of fifteen began working in a store at Bethel, Shelby Co., Mo., for P. & M. Miller, and remained three years in their employ. At the end of that time he became partner with J. G. Bauer. The firm title for the next three years was Bauer & Stahl, after which he formed a partnership with John D. Miller, under the firm name of Miller & Stahl. Both the above businesses were carried on in Nineveh, Adair Co., Mo., where he had moved to in 1868. In 1873 their store and contents, with no insurance, was burned, and the hard earnings of Mr. Stahl were swept away. He had a large amount of latent energy, and went to work with renewed vigor, establishing himself at Shibley's Point, Adair Co., Mo. February 22, 1874, he married Miss Sarah Shoop, who was born in Adair County, Mo., in 1854, and who became the mother of four children: Lillie A., Clauda C., Edwin R. and Carmine S. In 1880 Mr. Stahl was elected judge of Adair County, Mo., on the Republican ticket, and afterward moved to Kirksville, Mo., and assisted in the organization of the First National Bank of that city. He was director and stockholder, and the following year he was elected assistant cashier, holding that position until March, 1885, when, owing to his wife's health, he resigned his position and moved to Bentonville, Benton Co., Ark. On June 8, 1885, he organized the Benton County Bank, with a capital of $20,000, and was elected cashier of the same. May, 1887, the capital stock was increased to $50,000, paid up. Judge Stahl has been cashier of the same since its organization, and is a man of shrewd business capacity, and one whose honesty and integrity have never been questioned. The bank has prospered from the time of its organization and is doing a good business. This bank has the finest banking house in Northwestern Arkansas. Judge Stahl has always been very temperate in his habits, and is a warm supporter of temperance reform. He is a Master Mason of Lodge No. 56 and of Chapter No. 15, and he and his wife are members of the Cumberland Presbyterian Church, of which he has been a member for fourteen years, and all that time he has been a ruling elder.

John B. Steele, mayor of Rogers, Ark., and secretary of the Rogers Canning & Packing Company, was born in Bedford County, Tenn., in 1838, and is a son of C. D. and Catherine Steele, who were also Tennesseeans by birth. After residing on a farm until thirteen years of age he began serving an apprenticeship at the turner's and machinist's trades, and in connection with this attended school until 1859. From that time until the breaking out of the war he worked at the turner's trade, and at the latter date joined Col. Carroll's Arkansas Cavalry, and served in different companies for four years. He was lieutenant for the First Battalion Arkansas Cavalry, and was finally promoted to brevet-major. He was in a number of hotly contested battles, and was in over fifty skirmishes. He was wounded twice, was in prison six months, and was paroled from Vicksburg, Miss., at the close of the siege. After the close of the war Mr. Steele went to Texas, but after a short time returned to Arkansas, and engaged in the saw-mill business, which occupation he followed for about five years, and then turned his attention to merchandising at Springdale, Ark. About three years later he moved his stock of goods to Van Winkle Mills, but about six months later (in 1880) he abandoned this business and opened the Van Winkle Hotel, in Fayetteville, which he successfully managed for two years. He then returned to Van Winkle Mills, and spent one year in the wholesale and retail lumber business, when he sold out and followed the same occupation in Rogers for some time. Since 1885 he has held the position of mayor of Rogers, except about nine months, and has also been justice of the peace for several years. Since November, 1887, he has been connected with the Rogers Canning & Packing Company. In 1868 he was married to Miss Mary Van Winkle, who was born in Illinois in 1841, and by her is the father of three children: Guy C., Richard St. Clair and Harry. Mr. Steele is a stanch Democrat, and a member of the A. F. & A. M.

Isaac N. Steers may be mentioned as one of the prosperous farmers and stock raisers of Benton County, Ark. He was born in the "Keystone" State (Center County), November, 18, 1856, and is a son of Evans and Elizabeth (Mulholland) Steers, both of whom were born in Pennsylvania, the former in 1810. He was a mill-wright and farmer by occupation. He is a member of the Methodist Episcopal Church, South, and resides in Bartow, Fla. His wife died in Alleghany County, Va., in 1862, aged forty-one years. She was a member of the Baptist Church, and of Dutch descent. Isaac N. Steers was reared and educated in Alleghany County, Va. In 1879 he went to West Virginia, thence to Kentucky, and then to Cincinnati, Ohio, where he followed his trade, that of railroad carpenter, for six months. He then left that place, westward bound, and landed in Douglass County, Colo., where he worked at his trade until the fall of 1881, and then came to Arkansas. In 1885 he engaged in farming, and now has a pretty little home and a fine farm of 170 acres. He was married in Fayetteville, Ark., January, 6, 1885, to Mrs. Sallie Lamar (her former husband being also named Lamar); a daughter of John M. and Haynie (Smith) Lamar, and granddaughter of William Lamar, of French descent, a farmer and a soldier in the War of 1812. John M. Lamar was born in Anderson County, Tenn., July 7, 1804, and was captain of a company in the Black Hawk War. He was a farmer and merchant by occupation, and died in Nodaway County, Mo., August 16, 1877. His wife was born in Culpeper County, Va., February 15, 1806, and when a small child was taken by her parents to Anderson County, Tenn., where she grew to womanhood, and married Mr. Lamar. She was a member of the Missionary Baptist Church, a daughter of George Smith, and died in Nodaway County, Mo., August 20, 1844.

James B. Stephens is a son of William and Delilah (Short) Stephens, and was born in Tennessee December 20, 1824. The father and mother were born in North Carolina and Kentucky, respectively, the former being yet alive and almost one hundred years of age. The latter's birth occurred in 1811, and she died in 1883. After leaving North Carolina Mr. Stephens resided successively in Tennessee, Illinois, Iowa, and in 1843 located in Arkansas, where he yet resides. The following are his children: James B., Jeremiah, who was killed by lightning in Sebastian County, Ark., and Riley, Zerilda, Frances and Elizabeth, who are dead; Amanda, wife of Franklin Moore, died in 1865; Sarah, who died when a child; Nancy, wife of Joseph Merrill, died just before the close of the war; Cynthia A., who resides in California, the wife of J. J. Rogers, and William T. James B. Stephens served in the Mexican War under Scott, and belonged to the body guard of Gen. Franklin Pierce, who afterward became President of the United States. He has some interesting relics of that conflict in his possession. In 1850 he went to California and engaged in mining gold, meeting with good success. He was then engaged in stock raising for five years, and while in California married Matilda Watson. After returning to Arkansas he took for his second wife Miss Margaret Hughes, and she and her infant son, Franklin, died during the war, while Mr. Stephens was in the Union service. He served under Col. John E. Phelps, a son of ex-Gov. Phelps, of Missouri, as first lieutenant. December 21, 1865, Mr. Stephens married Elizabeth Douglass, who was born in Missouri. She became the mother of nine children: Margaret D., wife of Samuel Shipley; James R., William T., Sarah L., Cora A., Ollie B. (deceased), George F., Daisy B. and James B. Mr. Stephens represented Sebastian County in the State Legislature during the session of 1871, and was also captain of a company of the State Guard of Arkansas, receiving his commission from Gov. Powell Clayton. Mr. Stephens owns 220 acres of very fine land in the Osage Valley, and is a member of the Masonic fraternity and G. A. R. He is a Republican, and cast his first presidential vote for Franklin Pierce.

William Stevens is a Kentuckian, whose birth occurred in 1830. His father, George Stevens, was a native and farmer of North Carolina, and was there married to Miss Ellen Hise, the mother of William Stevens. The latter's early educational advantages were quite limited. He continued to reside with his parents until he was married, in 1852, to Elizabeth Powell, who died in 1859, having borne two children. The same year Mr. Stevens married his second wife, Ardia Prior, by whom he became the father of seven children. This wife died in 1875, and he married his third wife, a Mrs. Smith. After leaving Kentucky Mr. Stevens removed to Indiana, but only remained there one month, when he removed to Illinois, and there resided three years. He afterward took up his abode in Missouri, and after seven years' residence in that State went to Kansas, where he made his home until the close of the war. In 1867 he came to his present home in Arkansas, where he has since been engaged in agricultural pursuits on his valuable bottom land farm of 185 acres. He was not in active service during the war, but served in the State troops in the State of Kansas. He and family are members of the Missionary Baptist Church.

William Holland Steward may be mentioned as one of the prosperous and progressive farmers and stock raisers of Benton County, Ark. He was born in Bedford County, Va., December 23, 1829, and is a son of Josiah Edwin and Mary (Signor) Steward. who were born in Virginia February 24, 1805, and March 23, 1800, and died in Indiana in 1872 and December 30, 1886, respectively. The father was a farmer, and he and wife were members of the Protestant Methodist Church. The great-grandfather Steward was born in Scotland, and came to America, serving in the Revolutionary War. William Holland Steward was taken to Indiana by his parents when quite a small boy, and was there reared, educated and married, the latter event taking place in 1852, to Miss Lydia Ellen Coonfield, who was born in Marion County, Ind., October 27, 1833. Their union was blessed in the birth of ten children: Mary A., wife of Thomas Mason; George Newton (deceased), Elmira J., wife of Robert True; John A.; Martha A., wife of James True; Isaac E., William A., James W., Theodore J. and Richard A. Mr. Steward commenced life with small means, and met with severe losses during the late war, but by industry and good management has now a comfortable competency and a good and well-cultivated farm of 120 acres. He and family worship in the Methodist Episcopal Church, and have been worthy residents of Benton County, Ark., since 1854. Mrs. Steward's parents were Isaac and Lydia (Epperson) Coonfield.

J. K. P. Stringfield may be mentioned as one of the successful merchants and millers of Benton County, Ark., and holds the position of postmaster at War Eagle. He is a native of Benton County, born in 1845, and is a son of Nathaniel and Fidella (Stivers) Stringfield, who were born in Kentucky and Illinois, respectively. They were married in the latter State, and came to Arkansas about 1837, where they spent the remainder of their days, living to a good old age. J. K. P. Stringfield is the eighth of their twelve children, and his youthful days were spent in assisting his father on the farm and in attending the common schools. At the age of sixteen years he joined the Confederate army, and at the end of eight months returned home and began working at 70 cents per day, and afterward engaged in the saw-mill business as agent for P. Van Winkle, serving in this capacity for several years. In 1881 he engaged in general merchandising at War Eagle, and also became owner of the grist-mill at that place, which property he purchased from Mr. Blackburn. He has a large and well-selected stock of general merchandise, and also owns a branch store at Van Winkle Saw-mills. The water power which runs his grist-mill is the finest in Northwestern Arkansas, and the mill is very commodious and does a thriving business. Mr. Stringfield was married, in 1869, to Miss Emma Van Winkle, who was born in Benton County in 1852, and by her is the father of seven children: Luella (wife of W. T. Blackburn), Peter N., Alice, Mollie, Bertie, Lillie and James Berry. Mr. Stringfield is a Democrat, and is a Chapter Mason and a member of the I. O. O. F.

H. L. Stroud. The mercantile interests of Benton County, Ark., are ably represented in Rogers by Mr. Stroud. who was born in Pea Ridge, Ark., in 1858. He is a son of A. B. and Mary I. (Webb) Stroud, who were born in Tennessee, and are now residing in Carl Junction, Mo., and is the second of their seven children. His boyhood days were spent in following the plow and in attending the common schools and the Pea Ridge High-school. In 1878 his marriage with Miss Sallie Pace was consummated. She was also born in Benton County, her birth occurring in 1859. Their union was blessed in the birth of four children: Eva, Annie and Monty, who are twins, and Charley. Mr. Stroud engaged in agricultural pursuits after his marriage, but shortly after engaged in merchandising with his father. This he continued until 1886, when he purchased his present property, sold out his interest in the store at Pea Ridge, rented his farm, and is now residing with his family in Rogers, where he is devoting all his time and energy to his store. His stock of goods is large and well selected, and he is doing a prosperous business. He has in the course of erection a large brick store building, into which he will move his goods as soon as the building is completed. He is a consistent member of the Christian Church, and supports the principles of the Republican party.

George Washington Tate, farmer and stock-raiser of Benton County, Ark., was born in Newton County, Mo., October 26, 1845, and was reared to manhood in his native State. He received a fair business education, and at the age of twenty-four years went to Texas, where he was engaged in stock driving for six years, and then located in Benton County, Ark., where he was married, in 1875, to Miss Louisa Goad, and settled down to farming, at which he has been quite successful. Mrs. Tate is a daughter of Robert and Catherine Goad, and was born in Benton County, Ark., January 3, 1843. She is the mother of two sons: Robert Houston and Willie Edward. Mr. Tate's parents were Alexander and Patience (Cannon) Tate, both of whom were born in Tennessee. The father was a progressive and energetic farmer, and accumulated considerable property. He was a son of George Washington Tate. Mrs. Patience Tate was a devoted and affectionate wife and mother, and died in 1853, two years after her husband's death.

William A. Terry, president of the Bentonville Bank, and dealer in dry goods, merchandise, etc., at Bentonville, was born in Glasgow, Barren Co., Ky., in 1844, and is the son of Bennett W. and Ruth (McDanial) Terry. The father was born in Botetourt County, Va., in 1801, was of Irish descent, and a farmer by occupation. When a young man he immigrated to Kentucky, was married there, and there died in 1877. His wife was born in Virginia in 1805, was of Scotch-Irish descent, and died in 1877. She was the mother of nine children, eight of whom lived to be grown: Mrs. Josephine Hall, Mrs. Louise Jeffries, Mrs. Sarah Burks, Samuel (deceased), Louis D. (deceased), John F. (deceased), Christopher and William A. The last named was reared on the farm until fourteen years of age, and received a good practical education in the common schools. He then left home and began working for himself, as clerk in a dry goods house in Horsewell, Barren Co., Ky. He there continued for about two years, when the war broke out, and he enlisted in Company F, Sixth Regiment Kentucky Infantry, September, 1861, and was in the Confederate service from that time until May 20, 1865, when he surrendered at Glasgow, Ky. He was in the battle of Shiloh, first fight at Vicksburg, Baton Rouge, Murfreesboro, and all the engagements from Dalton to Jonesboro. He was held a prisoner for twenty days. After this he was sent to Kentucky as a recruiting officer, and held the rank of first lieutenant when he was eighteen years old. After the war he attended school for about five months, in Logan County, Ky., and at the end of that time he hired to a merchant at Red Sulphur Springs, in Macon County, Tenn., and had the management of the establishment. At the end of one year he gave up the position and went to Milligan, Tex., and clerked in a hotel three months, after which he clerked in a store on Brazos River for some time. He then sold sewing machines for the following six months. When he commenced he had $500. When he quit he was minus that sum. In 1868 he went to Dallas, Tex., and here clerked for three years. He then bought a stock of goods and commenced on his own responsibility at Breckinridge, Tex. At the end of one year he sold out and returned to Dallas, Tex. In October, 1871, he married Miss Kate Smart, a native of Oxford, Calhoun Co., Tex., born in 1849, and the daughter of Dr. John Smart, of Bentonville, Ark. Mrs. Terry died in 1873, and the following year Mr. Terry moved to Bentonville, Ark., where he has since been engaged in merchandising, and where he has met with good success in all his undertakings. He is a marked business manager, courteous, obliging and sociable. He married for his second wife Miss Susan Smart, sister of the first wife and a native of the same county, born in 1852. They have two living children: William A., Jr., and Kate. In April, 1887, Mr. Terry became interested in the

Bentonville Bank, was elected president of the same, and now holds that position. He is a Democrat in politics, casting his first vote for Tilden in 1876; is a member of the K. of P. and also ancient member of the K. of H.

Hon. Reuben S. Thomas, farmer and horticulturist, of Benton County, Ark., is a Culpeper County Virginian, born in 1832. He is a son of James and grandson of David Thomas, who was born in Wales. James Thomas was born in Virginia, and was married there to Lodama Tuller, who was also a native of that State, and with his family moved to Ohio about 1835. They located in Franklin County, where they both eventually died, the father's death occurring in 1853, at the age of fifty-seven years, and the mother's in 1884, at the age of eighty-four years. Reuben S. is the sixth of their seven children, and resided in Ohio until he attained his eighteenth year, when he determined to seek his fortune in the far West. He lived in the Rocky Mountains, where he was engaged in mining, until 1880, when he came to Arkansas and settled down on a farm in Benton County. His mining ventures met with varying success, his last venture being in Pima County, Arizona, where he sunk about $22,000. He afterward located in Maricopa County, and in 1877 was elected to the office of sheriff, and so efficient an officer did he make, and so fairly did he do his duty, that in 1881 he was elected to the State Legislature from that county, serving two years. On coming to Arkansas he purchased property, and is now a member of the Northwestern Real Estate Association, and is also agent for the Little Rock Fire Insurance Company and the California Fire Insurance Company of San Francisco. He was married in Arkansas to Miss Sarah A. Dalton, who was born in Cobb County, Ga. They have one child, Lola. Mr. Thomas is a warm Democrat, and is a Chapter Mason.

Elder William J. Todd, pastor of the Primitive Baptist Church at Rogers, Ark., was born in Andrew County, Mo., July 29, 1849, and is the sixth of nine children born to the marriage of Zapnath Todd and Sarah C. Stephens. Both parents were of Kentucky stock, and were married in Missouri, which was the father's birthplace. William J. Todd was reared, educated, married and ordained a minister of the Primitive Baptist Church in Missouri. While in Missouri he followed mercantile pursuits, and also carried on that business after coming to Rogers, in 1883. He is a man of great public spirit and enterprise, and is eminently fitted for an active business life. He has assisted materially in pushing forward many of the best enterprises of which Benton County can boast, and is now the president of the Rogers Canning and Packing Company, and is also president of the Benton County Horticultural, Agricultural and Mechanical Fair, and president of the Northwest Arkansas Horticultural Society. Besides the labor his connection with these institutions involves, he is pastor of the Little Flock Church, Oak Grove Church, and has regular appointments close to Lowell and on Pea Ridge. He was married to Sarah Z. Thornton, by whom he has an interesting little family of two children: Edna and Nellie.

J. M. Tucker, general merchant, Cherokee City, Benton Co., Ark., was born in Madison County, Ind., in 1840, and is a son of John and Angeline (Marsh) Tucker, natives of Ohio, and members of the Free-Will Baptist Church. The father was a successful farmer and merchant, and died in Southwest City, Mo. James M. Tucker was brought to Dallas County, Mo., by his parents when a child, and was there reared to manhood and educated. At the age of nineteen years he went to Colorado in 1860, but returned home in the fall of 1861, and entered the Confederate army, enlisting in Company E, Col. Hunter's regiment, in Price's army. He was in the battles of Pea Ridge, Lone Jack (being wounded five times in the latter battle), Cape Girardeau, Pilot Knob, Helena, Prairie Grove and a number of others of less note. He was captured twice, and each time succeeded in effecting his escape. After the war he resided for some time in Boone County, Mo., and helped to build the mills at Southwest City, McDonald Co., Mo. At the end of six years he sold his property in that town and went to Maysville, Benton Co., Ark., where he engaged in the mill and distillery business three years. He afterward made another trip to Colorado, but only remained six months, when he returned and located at Eureka Springs, where he sold family groceries and provisions for ten months. He then spent some time in Texas engaged in the cattle business, and after returning to Arkansas, located in Cherokee City, where he has resided since August 25, 1881. He is the oldest merchant in the place and is doing a prosperous business. He was married in Maysville, Ark., in 1876, to Miss Melvina Dabkins, a daughter of

Hugh Dabkins, of Tennessee, and by her is the father of three sons and three daughters. Mr. Tucker is a member of the Masonic fraternity, and is well known throughout Benton County, where he is esteemed and respected for his many sterling qualities.

J. M. Vandover, the popular liveryman at Rogers, Ark., was born in Butler County, Mo., in 1838, and is the eldest of twelve children, three of whom are living, born to the marriage of Theodore Vandover and Emeline Sandlin, which took place in Butler County, Mo. The father was born in the "Old Dominion," and at an early day moved to Kentucky, thence to Missouri, where he afterward made his home. His wife was of North Carolina stock. Their son, J. M. Vandover, was reared in his native State, and in 1859 went to Southern Arkansas, and at the breaking out of the war became a member of Company Second, Hempstead Rifles. His first experience in fighting was at Pea Ridge, where he was quite severely wounded. He served until the close of the war, his company being disbanded in Texas, and then returned to Hempstead County, Ark., and engaged in his old pursuit of overseeing. He soon afterward gave this up and went to Texas, where he met and married Miss Lizzie Dudley, who was born in Ripley County, Mo., in 1843. Belle M., William, Mattie and Riley C. are the children born to their union. After his marriage Mr. Vandover returned to Arkansas, and engaged in agricultural pursuits and also dealt in stock for about four years, which occupation proved a success financially. In 1870 he moved to Benton County, Ark., to benefit his family's health, and here has since made his home. He engaged in the livery and stock business, and is deservedly successful in his business enterprises. He owns a large amount of valuable city property in Rogers, and is also the owner of an excellent farm in Hempstead County, Ark. He and wife are members of the Methodist Episcopal Church, and he affiliates with the Democratic party.

Eugene Wager, a miller at Wager, Ark., was born in the French portion of Switzerland in 1821. He is a son of Joseph and Sophie (Clerc) Wager, the former being born in Wurtemberg, Germany, and the latter in Switzerland. There were four sons and three daughters, namely: Joseph Henry, an architect and painter, died in France; Eugene, the subject of this sketch; Isidore, a miller and mill-wright, died at Siloam Springs, Ark., and Gustave, a farmer in Iowa; Josephine (wife of Mr. L. Eplatenier), is dead, and Eugenia is married to E. Briot, of Chicago, and Cecile, married to the late Col. Arthur Jacobs, of Chicago. Joseph Wager having resided alternately in France and Switzerland, a portion of the children were born in France and others in Switzerland. In 1845 Eugene Wager left France for America, and after his arrival in this country hunting for a situation in a mill, was persuaded to go to Canada. Here he obtained employment, but his wish being to go West, he succeeded in the following spring in reaching Wisconsin, and at Milwaukee formed a close acquaintance with Mr. Solomon Juneau, the founder of the city. Through his influence he was enabled to better his condition considerably, and was employed in mills in East Troy and Whitewater. Here he was married, March 13, 1848, to Emeline Snider, and after living at Janesville a short time, at the request of Gov. Farwell, of Wisconsin, went to Madison to start up and operate his mill with the water power at that place. He next moved to Depere, where he resided for twenty-one years, engaged in milling, lumbering and mercantile business. Serious losses, mainly by fire, compelled him to retire from active business, and in 1864 he joined a party moving to Montana Territory, and there remained for nearly four years. On his return he concluded to make a journey in the South, and make the selection of a new home, when at last he located at Elm Springs, Washington Co., Ark. While here he purchased and restored the Thornberry Mill, and in 1876 he became the purchaser of what was then called the Valley Mills, but now the Wager Mills, on the Osage Creek, in Benton County, Ark. He still operates said mill, and resides here, and has imparted his name both to the post-office at that place and also the township. Mr. Wager and his wife are the parents of six sons and two daughters, namely: Francis E., a miner in Arizona; George O., a farmer and miner; Edwin G., a miner and merchant in Arizona; Orlando V., a merchant at Neosho, Mo.; Henry V., in Arizona, and William Wallace, at his father's. The daughters are: Sophie E., wife of Hugh Ritter, of Elm Springs, and Ida Jane, wife of J. F. Wasson, of Springtown, Ark.

William Wammack, a resident of Sulphur Springs Township, and son of

Richard and Matilda (Moxley) Wammack, was born April 21, 1843, in Wilson County, Tenn. The father was born in the same county, and received but a limited education, although by his own efforts and observation he has made up for this deficiency to a great extent. He was reared on a farm in his native county, and was there married to Miss Moxley, who was also born and reared in Wilson County. Their marriage resulted in the birth of twelve children, nine of whom are now living: Elijah B., William, Samuel M., James W., Leander, Mrs. Martha Mayo, George P.,Richard A. and Mrs. Julia A. Fair. Those deceased are Joseph P., Mary A. and Lavinia E. Kirkham. Elijah Wammack. grandfather of William Wammack, was born in Virginia, and immigrated to Tennessee when a young man, being one of the pioneer settlers of that country. His wife, Elizabeth (Patterson) Wammack, was born in North Carolina, near the lines of Virginia. The paternal grandparents, Joseph and Lavinia Moxley, were both natives of Virginia. Mr. Moxley was but fourteen years old at the breaking out of the Revolutionary War, but he joined the American army at that early age, and assisted in making his country free and independent. William Wammack remained in Tennessee until thirteen years of age, when he moved with his parents to Benton County, Ark. The country at that time was wild and unsettled, schools were scarce, and Mr. Wammack received but a common education. He remained with his parents until 1861, working on the farm, and was then married to Miss Elizabeth J. Harrell, daughter of Isaac and Clarissa (Asby) Harrell, who were from Rutherford County, Tenn. Nine children were the result of this union, five now living: Asbury O., Mrs. Nettie A. Davis, William F., Richard I. and Clarissa L. Those deceased were named John A., Martha L., Thomas E. and Robert E. After marriage Mr. Wammack followed farming on rented land until the breaking out of the war, when he went to Kansas, and there remained three years. He then returned to Benton County, Ark., and purchased eighty acres of timbered land in Osage Township. At the end of twelve years he traded for a farm in Dixon Township, where he lived for five years. He then sold out and purchased the farm where he now lives, which consists of 200 acres of land, fifty acres under cultivation. He also owns forty acres in Dixon Township. Mr. and Mrs. Wammack are members of the Cumberland Presbyterian Church.

L. C. Warner is the business manager of the Rogers *Republican*, and was born in York State in 1849. He has been connected with railroad life for many years, and has also given much of his attention to journalism, and has risen to considerable prominence in that calling. He was postmaster of Brookville, Kas., for six years, and at the present time is the owner of the Brookville *Transcript*, a breezy weekly paper published in the interests of the Republican party. Mr. Warner was married in Virginia to Miss Nettie Crandall, a native of New York, and by her is the father of two interesting children: Roy and Maurice. C. F. Honeywell, editor of the Rogers *Republican*, was born in the "Buckeye State" in 1868, and at the early age of fourteen years went to Kansas and purchased the Brookville *Transcript*, which he managed alone for four years, and is still a joint owner of the paper. He is a member of the Methodist Church and belongs to the Knights of Labor.

William D. Wasson, a prosperous general merchant of Springtown, Ark., and native of the State, is a son of Abner W. and Hannah (Trotter) Wasson, and was born in Carroll (now Boone) County, February 14, 1850. He grew to manhood in Washington County, Ark., and reading, writing and arithmetic were the extent of his scholastic attainments, as the facilities of that day were very meager for obtaining an education. However, by much private study, Mr. Wasson acquired a good practical education, and is well fitted for the business affairs of life. His early days were spent in following the plow and in learning the blacksmith's trade, but he abandoned this work in 1876 and engaged in the mercantile business at Springtown, Ark. His first ventures in this business were on quite a small scale, as his means were limited, but he is now worth about $10,000, with a stock valued at $5,000. He has a commodious and elegant brick store building, and a fine farm in the country which he manages in connection with his store. He is a man of much native ability, and his energy, enterprise and honesty make him a valuable citizen of the county. He was married at the age of twenty-six years to Miss Elizabeth R. Steele, who was born in Lawrence County, Ark., and is a daughter of Dr. M. D. Steele, of Elm Springs, Ark., and by her became the father of five children, four of whom are living: Bertha May, Ivy Belle, Fannie T. and David Leroy. Mr. Wasson is a Master and Royal Arch Mason. He and his family worship at the Methodist Episcopal Church, South. His father was born in Middle Tennessee in 1819, but from the time he was seven years old until he reached manhood, he was a resident of Alabama. He was of Scotch-Irish descent, a Mason, and a member of the Methodist Episcopal Church, South. His wife was born in Missouri and died in Washington County, Ark. She was also a member of the Methodist Episcopal Church, South, and was a daughter of David Trotter, who was a soldier in the War of 1812, and a resident of New Madrid County, Mo., at the time of the great earthquake.

James Franklin Wasson is a son of Abner W. and Hannah (Trotter) Wasson [for parents' history see sketch of William D. Wasson], and was born in Washington County, Ark., July 25, 1856, being reared to manhood and educated in his native county. His early days were spent in following the plow, and after starting out in life for himself he was engaged in agricultural pursuits for one year. He then dealt in stock one year, and in 1881 engaged in merchandising in Elm Springs, but a year later sold his stock of goods. He still continues to remain there engaged in buying stock and selling to ranchmen in the Indian Territory. In the fall of 1883 he located in Springtown and engaged in merchandising, as clerk, with his brother, W. D. Wasson. In 1884 he purchased his present homestead, and the same year was married to Miss Ida Wager. She was born in Wisconsin in 1863, and is the mother of two children: Lela Estelle and Fred Newton. Mrs. Wasson's parents, Eugene and Emeline (Snider) Wager, were born in France and New York State, respectively. The father is a miller by occupation, and is now residing at Wager, Benton Co., Ark., and is an enterprising and successful man. His wife is a member of the Presbyterian Church, and is a daughter of John Snider, a carpenter and mill-wright. Mr. Wasson commenced mercantile business, in partnership with R. J. McGaugh, September 1, 1888. He owns a fine farm of eighty acres in a high state of cultivation. He and his wife attend the Methodist Episcopal Church, South. He is a Mason.

Dick P. Wasson, dealer in general merchandise at Robinson, Ark., was born in Franklin County, Ark., January 13, 1854, but was reared and educated in Washington County. At the age of twenty-two years (1876) he was married to Miss Tennessee Terry, a native of Washington County, Ark., born in 1857, and a daughter of Thomas W. and Elizabeth (McGill) Terry, both of whom were born in Tennessee. The father was a farmer, a Mason, and died in Washington County, Ark. His widow still survives him. Just before his marriage Mr. Wasson engaged in the mercantile business at Springtown, Ark., in partnership with his brother, W. D. Wasson, and from the beginning made the business a success. In 1885 he removed to Robinson, where he has since resided and where he has, by industry and good management, built up a good trade. He owns the best store in the town and carries a stock of goods valued at $4,000, and, besides this property, owns two good farms, one in Washington County worth $1,600, and one in Benton County worth $1,200. His marriage was blessed in the birth of five children, three of whom are living: Sarah Connie, Lula Esther and Clifford Marvin. Mr. Wasson is a Mason, and he and family attend the Methodist Episcopal Church, South.

Thomas A. Watson, dentist of Bentonville, Ark., was born in Georgia, near Atlanta, in 1830, the son of James M. Watson and Anna W. (Harris) Watson. James M. Watson was a grandson of James Watson, and great-grandson of James Watson, who was a colonel in the Revolutionary War. The family of his grandson, Rev. Samuel Watson, now reside on the old home place in York District, S. C., and have in their possession the musket and sword that the grandfather carried in the Revolutionary War. The handle of the sword was broken by a bullet shot received while Col. Watson was in battle, and saved his life. James M. Watson, father of the subject of this sketch, was born in Pendleton District, S. C., in 1800, was of Scotch-Irish descent and was a cabinet workman, but in connection he also followed farming. James M. Watson left his native State when about twenty-six years of age and went to DeKalb County, Ga., where he married Miss Anna W. Harris in 1829, who was born May 9, 1808, and who died May 29, 1842. Mr. Watson died in Polk County, Miss., in 1884, having passed the last eighteen years of his life in that county. He was married three times, and was the father of sixteen children, there being eight to his marriage to Anna W. Harris, the mother of Thomas A. Watson. The latter received his education in the schools of Georgia, and at an early age became skillful in wood work, making wagons, buggies, household furniture, etc. In 1853 he married Miss Clementine R. Harris, who was born in Decatur March 10, 1839. Seven children were born to this marriage: Jeanette R., Cora A., Clementine R., B. E. Estella, William T., Joseph C. and T. E. Emmet. In 1857 Dr. Watson moved to Wood County, Tex., and during the war he was in the Confederate service three years, engaged in the manufacture of wagon-wheels for the Government. He was in Capt. Carter's company and Hubbard's regiment and Gen. Henry McCullough's division. He was located one year at Little Rock, one year at Fulton, Ark., and one year at Gilmer, Tex. He resided in Texas until 1869, when he moved to Bentonville, Ark., where he has since resided. He worked at his trade until about 1873, when he commenced learning the dentist's profession under Dr. A. C. Armstrong, of Bentonville. About 1874 Dr. Watson entered upon the practice of his profession, and has continued this ever since. He has resided in Benton County longer than any other dentist in the county, and is a skillful workman. He has a large trade, which extends to all parts of the county, and even into Washington County. He is a Democrat in politics, is an ancient member of the Masonic fraternity, and he and wife and four daughters are members of the Presbyterian Church.

John Watson, farmer, and native of Benton County, Ark., was born in 1840, and is a son of Daniel and Elizabeth (Rollins) Watson. The father immigrated to Arkansas in 1837, locating in Benton County, where he followed the life of an agriculturist. He is still living, and resides in Barry County, Mo., at a ripe old age. John Watson was educated in the common schools of his native county, and made his parents' house his home until he attained man's estate, at which time he entered the Confederate army as private in Company B, Eleventh Missouri Infantry, and served with the same from 1862 until 1865. He was in several battles, but was so fortunate as to escape unhurt. After returning to Benton County he engaged in tilling the soil, which occupation has received his attention up to the present date. He purchased his present farm, which consists of eighty acres, in 1866. His farm is in a fine state of cultivation, and is furnished with good buildings. Besides this farm he owns some property in Garfield. He was married in 1859 to Miss Mary Gaines, and by her is the father of three children: Eliza, Rebecca and Abraham. Both Mr. and Mrs. Watson are members of the Christian Church.

H. Weems, M. D., of Rogers, Ark., was born in Alabama on the 21st of October, 1852, and is a son of S. W. and B. P. (Kartley) Weems, who were born, respectively, in Alabama and Georgia. They are yet living, and reside in Mississippi. Dr. H. Weems is the second of their eight children (four living), and was reared in Mississippi and educated in the common schools. At the age of eighteen years he began clerking in a drug store, continuing in that capacity for four years. During this time he studied medicine privately, and afterward attended lectures in a school of pharmacy in Chicago, Ill. He afterward attended the medical department of the Vanderbilt University at Nashville, Tenn., and graduated as an M. D. from that institution in 1881. He soon after came to Arkansas, locating first in Coal Hill, Johnson County, where he practiced four years, meeting with fair success. He came to Rogers in 1883, and now ranks among the intelligent and successful young physicians of the county. In 1876 he was married, in Mississippi, to Miss M. A. Fullilove, who was born in Mississippi in 1856, and they have an interesting little family of four children: Thomas, M. A., Beatrice P. and Agnes E.

Leonard West, a retired merchant of Bentonville, Ark., was born in Randolph County, N. C., May 26, 1823, and is the son of David and Amelia (Varner) West, and grandson of Daniel West. The father was born in North Carolina in 1794, was of English descent and a farmer by occupation. He was married in North Carolina, and in 1824 he immigrated to Marion County, Ind., where he resided until 1839, when he moved to Polk County, Mo. He died in 1877. His wife, Amelia Varner, was born in Randolph County, N. C., in 1799, and was of German descent. She died in 1857, and was the mother of thirteen children, seven now living: Joel, Leonard, John, Robert, James, Mary (wife of B. Wilkinson) and Sarah (wife of Marion Farris). Leonard was only an infant when his parents moved to Marion County, Ind. He was reared and grew to manhood on the farm, and remained with his parents until twenty years of age. He went to Missouri in 1839, and about 1846 he began teaching and continued at this one term. Not liking the business he abandoned it, and in 1853 he commenced merchandising at Bolivar, Mo., and sold goods until the war. He was postmaster at Bolivar eight years under Pierce and Buchanan, and six months under Lincoln. In the spring of 1862 he went to Texas, and the same year he enlisted in Company K, Twenty-ninth Regiment Texas Cavalry. He was in the battles of Poison Spring, Elk Creek and numerous skirmishes, his duties being mostly scouting and raiding. He was in service about three years. After the war he sold goods at Pilot Point, Denton Co., Tex., two years, and in 1868 he became a resident of Bentonville, Ark., and for nineteen years from that time followed merchandising at that place. He sold his stock of goods in 1887, and since then has been living a quiet, retired life. He is an honest, upright citizen, and is respected by all who know him. He was justice of the peace in Bolivar, Mo., a short time; is a member of the Masonic fraternity, an Odd Fellow, a Democrat in politics, and is a member of the Christian Church.

James Larkin Monroe Weir, farmer of Benton County, Ark., is a son of Lawson Young and Charlotte (Williams) Weir, who were Tennesseeans, born September 16, 1827, and June 7, 1830, respectively. The father is a farmer and stock raiser, and resides in Cedar County, Mo. He and wife are members of the Methodist Episcopal Church South. His parents were John and Dicy F. (Grills) Weir. The mother's parents were Larkin and Catherine (Coonse) Williams. James L. M. Weir immigrated to Illinois in 1863, and at the end of three years located in Fayetteville, Ark. He was a successful farmer and stock raiser, and in 1870 engaged in the manufacture of tobacco in partnership with George B. Hunt. The enterprise was a failure financially, leaving Mr. Weir $500 in debt. By hard work he paid his indebtedness, and in 1873 was married to Miss Mary H. Dickson, a native of Benton County, Ark., born October 26, 1852, and a daughter of Ezekiel J. A. and Sophia J. (Morrison) Dickson. Soon after his marriage Mr. Weir located in Peirce City, Mo., and engaged in farming and stock raising. His labors met with good success, and in April, 1876, he moved to Bentonville, and made his home with his father-in-law, but shortly after the house in which they lived was burned to the ground, and Mr. Weir was again financially embarrassed. His wife had some land near Bloomfield on which they located, but her health began to fail, and he took her to Colorado Springs, and remained there one month, then to the mountains of Colorado, near the head of the Arkansas River, and stayed there one month; then they went to New Mexico and engaged in railroading, clearing $2,100 in eleven months. Mrs. Weir had fully regained her health by this time, and they returned to Bloomfield, where they have since resided. Four of their six children are still living: Charlotte B., Eliza A., Robert L. and Joe D. Mr. and Mrs. Weir are both members of the Methodist Episcopal Church South. Mr. Weir is a member of the A. F. & A. M: and I. O. O. F. lodges of Arkansas. He is an enterprising young citizen, and, by industry and perseverance under many difficulties has secured a good share of this world's goods.

Joseph D. White is a descendant of James White, who was born in North Carolina, and was a farmer by occupation. He came to Arkansas in 1836, settling on the farm now occupied by his son Joseph D. He held the office of justice of the peace for a number of years before the war, and was elected to the same position after the cessation of hostilities. He died in 1886, leaving a family of nine children to mourn his loss. He was a farmer, and a man who was esteemed and respected by all. Joseph D. White was born, reared and educated in Benton County, his birth occurring in 1855. His early days were spent in assisting his parents on the farm, and this he continued to do until his marriage, in 1879, to Miss Orleana J. Graham, of Washington County. He then began doing for himself, and partly by purchase and partly by inheritance is now the owner of 160 acres of excellent farming land; ninety acres are under cultivation and well improved. Mrs. White is the daughter of James Graham, and she and Mr. White are the parents of five children: Maude E., Pilot J., Ora M., Cynthia B. and James R. The parents are members of the Baptist Church.

Warren Harvey Wight, a farmer and stockman, residing about four miles east of Bentonville, Ark., was born in Spencer County, Ind., in 1836, and is a son of James H. and Celia (Springston) Wight, who were of Welsh and Irish descent, and were born in Philadelphia, Penn., in 1807, and Kentucky in 1795, respectively. Previous to the Revolutionary War three Wight brothers came to America, one locating in Pennsylvania, another in New York. The third died. James H. Wight was of Pennsylvania stock, and a son of James Wight, who immigrated to Spencer County, Ind. While residing in that county Abraham Lincoln assisted him many a day in splitting rails. In 1840 he came to Benton County, Ark., and entered 1,100 acres of land, and here died in October, 1882. His wife died in March, 1878, leaving two children: Warren H. and Simeon. Warren H. was only four years old when his parents moved to Benton County. At the age of nine years he began learning the shoemaker's trade, and also assisted his father on the farm. During the war he worked exclusively at his trade for the Confederate army, and after the cessation of hostilities began learning the blacksmith's trade, and was also engaged in raising fine stock, making a specialty of jacks and jennies. He now keeps from six to twelve jacks and from ten to eighteen jennies. He owns 640 acres of land in Benton County, and 160 acres in Barry County. He is a Democrat in politics, and is a member of the Masonic and I. O. O. F. fraternities. He was married in 1856 to Miss Lizzie Tennessee Webb, who was born in Bedford County, Tenn., in 1837. They are the parents of one child, Matilda Jane, wife of William Easley.

James M. Wilks is a native of the "Hoosier" State, born in 1835, and is a son of John and Elizabeth (Fields) Wilks. The father was born in Tennessee, and came to Indiana in the very early settlement of the State, and settled down to farming, but, thinking he could better his fortunes, he moved to Illinois in 1865, and in 1868 concluded to try Illinois. In 1872, however, he moved back to Illinois, and there died in 1878, leaving seven children: Henry, Jasper N., Andrew S., Edward, Francis M., Margaret and James M. The latter was educated in Illinois, and remained with his father until he attained man's estate. Owing to ill health he returned to Missouri in 1882, and followed the occupation of farming for two years, when he engaged in general merchandising, but met with reverses by fire in 1886, being burned out, and again returned to farming. A year later he again opened a general mercantile establishment, and is still engaged in that line of business. His stock is valued at $1,000, and he has a fair and increasing trade. In 1856 his marriage with Miss Mary A. Poe, of Iowa, was celebrated, and their union resulted in the birth of three children: John A., who is in partnership with his father; Francis M. and Frances Elizabeth. Mr. Wilks and family are among the esteemed citizens of the county, and are worshipers in the Christian Church.

Hon. Andrew C. Williams was born in Champaign County, Ohio, July 7, 1819, and is the son of Silas and Susanna (Cock) Williams. The father was born in North Carolina in 1782, and at the age of eight moved with his parents to Virginia, remaining in Grayson County until 1813, when the family moved to Ohio. Here he died in 1844. He was a farmer by occupation. The mother was born in Virginia about 1786, and died in Ohio in 1839. They were the parents of ten children, three now living: George and Enoch in Ohio, and Andrew C. in this county. The latter was reared on a farm in Ohio, where he lived until 1850, engaged in agricultural pursuits. He then moved to Oskaloosa, Iowa, engaging in the lumber business; was president of the National State Bank of that city for a time, was also interested in the First National Bank at that place, and also tilled the soil for some time. In 1869 he moved to Leavenworth County, Kas., and engaged in farming, and was also interested in milling. He represented that county in the State Legislature in 1871, and was county commissioner of his county one term. He was appointed Indian agent by Gen. Grant, and took the Wichita Agency and afterward the Pawnee Agency. He then purchased a farm near Arkansas City, Kas., and here resided until 1885, when he located where he now lives, in Flint Township, five miles northeast of Siloam Springs, where he has 120 acres, seventy under cultivation and ten acres in orchard. Four springs, which unitedly constitute one of the finest springs in the county, issue within a radius of ten feet, boil up in the level uplands, making a stream large enough to turn a mill wheel. October 3, 1839, Mr. Williams married Miss Ruth Stanton, a distant relative of Secretary Stanton. Five children were born to this union: Sarah (deceased); Hannah, wife of J. A. Stafford; Mary, wife of Mayor F. P. Schiffbauer, of Arkansas City, Kas.; Arabella, and Enoch (deceased). Mr. Williams is a Union Labor man, and he and family are members of the Friends Church.

Ben Wilson, a prosperous farmer residing near Garfield, Ark., was born in Illinois in 1832, and in 1836 was brought to Arkansas by his parents, and was here reared to manhood. He received but little education in his boyhood, owing to the scarcity of schools in Benton County at that day, and after the early death of his father continued to make his home with his mother, and did his share in helping to support the family. His early life was rather a hard one, but by perseverance and energy he succeeded in surmounting many difficulties, and is now a successful farmer of the county, owning 120 acres of upland, which he purchased in 1855. He did not serve in either army during the late war, but remained at home and tilled his farm. In 1855 he united his fortunes with those of Miss Minerva Harrison, of Washington County, and seven children blessed their union, two of whom are living at the present time: Debby Elizabeth and Delany H. His parents were James and Debby (Williams) Wilson, the former of whom was a farmer by occupation. He was a soldier in the War of 1812, and died soon after his removal to Arkansas.

Martin Wilson was born in Washington County, Ark., in the year 1843, and is a son of John and Rebecca (White) Wilson, who were natives, respectively, of Kentucky and Arkansas. The father was a farmer throughout life, and was killed during the late war by the Federal soldiers near Fayetteville on account of being a rebel. Martin Wilson made his parents' house his home until he entered the army in 1863. He enlisted in Cooper's Arkansas cavalry company, and served until the close of the war, when he was discharged at Springdale, Ark., and returned to his home and resumed his farm work. He was married in 1871 to Miss Tempy Graham, a daughter of Nelson and Eliza Graham, of Benton County, and by her is the father of four children: John N., Rebecca L., Cora B. and Charley L. Mrs. Wilson has been a consistent member of the Baptist Church for many years, and is a faithful wife and mother. Mr. Wilson owns forty acres of land in Benton County, whither he moved from Washington County, Ark., in 1871. His land is nearly all under cultivation, and is well improved.

Stephen B. Wing. Among the industries of Benton County, Ark., worthy of mention is the fruit evaporating establishment of D. Wing & Bro. Stephen B. Wing, the junior member of the firm, was born in the "Empire State" in 1845, and is a son of Benjamin and Eliza (Babcock) Wing, who were also natives of York State. The mother is dead, but the father is still living in his native State. The subject of this biography was reared and educated in New York, and from early boyhood has been engaged in the fruit evaporating business. Thinking that he could better his condition by moving westward, he came to Arkansas and located in Benton County, and has the largest fruit evaporator in the county, situated at Rogers, its capacity being 450 bushels per day. Mr. Wing and his brother also own an evaporator at Bentonville, and with their two establishments have evaporated at least as much as 450,000 pounds of apples annually. Their fruit is shipped to all the principal points in the United States, and is of very fine quality. This industry has proved of great benefit to the county, and has utilized fruit which otherwise would have been lost. This company has also followed the same business in Georgia. Mr. Wing was married in Arkansas to Miss Anna Clark, a native of Alabama, born in 1858, and their union has been blessed in the birth of one child, Winifred. Mr. Wing is a strong Republican, and a member of the A. F. & A. M.

W. B. Winstead, son of James and Elizabeth (Robbins) Winstead, was born in Hawkins County, Tenn., November 9, 1837. The father was born in the same place as his son, in 1814, and remained in that county until thirty-seven years of age, when he removed to White County, Tenn. He here remained until 1856, and then moved to Neosho County, Kas., and there received his final summons, in April, 1870. He followed the occupation of a farmer and stock raiser all his life. The mother was born in East Tennessee, is now living in Kansas, and is about seventy years of age. They were the parents of eleven children, only four now living. W. B. Winstead was the third child born in this family. He grew to manhood on a farm, and when a young man engaged in merchandising near Springfield, Mo. He went from there to Kansas, where he engaged in the same business, following this for three years altogether. After this he dealt in stock five years, and then farmed and dealt in stock in Kansas until 1881, when he moved to Benton County, Ark., where he has since followed the same occupation. While living in Kansas he was township trustee for six years. Mr. Winstead is the owner of 180 acres of land, 120 under cultivation. In 1864 Mr. Winstead married Miss Mary E. Krouse, a native of Pennsylvania, born in

Philadelphia about 1846. Eight children were born to this union: Charles W., Sarah E., Mary A., Josie F., James W., Bessie G., Martin H. and Henry H. Politically Mr. Winstead is a Democrat, but has never aspired to office, though he is regarded as a leading farmer and citizen. He was among the first of the Northern people in Benton County, and helped start the modern plan of farm cultivation here. He is a Master Mason and a good man. Mrs. Winstead is a member of the Methodist Episcopal Church.

John Riley Woods, farmer, ex-sheriff and ex-county clerk of Benton County, Ark., was born in Carroll County, Tenn., in 1828, and is a son of Dysart and Sarah (Holmes) Woods, who were born in Bedford County, Tenn., in 1806 and 1811, respectively. The father was of Scotch-Irish descent, and at the age of thirteen years was taken by his parents to Carroll County, and was there married in 1827 to Miss Holmes. In 1836 he became a resident of Pope County, Mo., and the following year came to Benton County, Ark., where he became the owner of 160 acres of land, and died in 1882. He was one of the very early settlers, a useful citizen, and his death was universally lamented. He was a son of John Woods, a North Carolinian, who immigrated to Bedford County, Tenn., and was there married, and moved to Carroll County, Tenn., in 1819, when Dysart was thirteen years of age. He died in Carroll County in 1846, at the age of seventy-two years. His father, Samuel Woods, was an early settler and resident of Tennessee, and a soldier in the Revolutionary War. Dysart Woods' wife died in 1859. They were the parents of fourteen children, ten of whom lived to be grown. Seven are now living, John Riley Woods being the eldest. He was about nine years old when his parents located in Benton County, Ark. He made his home with his parents until twenty-two years of age, and in 1849 was married to Miss Margaret Ann Woods, a daughter of Samuel P. Woods. She was born in Carroll County, Tenn., in 1832, and became the mother of fourteen children, ten living: Samuel L., John R., Jr., Dewitt C., William P., Cephas D., Margaret E., Sarah G., Finis H., Charles R. and Annie. In 1858 Mr. Woods was elected sheriff and *ex-officio* collector of the county. In 1860 he was elected county and *ex-officio* circuit court clerk and *ex-officio* recorder, being re-elected to the latter office in 1862. In April, 1882, his wife died, and in 1884 he was married to Jane Ellis, a daughter of David and Margaret Ellis. Mrs. Woods was born in Shelby County, Ill., in 1845, and is the mother of one child, Clyde. Mr. Woods is a Democrat, and his wife is a member of the Christian Church.

Levi Oliver Woods, a farmer residing two and a fourth miles east of Bentonville, Ark., is a native of the county, born in 1848. He is a son of Dysart and Sarah (Holmes) Woods, whose sketch appears in this work, and was reared on a farm. He made his home with his father until the latter's death, and in 1877 was married to Miss Nora Bates, who was born in Dade County, Mo., in 1855, and a daughter of Owen and Millie (Reed) Bates. Mr. and Mrs. Woods became the parents of three children: Millie, Francis Dysart and William Harrison. Mr. Woods resided on the old home farm, which consists of 132 acres, until 1887, and then removed to the farm of sixty-seven acres where he now resides. He has erected himself a nice residence, and has a cozy and comfortable home. He has always made Benton County his home, and has never been out of the county more than three months during his life. He has ever supported the principles of the Democratic party, and he and wife are members of the Cumberland Presbyterian Church. Mr. Woods' brothers and sisters who are living are as follows: John R., Nancy (wife of James Woolsey), Mary E. (wife of J. V. Lee), Cynthia A. (wife of J. J. Jefferson), David H. and Sallie M.

Joseph Newton Woods was born on the farm on which he now resides in 1852, and is a son of Samuel P. and Eliza G. (Dickson) Woods, both of whom were born in Tennessee in 1809. Samuel Woods, the grandfather of Joseph N., was born in the "Old North State," but became a resident of Tennessee in 1832. He afterward located in Benton County, Ark., where he passed the remainder of his days. Samuel P. Woods was married in 1831, and the following year located in Benton County, Ark., where he entered a large tract of land, on which his son, Joseph Newton, now resides. They were among the first white settlers of Northwestern Arkansas, and were compelled to suffer the hardships and privations incident to pioneer life. Here the father passed the remainder of his days, and died in 1882. He was a member of the first grand jury of Benton County and the last before the war and the first after the war. He was taken sick while in the grand jury court-room, on Wednesday, October 12, 1882, and

****

died the following Thursday, October 13, of cholera morbus. He and wife became the parents of eight children, four of whom are living: Robert D.; Eliza J., wife of A. J. Maxwell; John S. E. and Joseph N. The latter was educated in the common schools of the neighborhood, and was reared on his father's farm. In 1872 his marriage with Miss Nancy A. Chambers was celebrated. She is a daughter of James Chambers, and was born in Benton County in 1855. Their union has resulted in the birth of seven children: Harvey, James, Alexander, Allan, Grace, Nellie and an infant daughter. Mr. Woods always resided with his parents on the old homestead, and in 1880 assumed complete control of the place. He has 850 acres of land. His mother lives with him, and has a life lease on the old homestead. Mr. Woods is very conservative in politics, and he and wife are members of the Cumberland Presbyterian Church, his parents being also members of that church.

Henry B. Woolsey, farmer and nurseryman of Osage Township, three miles southeast of Bentonville, is a native of Hempstead County, Ark., born in 1830, and is the son of Samuel and Matilda (Thompson) Woolsey. The father was a Kentuckian by birth, the same occurring in 1787, and was also married in that State. In 1808 he moved to New Madrid, Mo.. from there to Hempstead County, Ark., in 1811, and in 1829 he moved to Washington County, of the same State, where he passed the last years of his life. He was one of the first settlers of both Hempstead and Washington Counties, and during his first year's residence in the former county his principal diet was buffalo meat. He was a great hunter, a skillful marksman, and was fond of the rude life of the pioneer. He was a soldier in the War of 1812, and fought the Creek Indians in the State of Kentucky. His father, John Woolsey, was born in New York State, was in the Revolutionary War, also the War of 1812, and in the latter war he and his son, Samuel, enlisted in the same company and regiment, and were at the battle of New Orleans. John Woolsey died in 1839, at the age of one hundred and five years. Samuel Woolsey's wife, Matilda Thompson, was born in Kentucky in 1791, and died in 1877. She was the mother of thirteen children, six of whom are now living, Henry B. being the tenth child. He was but an infant when his parents moved to Washington County, and here he was reared and educated. He worked on the old home place, which consisted of 200 acres, four miles west of the county seat, until twenty-four years of age, and in 1854 married Miss Margaret Neale, who was born in Boone County, Mo., in 1834. To their marriage were born six children: Josephine, wife of Richard Collins; James M., who died in 1880, at the age of twenty-one; Lillie G., wife of Alvin Dickson; Anna S., deceased, who died in 1876, at the age of six years, and George. Mr. Woolsey resided in Washington County, Ark., until 1857, when he became a resident of Bentonville, Ark., and worked in a wagon-shop. In 1861 he purchased eighty acres of land in Section 33, Township 20, Range 30, where he located and has since resided. About 1866 he started a nursery on a small scale, and continued to increase his stock year by year until about seven years ago, when his son-in-law, Alvin Dickson, became a partner, and since then they have devoted their time and attention to this work. They have at least 300,000 trees, at present writing, in fine growing order. Mr. Woolsey is one of the old settlers, and is a man well respected by his friends and acquaintances. He is a Democrat in politics, and Mrs. Woolsey is a member of the Methodist Episcopal Church South.

Isom M. Wright. Prominent among the successful and wealthy farmers of Benton County, Ark., may be mentioned Mr. Wright, who is deserving of special mention. He was born, reared, educated and married in Alabama, the first event taking place in 1826, and the latter in December, 1847. His wife, whose maiden name was Barbara Latham, was born in Alabama on the 20th of May, 1832, and by Mr. Wright became the mother of the following family : William A., James A., Celestia (wife of E. H. Pass), Elizabeth Jane (wife of Samuel Garret), Henry W., E. L. and Isaac J. In 1850 Mr. Wright moved to Fannin County, Tex., and after residing there about seventeen years came to Benton County, Ark., in the autumn of 1867, where he has been engaged in tilling his valuable farm of 290 acres. He is a Democrat, and during the late war served a few months in the Confederate army. His parents, William and Clarissa (Self) Wright, were born in North Carolina in 1800 and 1804, respectively. The father was reared in his native State, and was married in Alabama when he was about twenty-five years of age. He moved to Fannin County, Tex., in 1853,

BENTON COUNTY, ARKANSAS - BIOGRAPHICAL AND HISTORICAL MEMOIRS   232

****

and there resided until his death in 1872.   His wife died in Washington County, Ark., October 16, 1885.   The following are their children: Isom M., Susan E. (widow of J. F. Dabs), William Newton, Zina Catherine (wife of William Shaffin), Mary Adeline (wife of W. L. Gualtny), Jasper A., and Vina Jane (wife of Charles Johnson).

Archibald McKissick Yell, was born in Fayettville, Washington Co., Ark., and is a son of Alexander Curry and Martha D. (Coffee) Yell, who were born in Bedford County, Tenn., November 12, 1805, and in 1806, respectively. The father was a Master Mason, a successful business man, and died at Robinson, Ark., October 24, 1881.   He was a son of Moses Yell, an Englishman, and Methodist minister, who came to America.   The mother died in Fayetteville, Ark., March 25, 1849.   She was a daughter of Rice Coffee, a farmer.   Archibald M. Yell grew to manhood in Benton County, Ark., and received a common school education.   He received some help from his parents in starting out in life, and by successful investments is now the owner of a fine farm of 300 acres, with 200 under cultivation.   He is a Master Mason, and is an agreeable and intelligent gentleman.   His paternal uncle, Archibald Yell, was a soldier in the War of 1812, enlisting at the age of seventeen years.   He was elected to Congress from this district, but at the breaking out of the Mexican War he resigned his seat in that body and enlisted in that struggle.   He was commander of an Arkansas regiment, and was killed in that war February 23, 1847.

McNAIRY, TN, 169, 206
MEADE, KY, 204
MECKLENBURG, NC, 206, 207, 215
MEIGS, 133
MEIGS, TN, 183
MIAMI, OH, 156
MILLER, MO, 135
MONITEAU, MO, 205
MONROE, IN, 138
MONROE, MO, 130, 183
MONROE, OH, 193
MONROE, TN, 140, 142, 169, 187
MONTAGUE, TX, 146
MONTGOMERY, IL, 203
MONTGOMERY, KY, 147
MONTGOMERY, MO, 135, 197
MONTGOMERY, TN, 173
MONTGOMERY, VA, 203
MORGAN, GA, 200
MORGAN, IL, 182
MORGAN, TN, 195
MORROW, OH, 143, 184
NEOSHO, KS, 229
NEW MADRID, MO, 225
NEWTON, 214, 217
NEWTON, MO, 157, 164, 170, 221
NOBLE, IN, 143
NODAWAY, MO, 143, 219
NOXUBEE, MS, 173
OHIO, VA, 199
OHIO, WV, 185
ORANGE, NC, 154
OREGON, MO, 127, 169
OVERTON, TN, 8, 170
OZARK, MO, 185
PATRICK, VA, 213
PERRY, AL, 214
PICKAWAY, OH, 159
PICKENS, SC, 186
PIKE, 179
PIMA, AZ, 222
POLK, MO, 127, 130, 132, 133, 134, 165, 180, 183, 187, 188, 217, 226
POLK, MS, 225
POPE, 183
POPE, MO, 230
PULASKI, KY, 128
PULASKI, MO, 135, 139
PULASKI, VA, 175
RABUN, GA, 139
RABURN, GA, 187
RANDOLPH, IN, 210
RANDOLPH, NC, 140, 226
RAY, 204
RAY, MO, 204
RAY, TN, 143, 144
RED RIVER, TX, 168, 209
RICHARDSON, NE, 153
RICHLAND, OH, 130, 183, 184
RINGO, IA, 217
RIPLEY, MO, 223
ROANE, TN, 131, 132, 163, 203
ROCKBRIDGE, VA, 139

ROCKINGHAM, NC, 171
RUSH, TX, 209
RUTHERFORD, NC, 167, 193
RUTHERFORD, TN, 148, 149, 154, 201, 206, 207, 224
SAN DIEGO, CA, 173
SANGAMON, IL, 192, 206
SCHUYLER, MO, 212
SCHUYLKILL, PA, 158
SCOTT, 155
SCOTT, IL, 142
SCOTT, KY, 131, 158, 159, 181, 182
SCOTT, VA, 8
SEBASTIAN, 193, 219
SEVIER, 160
SHELBY, IL, 144, 203, 230
SHELBY, MO, 218
SHELBY, OH, 136
SHENANDOAH, VA, 138
SMITH, TN, 154, 157
SPARTANBURGH, SC, 195
SPENCER, IN, 227, 228
ST. CLAIR, MO, 192
ST. FRANCOIS, MO, 192
STARK, IL, 148
STE. GENEVIEVE, MO, 192
STEPHENS, TX, 216
STOKES, NC, 171, 213
SULLIVAN, 156
SULLIVAN, IN, 203
SULLIVAN, TN, 133, 155
SURRY, NC, 209
TARRANT, TX, 194
TEXAS, MO, 194
TIPPECANOE, IN, 192
TITUS, TX, 137
TRIGG, KY, 175
TRUMBULL, OH, 154
TUSCARAWAS, OH, 148, 150
UPSHUR, TX, 200
WALKER, GA, 208
WARREN, 164
WARREN, KY, 206
WARREN, OH, 136
WARREN, TN, 131, 164, 175, 190, 208, 212, 215
WASHINGTON, 1, 13, 20, 42, 43, 127, 139, 140, 143, 145, 146, 150, 167, 170, 171, 174, 175, 176, 187, 188, 196, 199, 208, 209, 216, 223, 224, 225, 229, 231, 232
WASHINGTON, IL, 151
WASHINGTON, KS, 137
WASHINGTON, MO, 126, 192
WASHINGTON, PA, 161, 184
WASHINGTON, TN, 177, 202

WASHITA, 135
WATAUGA, NC, 136, 161
WAYNE, IA, 186
WAYNE, MO, 192
WAYNE, NY, 137
WAYNE, OH, 145
WEBSTER, KY, 180
WELLS, IN, 145
WHITE, TN, 229
WHITFIELD, GA, 195
WILKES, NC, 213
WILSO, TN, 134
WILSON, TN, 156, 157, 224
WISE, TX, 129
WOOD, TX, 226
WOODFORD, IL, 129, 130
WRIGHT, MO, 185
YELL, 155, 156
COVEY
  W.B., 55
COW-SA-LOW-A, 66(2)
COWAN
  HENRY, 85
  J.W., 55(2)
  JAMES, 10
  ROBERT, 10
  W.L., 56
COWEN
  ROBERT, 24, 25
COX
  J.C., 80
  JOHN, 94, 95
COX (& HIBLER), 106
CRABAUGH
  GEORGE, 13
  SARAH, 13
CRAIG
  (& SONS), 86, 144
  ANNIE B., 144
  BESSIE, 144
  C.R., 53
  CARRIE M., 144
  CHARLES R., 58, 144
  EDDIE M., 144
  EDWARD A., 144(2)
  ELIZABETH, 196
  ETHEL, 144
  GEORGE M., 144
  JAMES L., 177
  JAMES R., 144
  JAMES T., 143(5), 144
  JAMES T. (& SONS), 144
  JANE (HENDERSON), 143
  JOHN, 144
  SAMUEL, 143(2)
CRAIG (& COTTON), 87
CRANDALL
  NETTIE, 224
CRANE
  (BROS.), 104
  ABIATHER, 144
  ADONIJAH, 144
  CLARA L., 144
  ELIHU, 144(2)
  ELLA L., 144
  EMILY J., 144
  GEORGE, 144
  JAMES E., 144(4)
  JAMES L., 144
  JOEL, 144
  JOHN, 144

  JOHN C., 144
  MARY I., 144
  MILO T., 144
  NANCY, 144
  ULYSSES G., 144
  WEALTHY, 144(2)
CRAVENS
  WILLIAM H., 103
CRAWFORD
  (BROS.), 93
CREEK
  BIG SUGAR, 3
  BRUSHY, 11
  BULL RUN, 165
  BUTLER, 12, 106
  ESCULAPIA, 3
  FLINT, 3, 11, 12, 20, 24, 100
  FORT WILSON, 129
  HONEY, 13, 52
  INDIAN, 3
  LITTLE CLIFTY, 3
  LITTLE SUGAR, 3
  OSAGE, 10, 172, 194, 216, 223
  PRAIRIE, 3, 37, 200
  SAGER'S, 11, 101
  SPAVINAW, 3, 6
  SPIDER, 3
  SUGAR, 2, 9, 37, 41, 173, 192
  WAR EAGLE, 3, 4, 12, 20, 108
CREELMAN
  ELIZA, 202
CRESSWELL (& BREEDLOVE), 104
CREW
  COL., 185
CROSS
  EDWARD, 56
CROUCH
  CLINTON, 131
CROUGH (& STAHL), 86
CRUM
  WILLIAM, 127
CUMMINGS
  T.B., COL., 189
CUNDIFF
  J.W., 98
CUNNINGHAM
  EDWARD, 9, 63
  M.D., 92
  W.D., 92
CURRY
  ANNIE, 144
  CATHERINE (BENNETT), 144
  DONNIE, 145
  ELLA, 144
  ETHEL, 145
  EULALA, 145
  GEORGE, 144, 145
  JAMES R., 144
  JOHN, 145
  JOHN W., 144
  LAFAYETTE, 144
  MARY E., 144
  N.C., 142
  PIERCE, 144
  WILLIAM J., 144
  WILLIAM J., DR., 144
  WILLIAM J., M.D., 144
CURTIS
  CAROLINE, 180

HUGH, 150, 151
JACOB S., 150(2), 151
JAMES, 150, 151
KATE, 151
MAUD, 151
ROBERT, 150
DODD
  CAPT., 179
DODGE
  COL., 74
DODSON
  MARY E., 128
  O.M., DR., 93
DODSON (& CARNEY), 86
DOGGETT
  JAMES S., 129
DONALDSON
  ALEXANDER B., 151
  CATHERINE, 151
  DAVID, 151
  ELIZA, 151
  ELIZA MYRTLE, 151
  ELIZABETH, 151
  JESSE D., 151
  LORENZO DOW, 151
  LORENZO L., 151
  M.N., 104
  MARGARET A. (NEWMAN), 151
  MARGARET ANN, 151
  MARTHA JANE, 151
  MARTHA L., 151
  MARY K., 151
  MATTHEW N., 151(2)
  MINNIE C., 151
  MISSOURI C., 151
  SOPHRONIA N., 151
  WILLIAM, 151(2)
DORKENS
  BENJAMIN H., 151
  CHARLES, 151(2)
  FANNIE (MACK), 151
  JENNIE S., 152
  JOHN W., 152
  THOMAS P., 152
DORSEY
  S.W., 56
DOSS
  J.A., 104
DOUGLAS
  M., 57(2)
  MAGGIE, 216
DOUGLASS
  ELIZABETH, 219
  ELLA, 191
  EMMA, 191
  H., 191
  J.D., 187
  M., 57
DREW
  COL., 76
DRYDEN
  NANCY C., 125
DUCKWORTH
  CHARLEY R., 152
  GEORGE, 166
  J.P., 152
  J.W., 152
  L.L., 163
  NANCY (ALEXANDER), 152
  ROBERT, 11
  SIDDIE, 152
  T.M., 54(2)
DUCKWORTH & BIXLER, 96(2), 152

DUDLEY
  LIZZIE, 223
DUDMON
  W.D., 175
DUFF
  JONATHAN, 61
DUFF (& JEFFREYS), 96
DUFF (& ROBERTSON), 96
DUFFEY & FRISTOE, 34
DUFFIE
  A.W., 86
DUMAS
  PHILIP, 61
DUMAS (& FREEMAN), 100
DUNAGAN
  AMANDA, 212
  ELDER, 212
DUNAGIN
  ALBERT, 153
  AMANDA, 152
  ANNIE, 153
  HIRAM, 152
  J., 57(4), 72(2), 121(2), 152(3)
  J.R., 83, 152
  JASPER, 14
  JOHN R., 152
  MARY (RUSH), 152
  MARY T., 152
  MATTIE, 152
  MINERVA, 152
  REBECCA, 152
  ROBERT, 152
  SARAH, 152
  W.D., 152
DUNAGIN & MITCHELL, 152
DUNAGIN (& MITCHELL), 95
DUNCAN
  ARMILDA C., 173
  CHARLES G., 65(2)
  THEBE, 184
DUNGAN
  J., 57(3)
DUNGIE & HUNTER, 86
DUNLOP
  W.S., 53
DUNN
  ANGELINE A., 51
  B.F., 54, 55, 88
  B.F. (& CO.), 153
  BENJAMIN F., 153
  ELIJAH FRANK, 153
  MARTIN, 153(2)
  MARY (PINE), 153(2)
  MARY BENNIE, 153
  MARY J., 216
  MR., 147
DURHAM (& BERRYHILL), 95

DUTTON
  MOSES, 110
DUVAL
  F., 96
  W.J., 53
DWYER
  W.H., 96(2)
DYER
  (BROTHERS), 96
  EURENE, 162
  V., 163

-E-

EAGLE
  J.P., 53
EARLY
  MISS, 125

WILLIAM, 41
EASLEY
  HANNAH, 155
  NANCY HAMILTON, 155
  STEPHEN, 155
  WILLIAM, 228
ECHOLS
  HARRIET A., 147
EDENS
  ELIZA, 208
EDWARDS
  ELIZABETH, 177
  ELIZABETH (ERWIN), 177
  JOHN, 11
  THOMAS, 177
EGY
  A.J., 105(3)
  ANNIE, 104
ELAM
  ALFRED, 153
  ALFRED M., 153
  ELIZABETH, 153
  ERA EARL, 154
  ETTA, 154
  HENRY, 153
  HIRAM A., 153(3)
  JAMES, 54, 153(3)
  JAMES E., 154
  JOHN, 153
  JOHN A., 153
  LOU ALLEN, 154
  LOUALLEN, 153(3)
  LOUISA, 153
  MARGARET, 153
  MARINDA, 154
  MARINDA (SHARP), 153
  MARY J., 153
  MYRTIE, 154
  NANCY, 153
  POLLY (EANS), 153
  RICHARD, 153
  SAMUEL, 153
  SUSAN, 153
  WILLIAM, 153
ELLIOTT
  ADALINE (BOWMAN), 154
  ADALINE B., 154
  CHARLES D., 154
  CLARISSA H., 154
  DAVID J., 154
  HARRY W., 154
  HUGH, 58
  JAMES, 154
  NANCY M., 137
  PEARL, 154
  S.G., 32
  S.N., 55, 69
  SAMUEL N., 154(2)
ELLIS
  DAVID, 230
  JANE, 230
  MARGARET, 230
  [BLANK], 68
ELLISON
  L. (& CO.), 98
ELZEY
  BENJAMIN, 141
  MARTHA, 141
ENGLAND
  JOSEPH, 209
  MIDDLETON, LANCASHIRE, 165
  YORKSHIRE, 172
ENGLISH
  JUDGE, 8

MATTHEW, 54
ENNIS
  R., 28
  T.A., 28
ENTERKIN (& SEWELL), 212
ENTERKINE
  ELLEN (SMILIE), 155
  JAMES, 154
  JOHN, 155
  JOSEPH, 154
ENTERKINE (& SEWELL), 101
EPLATENIER
  L., 223
ESLINGER
  J., 104
ESTES
  A.J., 121
  SENA, 161
EVANS
  B., 137
  CORNELIA, 130
  L.D., 62
  O., 57
  VIRGINIA A., 169
EWELL
  D., DR., 209
  HARRIET, 208
EWING
  J.M., 104
EWING & GILBREATH, 104

-F-

FAGAN
  ADA B., 141
  ELIZA, 140
  J.W., MAJ., 141
  JOHN, COL., 140
FAIN
  W.B., 57(2)
FAIR
  ALBERT, 155
  ANN, 155
  COMMODORE VANDERBILT, 155
  CORA ETHEL, 156
  EDWIN CLAUDIA, 156
  EDWIN F., 155
  EDWIN FRANKLIN, 155
  ELIJA ELLIS, 155
  ELLIS, 155(3)
  ELLIS HAMILTON, 156
  ELLIS N., 155
  EMMA B., 155
  EMMA VIVIAN, 156
  ENNIS LEE, 155
  FLOYD, 155
  GEORGE, 155
  GEORGE F., 155
  GEORGE FANNING, 155
  GRACE, 156
  HARVEY CUMMINS, 155
  HARVEY DICKSON, 155
  HUGH LANCING, 155
  JOHN, 155
  JOHN DICKSON, 155
  JOSEPH A., 155
  JOSEPH ASBERY, 155
  JOSEPH CLARK, 155
  JULIA A., 224
  LAURA, 156
  LEWIS, 155
  LOULA, 156
  LOVIC PIERCE, 155
  MARTHA EDNA, 156
  MARY ANN, 155, 156
  MARY E., 155

JOHN S.E., 231
JOSEPH N., 230, 231
JOSEPH NEWTON,
    230(2)
LEVI OLIVER, 230
MARGARET ANN, 230
MARGARET E., 230
MARGARET S. (BLACK),
    198
MARY (DICKSON), 190
MARY A., 149
MARY E., 230
MILLIE, 230
MISS, 198
NANCY, 230
NELLIE, 231
R.S., 190
ROBERT D., 231
SALLIE M., 230
SAMUEL, 9, 35(2),
    62, 149, 230(2)
SAMUEL L., 230
SAMUEL P., 61, 190,
    230(3)
SARAH (HOLMES),
    230(2)
SARAH G., 230
T.A., 88
W.H., 55
WILLIAM, 9
WILLIAM H., 190
WILLIAM HARRISON,
    230
WILLIAM P., 230
WOODS & CLAYPOOL, 86
WOODY
  W.B., 60
WOOLSEY
  ANNA S., 231
  GEORGE, 231
  HENRY B., 149, 231
  JAMES, 42, 84, 230
  JAMES M., 231
  JOHN, 231(2)
  JOSEPHINE, 231
  LILLIE, 149
  LILLIE G., 231
  MATILDA (THOMPSON),
    231
  SAMUEL, 231(3)
  W.T., 86
WOOTEN
  JESSE, 213
WRIGHT
  CELESTIA, 231
  CLARISSA (SELF), 231
  E.L., 231
  ELIZABETH JANE, 231
  HENRY, 209
  HENRY W., 231
  ISAAC J., 231
  ISOM M., 231, 232
  JAMES A., 231
  JANE, 185
  JASPER A., 232
  LEWIS, 202
  MARY ADELINE, 232
  SUSAN, 202
  SUSAN E., 232
  VINA JANE, 232
  WARREN, 42, 63
  WILLIAM, 231
  WILLIAM A., 231
  WILLIAM NEWTON, 232
  ZINA CATHERINE, 232
WYATT
  SAMUEL, 142

WYATT & BARTELL, 104

-Y-

YANTIS
  F.M., 68(2)
  IDA, 68
  OLIVER, 68
  S.J., 68(3)
  WILLIAM, 68
YARBERRY
  MR., 100
YELL
  ALEXANDER CURRY, 232
  ARCHIBALD, 56(2),
    232
  ARCHIBALD M., 232
  ARCHIBALD McKISSICK,
    232
  MARTHA D. (COFFEE),
    232
  MOSES, 232
  SARAH JANE, 206
YOES
  J., 57
YONCE
  MARY L., 137
YOUNG
  A.C., 42
YUNT
  ZEBE, 60

-Z-

ZINK
  ELIZA J., 203

www.ingramcontent.com/pod-product-compliance
Lightning Source LLC
Chambersburg PA
CBHW081432270326
41932CB00019B/3172